Protestantism and National Identity

This volume traces the complex contribution which protestantism made to national identity in the British Isles between the Stuart and Victorian ages. It therefore examines an essential – if ambiguous – foundation of British patriotism in the period when the United Kingdom was formed and emerged as a world power.

Often challenging existing work, the essays both question whether nationalism was a secular and 'modern' phenomenon, and ask whether protestantism could support any simple vision of a united, imperial and 'elect' Britain. Covering a wide variety of subjects, the authors show that whilst the reformed faith was always central to British self-awareness, it could also divide the peoples of Britain and Ireland, could cast doubt on their greatness, and could dissolve any insistence on the uniqueness of these nations. The collection thus takes the study of religion's contribution to nationality beyond simple acknowledge-ment of its importance, and suggests radical new ways to understand British and Irish development during the 'long eighteenth century'.

TONY CLAYDON is Lecturer in History, University of Wales, Bangor

IAN MCBRIDE is Lecturer in History, University of Durham

Protestantism and National Identity

Britain and Ireland, c. 1650–c. 1850

Edited by

Tony Claydon and Ian McBride

CAMBRIDGE
UNIVERSITY PRESS

PUBLISHED BY THE PRESS SYNDICATE OF THE UNIVERSITY OF CAMBRIDGE
The Pitt Building, Trumpington Street, Cambridge CB2 1RP, United Kingdom

CAMBRIDGE UNIVERSITY PRESS
The Edinburgh Building, Cambridge, CB2 2RU, UK
http://www/cup.cam/ac.uk
40 West 20th Street, New York, NY 10011–4211, USA   http://www.cup.org
10 Stamford Road, Oakleigh, Melbourne 3166, Australia

First published 1998

Printed in the United Kingdom at the University Press, Cambridge

Typeset in Plantin 10/12 pt [CE]

A catalogue record for this book is available from the British Library

ISBN 0 521 62077 5 hardback

Contents

vi   Contents

Britain, Ireland and the world

Contributors

DAVID ALLAN is lecturer in Scottish history at the University of St Andrews. He is the author of *Virtue, learning and the Scottish Enlightenment: ideas of scholarship in early modern history* (1993), editor of *In at The Deep End* (1996) and has written numerous articles on Scottish cultural and intellectual history. His *Philosophy and politics in later Stuart Scotland: neo-stoicism, culture and ideology in an age of crisis* will be published by Tuckwell Press in 1999.

TOBY BARNARD has been fellow and tutor in modern history at Hertford College Oxford since 1976. He is author of *Cromwellian Ireland* (1975) and *The English republic* (1982, new edn 1997). He has also edited (with Jane Clark) *Lord Burlington: architecture, art and life* (1995), and (with Dáibhí Ó Cróinín and K. Simms) *A Miracle of Learning: studies in manuscripts and Irish learning* (1998). He is completing a study of the Protestant Ascendancy in Ireland.

JEREMY BLACK is professor of history at the University of Exeter. His twenty-seven books include *A History of the British Isles* (Basingstoke, 1996), *Maps and history* (1997), *Maps and politics* (1997), and *The politics of Britain 1688–1800* (Manchester, 1993). Editor of *Archives*, he is a council member of the Royal Historical Society and the British Records Association.

TONY CLAYDON is a lecturer in history at the University of Wales, Bangor. He is author of *William III and the godly revolution* (Cambridge, 1996) – a study of Williamite propaganda after 1688 in England – and of articles on other aspects of late Stuart religion and political culture. He is currently working on a study of English attitudes to foreign protestants, c. 1650–c. 1750, and is an assistant editor of the new *DNB*.

TIM HARRIS is professor of history at Brown University, Providence, Rhode Island. He is author of *London crowds in the reign of Charles II: propaganda and politics from the restoration until the Exclusion Crisis* (1987) and *Politics under the later Stuarts: party conflict in a divided society, 1660–1715* (1993). He is the editor of *Popular culture in England, c. 1500–1850* (1995) and co-editor with Paul Seaward and Mark Goldie of *The politics of religion in Restoration England* (1990). He currently working on a major study of the political and religious upheavals in England, Scotland and Ireland in the later Stuart period entitled *British revolutions: the emergence of the modern state, 1660–1707* to be published by Penguin.

COLIN HAYDON is principal lecturer in History at King Alfred's College, Winchester. He is the author of *Anti-catholicism in eighteenth-century England, c. 1714–80: a political and social study* (1993). He has also edited (with John Walsh and Stephen Taylor) *The Church of England, c. 1689–1833: from toleration to tractarianism* (1993) and (with William Doyle), *Robespierre* (Cambridge University Press, forthcoming, 1999).

SCOTT MANDELBROTE is a fellow of Peterhouse, Cambridge, and of All Souls College, Oxford.

STEVEN PINCUS is assistant professor of history at the University of Chicago. He is the author of *Protestantism and patriotism: ideologies and the making of English foreign policy 1650–1668* (1996) as well as numerous essays on the politics, literature and culture of seventeenth-century England. He is currently finishing a book for Cambridge University Press entitled *The Glorious revolution and the origins of liberalism*.

IAN MCBRIDE is a lecturer in the department of history, University of Durham. He is the author of *The siege of Derry in Ulster protestant mythology* (Dublin, 1997) and *Scripture politics: Ulster presbyterians and Irish radicalism in the late eighteenth century* (Oxford, 1998), and has written articles on various aspects of Presbyterian politics and radicalism in eighteenth-century Ireland. He is currently working on a study of Irish political ideas between 1690 and 1800.

KATHLEEN WILSON is associate professor of history at the State University of New York, Stony Brook. Her book *The sense of the people: politics, culture and imperialism in England 1715–85* (1995), which won the 1996 Whitfield Prize, Royal Historical Society and the 1996 John Ben Snow Prize, North American Conference on British Studies, has just come out in paperback. She is currently finishing a study of empire and national identity in eighteenth-century Britain (Routledge, forthcoming) and is also progressing with her longer-standing project on theatre culture and modernity, 1720–1820.

JOHN WOLFFE is senior lecturer in religious studies at the Open University, and was formerly a Lecturer and British Academy post-doctoral research fellow in History at the University of York. He is the author of *The protestant crusade in Great Britain 1829–1860* (1991) and *God and Greater Britain: religion and national life in Britain and Ireland 1843–1945* (1994).

BRIAN YOUNG is lecturer in intellectual history at the University of Sussex. He is the author of *Religion and enlightenment in eighteenth-century England* (1998), and of numerous articles on eighteenth- and nineteenth-century British intellectual and religious history. He is currently at work on a study of intellectual secularisation and historiography in England from the mid-eighteenth to the early-nineteenth century.

Acknowledgements

In its early stages, the project which was to become this collection of essays was greatly helped by a conference held at the Institute of Historical Research, London, in July 1995. First versions of some of these papers were delivered at that conference, and many of the ideas and problems addressed by this volume had an initial airing. The editors would like to thank the staff of the institute – especially its director, Patrick O'Brien, and its administrative secretary, Bridget Taylor – for organising such a successful event, and for their hospitality over the weekend. The editors are also very grateful to all those who attended and participated in the conference: especially to Jonathan Clark, Linda Colley, Karen O'Brien and Frank O'Gorman, all of whom presented papers.

As the volume took shape, the editors received much encouragement, and had much good advice about the collection's overall shape and structure. For this, they would like to thank Linda Colley, Colin Kidd, Jeremy Black, and the anonymous readers for Cambridge University Press (any shortcomings in this area are naturally the editors' own responsibility). They are also grateful to the authors of the individual chapters for their patience and good humour in the face of endless editorial demands and directives. Finally, the editors would like to thank the staff of Cambridge University Press for wrestling with the vagaries of variously formatted floppy disks, and for producing a handsome final volume from an overly-eclectic mix of computer files and hard copy.

Abbreviations

AHR	*American Historical Review*
BL	British Library
BM	British Museum
Bod.	Bodleian Library, Oxford
CSPD	*Calendar of State Papers Domestic*
CUL	Cambridge University Library
EHR	*English Historical Review*
EUL	Edinburgh University Library
HJ	*Historical Journal*
HMC	Historical Manuscripts Commission
IHS	*Irish Historical Studies*
JBS	*Journal of British Studies*
JEH	*Journal of Ecclesiastical History*
JMH	*Journal of Modern History*
NLS	National Library of Scotland, Edinburgh
NLW	National Library of Wales, Aberystwyth
P&P	*Past and Present*
PD	Prints and Drawings
PRO	Public Record Office
RO	Record Office
SCH	*Studies in Church History*
SHR	*Scottish Historical Review*
SRO	Scottish Record Office, Edinburgh
SP	State Papers
SPCK	Society for Promoting Christian Knowledge
THSC	*Transactions of the Honourable Society of Cymmrodorian*
TRHS	Transactions of the Royal Historical Society
WHR	*Welsh History Review*

In footnotes, place of publication is London, England, unless otherwise stated.

Introduction

1 The trials of the chosen peoples: recent interpretations of protestantism and national identity in Britain and Ireland

Tony Claydon and Ian McBride

On 29 January 1689, the constitutional convention which had assembled in London to discuss the state of the nation after the flight of James II reached a moment of extraordinary consensus. A body which was deeply split between whigs and tories, which contained both future Jacobites and future ministers of William III, and which would continue to argue for two more weeks before deciding what to do about the disappearance of the monarch, unanimously agreed a resolution proposed by Colonel John Birch in its lower house and sent up to the assembled peers as soon as it had been approved. The resolution stated that 'it hath been found by experience, to be inconsistent with the safety and welfare of this Protestant Kingdom to be governed by a Popish Prince'.[1] The convention thus united its very disparate members in an unequivocal, and perhaps the first official, recognition of the essential protestantism of its nation. Through the wording of the resolution, people of every political persuasion had accepted that their realm was something so closely bound to the reformed faith that neither its interests, nor its constitution, nor its very identity, could be conceived without reference to that religion.

Throughout the period considered by this volume, this sense of the fundamental protestantism of Britain and Ireland was to have far-reaching consequences. To take only English constitutional examples, the desire to preserve the protestant nation was to produce a succession crisis in the years 1678–83, to legitimate the deposition of the king in 1688, to justify the union of England and Scotland in 1707, to import a foreign dynasty in 1714, to fuel a continuing crisis over catholic emancipation between the 1750s and 1829, and to encourage the electoral revolution of 1832 as anti-popish politicians sought a more 'popular' legislature that might defend their faith. Consequently, it is perhaps

---

[1] *Journals of the House of Commons*, X, 15; *Journals of the House of Lords*, XIV, 110.

superfluous to open this collection with a justification for exploring the links between religion and national identity in the late Stuart and Hanoverian kingdoms. We clearly cannot understand how contemporary British and Irish people thought about themselves or their nations without considering their faith. Yet some wider reflection on the prominence of British protestant nationalism within recent accounts of the 'long eighteenth century' may still be useful, if only because this subject has been so closely related to other historiographic developments. Because analysis of the links between British faith and nationality has had its origins in other areas of scholarly endeavour, it is important to look at how these other influences may have defined problems, shaped methodology, and perhaps imported distortions, into this field.

I

Perhaps the most important context for the recent study of 'Britishness' and protestantism has been the increasing interest in national identities across the historical profession. Since the 1960s, there has been an outpouring of works considering nationality, which have ranged across a wide variety of time periods, geographical areas and scholarly approaches.[2] Politically, the reason for this may seem obvious. After the containment of nationality as a contemporary problem after 1945, nationalism has erupted back into popular consciousness. In Europe alone, the east of the continent has been extensively remodelled by national movements, whilst in the west established nations have had to consider their relationship with the supra-national European Union, and have been challenged by regionalism from within. Yet whilst this explanation for the upsurge in scholarly interest is important, the fact that historians moved to analyse nationality somewhat before its political significance became clear suggests that there was more than this behind their interest .

Here the most vital change seems to have been the redescription of national identity as something constructed rather than natural. Over the last few decades, a number of historians have begun to explore the historical processes through which people came to conceive of themselves as belonging to a national group. For these scholars, there was nothing fundamental, organic or given about a person's national iden-

---

[2] Perhaps the most quoted of these studies have been Hugh Seton-Watson, *Nations and states* (1977); Benedict Anderson, *Imagined communities: reflections on the origin and spread of nationalism* (revd edn, 1983); Ernest Gellner, *Nations and nationalism* (Oxford, 1983); Anthony Smith, *National identity* (Reno, 1991). Some of the more influential works in the field have been collected in John Hutchinson and Anthony D. Smith, eds., *Nationalism* (Oxford, 1994).

tity. Rather, nationality had to be *created* as particular types of social and cultural interaction encouraged people to 'imagine' a national community where previously there had been only unrelated groups or individuals. Within this approach, the vital moment in the formation of identity came when individuals came to view an amorphous mass of people (most of whom they would never meet) as sharing a common history, destiny, culture or interests. This would commonly happen as a popular press, or mass political organisations, started encouraging their audiences to think of themselves as a nation sharing essential characteristics.[3] Obviously, such an approach to the study of identity had the excitement of novelty. It represented a break with older traditions of national history writing, which had never done much to question the origins or coherence of the units with which they dealt. More profoundly, however, it opened up a whole new field of historical scholarship by making nationality a subject of historical analysis. As long as nations were assumed to be natural divisions of mankind, then there would be no need to ask what processes had led to their formation. If, however, they were constructed, or 'imagined' communities, there was work to be done establishing exactly how they had been constructed, what forces had encouraged people to think of themselves in particular ways, and what political, social or economic interests might have been furthered by their promotion. To a large extent, it was the simple possibility of doing such work which drove interest in nationality, and which has contributed to recent analyses of the role of protestantism within 'Britishness'.

The other main spur to investigation in this field has been a general revival in the history of religion. In the past couple of decades, the study of the faith of historical actors has become more common and more varied in approach, and has moved out of the ghetto of ecclesiastical history to which it had been long confined.[4] The reasons for this renaissance are not entirely clear. Possibly the re-emergence of religion as source of dispute within contemporary conflicts has been a factor; but again, historiographic trends may hold more answers. Here, perhaps, interest has been sparked by the decline of traditional 'progressive' interpretation of the past, such as Anglo-American 'whiggism' or

---

[3] Anderson, *Imagined communities*, did most to popularise this approach.

[4] Some of the most strident claims for the centrality of religion within the period of this volume would include: Michael Finlayson, *Historians, puritanism and the English revolution* (Toronto, 1983); Mark Goldie, Tim Harris and Paul Seaward, eds., *The politics of religion in restoration England* (Oxford, 1990), especially the introduction; Tony Claydon, *William III and the godly revolution* (Cambridge, 1996); J. C. D.Clark, *English society, 1688–1832* (Cambridge, 1985); Clark, *The language of liberty, 1660–1832* (Cambridge, 1993).

Marxism. Within these old 'teleological' traditions, religious faith tended to be seen as a brake on the natural and unfolding development of mankind. It was a bulwark of conservative structures which would be swept away by an emerging liberal society or proletarian power, and it was treated as a irrationality which would be transcended by the intellectual enlightenment which was a central assumption of these interpretations. At best, therefore, 'teleological' scholarship ignored religion as irrelevant to the forward-looking forces which created new historical situations. At worst it denounced faith as a 'false consciousness' which distracted historical actors from their true vocations. Once, however, 'whiggism' and Marxism began to run into trouble (and their discreditation has been the main feature of historical scholarship in the later twentieth century), the significance of religion began to be reappraised. 'Revisionist' historians revelled in the new-found importance of a factor which had been overlooked by traditional interpretations, and some also found that they were forced to take faith seriously as it became the only explanation for developments which had traditionally been accounted for by liberal or proletarian advance, but which the revisionists themselves had ensured could no longer be analysed in these ways.[5] As a result, new areas of inquiry were opened up. Political, social, cultural and intellectual historians began to draw on the conclusions of their ecclesiastical colleagues, and greater efforts were made to understand the details of theological positions and to describe how faith moulded the worldview of historical actors.

Investigations of British protestant nationality have stood at the intersection of these broad historiographic trends. In part this has explained the popularity and dynamism of this particular part of the discipline. Scholars looking at the relationship between protestantism and Britishness have been fired by the excitement of wider investigations of national identity and religion: the contributions to this collection show how the field has been enriched by comparisons with other nationalities, by general theories of identity formation, and by increasingly subtle understanding of religious awareness, motivation and division. However, whilst such connections to more general trends demonstrate the crucial position of studies of British protestantism within current historical enterprise, they also point to some possible dangers with the approaches which have been adopted. In borrowing ideas from the wider interest in faith and nationality, historians of

---

[5] For one example of this, contrast Conrad Russell's retrospective collection of essays, *Unrevolutionary England, 1603–1642* (1990) which stressed early Stuart political stability, with his later work, *The causes of the English civil war* (Oxford, 1990) which depended on long-term religious instabilities to explain the breakdown of 1642.

eighteenth-century Britain and Ireland may have picked up analytical weaknesses along with strengths.

Briefly, there appear to be three main problems which the study of Britishness and protestantism shares with the wider historiographies. First, there is a preoccupation with 'the other'. As historians have tried to understand how collections of individuals came to imagine themselves as nations, they have borrowed the bi-polar approach of many anthropologists and literary critics, and have tended to concentrate on that which the national group has been defined against. They have argued that men and women can most easily be brought to think of themselves as a national community when they can be united in rejecting some external set of people, and so have examined how these outsiders, these 'others', are constructed as hostile aliens.[6] This interest in 'the other' can be seen in almost all works on identity formation.[7] As we shall see, it has affected the study of British and Irish nationalities through interest in the depiction of the catholic, continental and exotic peoples who were conceived as threatening the island nations. Yet whilst this approach has deepened our understanding of community formation (it is probably impossible to form any sense of identity without *some* rejection of things thought to lie outside), overconcentration on 'others' may have deflected attention from other features of nationality. For example, nationality tends to be depicted as almost entirely negative and exclusive within recent accounts. It is defined chiefly by describing what 'others' have been rejected in its formation, and rather less attention is paid to its 'positive' aspects – values which the community believes it embodies and in which it takes pride. Similarly, an approach centred on the 'other' suggests that national feeling is incompatible with more 'universal' sympathies embracing wider communities. In fact, there is much evidence to suggest that the relationship between nationality and universalism is more complex than this. Some national identities (for example, the old testament Jewish, and the modern American) include a sense of mission to the whole human race, and as several pieces in this volume make clear, the same was true of 'British' protestant identity in the late Stuart and Hanoverian period.[8]

---

[6] Among the most influential works have been Frederick Barth, ed., *Ethnic groups and boundaries* (Bergen, 1969); Edward Said, *Orientalism* (1978); and Peter Sahlins, *Boundaries: the making of France and Spain* (Berkeley, 1989).

[7] Most relevantly here, 'otherness' is central to Linda Colley, 'Britishness and otherness: an argument', *JBS*, 31 (1992), 309–29.

[8] For later Hebrew internationalism see the texts of later old testament prophets, e.g. *Isaiah* 49:6. For an interesting discussion of the connections between nationalism and universalism, and their application to America, see Conor Cruise O'Brien, *God land: reflections on religion and nationalism* (1988).

A second general weakness of recent scholarly trends has been to suggest that national feeling is something relatively modern. Because attention has shifted to the *creation* of identities, many have been drawn to study the pre-conditions for this fabrication, and have concluded that real nationality was impossible before such recent developments as a literate and press-reading population, or mass political movements. If large numbers of people are to imagine themselves a community, the argument runs, modern means of communication and politicisation are essential. As a result, nationality was seen emerging no earlier than the late eighteenth century. If some vague feeling of nationhood was admitted before that time, its conversion into the more significant nation*alism* (usually conceived as a mass movement demanding that political structures reflect the autonomy of the nation) was always delayed until the era of the French revolution.[9] Within British historiography, this tendency has been seen in studies which argued for novel forms of identity in the Georgian era, and which dismissed earlier feelings of nationality as politically unimportant.[10] However, while it is certain that the expansion of popular politics in the eighteenth century affected the nature of nationality, it is far less clear that true national identity, or even nationalism, was unsustainable before this time. As contributions here demonstrate, a sense of nationality – even a politically significant one – seems to have been well established in the British realm by the mid-Stuart period.[11] Either the Britannic islands developed the popular press and political movements necessary to sustain national feeling much earlier than the French revolutionary era, or other, much older, cultural forms such as chronicles, sermons, liturgies, ballads and ceremonies proved as capable of propagating nationality and allowing people to imagine themselves part of a wider community.[12]

[9] See E. J. Hobsbawn, *Nations and nationalism since 1780* (Cambridge, 1990); John Brueilly, *Nationalism and the state* (Manchester, 1982), p. 4; Hans Kohn, *The idea of nationalism: a study of its origin and background* (New York, 1945), p. 1; Gellner, *Nations*, pp. 39–40; Anderson, *Imagined communities*, p. 11.

[10] For the origins of politically significant nationalism in the eighteenth century, see Gerald Newman, *The rise of English nationalism: a cultural history, 1740–1830* (1987); and to a lesser extent, Linda Colley, *Britons: forging the nation, 1707–1837* (New Haven, 1992).

[11] See also, Peter Furtado, 'National pride in seventeenth-century England', in Raphael Samuel, ed., *Patriotism: the making and unmaking of British national identity* (3 vols., 1989), I, pp. 44–56; Liah Greenfeld, *Nationalism: five roads to modernity* (Cambridge, MA, 1992), ch. 1.

[12] For such media see David Cressy, *Bonfires and bells: national memory and the protestant calendar in Elizabethan and Stuart England* (1989); Richard Helgerson, *Forms of nationhood: the Elizabethan writing of England* (1992); John N. King, *Tudor royal iconography* (Princeton, 1989). For early national identities, see Susan Reynolds, *Kingdoms and communities in western Europe, 900–1300* (Oxford, 1984); Anthony D. Smith, *The ethnic origins of nations* (Oxford, 1984); John A. Armstrong, *Nations*

Finally, whilst study of British protestantism and nationality has benefited greatly from the renaissance in religious history, this surge in interest has also had dangers. The most pressing of these is a tendency to over-play faith as a historical dynamic. So enthusiastic have 'revisionist' scholars been for new, theological, explanations of developments, that they have tended to concentrate upon them to the exclusion of other factors. In our area, this temptation is evident in what one contributor describes as a tendency to view protestantism as constituting (rather than being merely a constituent in) national identity.[13] In fact, national identities are always more complex and multifaceted than this view suggests. As the pieces here demonstrate, protestantism was only ever one element in British nationalities, and it always interacted with beliefs about the constitution, race, language, and relations between local and European culture. Thus, as with identity, so with religion. Study of 'British' protestant nationality benefits greatly from its central position within current scholarship; but this position brings hazards as well as rewards, and historians must be careful to select very carefully from the wider academic projects.

II

Having looked at the general state of the field, it is important to focus attention more narrowly on the relationship between protestantism and national identity in Britain and Ireland between the mid-seventeenth and mid-nineteenth centuries. What precise approaches have been adopted here over the past years; what progress has been made; and what contribution can be made by the essays within this volume? In answering these questions, it can be useful to separate England from the wider entity of Britain and Ireland. Not only do historians of England tend to form a separate (generally anglo-centric) school from students of the whole archipelago, but the study of English history in isolation allows examination of certain trends which can get lost in the complexities of multinational interaction with which wider 'British' scholars have become involved.

In England, the starting point for most discussion of religion and national identity has been a model of their relationship which has placed the reformed faith at the very centre of English feeling. This model was

before nationalism (Chapel Hill, 1982). For the emergence of an English public sphere in the late seventeenth century, see Jürgen Habermas, *The structural transformation of the public sphere* (English trans., Cambridge, 1992); Steven Pincus, '"Coffee politicians does create": coffee houses and restoration political culture', *JMH*, 67:4 (1985), 807–34.

[13] See below, p. 93.

derived from work by historians of the Tudor era (particularly from the
studies of William Haller on John Foxe's 'Book of martyrs') which
argued that the sixteenth-century reformation had produced a peculiar
feeling of national election because it allowed people to see themselves
as uniquely blessed in their possession of the true, protestant creed.[14]
This paradigm was carried forward into the eighteenth century by a
number of other historians, most notably Linda Colley, who – whilst not
accepting the model uncritically – used it at least as a starting point for
discussion.[15] Given the influence of this interpretation on studies of late
Stuart and Hanoverian England, it is worth examining in some detail.

At base, the interpretation which scholars of the eighteenth century
borrowed from Tudor specialists was very simple. It revolved around
two central assumptions, both of which suggested that nationality was a
sub-set of protestantism. The first of these assumptions was that the
early modern sense of Englishness was founded on a profound horror of
a papist 'other'. According to this view, the dominant sentiment among
Tudor Englishmen was hostility to Roman catholicism, and to the
panoply of associated conspiracies against godly protestantism which
contemporaries labelled 'popery'. In this interpretation, the English saw
popery as the very antithesis of virtue. It was an anti-christian perversion
of the true faith which became a convincing explanation of all misfortunes, evils, instabilities and oppressions. Within this worldview, 'Englishness' emerged in opposition to popish horrors. The English could
see themselves as profoundly fortunate that they (almost uniquely
within Europe) had escaped the bondage of catholicism; and they could
view other nations as more completely alien, since they were not only
distant and unfamiliar, but essentially corrupted. They were thus given
a heightened, ideological sense of the borders of their nation; and were
provided with a sense of a national character which had rejected the
sensuous debauchery, priestly persecution and monarchical tyranny
which were thought to be the defining vices of catholicism.[16]

The second assumption behind the 'Tudor' model of protestantism
and nationality, was that the English thought of themselves as an 'elect
nation'. In this view, early modern Englishmen's sense of themselves as
the unique adherents of God's true faith, led them to believe that they
were the successors of the old testament Jews, and that they enjoyed a

---

[14] William Haller, *Foxe's 'Book of Martyrs' and the elect nation* (1963).
[15] Colley, *Britons*, ch. 1.
[16] Peter Lake, 'Anti-popery: the structure of a prejudice', in Richard Cust and Ann
Hughes, eds., *Conflict in early Stuart England* (1989), pp. 72–106; Robert Clifton, 'Fear
of popery', in Conrad Russell, ed., *The origins of the English civil war* (1973),
pp. 144–67; C. Z. Weiner, 'The beleaguered isle: a study of Elizabethan and early
Jacobean anti-catholicism', *P&P,* 51 (1971), 27–52.

similarly privileged relationship with the deity. Noticing the parallels between the Hebrews' situation surrounded by unbelieving pagans, and their own position in a largely popish continent, the English came to think that they too were God's 'chosen people'. They came to believe they were the objects of God's special love; they thought that they too received his special care and protection; and they argued that they too had entered into a peculiar covenant with heavenly powers, in which they gained providential blessing in return for their continuing efforts to sustain and extend true, protestant worship. This sense of divine election added three main features to those produced by the basic drive of anti-popery. First, it bred a feeling of uniqueness. The English came to feel that they alone had been favoured by God, and had been singled out from the general run of mankind. Second, 'election' produced a peculiar vision of national history, in which the English began to interpret their national past as a re-run of the old testament. In this vision, the English story – an analogy for the Israelite story – was a series of trials of a chosen people. It was a record of God's tests of his children, of his leading them into temptations, of his judgements, and – most importantly – of his sudden providential deliverances in the face of terrible danger. Finally, the English sense of election fed an enhanced sense of destiny. Combining the feeling of uniqueness, and the peculiar view of the national past, Englishmen came to believe that the culmination of God's plans for them would be pre-eminence. Once they had come through their trials, the chosen people would be raised to a privileged position at God's right hand.[17]

This, then, was the basic model of a protestant national identity which scholars of the eighteenth century borrowed from the early modern period. In the recent spate of studies of Georgian national identity, it has played a large part. In the work of Linda Colley, for example, notions of patriotic anti-popery and elect nationhood have loomed large. The reason for this easy borrowing of the 'Tudor' model has been a glut of evidence that eighteenth-century Englishmen did in fact continue to view their world as their predecessors had done. For example, in this volume Colin Haydon demonstrates how common anti-popery was in the eighteenth century and how it was bound up with the identity of contemporary people – especially enabling them to recognise what was foreign. As Haydon shows, Georgian men and women were reminded of the 'outlandishness' of Roman catholicism (the territorial nature of the adjective is significant) through a host of cultural forms.

---

[17] For aspects of these beliefs, see William Lamont, *Godly rule: politics and religion, 1603–1660* (1969); Paul Christianson, *The reformers and Babylon: English apocalyptic visions* (Toronto, 1978).

Similar evidence can be seen in John Wolffe's discussion of a continuing anti-popish patriotism at the end of the Hanoverian period, and there is more in the evangelical protestant imperialism explored by Kathleen Wilson. Even Steven Pincus – whose stimulating and controversial essay on English nationalism does much to question the role recently assigned to religion in constructing Englishness – admits that protestantism was crucial to national feeling. Pincus contends that late Stuart Englishmen had become wary of anti-catholic crusades, and argues that they defended their national faith primarily on traditional and legal, as opposed to outdated providential, grounds. He nevertheless maintains that the English people's defence of their religion was central to their sense of nationhood, and dictated their actions in the 1688 revolution.

Yet whilst the basic idea of a protestant Englishness does have much to commend it, the model also has certain problems which must lead to doubts about its effectiveness as a tool of historical analysis. In particular, recent historiographical trends have undermined any simple connection between faith and nationality. Ironically, the most direct criticisms of a simple, protestant Englishness came from the field in which the notion originated. As Tudor and early Stuart specialists began to look more closely at the theory that early modern protestants saw themselves as a chosen people, they began to see considerable difficulties with it, and even began to question whether the reformed religion could ever have served as the basis for national feeling.

The doubts sprang from study of what sixteenth-century protestants said about the 'true church'. At first sight, this need not have been a problem, since, in Tudor terminology, the true church was simply the community of the faithful. It was the phrase used to describe those who would be saved by God, so it should have been easy to identify it with the faithful British nation whose protestantism ensured they accepted and lived by the true religion. However, as scholars looked more closely at accounts of this true church, the less likely it appeared that early modern people would make this identification. On examination, subjects of the Tudors and early Stuarts appeared to have thought of the true church as a mystical body, which existed on a different plane to human creations such as states or nations. Particularly, it was believed that God's true community was created as the unfettered Holy Spirit converted people to the gospel faith, and it was thought improbable that the deity would confine its attention to one nation – or convert all the people within a particular country – when calling folk into this community. Once this was appreciated, it became clear that the protestant faith could act as the solvent, as well as the cement of national feeling. Since protestants thought it unlikely that their true church was the same as the

English nation, their sense of themselves as Christians would cut across their sense of themselves as English.

As scholars studied this complexity further, two particular problems emerged. The first was the position of foreign protestants. As Tudor Britons surveyed their world, it was clear that there were godly people who lived outside their islands and nations. There were substantial protestant populations in Germany, Switzerland, Scandinavia and Holland; and isolated communities of the reformed existed in France, Austria, Savoy and elsewhere. In all these places early modern protestants might see branches of their true church. Recognising this, English people demonstrated considerable sympathy and solidarity with certain foreigners and so revealed an identity which transcended national boundaries. Tudor and early Stuart Englishmen wrote foreign protestants into their accounts of their history, they called for their protection against hostile powers, they talked of the ties that bound them together, and they made efforts to unite with them in single churches or even single polities.[18]

Whilst such universalism undermined any simple English election on an international level, a second problem with the definition of the true church weakened it in the domestic sphere. Early modern scholars found that those they studied were as unlikely to see God's community encompassing all Englishmen, as they were to see it excluding all foreigners. Some of the groups rejected as ungodly by Tudor protestants were obvious enough. The refusal of catholic recusants to join in the reformation made it inevitable that many English subjects would be seen as an alien threat living within the borders of the realm, whilst low standards of religious understanding, piety and personal morality among other sections of the population led contemporaries to denounce such reprobates' failure to live up to the nation's status as chosen people.[19] More subtle, but easily as significant, was the problem that even committed protestants might fail to recognise one another as God's true people. Perhaps because the protestant faith encouraged its adherents to view personal interpretation of the bible as the source of religious authority, early modern Englishmen tended to diverge in their ideas about the precise nature of godly belief and life, and this made it difficult to unite everybody through a sense of belonging to God's true community. By the mid-seventeenth century, this diversity had taken its toll.

[18] For this, see Patrick Collinson, *The birthpangs of protestant England* (Basingstoke, 1988), ch. 1; Katherine R. Firth, *The apocalyptic tradition in reformation Britain* (Oxford, 1979), pp. 106–9; Richard Bauckham, *Tudor apocalypse* (Oxford, 1978), p.86.

[19] For this, see Collinson, *Birthpangs*, ch. 1; Christianson, *Reformers and Babylon*; Lamont, *Godly rule*; Michael McGifford, 'God's controversy with Jacobean England', *AHR*, 88 (1983), 1151–74.

Although a protestant church was established by parliamentary statute, disputes and divisions became common among its members, and some groups found they could not be comprehended within its structures.[20] In this situation it was again easy for people to view the true church as something less extensive than the secular nation.

The full scale of the difficulties caused by the ungodly within the realm are best illustrated by accusations of popery in the Tudor and early Stuart era. Unfortunately for any simple model of protestant nationality, these were not simply directed outwards to label foreigners and define the boundaries of the nation. They were also hurled at fellow Englishmen, thus confusing that labelling and definition. Obviously the English catholics were denounced as popish, as were the debauched and impious, whose failure to attend to God's truth was blamed on catholic influence. More damagingly, however, the accusations were made in debates between zealous protestants. People who were used to justifying their split from the church of Rome on the basis that it was a limb of the antichrist (and who were used to finding popery lurking behind any opposition), easily extended their hostile rhetoric to those who disagreed with them on doctrine, liturgy or church government. Thus supporters of the established church came to accuse dissidents of allying with catholicism in their attacks upon the ecclesiastical settlement.[21] In response, dissidents began to construct a case against the establishment. Building on a tradition which saw persecution as the characteristic mark of popery (protestants had always been keen to stress their faith's transmission from early Christians through groups of medieval 'heretics' who had been attacked by the false Roman church), dissidents dressed official attempts to impose religious uniformity as persecution, and so turned the charge of popery back upon the official church.[22] Here, English people were disagreeing about the nature of the popish threat which was supposed to unite them. There was, therefore, a danger that the vision of England as Israel might collapse from within.

Given these early modern problems with protestant Englishness, it is worth asking whether the reformed faith could ever have been a sound basis for a unifying national identity. The protestant community's sense

[20] For the best recent discussions of divisions within the church, see Nicholas Tyacke, *Anti-Calvinists* (Oxford, 1987); Kenneth Fincham, ed., *The early Stuart church* (Houndmills, 1993); Anthony Milton, *Catholic and reformed* (Cambridge, 1995). More radical groups who split from the church can be traced in Christianson, *Reformers and Babylon*.

[21] This happened particularly after the civil war, as episcopalians reminded audiences of the horrors of puritan rule, see Tim Harris, *London crowds in the reign of Charles II* (Cambridge, 1987), ch. 6.

[22] See above footnote 17 and Paul Christianson, 'From expectation to militance: reformers and Babylon in the first two years of the Long Parliament', *JEH*, 24 (1973), 225–54.

of the true church as something mystical rather than human; its appeal to foreigners; its universalist mission to convert all mankind; its tendency to fissure; its easy adoption of the divisive rhetoric of anti-popery in internal disputes; and its suspicion of attempts to impose conformity as popish persecution: all these made protestantism an unlikely bedrock of nationality in the early modern period. And if such doubts about a simple protestant Englishness are important for sixteenth and early-seventeenth-century scholarship, they are as crucial to study of the next 200 years. As contributions to this collection repeatedly illustrate, the English continued to feel supra-national affinities with foreign protestants, and were pulled by a universalist mission to convert the whole world (see for example, the chapters by Black, Young, Wilson and Wolffe). In this later period too, and again as illustrated by the essays by Black, Young, Wolffe and Haydon, the English argued among themselves on matters of faith, and so weakened any unifying protestant nationality.

III

England, as Liah Greenfeld has recently reminded us, was the first nation in the world.[23] A combination of well-defined territorial boundaries, a high degree of administrative centralisation and a vernacular language of government all helped to make possible the articulation of a national consciousness during the religious upheavals of the sixteenth century. But the model of collective identity on which the English drew was equally available to other bible-centred cultures. The old testament language of nationhood, with its covenanted sense of chosenness and its providential reading of historical events, was also taken up by protestants in Scotland and Ireland. In both those kingdoms ecclesiastical scholars compiled historical narratives which presented the reformation as the recovery of an indigenous, pure Christianity from the encroachments of an alien Roman tyranny. Moreover, the rise of print capitalism, which made possible the construction of 'imagined communities' of readers, was not confined to England.[24] As Scott Mandelbrote explains below, biblically centred literacy consolidated communities of English speakers in all three realms – albeit at the cost of dividing them further from those using varieties of Gaelic.

   In constructing their own myth of national election, the English rarely gave much thought to protestants in other parts of the British Isles. Yet any discussion of early modern Englishness naturally raises questions

[23] Greenfeld, *Nationalism*, ch. 1.   [24] Anderson, *Imagined communities*, esp. ch. 3.

about the other inhabitants of the archipelago, and about the role of religion in the political relationship between the three kingdoms. After all, England's transformation from dynastic realm into territorial nation-state was part of a wider process of state formation which saw the extension of metropolitan authority over the rest of these islands.[25] Broadly speaking, the creation of a unified British state, beginning with the demonstration of English political and military hegemony in the 1650s and ending with the emancipation of catholic Ireland, coincides with the time-span covered by this book. As Allan and McBride show below, the protestant peoples of Scotland and Ireland possessed their own national myths distinct from, but related to, the English pattern. Indeed their experience of seventeenth-century warfare – when the intervention of external forces had proved decisive – may have been particularly amenable to providential interpretations.[26] It would be profoundly misleading, therefore, to write the history of the British monarchy from a purely anglo-centric perspective. Rather we should follow J. G. A. Pocock's example and approach the subject as a 'problematic and uncompleted experiment in the creation and interaction of several nations'.[27] At this point, then, it is necessary to enter the territory of the 'new British history' and to examine more closely the role of protestantism in the development of the three kingdoms.

The natural point of departure for such an inquiry is Linda Colley's *Britons.* The central theme of her stimulating and wide-ranging book is the construction of a British identity in the period between the union of 1707 and the accession of Queen Victoria. She claimed this identity was defined during a series of wars against catholic, absolutist France, and was founded on a common protestant faith. To the question, 'who were the British, and did they even exist?', Colley replied that 'protestantism could supply a potent and effective answer, perhaps the only satisfactory answer possible'.[28] She thus extended her conception of elect nation-

---

[25] Recent literature on this includes R. G. Asch, ed., *Three nations – a common history?* (Bochum, 1993); Brendan Bradshaw and John Morrill, eds., *The British problem, c. 1534–1707* (1996); Steven G. Ellis and Sarah Barber, eds., *Conquest and union: fashioning a British state, 1485–1725* (1995); Alexander Grant and Keith J. Stringer, eds., *Uniting the kingdom? The making of British history* (1995). The trend towards the new British history has been greeted with scepticism as well as enthusiasm: see Tony Claydon, 'Problems with the British problem', *Parliamentary History*, 16:2 (1997), 221–7.

[26] For the Irish case, see Nicholas Canny, 'The formation of the Irish mind: religion, politics and Gaelic Irish literature, 1580–1750', *P&P*, 95 (1982), 91–116.

[27] J. G. A. Pocock, 'The limits and divisions of British history: in search of the unknown subject', *AHR*, 87 (1982), 318. For examples of a British approach, see R. S. Thompson, *The Atlantic archipelago: a political history of the British Isles* (Lewiston, 1986); Hugh Kearney, *The British Isles: a history of the four nations* (Cambridge, 1989).

[28] Colley, *Britons*, p. 53.

hood, based on reformed Christianity, to embrace all of Britain. In doing so, Colley deserves credit for placing a range of new questions onto the historiographical agenda. In the past, historians and political scientists had tended to categorise 'Britishness' as a legal concept rather than a cultural identification (a kind of citizenship rather than nationality). Part of Colley's achievement was to show that Britishness had deeper roots in the historical consciousness and experience of eighteenth-century people.[29] Yet this picture of a strong protestant consensus was only achieved at the expense of excluding Ireland; while Colin Kidd has recently put forward an alternative interpretation of the emergence of 'North Britishness' in eighteenth-century Scotland, which emphasises anglicisation rather than a genuinely comprehensive British nationhood.[30] It is time, therefore, to take a closer look at the role of a common protestant heritage in the development of a wider British solidarity.

In an exemplary exercise in 'three-kingdoms' history, Tim Harris' essay below casts considerable doubt on whether the reformed faith could produce a common national feeling. Considering the reign of Charles II, he shows that religion's main role in the period was to destabilise the already difficult problem of ruling different 'British' realms.[31] Among Englishmen fearful for the security of their faith and their liberties, Scotland and Ireland continued to be viewed as testing grounds where experiments in popery and absolutism could be conceived; whilst past population movements (such as the influx of English and Scots into Ulster), coupled with the varying results of the sixteenth-century reformation, meant that religious divisions cut across all the kingdoms and left minorities in each. It was the consequent temptation to construct denominational alliances across borders which made the interrelations between the three Stuart monarchies so complex and troublesome. Most particularly, Harris shows that the integrative potential of anti-popery in the decades after 1660 was checked by a rival 'other'. Churchmen detected something as devilish as Rome in the forces of protestant dissent represented in all three kingdoms, and made strenuous efforts to root it from all its refuges.

Of course, the chaotic situation described by Harris was transformed by the revolution of 1689–91. The events of these years – though arising from instabilities within the *English* polity – rapidly became a second war

[29] Bernard Crick, 'The English and the British', in Bernard Crick, ed., *National identities: the constitution of the United Kingdom* (Oxford, 1991), p. 97.

[30] On Ireland, see Colley, *Britons*, p. 8: For Scotland, see Colin Kidd, 'North Britishness and the nature of eighteenth-century patriotisms', *HJ*, 39 (1996), 361–82.

[31] See also T. C. Barnard, 'Scotland and Ireland in the later Stewart monarchy', in Ellis and Barber, eds., *Conquest and union*, pp. 250–75.

of the three kingdoms. The decisive battles of the era were fought on Scottish and Irish soil, and soon led to a closer integration of the three realms as the victorious forces in London consolidated their gains. From a British perspective, the revolution settlement, the union of 1707 and the Irish declaratory act of 1720 formed part of a single process in which the supremacy of the Westminster parliament was formally established.[32] Given this, it was possible that a new national consciousness could emerge from these constitutional changes. As Colley has argued, it was also possible that protestantism could act as midwife to this new consciousness, and so take the role it had failed to fulfil in the seventeenth century. In order to gauge whether this actually occurred, however, it will be convenient to consider Scotland and Ireland separately.

The Anglo-Scottish union of 1707, designed above all to safeguard the protestant succession, can be said to represent a common commitment to the reformed faith, or at least a common hostility to the catholic 'other'. Since the sixteenth century, a shared biblical vocabulary, combined with the extension of English-language print culture, had stimulated periodic bursts of enthusiasm for the idea of an imperial British monarchy, particularly north of the border. Many presbyterian reformers, including John Knox himself, had envisioned a dynastic union within the apocalyptic context of the battle against the Roman antichrist.[33] The prospect of a pan-British millennium was revived in the 1640s when the covenanters fought for a federal union of kingdoms and churches, this time on Scottish presbyterian terms.[34] But this adherence

---

[32] D. W. Hayton, 'The Williamite revolution in Ireland, 1688–91', in Jonathan Israel, ed., *The Anglo-Dutch moment* (Cambridge, 1991), pp. 185–213; W. A. Maguire, ed., *Kings in conflict: the revolutionary war in Ireland and its aftermath* (Belfast, 1990). The most recent survey of the Anglo-Scottish union is Mark Goldie, 'Divergence and union: Scotland and England, 1660–1707', in Bradshaw and Morrill, eds., *British problem*, pp. 220–45. For the background see B. P. Levack, *The formation of the British state* (Oxford, 1987). David Hayton offers an interesting comparative perspective in his 'Constitutional experiments and political expediency, 1689–1725', in Ellis and Barber, eds., *Conquest and union*, pp. 276–305; see also Daniel Szechi and David Hayton, 'John Bull's other kingdoms: the English government of Scotland and Ireland', in Clyve Jones, ed., *Britain in the first age of party 1680–1750* (1987), pp. 241–80.

[33] Arthur H. Williamson, *Scottish national consciousness in the age of James VI* (Edinburgh, 1979); 'Scotland, antichrist and the invention of Great Britain', in J. Dwyer, R. A. Mason and A. Murdoch, eds., *New perspectives on the politics and culture of early modern Scotland* (Edinburgh, 1982), pp. 34–58; Roger A. Mason, 'Scotching the Brut: politics, history and national myth in sixteenth-century Britain', in Roger A. Mason, ed., *Scotland and England, 1286–1815* (Edinburgh, 1987), pp. 60–84; Roger A. Mason, 'The Scottish reformation and the origins of Anglo-British imperialism', in Mason, ed., *Scots and Britons: Scottish political thought and the union of 1603* (Cambridge, 1994), pp. 161–86.

[34] S. A. Burrell, 'The apocalyptic vision of the early covenanters', *SHR*, 43 (1964), 1–24.

to the ideal of reformation was not capable of transcending the competing theological and ecclesiological systems which had their roots in
conflicting interpretations of protestantism.[35] After the restoration, the
suppression of Cameronian conventicles in the south-west toughened
the militant anti-Englishness which existed on the fringes of presbyterianism, while the ejection of episcopalian ministers after 1690 alienated
a majority of the Scottish political nation from both the revolution
settlement and later from the union. The continuing adherence of the
Scottish episcopalians to a Roman catholic pretender is only the most
startling example of the profound faultlines *within* Scottish protestantism which must cast doubt on the integrative potential of anti-
catholicism.

Even within the established church itself, the union was accepted with
resignation rather than enthusiasm. The unified British kingdom was
unusual in many respects, but none was more startling than its combination of a single sovereign legislature with a dual ecclesiastical establishment. The preservation of two separate and mutually opposed national
churches, each with their own claims to antiquity and territorial
autonomy, had profound implications for the development of national
consciousness. On a practical level there was the question of whether
the future of the Scots kirk could be entrusted to the Westminster
parliament, with its in-built anglican majority in the Commons and its
episcopal component in the Lords. On an ideological level, there were
rival doctrinal positions concerning the role of the civil magistrate in
Christ's kingdom. Although the security of the kirk was guaranteed in
the union settlement, the Court of Session could now be overruled by
the House of Lords, as the Edinburgh authorities discovered in 1709
when they imprisoned the Rev. James Greenshields for worshipping
according to 'the English service'.[36] Worse was to follow under the tory
regime of 1710–14, when freedom of worship was granted to the
episcopalian clergy, and the right of nominating ministers was restored
to lay patrons – a direct affront to the 'two-kingdoms' ecclesiology which
rejected the supremacy of the civil power over the ecclesiastical sphere.

At first glance, then, the prospect that protestantism might underwrite
political unification was unlikely. However, from 1690 onwards, as
recent work by Colin Kidd has demonstrated, presbyterian controversi-
alists were increasingly pushed onto the defensive as they accommo-
dated themselves to the political realities of the post-revolution British

[35] Jane Dawson, 'Anglo-Scottish protestant culture and integration in sixteenth-century
Britain', in Ellis and Barber, eds., *Conquest and union*, pp. 87–114.
[36] A. Drummond and J. Bullock, *The Scottish church, 1688–1843* (Edinburgh, 1973),
p. 17.

state. Faced with a vocal episcopalian-Jacobite opposition at home, and the entrenchment of a conservative whig establishment in London, they struggled to preserve an orthodox presbyterianism while shaking off their seventeenth-century associations with religious enthusiasm, social subversion and political extremism. Hence the cautious whig constitutionalism of Robert Wodrow's epic *History of the sufferings of the church of Scotland* (1721–2), which played down the covenants in favour of the Williamite deliverance, the revolution settlement and the Hanoverian succession. In the second half of the century, Wodrow's mildly apologetic tone accelerated into full-scale revisionism, as William Robertson and his 'moderate' party trimmed their sails to the prevailing winds of erastian, latitudinarian Christianity.[37]

The result was an anglo-centric view of history and politics which celebrated the revolution of 1688 as the fountainhead of civil and religious liberty, freedom of the press, the diffusion of knowledge and religious toleration.[38] Thus moderate ministers such as Adam Ferguson were able to merge the rhetoric of civic humanism with the more traditional form of the Jeremiad sermon to rally their congregations around an inclusive Britishness in the face of the Jacobite threat in 1745.[39] This ideological transformation was linked to broader attempts to reconstruct England's 'vulgar' whiggism with the aid of the new political science and sociology produced by the Scottish enlightenment.[40] Although this intellectual efflorescence is usually associated with the moderates, it has been shown that their orthodox rivals in the 'popular' party were moving in the same direction.[41] In place of the narrowly sectarian framework of the seventeenth century their increasingly evangelical outlook allowed them to adhere to a heightened sense

---

[37] I. D. L. Clark, 'From protest to reaction: the moderate regime in the church of Scotland, 1752–1805', in N. T. Phillipson and Rosalind Mitchison, eds., *Scotland in the age of improvement* (Edinburgh, 1970), pp. 200–24.

[38] Richard B. Sher, '1688 and 1788: William Robertson on revolution in Britain and France', in Paul Dukes and John Dunkley, eds., *Culture and revolution* (1990), pp. 98–109.

[39] Richard B. Sher, *Church and university in the Scottish enlightenment* (Princeton, 1985), ch. 1.

[40] Duncan Forbes, *Hume's philosophical politics* (Cambridge, 1976); Duncan Forbes, 'Sceptical whiggism, commerce and liberty', in A. S. Skinner and T. Wilson, eds., *Essays on Adam Smith* (Oxford, 1975), pp. 179–201; N. T. Phillipson, *Hume* (1989). Also relevant are Rosalind Mitchison, 'Patriotism and national identity in eighteenth-century Scotland', in T. W. Moody, ed., *Historical Studies 11: Nationality and the pursuit of national independence* (Belfast, 1978), pp. 73–95, and Nicholas Phillipson, 'Politics, politeness and the anglicisation of early eighteenth-century Scottish culture', in Mason, ed., *Scotland and England*, pp. 226–46.

[41] Friedhelm Voges, 'Moderate and evangelical thinking in the later eighteenth century: differences and shared attitudes', *Records of the Scottish Church History Society*, 22 (1985), 153–7.

of British patriotism. Their conception of British Israel was an expansive imperial one, with strong transatlantic connections, which left them deeply divided over the justice of war with the American colonies.[42] During the revolutionary crisis of the 1790s, the kirk stood as a central pillar of the established political and social order, with both parties committed to a British conservatism whose ideological content had little that was distinctively Scottish.[43]

At this point, however, it is necessary to register a few reservations. First, we must be careful not to overestimate the degree of consensus. In 1736 the refusal by a third of the kirk's ministers to read proclamations condemning the Porteous riots revealed the continuing hostility of the presbyterian clergy to government interference in spiritual affairs. This opposition to erastianism was entrenched in the hardline secession churches, where an attachment to the covenants and the rejection of the ecclesiastical supremacy claimed by the crown remained articles of faith. Indeed a number of seceder ministers played a prominent part in the radical agitation of 1790s, as did the tiny sect of covenanters.[44] The second reservation concerns the ambivalent, flexible and transferable character of the protestant-nation paradigm. As David Allan's essay illustrates, the language of protestant nationhood could be used in a defensive Scottish sense as well as an inclusive British sense. While protestantism continued to underpin national identity, the chosen people might describe themselves variously as Scots or Britons or both. This flexibility is demonstrated most dramatically in the career of John Witherspoon, the popular party leader who emigrated to become

[42] Ned C. Landsman, 'Presbyterians and provincial society: the evangelical enlightenment in the west of Scotland, 1740–1775', in John Dwyer and Richard B. Sher, eds., *Sociability and society in eighteenth-century Scotland* (Edinburgh, 1993), pp. 194–209; 'Witherspoon and the problem of provincial identity in Scottish evangelical culture', in Richard B. Sher and Jeffrey R. Smitten, eds., *Scotland and America in the age of enlightenment* (Edinburgh, 1990), pp. 29–45; Robert Kent Donovan, 'The popular party of the church of Scotland and the American revolution', in *Scotland and America*, pp. 81–99; Robert Kent Donovan, 'Evangelical civic humanism in Glasgow: the American war sermons of William Thom', in Andrew Hook and Richard B. Sher, eds., *The Glasgow enlightenment* (East Linton, 1995), pp. 227–45.

[43] T. M. Devine, 'The failure of radical reform in Scotland in the late eighteenth century', in Devine, ed., *Conflict and stability in Scottish history 1700–1850* (Edinburgh, 1990), pp. 50–64; Emma Vincent, 'The responses of Scottish churchmen to the French revolution, 1789–1802', *SHR*, 73 (1994), 191–215; Colin Kidd, 'The kirk, the French revolution and the burden of Scottish whiggery', in Nigel Aston, ed., *Religious change in Europe 1650–1914* (Oxford, 1997), pp. 213–34.

[44] John Brims, 'The covenanting tradition and Scottish radicalism in the 1790s', in Terry Brotherstone, ed., *Covenant, charter, and party: traditions of revolt and protest in modern Scottish history* (Aberdeen, 1989), pp. 50–6; John D. Brims, 'The Scottish "Jacobins", Scottish nationalism and the British union', in Mason, ed., *Scotland and England*, pp. 247–65.

president of the College of New Jersey in 1766. Witherspoon's classic revolutionary sermon, *The dominion of providence over the passions of men* (1776) is a striking illustration of how easily the paradigm of national election could be transposed from his native land to the context of the rebellious colonies.[45]

While the relationship between England and Scotland contained many anomalous features, the position of Ireland under the Stuart and Hanoverian dynasties was unique. The kingdom of Ireland was of recent, sixteenth-century origin, and its subordinate status as a possession of the English crown was underlined in 1603, 1660 and 1689, when the settlement of the throne was decided in London without reference to the Irish political nation.[46] Ireland was not included in the Brutus legend, the medieval origin-myth which told how England, Scotland and Wales had once comprised a single British kingdom, nor did Tudor or Stuart propagandists attempt to re-write the history of the British Isles from an inclusive, three-kingdoms standpoint. The otherness of Ireland was underlined both by the perceived barbarity of its catholic majority and the very real dependence of its protestant minority, revealed most graphically in the rebellions of 1641 and 1689. English apologists exploited varieties of conquest theory to justify Ireland's colonial status, and from the 1690s a series of measures – most infamously the suppression of the Irish woollen industry – eroded still further the privileges of the Dublin parliament. Finally in 1720 the declaratory act asserted the legislative supremacy of Westminster over the kingdom of Ireland.[47]

The main cause of Irish exceptionalism, of course, was the peculiar position of the dominant protestant group – a position created in the hundred years before Cromwell's invasion. An initial lack of resources to promote the reformed faith, and the great success of a missionary counter-reformation in the later sixteenth century, had encouraged

---

[45] Richard B. Sher, 'Witherspoon's *Dominion of providence* and the Scottish jeremiad tradition', in Sher and Smitten, eds., *Scotland and America*, pp. 46–64.

[46] For the constitutional status of seventeenth-century Ireland, see M. Perceval- Maxwell, 'Ireland and the monarchy in the early Stuart multiple kingdom', *HJ*, 34 (1991), 279–95; C. E. J. Caldicott, 'The Irish parliament and the états of Languedoc 1640–1689: regional assemblies and the doctrine of law', in L. M. Cullen and L. Bergeron, eds., *Culture et pratiques politiques en France et en Irlande XVIe–XVIIIe siècle* (Paris, 1991), pp. 5–21; Aidan Clarke, 'Colonial constitutional attitudes in Ireland, 1640–1660', *Proceedings of the Royal Irish Academy*, 90C (1990), 357–75. For the later period see J. C. Beckett, 'Anglo-Irish constitutional relations in the later eighteenth century', *IHS*, 14 (1964).

[47] P. H. Kelly, 'Ireland and the Glorious Revolution: from kingdom to colony', in R. Beddard, ed., *The revolutions of 1688* (Oxford, 1991), pp. 163–90; Isolde Victory, 'The making of the 1720 declaratory act', in Gerard O'Brien, ed., *Parliament, politics and people: essays on eighteenth-century Irish history* (Dublin, 1989), pp. 9–29.

renewed protestant efforts under the early Stuarts which had included vigorous imposition of English state power, grants of land to the church, and the importation of new waves of enthusiastic protestants (from the English clergy who invaded Irish ecclesiastical posts to the Scots planters who moved into Ulster).[48] This history of attempted conversion, resistance and reaction had resulted in an anglican church which was legally established, well-endowed and professionally staffed; but which was also orientated to a small group of relatively recent settlers, and whose prevailing ethos alienated it from the bulk of the Irish people. The anglicans might, therefore, exalt in their self-image as guardians of the national faith – but any celebration was marred by awareness of their position as a minority church catering only for the New English. As Toby Barnard shows below, the church's position was also complicated by denominational clashes within protestantism which were often re-enforced by the ethnic divides between Englishmen and Scots.

Obviously, such a situation suggests that the established protestant church could never provide a means of integrating the bulk of the Irish population into a wider 'British' identity, or even of uniting them in a common Irish nationhood. The church's very explanations for its failure to make inroads into native superstition distanced it further from those it wished converted. Whilst failure was attributed to a variety of factors (from insufficient numbers of clergy and the language barrier to 'the very inborn hatred of subdued people to their conquerors'),[49] many clergy explained the resilience of catholicism by a crude distortion of predestinarian theology. All over the British Isles protestants believed that they were chosen, but nowhere else did they come into such direct conflict with the reprobate. Old testament examples were employed to underline the necessity of completely segregating the godly settlers from the idolatrous natives. The irredeemable nature of the Irish was apparently confirmed by the bloody rebellion of 1641, prompting one anglican bishop to observe that the English interest had learned 'how dearly the Israelites paid for their cruel mercy in not extirpating the idolatrous Canaanites'.[50] The same message was enshrined in the foundation text of Irish protestant providentialism, Sir John Temple's

[48] For reformation and counter-reformation, see Alan Ford, *The protestant reformation in Ireland, 1590–1641* (rev. edn, Dublin, 1997); Canny, 'Formation of the Irish mind'; Colm Lennon, 'The counter-reformation in Ireland, 1542–1641', in Ciaran Brady and Raymond Gillespie, eds., *Natives and newcomers: essays on the making of Irish colonial society, 1534–1641* (Dublin, 1986), pp. 75–92.

[49] William Bedell, 1634, quoted in Alan Ford, 'The protestant reformation in Ireland', in Brady and Gillespie, eds., *Natives and newcomers*, p. 73.

[50] Daniel Harcourt, quoted in Ford, *Protestant reformation*, p. 221.

The Irish rebellion (1646),[51] whilst the liturgical calendar of the church of Ireland adopted 23 October (the anniversary of the outbreak of the 1641 massacres of protestants) as its own, specifically Irish, day of commemoration.

Given the close connection between protestantism and anglicisation, it might be assumed that the church of Ireland was destined to remain exclusive and elitist in its mission. There is certainly a direct line of descent from the idea of a distinctive 'protestant interest' formulated in the turbulent years between 1641 and 1660 to the late-eighteenth-century 'protestant ascendancy'.[52] However, as Toby Barnard and Ian McBride emphasise, this sense of chosenness was compatible with a variety of overlapping national identifications – Irish, English, and even on occasion British. The Williamite victories of 1690–1 confirmed the settler community's monopoly of power, contributed new dates to the protestant calendar, supplied the protestant community with its totemic great deliverer in the shape of William III, and reinforced the congruence between ethnicity, confession and political allegiance.[53] Yet whilst Irish protestants were initially happy to describe the Williamite revolution as a war of conquest,[54] their ethnic and religious inheritance did not guarantee their acquiescence under metropolitan rule. While Edinburgh and Glasgow advertised their north Britishness, the trend in eighteenth-century Dublin and Belfast was one of divergence rather than assimilation. Constitutional tussles with the metropolis, the steady growth of a polite public sphere in the cities, and a noticeable (if partial) spread of 'enlightened' attitudes to religious division, meant that hybrid formulations such as 'the English in Ireland' would eventually give way to a prouder sense of Irish nationhood. Gradually a potentially inclusive (because pre-catholic) Gaelic antiquity replaced English colonisation as the origin myth of ascendancy identity.[55]

In the old nationalist historiography (where eighteenth-century patri-

---

[51] For extracts see Seamus Deane *et al.*, eds., *The Field Day anthology of Irish Writing* (Derry, 1991), I, pp. 221–5.

[52] T. C. Barnard, 'The protestant interest, 1641–1660', in Jane Ohlmeyer, ed., *From independence to occupation* (Cambridge, 1995), pp. 218–40; James Kelly, 'The genesis of "Protestant Ascendancy": the rightboy disturbances of the 1780s and their impact upon protestant opinion', in Gerard O'Brien, ed., *Parliament, politics and people: essays in eighteenth-century Irish history* (Dublin, 1989), pp. 93–127.

[53] James Kelly, '"The glorious and immortal memory": commemoration and protestant identity in Ireland 1660–1800', *Proceedings of the Royal Irish Academy*, 94C (1994), 25–52.

[54] J. I. McGuire, 'The church of Ireland and the "Glorious Revolution" of 1688', in Art Cosgrove and Donal McCartney, eds., *Studies in Irish history presented to R. Dudley Edwards* (Dublin, 1979), pp. 141, 144.

[55] For a comparative study, see Colin Kidd, 'Gaelic antiquity and national identity in enlightenmnent Ireland and Scotland', *EHR*, 109 (1994), 1197–214.

otism was inevitably cast as the precursor of later separatist movements)
the reformed faith was treated as irrelevant, if not hostile, to the
development of national consciousness. While patriots such as Jonathan
Swift were praised for their mordant articulation of anti-English
feeling, they were censured for their religious exclusivity, an ambiva-
lence which can still be detected in some recent scholarship.[56] Contrary
to nineteenth-century assumptions, however, it can be seen that protestantism did shape Irish national identity in important ways. Just as the
Scottish kirk feared for its security under the union, so too the church of
Ireland had its own corporate interests to defend against metropolitan
governments who periodically found it necessary to intervene on behalf
of Roman catholics and protestant dissenters in the interests of international diplomacy or domestic tranquillity. It is no accident that some
of the first patriotic writers to give voice to Irish constitutional grievances were church of Ireland clergymen. Archbishop William King and
Dean Jonathan Swift can be seen as the Irish counterparts of Robert
Wodrow, trying to protect the integrity of an anglican church in the face
of a metropolitan government which favoured compromise with the
presbyterian dissenters of the north. Indeed it was within the church
episcopate, riven by disputes over the distribution of patronage, the
appellate jurisdiction of the Irish House of Lords, and the repeal of the
sacramental test, that the idea of antithetical Irish and English 'interests'
first took hold.[57]

Returning to the British level, then, what conclusions can be drawn
about the impact of religious divisions on nation-building during the
long eighteenth century? First and foremost, the essays included in this
volume all confirm the primacy of protestantism in the early modern
collective consciousness. Anti-popery, as David Hempton has written, is
'probably the most ubiquitous, most eclectic and most adaptable
ideology in the post-reformation history of the British Isles'.[58] But the
picture of national identity that emerges from this volume is less one of a
dominant consensus, than of a frequently contested terrain. As in
England, so across the three kingdoms, it is the ambivalent, contradictory character of protestantism, its ability to function both as a

---

[56] For recent examples of a teleological approach, see Joseph McMinn, 'A weary patriot:
Swift and the formation of Anglo-Irish identity', *Eighteenth-century Ireland*, 2 (1987),
103–13; Sean Murphy, 'Charles Lucas, catholicism and nationalism', *Eighteenth-
century Ireland*, 8 (1993), 83–102; Neil Longley York, *Neither kingdom nor nation: the
Irish quest for constitutional rights, 1698–1800* (Washington, DC, 1994).

[57] Patrick McNally, ' "Irish and English interests": national conflict with the church of
Ireland episcopate in the reign of George I', *IHS*, 29 (1995), 295–314.

[58] David Hempton, *Religion and political culture in Britain and Ireland* (Cambridge, 1996),
p. 145.

stabilising and a disruptive force, that is striking. Protestantism certainly defined the outer circle of nationality, ensuring that catholic Ireland would remain the one unasssimilable element within these islands. But it was by no means inevitable that a shared repudiation of Rome would be sufficient to dissolve the inherited ideological differences between the protestant communities of the three kingdoms. The patterns of integration and division which characterised the emergence of the imperial British state were certainly shaped by cultural affinities, but geography, economic and demographic development, and the distribution of patronage to provincial elites all played a part.

IV

So far in this introduction much doubt has been cast on any simple connection between religious and national identities. Looking at the work of many scholars, it appears that the internal ambiguities of the protestant faith, the divisions between protestants in different parts of the islands, and the difficulties of translating a shared belief in protestantism into an embracing set of institutions, all conspired to disrupt any confident sense of 'British', or even more narrowly 'English', feeling. Yet, despite all the qualifications that have been made, it would be as distorting simply to abandon the simple model of protestantism and nationality as it would have been to leave it unchallenged. Whilst eighteenth-century Britons had trouble reconciling their faith and their national identity, there is too much evidence that many thought the two were interlinked for the idea of close connection to be denied. Scholars must therefore find a way of writing about protestantism and national identity which acknowledges their interdependency, but gives due weight to the mismatches between them. They need to find an analysis which takes seriously both the weaknesses in any simple model of faith and identity – but which also accounts for its compelling explanatory force.

A promising way forward here is to redirect attention away from *descriptions* to *aspirations*. One might uphold the idea that the elect, godly nation was central to eighteenth-century thought, but one could suggest that this ideal was an objective for the community, rather than an agreed depiction of it. In other words, one could argue that subjects of the Stuarts and Hanoverians thought they *ought* to be an ideal protestant people, but that they recognised that in their current state of imperfection they were not. They may have believed that the British and Irish had a mission to become pure, protestant and chosen nations; but their chief responses to this mission may have been regret at the shortfallings and confusions which stood in its way, and an acute sense of the difficulty of the struggle which its fulfilment would entail.

Treating protestant nationhood in this way – as an anxious aspiration, rather than as a triumphal description – seems to have several advantages. First, and most obviously, an aspirational model of protestant national identity appears to match what the British and Irish actually said about their situation. When eighteenth-century people contemplated their country and its faith, it is true that they frequently saw themselves as objects of God's special concern. Yet this sense of divine selection did not produce a feeling of security. Rather, the dominant tone in most discussions of British and Irish relations with God was one of lamentation and alarm. For example, the contemporary sermons preached on state occasions (the literary products which did most to establish and explore protestant nationality) were almost always jeremiads. Applying the words of old testament prophets, preachers cautioned that the people were not living up to their elect status, that God would punish them for their backslidings, and that their divine status was in jeopardy if they did not make urgent efforts to repentance, purgation and reform.[59] In these sermons, the lesson of the analogy with Israel was not that God loved his faithful nation. Instead, the history of the Jews taught that election had never been secured, and that even a favoured people could be scattered by divine wrath if they did not make constant exertions to re-earn their special status.

Such indications that the idea of a godly community was prescriptive rather than descriptive ran through many of the cultural forms and movements of the era. In fact, there is a case for arguing that concern about the gap between ideal and reality was the central dynamic of late Stuart and Hanoverian society. Recent work by scholars of the period has shown how much contemporary effort was directed towards remodelling – or at least reconceptualising – the national community so it more closely met the image of a protestant country. For example, the historiography of religion has begun to emphasise the overwhelming sense of mission among late Stuart and Hanoverian protestants. It has stressed an acute sense that the country was still unconverted and that all faced the urgent task of completing the work of the sixteenth-century reformers. These attitudes have led some scholars to talk of a 'long reformation' – a continuing campaign of religious renewal and

---

[59] For such jeremiads, see Claydon, *William III*, p.130; Paul Langford, 'The English clergy and the American revolution', in Eckhart Hellmuth, ed., *The transformation of political culture: England and Germany in the late eighteenth century* (Oxford, 1990), pp. 275–308; Boyd Hilton, *The age of atonement: the influence of evangelicalism on social and economic thought, 1785–1865* (Oxford, 1988); and forthcoming work by James Caudle.

conversion stretching from the Tudor to the Victorian era.[60] Similarly, other works have underlined the persistent importance of calls for protestant renewal in mainstream political discourse. Governments legitimated themselves through such appeals, politicians argued about the denominational divisions which stood in their way, the press judged public figures on their record in such areas, and social and imperial projects were launched and debated with reference to the cause.[61] Again, the basic role of protestant messages has been recognised in contemporary art and culture, and this collection itself considers many cases where attempts to transform the British nations into more per-fectly godly communities generated new initiatives, changed contem-porary perceptions, or gave rise to bitter debates (the several essays dealing with approaches to non-protestant British subjects are obviously most relavent here). In all these cases, contemporary action seems to have been driven by a desire to elide national and confessional alle-giances. The dynamism of the era was often the product of the drive to create a truly protestant nation; and the divisions of the time were often rooted in disagreements about the correct strategy to reach this goal.

The second, and for this volume the most relevant, advantage of the aspirational model of faith and nationality is that it provides a relatively subtle account of late Stuart and Hanoverian identities. The crude notion of protestant Britishness introduced earlier foundered on the difficulty of reconciling religion and nationhood. By contrast, the notion of protestant nationality as an unrealised objective can cope with this problem better because it permits the scholarly balancing act mentioned above. On the one hand, it upholds the obvious centrality of the reformed faith to a sense of Britishness. Identity is constructed as much through objectives as through perceived achievements, so the British

---

[60] See especially, Nicholas Tyacke, ed., *England's long reformation, 1500–1800* (1998), particularly the articles by Jeremy Gregory and Jonathon Barry; and Jeremy Gregory, 'The eighteenth-century reformation: the pastoral task of the anglican clergy after 1689', in John Walsh, Colin Haydon and Stephen Taylor, eds., *The church of England, c.1689–c.1833* (Cambridge, 1993).

[61] See, for example, Colley, *Britons*, ch. 1; Claydon, *William III*; Hilton, *Age of atonement*; Jeremy Black, 'The catholic threat and the press in the 1720s and 1730s', *Journal of Religious History*, 12 (1983), 364–81; John Wolffe, *The protestant crusade in Britain* (Oxford, 1991); the essays by Gregory, Smith, Spurr, Rose and Elbourne in Walsh *et al.* ed., *Church of England*; Dudley Bahlman, *The moral revolution of 1688* (New Haven, 1957); and the rest of the huge literature on moral reform which is perhaps best approached through the footnotes to Robert B. Shoemaker, 'Reforming the city: the reformation of manners campaign in London', in Lee Davison, Tim Hitchcock, Tim Kearns and Robert Shoemaker, eds., *Stilling the grumbling hive: the response to social and economic problems in England* (1992), and through the essay by Joanna Innes in Hellmuth, ed., *Transformation of political culture*.

nations could still be described as essentially 'protestant' even though nobody would claim they had actually attained perfect reformation. On the other hand, the aspirational model takes seriously the shortcomings of the British nations as protestant communities. It suggests that contemporaries themselves were deeply aware of these shortcomings, and even incorporates this awareness in their self-perception by portraying them as people with a mission to *create* a fully protestant society. With this balance struck, a much more successful account of the ideal of an elect nation can be constructed. The ideal can be seen as crucial to the late Stuart and Hanoverian worldview, but it can also be seen as fluid and contested. Since a protestant national community was to be realised in the future, rather than celebrated now, its precise form was not settled. There was, therefore, still room for ambiguity about how it could be achieved, who could belong, or how exactly its godliness would be manifest. With elect nationhood still only an objective, it was debatable whether all protestant Britons would be included; whether there were ways to embrace non-protestant Britons; what the defining marks of the community would be; and whether England, Britain, or something imperial, European or even global was meant. Looking at the issue in this way appears to get us much closer to the full complexity of protestant and national identities in this period. As all the contributions to this collection make clear, late Stuart and Hanoverian Britons did put faith at the centre of their identity. Yet because that faith was largely an aspiration, the basic foundation in protestantism did not always lead to national triumphalism, clarity or unity.

England

2 'I love my King and my Country, but a Roman Catholic I hate': anti-catholicism, xenophobia and national identity in eighteenth-century England

Colin Haydon

It is not hard to see why the links between religion and national identity interested historians in the 1990s. To begin with, the times in which they wrote drew attention to the subject. With the collapse of communism, for example, racial and religious conflicts resurfaced in eastern Europe. Yugoslavia crumbled as catholic Croatians, orthodox Serbs and muslim Bosnians took up arms, and in Poland, the catholic church re-emerged as a potent political force. In Northern Ireland, too, both the IRA's war, and the 'peace process', threw into stark relief the issues dividing the loyalist and nationalist communities – and as Steve Bruce forcefully contended, religion was central to that conflict.[1] In addition, for historians of eighteenth-century Britain, religion became a subject of immense importance. After the neglect of the 1950s, 1960s and 1970s, Jonathan Clark's *English society, 1688–1832* (1985) sought to 'reintegrate religion into . . . [our] historical vision' of the Georgian era.[2] It succeeded in doing so, as did studies by other scholars such as Grayson Ditchfield, Jeremy Gregory, David Hempton, Stephen Taylor and John Walsh. Consequently, many historians came to accept Jeremy Black's judgement that anti-catholicism was 'arguably the prime ideological commitment of most of the population';[3] or Linda Colley's statement that 'Protestantism was the foundation that made the invention of Great Britain possible.'[4] Such an acceptance would not have been widespread twenty years before.

I

The main contribution of anti-catholicism to national identity in the Georgian era was to construct the European continent as fundamentally

[1] Steve Bruce, *God save Ulster!* (Oxford, 1986); and *The edge of the union* (Oxford, 1994).
[2] J. C. D. Clark, *English society, 1688–1832* (Cambridge, 1985), p. ix.
[3] Jeremy Black, *Natural and necessary enemies* (1986), p. 161.
[4] Linda Colley, *Britons* (New Haven/London, 1992), p. 54.

alien. If, in the nineteenth century, protestant Englishmen saw Irish catholics as 'the other', whose many failings negatively defined and extolled the former's values,[5] continental papists were 'the other' for protestant Britons in the preceding century. To begin with, catholic monarchs and their nobilities were pictured in an unfavourable light. Their political systems appeared inimical to concepts of liberty; and 'popery and tyranny' and 'popery and arbitrary power' became two of the most common political slogans of the age. In particular, France was depicted as the apogee of catholic despotism. Louis XIV seemed the archetypal popish tyrant – described in almanacs as 'the Bully King' or the 'King of Wooden Shoes'[6] – whilst in 1737 a publication entitled *The Hyp-doctor* saw Louis' successor as 'an absolute tyrant' whose rule was grounded on 'the Bastile . . . Lettres de cachet . . . [and] the Wheel'.[7] Within this view of the world, there was limited appreciation of the various brakes on French monarchical power or of changes respecting it before 1789.[8] At the same time, continental elites seemed to bolster, rather than mitigate, despotism. Spanish grandees were depicted as proud and cruel; French noblemen appeared foppish and debauched (until the revolution, after which the extinction of their old-world manners was lamented);[9] and catholic aristocracies were denounced for allowing the representative institutions of their country to fall into obsolescence. Only Austria escaped general censure, and then only because it was Britain's ally for much of the early century.[10]

Popish priests abroad were also subjects for attack. Their teaching was represented as a corruption, indeed a perversion, of the gospels; and it was thought small wonder that they sought to deny the laity vernacular bibles. On the continent, the English presumed, the veneration of relics and the promotion of false doctrines, such as Mariolatry and transubstantiation, obscured true religion and hence endangered souls. In addition, 'heretics' were treated cruelly, as prints of the Inquisition's dungeons in Spain or accounts of the 'Thorn massacre' (1724) graphically emphasised. '*Popery* is at this Day', one preacher declared in 1719, 'what it always was, a *bloody* Religion, which teacheth the Persecution of *Protestants* with Fire and Sword, and other *inhumane Severities*.'[11] The clergy also seemed self-seeking. Great ecclesiastics wanted political

[5] R. F. Foster, *Paddy and Mr Punch: connections in Irish and English history* (Harmondsworth, 1993), pp. 171–94.

[6] Bernard Capp, *Astrology and the popular press: English almanacs, 1500–1800* (1979), p. 248.

[7] Black, *Natural and necessary enemies*, p. 186.

[8] Ibid., p. 192.   [9] BM, PD, 4,754, 9,410.

[10] Black, *Natural and necessary enemies*, p. 192.

[11] Thomas Knaggs, *The cruelty and tyranny of popery* (1720), pp. 11–12.

power; and monks and nuns contributed little or nothing to the society that supported them. Nor was the church's wealth used wisely. It 'is a very shamefull thing', one English visitor to Loretto observed, 'that so vast a treasure of jewels and other riches should lye buried there [in the churches], while all the inhabitants of the town almost are starving'.[12] As for clerical vows of celibacy, they were often a blind for lechery or unnatural vice. The case of a French girl, Catherine Cadière, seduced by her confessor, was extensively – and gleefully – reported in the British press in the 1730s.[13]

By contrast with the proud catholic rulers and the great churchmen, the masses of the continent appeared poor and servile. In prints depicting eighteenth-century French society, the peasants are bowed and emaciated, wearing wooden shoes, the symbol of their servitude.[14] In Hogarth's *The roast beef of old England*,[15] even the French soldiers have holes in their clothes and are scrawny. Two are eating *soupe maigre*. Again, in Hogarth's *The invasion* (1756),[16] soldiers roast frogs at an inn – called 'La Sabot Royal' [*sic*], with a wooden shoe as its sign – which advertises 'Soup Meagre' as the chief delight on its menu. Such images reflected the view that popery and poverty went inevitably together. Unlike protestantism (which encouraged industry and thrift), popery, with its numerous holidays and indiscriminate charity, encouraged idleness. Richard Woodward, preaching in Dublin in 1764, observed that the reformation had rightly effected the 'Restoration of so many Days lost to Labour, under the Name of Holydays'.[17] The continental peasantry was also seen as cowardly and credulous. In *The roast beef of old England*, people kneel around a priest holding the host, whilst three old women 'see' Christ's image on the skin of a fish. By comparison, the lower orders in England were depicted as well fed and happy, enjoying freedom under the law and the benefits of a rational church's teaching.

This essential connection between catholicism and the perversions of the continent affected attitudes to British adherents of the Roman faith. Twentieth-century patrician catholic families are often depicted as 'more English than the English', but this is not how their forebears seemed to eighteenth-century protestants. Their continental connections gave

---

[12] Jeremy Black, 'The catholic threat and the British press in the 1720s and 1730s', *Journal of Religious History*, 12:4 (1983), 366.
[13] Colin Haydon, *Anti-catholicism in eighteenth-century England, c. 1714–80* (Manchester, 1993), p. 38.
[14] BM, PD, 4,679, 4,790, 4,792.   [15] Now in the Tate Gallery, London.
[16] BM, PD, 3,446, plate 1.
[17] Richard Woodward, *A sermon preached at Christ-Church, Dublin, on 13 May, 1764* (Dublin, 1764), p. 4.

them a cosmopolitan character, which cut them off from true English-ness. Catholics, for instance, were often educated in colleges abroad. At a school like Douai, they may well have acquired traces of foreign manners (even, perhaps, the hint of an accent),[18] and in later life, they might travel abroad to visit shrines and pilgrimage centres. Priests, trained at Douai, Lisbon, Rome, Seville or Valladolid, could seem similarly 'un-English'. They conducted their services in Latin, and their breviaries and devotional works were often brought from the continent (or so at least it was purported). Emphasising these foreign links, the only legal catholic services in England before 1791 were those held in the embassy chapels, maintained in London by Bavaria, the Empire, France, Naples, Portugal, Sardinia, Spain and Venice. The chapels – and especially the Sardinian – were lavishly decorated;[19] and in such settings, the many protestant visitors could witness mass celebrated with full baroque pomp, and might contrast Roman rites and buildings with the relative simplicity of anglican worship and decoration.[20] Some country-house chapels were impressive too, and that at Wardour, built for the eighth Lord Arundell, was magnificent. Arundell had undertaken the grand tour with the Jesuits and his agent in Rome, Fr John Thorp SJ, supplied him with a range of possible Italianate designs. The chapel, started in 1770 and opened in 1776, was filled with continental works of art; and the altar, with a tabernacle and throne in silver gilt, was designed by Jacomo Quarenghi. Its *verde antico* sarcophagus was a gift from the pope.[21]

To this cultural threat from the catholic continent, the political dimension of Jacobitism was added. In St Peter's in Rome, there is the splendid monument to the exiled Stuarts. That the remains of 'James III', 'Charles III' and 'Henry IX' lie buried in the chief shrine of catholicism would have seemed entirely appropriate to George III's protestant subjects, for, in the eighteenth century, it was through Jacobitism that the catholic threat was chiefly perpetuated. As Arthur Ashley Sykes put it in 1746, '*Foreign Jurisdiction* in the *Pope*, and a

---

[18] It was said of the celebrated collector of antiquities Charles Townley (1737–1805), who had been educated at Douai, that 'he never spoke his native tongue but with some hesitation, and had frequent recourse to French and Italian words to remove his embarrassment': T. D. Whitaker, *An history of the original parish of Whalley* (3rd edn, revd, 1818), p. 486. I am grateful to Gerard Vaughan for this reference.

[19] Roderick O'Donnell, 'The architectural setting of Challoner's episcopate', in Eamon Duffy, ed., *Challoner and his church* (1981), pp. 64–70.

[20] Eamon Duffy, '"Poor Protestant flies": conversions to catholicism in early eighteenth-century England', in Derek Baker, ed., *Religious motivation: biographical and sociological problems for the church historian, SCH*, 15 (Oxford, 1978), 296–7.

[21] O'Donnell, 'Architectural setting', pp. 60–2.

Foreign Pretender to our Crown, are inseparable.'[22] Despite the Stuarts' negotiations with Sweden, Russia and Prussia, catholic France and Spain seemed to be the claimants' natural supporters, and were depicted as such in propaganda at home. If triumphant, it was trumpeted, the Stuarts would impose an alien, authoritarian political regime on Englishmen and restore popish idolatry. For example, in one print, *The invasion or Perkins [sic] triumph* (1745), James Edward is brought to London in a coach by Louis XV and the pope,[23] whilst in another, *The chevaliers [sic] market* (1745), Magna Carta and the bible are cast on the ground and cleared away by a street sweeper.[24] 'Had the Pretender succeeded in his Rebellion in Great-Britain', declared the *Weekly Journal, or, British Gazetteer* in 1716, 'he . . . [would] without doubt [have] erected such a bloody Tribunal, as they have among the Spaniards'.[25] Such close mental association between catholicism and Jacobitism had a foundation in reality. Early in the eighteenth century, English papists did seem thoroughly committed to James Edward's cause. They widely refused to swear allegiance to George I.[26] They also predominated in the higher ranks of the 1715 English rebel forces, and Paul Monod has estimated that they constituted between two-thirds and three-quarters of the English rebel army as a whole.[27] One preacher's view of such people was simple: 'He that can bear to think of a *Popish* Pretender, and an *arbitrary French* Government, deserveth not to *tread* on *English* Earth, or *breathe* in *English* Air.'[28] English papists' connections with Jacobites abroad were, therefore, very disturbing. Take, for example, two catholic gentry families from south Warwickshire, the Sheldons and the Bishops. William Sheldon was a member of the Jacobite masonic lodge at Rome,[29] whilst Henry Bishop, who later became a Franciscan, fought on the French side at Fontenoy.[30] Amassing such evidence, the English constructed catholicism as the most dangerous part of the external threat facing their country. It was all the more alarming for its adherents within the state. English catholics'

[22] [A. A. Sykes], *The reasonableness of mending and executing the laws against papists* (1746), pp. 31–2.
[23] BM, PD, 2,636. [24] Ibid., 2,660.
[25] *Weekly Journal, or, British Gazetteer*, 24 Mar. 1716.
[26] Edgar E. Estcourt and John Orlebar Payne, eds., *The English catholic nonjurors of 1715* (n.d., repr. Farnborough, 1969).
[27] Haydon, *Anti-catholicism*, pp. 81–2; Paul K. Monod, *Jacobitism and the English people, 1688–1788* (Cambridge, 1989), p. 322.
[28] John Billingsley, *A sermon preach'd on the thanksgiving, January 20, 1714/15* (1714) [sic], p. 21.
[29] W. J. Hughan, *The Jacobite lodge at Rome, 1735–7* (Torquay, 1910), pp. 14, 37.
[30] John Kirk, *Biographies of English catholics in the eighteenth century*, ed. J. H. Pollen and Edwin Burton (1909), p. 26.

cultural connections and their supposed political allegiances were thought to dispose them to disloyalty.

II

How were such attitudes to catholicism propagated and sustained? Sermons were one staple means of disseminating anti-popish ideology and, in the first half of the century, of reviling the 'popish pretender' and his supporters on the continent. Each year on the fifth of November, anglican churches held a special service commemorating the thwarting of the 'gunpowder plot' and William III's triumph in 1688–9; and since the liturgy made provision for a sermon, preachers could draw parallels between past and current dangers from popery. During the Jacobite rebellions, much could be made of the catholics' foreign links. Thanksgiving services were also held to celebrate the failures of the 'Fifteen' and the 'Forty-five' – failures which, the preachers declared, were the work of providence.[31] In time of war too, sermons might attribute victory to the hand of God. It 'hath . . . pleased the Lord of Hosts', Josiah Woodward told the City of London's aldermen in 1706, 'to crown our late campaigns with astonishing success, with the most compleat and honourable victories that many ages can produce.'[32] Britain thus seemed a new Israel, favoured by God, with her popish adversaries the counterparts of the Jews' heathen enemies. Hence the splendid title of one 1763 sermon, *The triumph of Israelites over Moabites, or protestants over papists.* Some preachers stressed Britain's obligations to foreign protestants, and, in 1760, Whitefield raised collections of over £400 for the 'distressed Protestants in *Prussia*', suffering as a result of the Seven Years War.[33] Sermons attacking popery were easily understood by an ill-educated congregation, especially when they focused on popish brutality rather than Rome's doctrinal errors. Certainly the cruelty of foreign papists was a stock theme, substantiated by accounts of the Inquisition, *autos-da-fé*, and the Spaniards' depredations in the new world. Stories of this kind fed the popular appetite for horror.

The race relations act of 1976 outlawed the use in public places of 'words which are threatening, abusive or insulting, in a case where . . . hatred is likely to be stirred up against any racial group . . . by the

---

[31] Haydon, *Anti-catholicism*, p. 95; Françoise Deconinck-Brossard, 'The churches and the '45', in W. J. Sheils, ed., *The church and war, SCH*, 20 (Oxford, 1983), 259.

[32] D. Napthine and W. A. Speck, 'Clergymen and conflict, 1660–1763', in Sheils, ed., *Church and war*, 237.

[33] John Gillies, *Memoirs of the life of . . . George Whitefield* (1772), pp. 231, 234.

matter or words in question'.[34] The statute thus recognised that vocabulary can be an expression of, and a conduit for, prejudice – and so it was in eighteenth-century England. 'Popery', 'popish' and 'papist' were abusive words. Along with their theological significance – that the papists' faith centred not on Christ but on the pope – they branded catholics as a group whose political allegiance lay, as Locke had argued, with 'another prince'.[35] Catholics were naturally riled by this vocabulary, as the parson of Woolhampton, a rural parish in Berkshire, observed in 1767. 'My good neighbours', he noted, 'seem now to be a little ashamed of ye name of *Papists*, by which . . . they don't love to be called, & wod. disown it, & say they are not *Papists*, but good *Catholicks*.'[36] Similarly, 'Romish' – 'Romish superstitions', 'Romish rites' – evoked images of the eternal city and its baroque churches with their candles, incense, magnificent paintings and flamboyant alien worship. Another pointed adjective was 'outlandish'. 'I will have your house down, you outlandish bouger', a certain Thomas Lebarty was told in the Gordon riots.[37] Lebarty was an Italian and this suggests the word's contemporary meaning. Dr Johnson defined it literally in his *Dictionary* (1755) as 'not native; foreign'; and it is significant that it was often applied to the catholic minority in England generally. Catholic culture was essentially continental, 'unEnglish'.

Historians of early modern France have shown much interest in the folkloric dimension of oral culture. One wonders whether English folklore buttressed the sense that catholicism was fundamentally 'unEnglish'. In fact, evidence that it did so is limited. Folk tales might recall popish atrocities. According to Defoe, popery was 'the Hobgoblin, the Spectre with which the Nurses fright the Children, and entertain the old Women all over the Country'.[38] However, stories seem to have concentrated on domestic events – notably the Marian persecutions and Monmouth's rebellion – so they may not have helped to emphasise the alien nature of catholicism.[39] Even so, there were visual reminders of the

---

[34] 1976, c. 74, § 70.

[35] John Locke, *Epistola de tolerantia/A letter on toleration*, ed. R. Klibansky and J. W. Gough (Oxford, 1968), p. 133.

[36] Wiltshire RO, Salisbury Diocesan Archives, DI/9/1/3, return of W. Deane, 21 Nov. 1767.

[37] George Rudé, 'The Gordon riots: a study of the rioters and their victims', *TRHS*, 5th ser., 6 (1956), 113, n. 1.

[38] [Daniel Defoe], *The great law of subordination consider'd* (1724), p. 20.

[39] Haydon, *Anti-catholicism*, pp. 43–4; Lord Macaulay, *The history of England from the accession of James the Second*, ed. C. H. Firth (6 vols., 1913–15), II, p. 635. Sometimes, too, folklore showed catholicism in a favourable light. Its priests were credited with magical powers; miracles, it was said, were still worked at its shrines. Protestants, of course, strongly disliked such claims. I hope to examine this important subject in detail elsewhere.

catholic threat from abroad in earlier times. Across southern England, there was the chain of hills on which beacons had been lit during the 1588 armada crisis, and the Monument in London had a plaque attributing the 1666 fire – which had, of course, occurred in time of war – to 'the treachery and malice of the Popish faction'. Until the middle of the eighteenth century, there was a very similar inscription in Pudding Lane, where the fire began.[40] In the Tower of London, visitors to the Spanish armoury saw relics of the armada, including a gun disguised as a holy-water sprinkler.[41] Given the scarcity of evidence of response to such objects, it is impossible to gauge popular reactions. However, the very display of such relics must have promoted a garbled version of English history, in which the defeat of popery was the nation's constant and greatest task.

For the literate, there was a profusion of anti-popish books. Some were scholarly treatises, but, since many divines regarded the intellectual battle against Rome as won, a good number were aimed at a humbler market.[42] The SPCK's *Protestant catechism* denounced Roman theology in twenty-four pages and in simple language which could be easily grasped.[43] Some works were adapted for a popular readership. In 1753, John White produced a sizeable book *The protestant Englishman guarded against the arts and arguments of Romish priests and emissaries,* but two years later, he issued a much smaller work based on it, *A new preservative against popery,* so that, by virtue of its reduced size and cost, and simpler content, it might be more easily dispersed 'among the lower People'.[44] In the eighteenth century, bowdlerised versions and excerpts of Foxe's 'book of martyrs' were printed, sustaining the belief that the English were an elect people.[45] Similarly, in the early nineteenth century, much-loved copies of Bunyan's *Pilgrim's progress,* with its anti-popish passages, might still be found in countless cottages.[46] Newspapers, pamphlets and

---

[40] W. E. H. Lecky, *A history of England in the eighteenth century* (new edn, 7 vols., 1892), I, p. 342.

[41] J. Anthony Williams, 'Change or decay? The provincial laity, 1691–1781', in Duffy, ed., *Challoner and his church,* pp. 48–9.

[42] John Walsh and Stephen Taylor, 'Introduction: the church and anglicanism in the "long" eighteenth century', in John Walsh, Colin Haydon and Stephen Taylor, eds., *The church of England, c. 1689–c. 1833: from toleration to Tractarianism* (Cambridge, 1993), pp. 57–8.

[43] *A protestant catechism: shewing the principal errors of the church of Rome. In four parts* (1766).

[44] J. White, *A new preservative against popery* (1755), p. iv.

[45] Haydon, *Anti-catholicism,* pp. 28–9; Colley, *Britons,* pp. 25–8; Eirwen Nicholson, 'Eighteenth-century Foxe: evidence for the impact of the *Acts and monuments* in the "long" eighteenth century', in David Loades, ed., *John Foxe and the English reformation* (Aldershot, 1997), pp.143–77.

[46] Clark, *English society,* p. 166.

printed sermons also portrayed Britain as protestantism's champion and detailed instances of catholic intolerance and vice in Europe. Much was made of the sufferings of the Huguenots and of Salzburg's protestants, expelled by the archbishop's patent of 1731, and one pamphlet covering the Cadière affair went through at least eleven editions.[47] As for almanacs, they were virulently anti-catholic and xenophobic. In late Stuart times, some 400,000 were sold annually in an England with a population of 5 million,[48] and Francis Moore, it was said, came to provide the 'creed of the common people'.[49] Whilst it is not clear exactly who purchased such productions,[50] their message was plain as anti-popery was promoted through attacks on catholic rulers, chronologies which listed protestant triumphs and popish atrocities, and eager predictions of the fall of the papal antichrist (the Lisbon earthquake of 1755 marked, according to 'Moore', the start of this apocalypse).[51] By contrast, chapbooks contain little anti-catholic material. Perhaps, however, this is to be expected, given the timeless quality Margaret Spufford has observed in such publications in the seventeenth century.[52]

In 1981, Bob Scribner investigated the role of prints in transmitting the ideas of the German reformation to the illiterate and semi-literate populace.[53] In eighteenth-century England, prints could likewise show the 'meaner sort' the iniquities of popery. However, one must observe that the illiterate could not – on their own – fully appreciate prints with captions, whilst the nature of the prints' market/public is problematical.[54] Nevertheless, English satirical prints were produced in large numbers, either as illustrations for books or to be sold separately, and many dealt with religion, having popery as a favourite target.[55] Though Hogarth's repulsive *Transubstantiation satirized* (1735) was an exception,[56] theological subjects were rarely treated (since the points were

---

[47] *The case of Mrs. Mary Catharine Cadiere* (11th edn, 1732).

[48] Capp, *Astrology*, p. 23.

[49] Paul Langford, *A polite and commercial people: England, 1727–1783* (Oxford, 1989), p. 281.

[50] Jonathan Barry, 'Literacy and literature in popular culture: reading and writing in historical perspective', in Tim Harris, ed., *Popular culture in England, c. 1500–1850* (Basingstoke, 1995), p. 75.

[51] Capp, *Astrology*, p. 252.

[52] Margaret Spufford, *Small books and pleasant histories* (1981), p. 219.

[53] R. W. Scribner, *For the sake of simple folk: popular propaganda for the German reformation* (Cambridge, 1981).

[54] Eirwen Nicholson, 'Consumers and spectators: the public of the political print in eighteenth-century England', *History*, 81 (1996), 5–21.

[55] John Miller, *Religion in the popular prints, 1600–1832. The English satirical print, 1600–1832* (Cambridge, 1986), p. 15.

[56] BM, PD, 2,156. In it, the Christ child is fed into a mill which makes the host from his body.

hard to convey in picture form); but the papists' politics were much more easily lampooned, and much was made of the catholics' 'outlandish' connections. In one print noted above, *The chevaliers market*, the pretender is not only attacked as a popish zealot and would-be tyrant, but Jacobitism is also portrayed as an essentially foreign movement. Around the market cross, vendors sell 'Gaggs and Spanish Padlocks', 'Woode[n] Shoe[s] A la mod PARIS', and 'FROGS for a Fricacee'. One stall has 'Holy RELICKS from JERUSALEM ITALY FRANCE SPAIN & other Catholick Countries'.[57] A bitter print of 1779, *The family compact*, attacked the alliance of France and Spain against Britain during the American war. It was shown as the work of the devil, wearing a papal tiara.[58] Another theme which was easily illustrated was that of popish cruelty. Foxe's *Acts and monuments* was amply illustrated with gory woodcuts of the Marian martyrs' sufferings at the stake. Eighteenth-century versions might include pictures of later events, such as the 1641 Irish massacre[59] or the Calas affair.[60] The Inquisition's cruelty was also depicted in prints. Samuel Chandler's *History of persecution* (1736) contains pictures of an interrogation, the torture chamber, and an *auto-da-fé*.[61]

The 'outlandish' character of catholicism was also emphasised in pope-burning demonstrations held on 5 November, on royal birthdays, coronation days, and, in the early eighteenth century, on Queen Elizabeth's accession day (17 November). A woodcut of a pope-burning from 1717 shows an effigy of the pretender, clutching a pair of wooden shoes, consigned to a bonfire.[62] When the pope's effigy was burnt at Chichester on coronation day 1714, it was attired in full Romish splendour: 'richly dress'd in his proper Habit . . . on his Head a Tripple Crown; his Vestment was a Scarlet Cassock . . . at his Girdle Two Golden Keys, and within the bending of his left Arm stood his Crosier Gilt with Gold'. The accompanying figure of the pretender had a 'Hat lac'd after the French Mode', whilst a person representing the devil carried 'a large pair of Wooden-Shoes in his Hand'.[63] In an elaborate display at Deptford, organised in 1745 on George II's birthday, such symbolism was again used to great effect. The parade consisted of:

1. A highlander in his proper dress carrying on a pole a pair of wooden shoes with this motto, *The Newest make from Paris*. 2. A Jesuit, in his proper dress,

---

[57] Ibid., 2,660.   [58] Ibid., 5,567.
[59] Paul Wright, ed., *The new and complete book of martyrs* [1785?], facing p. 947.
[60] Ibid., facing p. 879.
[61] Samuel Chandler, *The history of persecution* (1736), facing pp. 189, 245, inserted after pp. 280, 290, 292.
[62] BM, PD, 1,607, p. 8.
[63] *Flying Post: or, the Post-Master*, 30 Oct.–2 Nov. 1714.

carrying on the point of a long sword, a banner, with this Inscription in large letters Inquisition, Flames and Damnation. 3. Two Capuchin Friars, properly shaved habited and accoutred with flogging ropes, beads, crucifixes etc. One of them bore on a high pole a bell, mass book and candles to curse the British nation with . . . 4. The Pretender, with a green ribband a nosegay of Thistle etc. riding upon an ass, supported by a Frenchman on the right and a Spaniard on the left, each dressed to the height of the newest modes. 5. The Pope riding on his Bull . . .[64]

Many people could witness, or take part in, pope-burning demonstrations. At Chichester, the initial procession wound through 'the Principal Streets of the City',[65] whilst at Aylesbury, in 1716, the effigies of the pope, the pretender, and the earl of Mar 'were carry'd through the Town with Musick before them'.[66] Large crowds could also gather round a bonfire, and the displays could be fun as well as instructive.

Between 1714 and 1760, the function of such ceremonies, with respect to politics, was clear. It was to counter the anti-Hanoverian sentiment that was so marked in the years after George I's accession and which swelled again in the early 1740s (the result of George II's provisions for his electorate during the war of the Austrian succession). George I and his son were Teutonic and uncharismatic. The former was perceived as Lutheran, the latter latitudinarian, in his religion. Despite all this, however, the Hanoverian monarchs were preferable to a '*Popish Pretender*, back'd with [*sic*] a Foreign Power',[67] and the pope-burnings repeatedly publicised this message. There are numerous accounts of the displays, notably in contemporary newspapers, and they often describe the symbolism at some length. Usually though, such descriptions cover larger, urban spectacles. Village celebrations were less elaborate: sometimes they consisted of little more than the burning of a few sticks, surmounted by a paper tiara, and sometimes the crowd had to use its imagination. When a bonfire was held at one Warwickshire village in 1735, the participants put on faggots and sticks. They told the curate that they had burnt 'the Pope and the Devil, and then held up their Hats and Hallowed'.[68] However, whilst such local ceremonies lacked the sophistication of the better-known publications or urban festivities, they do attest to the protean nature of anti-catholic cultural forms. In the eighteenth century, anti-popery was promulgated through a rich variety of media. Many of these were well calculated to gain a mass audience.

[64] W. A. Speck, *The butcher: the duke of Cumberland and the suppression of the '45* (Oxford, 1981), p. 69.
[65] *Flying Post: or, the Post-Master*, 30 Oct.–2 Nov. 1714.
[66] Ibid., 12–14 June 1716.
[67] Thomas Linford, *God, a tower of salvation to the king* (1715), p. 21.
[68] Worcester (St Helen's) RO, 797.6 (iii), BA 2,632, deposition of Randal Bevans, 29 Apr. 1736.

III

Despite the ubiquity of anti-catholicism in Georgian England, expression of hostility was not uniform across the period. Not surprisingly, given that anti-popery contained a large xenophobic and political element, it was in time of war that the sentiment intensified, and it was France – Britain's chief rival and adversary in successive conflicts – which was particularly vilified. Almanacs portrayed Louis XIV as a monster in the war of the Spanish succession.[69] During the Seven Years War, the Sussex shopkeeper and diarist Thomas Turner noted crossly, 'What seems very surprising to me in the Duke of Newcastle is that he countenances so many Frenchmen, there being ten of his servants, cooks etc. which was down here of that nation.'[70] It was popularly believed that the French would fight in a treacherous fashion – a favoured tactic was thought to be arson in their enemies' towns, ports and dockyards.[71] And in the war of the Austrian succession, the Laudable Association of Antigallicans was founded. At its branch meetings – its chief general meeting was predictably held on St George's day – it disseminated propaganda about the detestable character of the French nation and its religion. It also tried to promote British manufactures with a view to keeping out French imports and, in wartime, arranged for young men to be trained in the navy.[72] Other popish enemies seemed only slightly less hateful. In 1738 and 1739, the Spaniards' treatment of Captain Jenkins outraged national pride and English xenophobia was fed by tales of Spanish cruelty and the 'Black Legend'. Accordingly, after his capture of Porto Bello in 1739, Admiral Vernon was lionised as a latter-day Drake or Ralegh.[73] And following the 'diplomatic revolution' and its offensive alliance with France in the Seven Years War, Austria, previously treated with relative leniency, was attacked as a cruel, persecuting state.[74]

Given such wartime attitudes, catholics were easily depicted as a fifth column. If the opportunity arose, some believed that they might come

---

[69] Capp, *Astrology*, p. 248.

[70] David Vaisey, ed., *The diary of Thomas Turner, 1754–1765* (Oxford, 1984), p. 160.

[71] Haydon, *Anti-catholicism*, p. 57.

[72] Ibid.; Linda Colley, 'Radical patriotism in eighteenth-century England', in Raphael Samuel, ed., *Patriotism: the making and unmaking of British national identity* (3 vols., 1989), I, pp. 172–5.

[73] Kathleen Wilson, 'Empire, trade and popular politics in mid-Hanoverian Britain: the case of Admiral Vernon', *P&P*, 121 (1988), 74–109; Nicholas Rogers, *Whigs and cities* (Oxford, 1989), pp. 58–9, 235–6, 374–6, 397.

[74] Jeremy Black, 'Ideology, history, xenophobia and the world of print in eighteenth-century England', in Jeremy Black and Jeremy Gregory, eds., *Culture, politics and society in Britain, 1660–1800* (Manchester, 1991), p. 192.

out in open rebellion. 'If France or Spain . . . would venture 1000 men . . . upon our English Shore', declared one Oxfordshire parson in 1739, they 'would quickly have 10000 [Catholics] to joyn them . . . from ye beck of their Popish Spiritual Superiors.'[75] Unsurprisingly, such concerns had their mirror-image in catholic Europe. During the war of the Austrian succession, Maria Theresa ordered the expulsion of the Jews from Bohemia and major Moravian cities: she believed that they wanted her enemies to triumph.[76] Similarly, during the Seven Years War, it was feared in France that a Huguenot rising might occur.[77] In fact, after the disaster of the 'Fifteen', the possibility of a significant catholic rising quickly receded: yet, for protestants, there remained the fear that the papists might seek to undermine the state through clandestine activity in time of war. In 1745, the authorities in King's Lynn regarded the foreign correspondence of some catholics there as highly suspicious.[78] Were they the agents of hostile powers? Methodists, during the war of 1739–48, were denounced as papists in disguise, and the Wesleys themselves, it was claimed, had received Spanish bribes to raise a disloyal plebeian army.[79] The bulk of catholics, unable – or too fearful – to assist the nation's enemies, might rejoice, protestants suspected, in the nation's defeats. In December 1756, a corn riot occurred at Hereford. A local popish farmer had apparently 'been heard to Say that he rather would Sell to the french for 5. Shill. than to his own Country for 7. shs. 6 pen'. The mob, composed of women, mindful of such perversity, enacted a fitting inversion ritual. They ducked him in the river, like a scold, 'till he was almost drownded'.[80]

Invasion scares naturally heightened suspicions about the popish minority. In 1745, the authorities' concern about the King's Lynn papists had as its background the belief that the French navy, said to be making 'a vast Embarkation', might land near the town.[81] At Portsmouth, too, it was feared in that year that the local catholics might revolt, coordinating their action with the French fleet's arrival.[82] Portsmouth's great dockyard seemed an obvious target for treachery. Later, in 1770, a fire broke out there, and, according to a radical paper, *The*

---

[75] Oxfordshire Archives, MS Oxf. Dioc., c. 651, f. 68.
[76] Robert A. Kann, *A history of the Habsburg empire, 1526–1918* (Berkeley, 1974), pp. 189–90. The orders were later largely rescinded.
[77] D. D. Bien, *The Calas affair: persecution, toleration and heresy in eighteenth-century Toulouse* (Princeton, 1960), p. 72.
[78] PRO, SP Domestic, 36/76/259.
[79] John Walsh, 'Methodism and the mob in the eighteenth century', in G. J. Cuming and Derek Baker, eds., *Popular belief and practice, SCH*, 8 (Cambridge, 1972), 226.
[80] NLW, 478 E, f. 16v.
[81] Albert Hartshorne, ed., *Memoirs of a royal chaplain, 1729–1763* (1905), p. 113.
[82] PRO, SP, 36/76/1; 36/76/414; 36/76/420.

Whisperer, it was started by papists.[83] Prints designed to excite patriotism made light of invasion threats. In Hogarth's second *Invasion* plate, brawny English soldiers and sailors, nourished on beef and beer, mock a daub of the French king at the Duke of Cumberland inn. A civilian willingly enlists.[84] All are eager to fight the French whose forces (depicted on the first plate of the prints) are accompanied by a monk, with chains, a wheel and a gibbet.[85] The reality for civilians, understandably, was liable to be different. As a Hampshire parson pointedly joked to a friend in 1756, he rejoiced in his recovery from illness since 'now, shd. the French come, I can run away like an Englishman'.[86] In 1779, when a Franco-Spanish invasion plan came close to success, there was pandemonium along parts of the south-west and south coast. As the armada sailed towards Plymouth, it produced panic, with the inhabitants making 'every possible exertion to move off with their families to Truro, Tiverton' and other inland towns.[87] Then, the following year, when the Gordon riots erupted, external dangers were again linked to internal conspiracy. Some espoused the paranoid thesis that the riots were the work of catholic *agents provocateurs*. By causing chaos in the capital, they would break the nation's war effort.[88] Even so, it was in 1745, as Charles Edward Stuart advanced into England and a French invasion was anticipated, that fears of catholic treachery reached their zenith. Across the kingdom they were manifested in popular panics akin to the French *grande peur* of 1789 or to the anti-popish alarms which had swept England prior to the civil war and in 1688.[89] Those English *peurs* had originated in rumours that the papists or James II's Irish soldiers were moving against the protestant population. As Defoe noted, at the time of the 1688 revolution, a 'universal alarm . . . spread over the whole kingdom . . . of the Irish being coming to cut every bodies throats';[90] now, in 1745, it was widely expected that the catholics would try to assist James' grandson.[91] For example, when the Lancashire

---

[83] *The Whisperer*, 86 (1771), 537–44.   [84] BM, PD, 3,454.

[85] Ibid., 3,446.   [86] Hampshire RO, photocopy 605, 70.

[87] A. Temple Patterson, *The other armada: the Franco-Spanish attempt to invade Britain in 1779* (Manchester, 1960), p. 182.

[88] Rudé, 'Gordon riots', pp. 101–2. Such ideas persisted in the era of the French revolution. Was it not possible that agents of the revolution were masquerading as refugees? Accordingly, security measures were introduced by the 1793 'Act for establishing regulations respecting aliens arriving in this kingdom, or resident therein, in certain cases' (33 Geo. III, c. 4).

[89] Georges Lefebvre, *La grande peur de 1789* (Paris, 1932); Robin Clifton, 'The popular fear of catholics during the English revolution', *P&P*, 52 (1971), 23–55; John Miller, *Popery and politics in England, 1660–1688* (Cambridge, 1973), pp. 259–61.

[90] Daniel Defoe, *A tour through the whole island of Great Britain* (Everyman edn, 1974), I, p. 294.

[91] Loyalist propaganda linked the dangers from France and popery. Lord Hardwicke told

militia was dismissed, its members refused to part with more than 200 of their arms. They durst not go home without them, for fear of their popish neighbours.[92] Similarly, it was said that 'great numbers of men, horse, and arms, were concealed . . . in subterraneous passages' under Lady Petre's house at Lower Cheam, Surrey.[93] Again, at Sarnesfield in Herefordshire, a cellar belonging to the catholic Monington family was reported to contain a cache of arms 'design'd for an ill Use'.[94]

Along the south and east coasts, there were further anxieties or alarms, with some born of the apprehension – official or otherwise – that local papists might be working with the French or the Jacobites. They were widespread not least because it was unclear where a French landing might be made. In Hampshire, a loyal association was formed and some argued that 'the Lower Sort of the People' should be armed as a security measure.[95] We have seen the concerns of the authorities at King's Lynn, and there the days 8–10 December 1745 saw the 'greatest confusion' in and around the town, with some inhabitants thinking of leaving and packing their valuables.[96] 'His majesty's bakehouse at *Dover* . . .', the *Gentleman's Magazine* noted, was 'burnt . . . not without suspicion of these wicked people [i.e. the catholics].'[97] Popish gentlemen living near the coast could also fall under suspicion. Maldon in Essex would have been a suitable point for a French landing, since it was possible to march from there to London without crossing the Thames. Unsurprisingly, then, the arrival of a large number of people at Sir Edward Southcott's mansion at Witham, a few miles away, excited some apprehension.[98] At Lynsted, near the Isle of Sheppey, Lord Teynham's home was searched by the authorities.[99]

As for anti-catholic rioting, it mostly occurred in wartime – in 1745–6 (during the war of the Austrian succession) and in 1780 (during the war of American independence).[100] In view of this, the fact that anti-papist violence was limited after the 'Fifteen',[101] despite the conspicuous

Archbishop Herring, 'representing the Pretender as coming (as the truth is) under a dependence upon French support; I say, stating this point, together with Popery, in a strong light, has always the most popular effect': R. Garnett, 'Correspondence of Archbishop Herring and Lord Hardwicke during the rebellion of 1745', *EHR*, 19 (1904), 535.

92 PRO, SP, 36/76/65.
93 Estcourt and Payne, eds., *English catholic nonjurors*, p. 304, n.
94 British Library, Add. MS 32,705, fs. 270, 272.
95 Haydon, *Anti-catholicism*, pp. 141–2; cf. Speck, *Butcher*, p. 71.
96 Hartshorne, ed., *Memoirs of a royal chaplain*, p. 113.
97 *Gentleman's Magazine*, 15 (1745), 555.   98 PRO, SP, 36/76/322.
99 PRO, SP, 36/76/118.
100 During the Seven Years War, too, a mass-house was attacked in Liverpool (1759): R. J. Stonor, *Liverpool's hidden story* (Billinge, 1957), p. 32.
101 Haydon, *Anti-catholicism*, pp. 97–8.

catholic turn-out, is not altogether surprising. Britain was then at peace with catholic Europe, and there was not an immediate threat from popish states. At time of conflict, however, the story was different. The 1780 Gordon riots displayed a pronounced xenophobic element. Early in the troubles, the Sardinian embassy chapel was attacked by a mob and the Bavarian embassy's chapel was wrecked and plundered by rioters.[102] The chapels of the Portuguese envoy and other catholic ambassadors were thought to be in danger and the xenophobic current is nicely revealed by the rumour that the Russian embassy chapel was threatened with attack too.[103] Other, more minor, incidents showed the mobs' dislike of foreigners. We have already noted the case of Lebarty, the Italian threatened in the disturbances. It was said that no Frenchman dared to show his face in the streets,[104] whilst some claimed that French agents had started the violence.[105] Anti-Irish feeling also surfaced in 1780. In some parts of the metropolis, effigies of St Patrick were burnt in the street,[106] and Irish alehouses were attacked in Golden Lane and in Southwark. One woman, a certain Susannah Clark, supposedly demanded that Cornelius Murphy's house should come down: 'for Mr. Murphy's was a Roman Catholic's house' and 'if they were not Roman Catholics, why did they keep Irish wakes there?'[107] Since France's and Spain's intervention in the American war was proving disastrous for Britain, the Gordon rioters' fusion of xenophobia and anti-popery is entirely understandable. 'I love my King and my Country, but a Roman Catholic I hate', declared one of the rioters, a soldier.[108]

The violence which occurred in 1745–6 was widespread, but again, it appears to have been shaped by wartime fears. It is significant that some of the best documented disturbances occurred on, or not far from, the Yorkshire/north-east coast, where there may have been fears of a French landing,[109] and the rioters were often sailors or dockyard workers. When it was learnt that the papists of Egton in Yorkshire had 'made great rejoicings' following the government forces' defeat at Prestonpans, the 'Ship carpenters of Whitby . . . took there [*sic*] Axes and Cleavers to hack and hew the said papists in pieces' – though they were dissuaded from this course.[110] At Sunderland, 'a number of people, consisting

[102] Rudé, 'Gordon riots', p. 95.
[103] PRO, SP, 37/20/81. 'Popery' was scrawled on the Russian embassy chapel.
[104] Rudé, 'Gordon riots', p. 113, n. 1.   [105] Ibid., p. 101.
[106] Haydon, *Anti-catholicism*, p. 234.   [107] Rudé, 'Gordon riots', pp. 110–11.
[108] PRO, SP, 37/21/327.
[109] F. J. McLynn, *The Jacobite army in England, 1745* (Edinburgh, 1983), p. 171.
[110] Rupert C. Jarvis, *Collected papers on the Jacobite risings* (2 vols., Manchester, 1971–72), II, pp. 313–14.

chiefly of sailors, went . . . to the popish mass-house . . . [and] pulled down . . . [the] altar and crucifix, together with all the seats, the priest's robes, all . . . [the] books, the furniture, and every individual thing in the room, and burnt them in a fire in the street'.[111] At Stokesley in Yorkshire, a mob plainly equated the Hanoverian cause with anti-popery and patriotism. Some boys did some damage to a mass-house and when a ringleader, a sailor, was apprehended, his associates, numbering 'near 200, and being joined by some young fellows, march'd in order (with drum beating and colours flying)' and intimidated the local JP. Afterwards, they went to the chapel, broke in, tore it to pieces, 'march'd with their booty to the Market-cross', and burnt it. One rioter made a speech, telling the rest 'of the great service they had done to their king and country, in destroying the Mass-house that day', and the crowd cried '*God save king* GEORGE, *and down with the Mass.*'[112]

IV

Anti-catholicism, then, was an ideology which promoted national cohesion, countering, though not submerging, the kingdom's political divisions and social tensions. It showed what it was – despite these – to be English by emphasising what it was to be 'unEnglish'. As has been said, anti-Hanoverian feeling ran high in the early 1740s. George II was unpopular on account of his German origins and attachments and his personality. Still, in 1745, his failings shrank beside those of a popish claimant reared in catholic Europe. If '*Popish-Tyranny* . . . be really the *heaviest Curse* that can befall an unhappy People', one preacher argued, the nation, 'as *Christians*, as *Protestants*, as *true Englishmen*', had to support the Hanoverian regime.[113] Similarly, many facets of whig rule might seem harsh, but when comparisons were made with catholic Europe, English aristocrats appeared benign and the English constitution free. Even when popular rights were eroded, the kingdom's lower orders seemed well fed and industrious by contrast with the peasantry of France. The church of England deployed anti-popish teaching in analogous ways. Because of its doctrinal fuzziness, and the nonjurors' schism, its identity was vague. Nevertheless, the church's position could, in part, be delineated by reference to the Romish doctrines rejected by anglicans. As J. R. R. Tolkien was later nastily to put it: 'Hatred of our [i.e. the catholic] Church is after all the only real foundation of the C of E.'[114] Anti-catholicism's functions might, moreover, be interpreted in

[111] *Gentleman's Magazine*, 16 (1746), 42.   [112] Ibid., p. 40.
[113] John Wiche, *Englishmen urged to loyalty* (Salisbury, 1745), p. 17.
[114] A. N. Wilson, *C.S. Lewis: a biography* (1990), p. 195.

psychoanalytical terms. By a process of displacement, it could be argued, potential aggression in society was focused on foreign papists or their domestic coreligionists. Unrecognised dark impulses were projected on to scheming Jesuits or wayward priests. Hence, loyalty was inculcated to the state and national institutions, including the church of England.

Anti-catholicism was, therefore, important in developing an English national identity, but some qualifications are needed to this general thesis. One must not assume that the intensity of anti-popish feeling was uniform. It was especially strong among certain groupings – for instance, non-conformists, methodists and rational dissenters – and (as this chapter has at points illustrated) soldiers and sailors were prominent among 'No Popery' rioters. Anti-popery was geographically patchy, seeming marked in places where Marian martyrs originated, were captured or burnt,[115] and in coastal regions, with folk memories of the French or Spanish threat.[116] Lancashire was peculiarly marked by sectarian tension. Again, good or poor relations with catholic neighbours could mitigate or fuel prejudice, with some humble people being attracted to catholicism by its quasi-magical practices, and popular Jacobitism eroding hostility. For the elite, the grand tour could confirm, but also modify or dispel, dislike. Moreover, anti-catholicism did not always produce social bonding amongst protestants.[117] Dissenters saw too much 'popery' in the church of England's tenets and attacked them accordingly. One pamphlet of 1735 connected non-conformist rhetoric against Rome with 'intemperate zeal and invectives' against anglicanism.[118] Further fissures were created after 1760, when an increasingly enlightened and cosmopolitan elite became more tolerant of catholics, and, with the collapse of the Jacobite movement, was able to treat the minority with growing leniency. Such a stance was at odds with that of many sober, middle-class dissenters, and methodists, who disliked it on theological grounds. And when this tolerance found expression in the first catholic relief act (1778), it provoked the plebeian violence of the Gordon riots, most infamously in London, but also in the provinces.[119] Edward Gibbon felt utterly alien from the rioters. They were, he wrote, 'Puritans such as they might be in the time of Cromwell . . . started out of their graves', and he went on to decry the 'dark and diabolical fanaticism, which I had supposed to be extinct, but

---

[115] Haydon, *Anti-catholicism*, p. 264.   [116] Cf. Clifton, 'Popular fear', p. 49.

[117] David Hempton, *Religion and political culture in Britain and Ireland* (Cambridge, 1996), p. 174.

[118] James E. Bradley, review of Haydon, *Anti-catholicism, Albion*, 27:2 (1995), 313.

[119] Colin Haydon, 'The Gordon riots in the English provinces', *Historical Research*, 63 (1990), 354–9.

which actually subsists in Great Britain perhaps beyond any other Country in Europe'.[120] Later, radicals saw the subject of rank and anti-catholicism in another light. In a print of 1826, *The* NO POPERY! *cry*, anti-popery is shown as an establishment stratagem for duping the poor and diverting them from radical activity. 'We', conservative politicians declare in the accompanying verses, 'know not a word of its [*sic*] true.'[121] For those who thought in this way, anti-catholic propaganda was just an infuriating confidence-trick.

Attitudes to popery did not only create troubles between different groupings and ranks in English society in the eighteenth century: they could also produce Anglo-Scottish tension. In 1778–9, it was expected that a catholic relief bill, modelled on that for England, would be passed for Scotland. But whilst the anglican bishops had sanctioned the English legislation, those imbued with the kirk's granite teaching were made of sterner stuff. Bitter resolutions denounced any change in Scotland. There 'is reason to believe that the British Legislature, is in a great degree unacquainted with the general sentiments of the inhabitants of Scotland, upon this subject', declared the Friends of the Protestant Interest in Edinburgh.[122] Constitutional arguments were powerful: '*Repealing the Scots acts against Popery would be a direct infringement of our constitution. It would not only contradict the general spirit of our law, but would be an express violation of the Claim of Right 1689, and of the Union 1707,* or rather of an essential condition of the very existence of that treaty.'[123] 'Scotsmen', it was bluntly noted, 'are not ignorant of their rights, nor are they yet afraid to plead the titles which support them';[124] whilst it was claimed that 'such a repeal . . . may produce more dangerous consequences to the British empire, than any thing done, or happened with respect to America'.[125] Many separate group-ings protested against the proposed bill. More than twenty-three Scottish boroughs did so, and no fewer than 20,000 people signed the petition against it raised in the bounds of the synod of Glasgow and Ayr within three weeks.[126] Declarations came from numerous objecting bodies – for example, the trades and inhabitants of Dunfermline (for 'Motives of loyalty, of patriotism, of religion'), the heritors and inhabi-tants of Logie, the magistrates and others of Newton upon Ayr, and the kirk session of Dundonald.[127] There were riots in Edinburgh and

[120] J. E. Norton, ed., *The letters of Edward Gibbon* (3 vols., 1956), II, pp. 243, 245.
[121] BM, PD, 15,125.
[122] *Scotland's opposition to the popish bill* (Edinburgh, 1780), pp. 10–11.
[123] Ibid., p. 324.   [124] Ibid., p. 311.   [125] Ibid., p. 233.
[126] Eugene Charlton Black, *The association: British extraparliamentary political organization, 1769–1793* (Cambridge, MA, 1963), pp. 138–9.
[127] *Scotland's opposition*, pp. 13–14, 60, 160–1, 271–3.

Glasgow and the scheme was dropped early in 1779.[128] Yet the episode taught a clear lesson. Anti-catholicism might help to underpin the union, as Linda Colley has argued.[129] However, when politicians acted ineptly, it could also whip up anti-English sentiments in Scotland, uniting Scots from very different backgrounds in patriotic anger, and highlighting the tensions which still existed between the two nations.

Nevertheless, anti-catholicism gave the English a very clear vision of their history. Foxe's *Acts and monuments* had inspired the view that the protestant English were a chosen people. Their faith had survived despite Mary's burnings, whilst Philip I, king of England, was banished from historical memory.[130] The defeat of the armada, the thwarting of the 'gunpowder plot' and the ruin of James II's schemes were viewed as part of God's design. As we have seen, eighteenth-century preachers also saw contemporary success in war and the defeat of Jacobitism in providential terms. Only after the defeat of popery and tyranny could the English achieve their destiny – to enjoy liberty at home whilst ruling a vast empire overseas. Such ideas remained central to the English sense of identity throughout the nineteenth century. Indeed, they gained strength from the conviction that, in part, the national mission lay in spreading anglicanism across the globe. Even Macaulay, whose sense of religion seems so shallow, conventionally acknowledged that the successes of the Victorian age were ultimately owing to 'Him who raises up and pulls down nations at his pleasure'.[131] Concepts of linear advance underlay both secular and ecclesiastical history. The whig story of constitutional and imperial progress remained, despite academic attacks, the nation's perception of its past. As von Ranke stated, 'Macaulay decided the victory of the Whig view.'[132] English protestantism was likewise seen as growing slowly but inexorably to fruition, often from roots in the middle ages. The constitutions of Clarendon and Wycliffe's theology appeared as precursors of the reformation. Political and religious developments marched in parallel. Such notions have persisted in the twentieth century, too. Revealingly, two of Sir Arthur Bryant's popular works were entitled *Protestant island* (1967) and *Freedom's own island* (1986), whilst, even in the 1990s, anxiety about the European union derived in large measure from the knowledge, or subliminal sense, that England's protestant past was different from her continental neighbours' history.

[128] Black, *Association*, pp. 142–4.   [129] Colley, *Britons*, pp. 35–6, 53–4.

[130] In the *Dictionary of national biography*, the entry simply reads: 'PHILIP II OF SPAIN (1527–1598). [See under MARY I, queen of England]'.

[131] Macaulay, *History of England*, III, p. 1,312.

[132] Leopold von Ranke, *A history of England, principally in the seventeenth century*, ed. C. W. Boase and G. W. Kitchin (6 vols., Oxford, 1875), VI, p. 29.

3 Confessional state or elect nation? Religion and identity in eighteenth-century England

Jeremy Black

The demolition of the Berlin wall could serve as a handy symbol for the decline of class-based analyses of history, more particularly of political history. Throughout the twentieth century, Marxist and Marxisante historians have made class-based analysis all-encompassing; and have sought to embrace not only economic and social history, but also its political, religious and cultural counterparts. This approach has never been very convincing on an empirical basis: but, with the collapse of the states which have done most to sponsor it, it has come to seem redundant even as a historical review.

This decline of Marxism in the 1980s interacted with the rise of new intellectual questions: not least the process by which states and societies gained a sense of identity and identified themselves. Moreover, these intellectual issues were given added point in the 1990s by an apparent re-configuration of the European political space, which served to place questions of identity at the heart of contemporary analysis. At the end of the twentieth century it has become possible to see Europe as a continent torn between cosmopolitanism and a set of political beliefs and identities (summarised as nationalism) which have been considered exclusive rather than inclusive. In such a view, the broad 'continental' sense sponsored by the end of the 'Cold War', the development of the European union, and the proposed eastward expansion of NATO, has met a nationalism defined and expected to act in response to the dictates of religion and ethnicity – both forces which have been understood as confrontational and divisive.

If intellectuals, who have spent much of the century ignoring national identities, began to dissect – if not entirely subvert – them by considering nations as 'imagined communities', they nevertheless recognised that identity was a subject worthy of serious attention: both in terms of current political debate and with reference to an academic agenda.[1] One society which claimed attention was eighteenth-century England.

---

[1] B. R. Anderson, *Imagined communities: reflections on the origin and spread of nationalism* (2nd edn, 1991); E. Hobsbawn, *Nations and nationalism since 1780: programme, myth,*

Interest in the subject, though generated relatively late, reflected the conflation of two approaches. First, the period 1688 to 1815 was recognised as one when Britain (the political entity of which England formed the core) was of great importance in global history. This was due to the country's role to the fore of industrialisation and social change, to the ferment of British culture, to the success of British armed forces and to Britain's importance as an alternative to the norms of political society on the European continent both before and after the French revolution. Second, eighteenth-century England had attracted scholarly attention centred on the project of emphasising the role of religion. In recent work on the period, religion has not simply been seen as a system of faith, but has been interpreted as the primary means of creating political and ideological cohesion, and as the language through which such cohesion was discussed and challenged.

The most influential work to adopt this latter agenda was Jonathan Clark's *English society, 1688–1832* (1985).[2] This provided a theme for what had hitherto been somewhat mechanical accounts of English political activity by asserting that continuity was the result of an active conservative ideology rather than of the political calculation which had dominated the works of Sir Lewis Namier.[3] Clark put religion at the centre stage of English conservatism, and by seeing this conservatism as vigorous and successful, not merely reactive, he put faith at the centre of English stability and identity.[4] In his book, England was presented as an anglican church-state.[5] For Clark, the eighteenth century saw an *ancien regime* society, buttressed by the hierarchical ideology of a popular established religion. This analysis served to re-focus eighteenth-century studies: not least because the controversy it created led to a great interest in the period and obliged scholars to adopt positions as no other recent work on the century had done.

The active role of religion was also prominent in another influential work: Linda Colley's study of Georgian national feeling, *Britons: forging the nation* (1992).[6] Far from presenting nations as organic historic phenomenon, characterised by cultural and ethnic homogeneity, Colley saw them as imagined communities, culturally and ethnically diverse,

---

reality (Cambridge, 1990); R. Samuel, ed., *Patriotism: the making and unmaking of British national identity* (1989); R. Porter, ed., *Myths of the English* (Cambridge, 1992).

[2] J. C. D. Clark, *English society, 1688–1832* (Cambridge, 1985).

[3] Lewis Namier, *The structure of politics at the accession of George III* (revd edn, 1957) and *England in the age of the American revolution* (2nd edn, 1963).

[4] For support for this view see J. J. Sack, *From Jacobite to Conservative: reaction and orthodoxy in Britain, c.1760–1832* (Cambridge, 1993).

[5] See also, J. C. D. Clark, 'England's *ancien régime* as a confessional state', *Albion*, 21 (1989), 450–74.

[6] Linda Colley, *Britons: forging the nation 1707–1837* (New Haven, 1992).

and needing artificial construction. Her account of Georgian loyalism, therefore, was a study of how an idea of Great Britain was created, and how it was superimposed onto older alignments and loyalties. In this story, protestant identity (along with success in war and the profits of empire) was central. Colley argued that the sense of Britain as an elect nation, and the perception of a contrast between a godly island and a popish continent, gave eighteenth-century Britons one of their strongest self-definitions.[7] Where Clark's vision was traditionalist, constantly emphasising survivals rather than origins, Colley's idea of protestantism was dynamic, modern and much more compatible with John Brewer's emerging 'fiscal-military' state than with Clark's confessional society.[8] Another important difference was that Clark had little to say about anti-catholicism. His 'other' was protestant non-conformity, and especially unitarianism. For Colley, by contrast, protestantism seemed at times little more than anti-popery. She ignored the challenge posed by dissenters, and the need on the part of the national church to respond to it.

Yet although Clark and Colley are notorious for providing contrasting views of the eighteenth century, there are in fact surprising structural similarities in their accounts of religion and nationality, which are shared by much of the other recent work on this field. At base, both offer views of the period centred on a sort of *Zeitgeist*, or spirit of the age. For each author, religion played the defining role in the *Zeitgeist*, and was crucial to the creation and maintenance of identity. For both historians, religion was both structure and agency: practice and discourse. In their work, faith reflected and sustained a largely unquestioned and hegemonic ideology. It dominated action and the possibilities of discussion, and tended to maintain the population in one particular vision of themselves. However, whilst Clark and Colley's work has been stimulating, and has been typical of much of the other recent scholarship of religion and national identity, there are problems with their approaches to the field. First and foremost, the dangers of treating religion as a hegemonic ideology must be recognised. Historians may stress the power of particular sets of ideas, but to go beyond this to suggest that one vision became a dominant discourse runs considerable risks. It may become self-validating; it has severe limitations in describing what was generally a diverse situation; it may neglect the complexity and compromises within discourses itself; and it may miss

[7] See also, Linda Colley, 'Britishness and otherness, an argument', *JBS*, 31 (1992), 309–29.
[8] For the idea of a fiscal-military state, see John Brewer, *The sinews of power: war, money and the English state, 1688–1783* (1989).

the extent to which supposedly hegemonic worldviews were actually divisive and polemical.

II

To begin to explore these problems, it is worth reflecting on the dominant patriotic discourse of the eighteenth century. As described in much scholarship, this consisted of an intense anti-French and anti-popish xenophobia; an easy pride in English protestantism, prosperity and personal liberty; and a pragmatic opposition to foreign powers which threatened the balance of power in Europe. Treated casually, this protestant-centred patriotism could be presented as a kind of *Zeitgeist*. It could be shown to have dominated public discussion in the eighteenth century; it could be proved to have controlled the attitudes of many Englishmen; and could be presented as the natural product of English traditions, political circumstances and national interest.[9] In short, it could be dressed as the sort of hegemonic discourse on which much recent work on religion and national identity has rested. Yet deeper interrogation of English patriotism raises doubt about the picture. On investigation, the sense of nationality so often described may not have been so effortlessly dominant, and its centrality in modern accounts of the period may appear to have distorted historical understanding.

To see this, one can consider how the traditional English patriotism came to be established. Clearly this vision of nationality was given a tremendous boost and fresh definition by the 'Glorious Revolution'. In 1688–9 the protestant William III replaced the catholic king, James II, and led England into a new hundred year war against French popery and absolutism. Yet whilst these events were an important advance for a particular view of England, they did not secure that view instant dominance, or allow the nation to unite around it. In fact, the revolution produced a number of competing theses of patriotism. Alongside praise for William as a protestant and providential blessing on the nation were Jacobite, country and tory views of the new king as a usurper and of an England suffering depredations under his tutelage.[10] These other views were perfectly viable, and attracted considerable support in the 1690s. They were marginalised – not because of any inherent absurdity, or necessary incompatibility with English national character – but simply because the circumstances of William III's reign allowed him a political

---

[9] See, for example, Colley, *Britons*, ch. 1.

[10] For William as a providential blessing, see Tony Claydon, *William III and the godly revolution* (Cambridge, 1996); for opposing views see ibid. pp. 122–6, 215–21; Paul Monod, *Jacobitism and the English people, 1688–1788* (Cambridge, 1989).

and polemical victory over his opponents. Most importantly, William proved able to win the military struggle over the English succession which followed 1688. He could, therefore, exclude his opponents from power, and condemn critics of his vision of nationality as disloyal. In addition, William's military victory coincided with a dramatic expansion of public politics. In the 1690s, the advent of annual parliaments, the ending of pre-publication censorship (1695), and the development of a considerably more active press, meant that polemical politics began to produce more and different kinds of sources. As a result, the particular patriotic discourse associated with the victors of the revolution was widely disseminated, and gained the highest profile in the culture of print, as well as on government record. Over the years after 1688 it displaced rivals, both in the respectable discussion of the time, and in the records (especially the most-consulted metropolitan and printed texts) which historians would use to reconstruct that discussion.[11]

The consequence of this victory for Williamite patriotism has been to distort, not only Georgian Britons' view of their world, but even later historical understanding of the period. Much of the scholarship dealing with the century after 1688 has been soaked in the sort of whiggism promoted by that event, with the result that many of the ambiguities and complexities of the period have been lost. Until recently, for example, historians of the eighteenth century were almost as effective as Williamite politicians in marginalising the Jacobite and other dissonant voices which were unsuccessful in the political struggles of the late Stuart era. Consequently, the protestant and whiggish vision associated with the victors has come to seem natural to the English, and the coherence and potential persuasiveness of alternative worldviews has been obscured.[12]

Similarly, too little attention has been paid to the exclusivity and polemical nature of the eventually dominant patriotism. Its victory has hidden the fact that it was directed against those critical of William, that it was therefore necessarily divisive, and that (far from uniting the nation

---

[11] For comment on the expanding public sphere see, Geoffrey Holmes, 'The electorate and the national will in the first age of party', in Holmes, ed., *Politics, religion and society in England, 1679–1742* (1986) pp. 1–34; G. C. Gibbs, 'Press and public opinion: prospective', in J. R. Jones, ed., *Liberty secured? Britain before and after 1688* (Stanford, CA, 1992); J. A. Downie, *Robert Harley and the press: propaganda and public opinion in Britain in the first age of party* (Cambridge, 1979). For William's intervention in this public sphere, see Claydon, *William III*, especially ch. 2.

[12] Paradigmatically in the classic and influential 'whig' texts: Thomas Babington Macaulay, *History of England to the death of William III* (4 vols., Heron books edn, 1969), (originally published 1848–55); G. M. Trevelyan, *The English revolution, 1688–1689* (Oxford, 1938); David Ogg, *England in the reigns of James II and William III* (Oxford, 1955).

in a universal ideology) it derived much of its early drive from its partisan character.[13] Again, and even in very recent works, William's victory in 1688–91 has been made to appear desirable because it was necessary for national development. It has been seen as the opportunity for England to move into the first rank of European powers, and as the moment when its internal political structures diverged (very fruitfully) from continental norms.[14] As part of this interpretation, discussion of England's national interest has shared the Williamite assumption of the need to oppose France, when in fact any notion of 'national interest' is theoretically problematic. Ideas of national interest are inseparable from ideologies which define a country's role and destiny – so, in reality, enmity with France was only 'natural' to people who had already decided that catholicism, Bourbon absolutism and continental predominance were the antithesis of Englishness.[15] Also, and finally, Williamite insistence that Jacobite and tory enemies were bigoted dogmatists, led to the construction of religious tolerance as a cardinal English virtue. Later commentators (notably Voltaire, and 'whig' historians) accepted this vision, and England came to be seen as a land of precocious religious liberty.[16] In truth, under the 1689 act 'for exempting their majesties protestant subjects dissenting from the church of England from the penalties of certain laws' – the concessionary but restrictive formulation of what is better know as the toleration act – unitarians, catholics and non-Christians did not enjoy rights of public worship, and catholics were subject to penal statutes, as were anti-trinitarians under the 1697 blasphemy act.[17]

---

[13] For the sheer effort put into Williamite propaganda, see Claydon, *William III*; Lois G. Schwoerer, 'Propaganda in the revolution of 1688–9', *AHR*, 82 (1977), 843–74; Mark Goldie, 'The revolution of 1689 and the structure of political argument', *Bulletin of Research in the Humanities*, 83 (1980), 473–564; David Hayton, 'The propaganda war', in W. A.Maguire, ed., *Kings in conflict: the revolutionary war in Ireland and its aftermath, 1689–1714* (Belfast, 1990), pp. 106–21.

[14] For example, see Brewer, *Sinews of power*; Patrick O'Brien, 'The political economy of British taxation, 1660–1815', *Economic History Review*, 2nd ser., 41 (1988), 1–32.

[15] For some discussion of the contested – rather than the self-evident – nature of the assumptions behind eighteenth-century foreign policy, see Jeremy Black, *A system of ambition? British foreign policy, 1660–1791* (1991), ch. 8.

[16] For Voltaire see J. C. Collins, *Voltaire, Montesquieu and Rousseau in England* (1980); G. Bonno, 'La culture et la civilisation Britanniques devant l'opinion française de la paix d'Utrecht aux *Lettres Philosophiques*, 1713–34', *Transactions of the American Philosophical Society* (1948). Macaulay noted the esteem in which the 1689 toleration act had been held as 'the Great Charter of religious liberty', and (whilst pointing out its limitations) lauded it as ending a 'persecution which had raged during four generations', Macaulay, *History*, II, pp. 461–8.

[17] For a view of the limited aims of the toleration act, see Richard Ashcraft, 'Latitudinarianism and toleration: historical myth versus political reality', in Richard Kroll, Richard Ashcraft and Perez Zagorin, eds., *Philosophy, science and religion in England, 1640–1700* (Cambridge,1991).

This analysis of eighteenth-century patriotism demonstrates the danger of accepting an influential ideology on its own terms. Once a particular view dominates the historical record (particularly the printed record of metropolitan political culture) it is too easy to forget that other views were, and still should be, available. Most dangerously, the easy hegemony which this process of self-validation bestows can discourage historians from looking for opposition to, and weaknesses in, their *Zeitgeist*. Particularly with the religiously centred ideologies which have dominated recent work on the eighteenth century, too little attention can be given to the divisions of faith which undermined any effortless ideological dominance; or to the messy compromises which were often made once the discourse met complex conditions on the ground.

Evidence of religious diversity in eighteenth-century England is clear, and suggests that both Jonathan Clark and Linda Colley underplayed the divisiveness of faith in their period. Colley, for example, failed to place sufficient weight on the rivalry between non-conformity and the church of England, and she under-rated the divisions within the latter – an issue faced in Clark's more recent work.[18] Colley's thesis of a unifying anti-popery can account for the Gordon riots of 1780, but not for the politically more threatening Sacheverell riots, nor for the Priestley riots in 1791, both of which stemmed from the deep tensions between church and dissent.[19] Sacheverell was able to command attention in 1709 with his argument that the church was in danger from a dissenting conspiracy fostered by the whigs, and the issue which he raised rumbled on through the next hundred years. Thus the occasional conformity act of 1711 and the schism act of 1714 (designed respectively to prevent dissenters circumventing the test acts by communicating once a year, and to prevent them receiving a separate education) were passed by Queen Anne's tory ministry, but were both repealed amid great controversy by the whigs under George I. Soon after, a degree of anti-establishment anti-clericalism was visible in the early whig ascendancy, and was evident in Viscount Stanhope's desire to repeal the religious tests. His campaign led to a dilution of the corporation acts (so that dissenters could take a role in local government) but the controversial test act remained much more effective at the national level, and excluded those not willing to take anglican communion from public office. Moves to repeal the legislation were made in 1736, 1739, 1787 and 1790, but

---

[18] Especially, J. C. D. Clark, *The language of liberty, 1688–1832* (Cambridge, 1994).

[19] For these anti-dissenting riots, see R. B. Rose, 'The Priestly riots of 1791', *P&P,* 18 (1960), 68–88; Geoffrey Holmes, 'The Sacheverell riots: the crowd and the church in early eighteenth-century London', in Paul Slack, ed., *Rebellion, popular protest and the social order in early modern England* (Cambridge, 1984), pp. 232–62.

their repeated defeat kept the tension alive, and fed into the 'Church and King' riots against Priestley in 1791.

So basic, in fact, was the division between anglicans and their opponents, that it can be seen behind some of the other fissures evident in Georgian society. For example, a religious foundation to English electoral behaviour (especially to party division) has recently been emphasised for the late eighteenth century, and the rift has been regarded as essential to both the continued nature of local political divisions and to the configuration of the national debate between Pitt the Younger's ministry and the whig opposition.[20] In the absence of a modern structure of party organisation, confessional links provided the basis of community and sociability that was vital in the development and maintenance of political alignments. Religion was also a way to mobilise passion and support. More profoundly, it is possible that the religious foundation to electoral behaviour went beyond politics, and was related to the embryonic ideas of class and the cultural influences brought by economic development. Religious-party allegiance was very different from localised loyalties based on landed estates or clientage. By linking people who perceived common interests in different parts of the country, it may have been central in the emergence of more 'national' – but more divisive – consciousnesses such as class.[21]

Obviously there is a danger that tension between church and dissent can be exaggerated. As we shall see below, divisions were sometimes less clear-cut and comprehensive than might be suggested; and people at all levels of society worked to avoid differences growing into dangerous ruptures. Sir Robert Walpole, for instance, struggled to accommodate non-conformity throughout his career – both silencing the anglican convocation which threatened crusades against dissent in 1717, and issuing annual indemnity acts through the 1720s and 1730s which excused many from the rigours of the religious test. Similarly whig bishops preached moderation in dealings with non-conformists; protestant unity remained a prominent theme in public polemic; and dissenters stressed their loyalty to the Hanoverian state (especially during the Jacobite risings in 1715 and 1745) by emphasising a broad, protestant

[20] J. Barry, 'The press and the politics of culture in Bristol, 1660–1775', in Jeremy Black and Jeremy Gregory, eds., *Culture, politics and society in Britain, 1660–1800* (Manchester, 1991), p. 52; J. E. Bradley, *Popular politics and the American revolution in England: petitions, the crown and public opinion* (Macon Ga., 1986), pp. 211–12; Frank O'Gorman, *Voters, patrons and parties: the unreformed electorate of Hanoverian England, 1734–1832* (Oxford, 1989), pp. 350–2, 359–68; J. A. Phillips, *Electoral behaviour in unreformed England* (Princeton, 1982).

[21] An argument classically expounded in Harold Perkin, *The origins of modern English society* (1966).

patriotism which could include them as well as the established faith.[22] As a result, open conflict between the two communities was generally avoided; and intense rivalry was usually limited to specific localities.[23] However, despite these caveats, enough has been said about the rivalry between church and non-conformity to demonstrate that there was no easy protestant consensus in England. The split between anglican and dissenter was a basic political and ideological one, which ensured that protestant identity was a contested area. Civic culture in England was an arena for active debate, and, in so far as there was a common idiom, it was used to promote different views and was an expression of genuine pluralism. Such a conclusion threatens both Colley and Clark's most influential interpretations of religion and identity in the eighteenth century. Religious diversity suggests that there was no unifying protestantism on which a strong feeling of 'Britishness' could be based, and (whilst the vision of an anglican hegemony does not require that there be absolutely no opposition to the predominant faith) the degree of open religious debate evident in eighteenth-century England must question any easy notion of a confessional church-state.

The tension between church and dissent, then, poses a problem for historians trying to establish any easy link between a prevailing faith, and a dominant identity in the Georgian era. Yet there are more difficulties than this. For example, there were divisions *within* the different denominations. English presbyterians, for example, argued over the scriptural basis of doctrine; early methodists divided over predestination; and anglicans debated a wide range of religious issues which are discussed in another contribution to this collection.[24] Moreover, close examination of particular neighbourhoods reveals that bold statements of religious identity in metropolitan print culture were often not reflected in actual local conditions. Colley's vigorous anti-popery, or Clark's anglican ascendancy, may have been stated as facts or goals in

---

[22] See, for example, Samuel Chandler, *Great Britain's memorial against the pretender and popery* (1745). The pattern largely continued in the Napoleonic wars. There were loyal dissenters' addresses in 1792, 1795 and 1800; and some non-conformists preached patriotism – see, for example, Abraham Ress, *The privileges of Britain: a sermon preached at the meeting-house in the Old Jewry on Thursday 29 November, 1798, being the day appointed for a general thanksgiving* (1798). Other dissenters, however, stayed silent on the need to oppose France: see D. Lovegrove, 'English evangelical dissent and the European conflict, 1789–1815', in W. J. Sheils, ed., *The church and war, SCH*, 20 (Oxford, 1983), 263–76.

[23] In some localities, collaboration between the two sides was evident, see for example, A. Urdank, *Religion and society in a Cotswold vale: Nailsworth, Gloucestershire, 1780–1865* (Berkeley, 1992).

[24] See Michael R. Watts, *The dissenters. Volume one: From the reformation to the French revolution* (Oxford, 1978), pp. 371–82, 428–34; Henry D. Rack, *Reasonable enthusiast: John Wesley and the rise of methodism* (1992), pp. 198–202; ch. 3 below.

national literature: but, in reality, people wished to avoid disrupting local communities and had to find ways of living with heterodox neighbours. Indeed, a recent study of anglican cultural patronage in Bristol suggests that compromise may have been a necessary price to pay for a leading role in communities. Bristol's anglican churches retained their dominance of artistic patronage in the city, but they did so only by cooperating with lay or dissenting groups on which they relied for finance and support.[25]

Further examples of compromise are easy to find. For instance, whilst one can demonstrate the strength of anti-popery in eighteenth-century England (an enormous number of crude attacks upon catholics were made in newspapers, pamphlets, prints and books, and a vigorous public culture of anniversary celebrations survived throughout the century), it is less clear that there was a coherent or homogenous *practice* of anti-catholicism amongst the general population.[26] Obviously the degree of religious antagonism towards catholics can be difficult to measure, because it may have operated at the level of endogamy, discrimination and petty insult which did not attract official attention; but even so the case for common direct hostility is slight. Outside particular neighbourhoods at particular times, there is little evidence for serious tension between catholics and others in communities, instances of violence were few, and at the elite level, at least, social relations steadily improved.[27] Catholics could and did vote; and whilst protestant clergymen sometimes surveyed the number of catholics living within their areas (as Archbishop Blackburn did in the diocese of York in the 1730s) these surveys were relaxed in tone, and rarely suggested that their subjects were a social or political threat.[28] Thus when the penal laws against catholics began to be eased from the 1770s onwards, the legislative code may simply have been catching up with popular attitudes. Anti-popery, therefore, may have been a key element of public discussion in eighteenth-century England, but its constant use did not result in a homogenous campaign of anti-catholicism. Indeed, close study of the rhetoric might lead one to expect this.

[25] Jonathan Barry, 'Cultural patronage and the anglican crisis, Bristol c.1689–1775', in John Walsh, Colin Haydon and Stephen Taylor, eds., *The church of England c.1689–c.1833: from toleration to tractarianism* (Cambridge, 1993), pp. 191–208.

[26] For a recent survey of English anti-popery, see Colin Haydon, *Anti-catholicism in eighteenth-century England* (Manchester, 1993).

[27] For something of the flavour of catholic life in the later century, see Eamon Duffy, 'Richard Challoner: a memoire', in Duffy, ed., *Challoner and his church: a catholic bishop in Georgian England* (1981), pp. 1–26.

[28] Though there was clerical suspicion of catholics in Kent in 1758–61, see Jeremy Gregory, ed., *The speculum of Archbishop Thomas Secker* (Woodbridge, 1995), pp. xxviii–xxix.

Anti-popery was an extremely eclectic discourse, which could operate in different ways in different social, political and cultural contexts, and could identify a multiplicity of different evils according to circumstance. Rarely did it advocate open hostility to English catholics. Rather, the religious persecution and social disruption implied by such hostility were often denounced as 'popish' in themselves – so that the recognition of actual religious pluralism created an ambiguity within the ideology itself.[29]

Similar compromises and ambiguities can be seen in attitudes to nonconformity. As we have seen, the tension between church and dissent was a fundamental political and ideological division in England. Yet again at the social – or the raw physical – level, there seems to have been no sustained or coherent crusade against dissent. It is true that protest against methodists was sometimes violent, and was usually ignored by the authorities; and it is true that rioters in 1710 and 1791 targeted dissenting meeting houses.[30] However, as in the case of catholics, dissenters found they could generally live peacefully among anglican neighbours (despite the vigorous polemics, and occasional outrages against them) and non-conformists found many ways to integrate into mainstream politics and culture. In local communities, such as Great Yarmouth, a workable accommodation was gradually worked out after the toleration act; and the decline in church courts and ecclesiastical authority hastened by that legislation allowed a 'freedom' to diverge from orthodoxy.[31] Clerical investigations into dissenter numbers rarely challenged the right of people to worship outside the church in their homes or meeting houses, and throughout the eighteenth century non-anglicans found ways – especially through occasional conformity and indemnity acts – to evade the laws against them.[32] Again, as with catholics, the very discourses used by the religious majority to discuss the heterodox came to accept the realities of diversity. Whilst all anglican polemic deplored schism from the church and the spiritual pride which prompted it, most rejected a return to enforced uniformity

---

[29] At the very moment of protestant victory in 1688, Gilbert Burnet – a leading protestant propagandist – warned his audience not to imitate papists by persecuting others. Gilbert Burnet, *A sermon preached in the chappel of St James' before his highness the prince of Orange, 23 December* (1689), pp. 28–30.

[30] For attacks on methodists, see Rack, *Reasonable enthusiast*, pp. 271–5; John Walsh, 'Methodism and the mob'; G. J. Cummings and Derek Baker, eds., *Popular belief and practice, SCH*, 8 (Oxford, 1977), 213–27.

[31] P. Gauci, *Politics and society in Great Yarmouth, 1660–1722* (Oxford, 1996). For the situation more generally, Watts, *Dissenters*, I, chs. 4–5.

[32] For clerical surveys, see J. Broad, ed., *Buckinghamshire dissent and parish life, 1669–1722* (Aylesbury, 1993).

as counter-productive, or labelled it an anti-Christian sin of uncharity as bad as schism itself.[33]

Overall, therefore, close examination of real conditions shows that the religious homogeneity assumed or called for in much eighteenth-century rhetoric was neither unchallenged, nor rigidly enforced. A lack of such homogeneity must question any simple notion of religious hegemony, and the possible role of confessional solidarities serving as the basis for national ones. Of course, it can be argued that hegemony does not require absolute conformity. Religious attitudes can dominate by setting the grounds for debate, or by governing the assumptions used in argument, far more easily than by forcing total acceptance. It is possible that anti-popery or anglicanism did influence eighteenth-century minds, at least to this extent. Yet the evidence marshalled above demonstrates that any religious basis for national identity must have been more ambiguous, complex and confusing than is often suggested in work on this subject, and demands that historians do more to check the solidity of the ideologies they describe.

III

If close examination of religious conditions in England may help us get behind an oversimplified *Zeitgeist*, then adding a European dimension throws up more doubts about any uncomplicated protestant identity. If historians cease to study England in isolation, and consider it merely as one of a number of continental societies, then parallels with other countries emerge which underline the ambiguities within English nationality. Neither Colley, nor Clark, went far in considering Britain as part of a larger, continental whole (despite the former's interest in England's clashes with continental powers, and the latter's borrowing of the term *ancien régime* to describe the society he saw on the British side of the Channel). This is a problem, because concentration on the European context highlights further difficulties with the approaches they adopt.

Of course, there might be dangers with treating England as a run-of-the-mill European state. Historians assuming an English exceptionalism have pointed to many unique aspects of the island nation, which might devalue international comparisons.[34] In the field of faith and identity, there was the unusual nature of the anglican establishment, and its

---

[33] This mixture of attitudes was clearly evident among those clergy who had promoted the toleration act in 1689: see Claydon, *William III*, pp. 164–77.

[34] Some of the issues involved in assessing English exceptionalism are discussed in Jeremy Black, *Convergence or divergence: Britain and the continent* (1994).

remarkable position in national life. The church of England was extraordinarily closely bound to the nation since it was not only the official
religion of the governing state, but was an ecclesiastical institution and
theological system virtually peculiar to one country. However, whilst
anglicanism did have some unique features, parallels with conditions
elsewhere in the continent were closer than might appear. For instance,
state churches had become the norm in Europe by the eighteenth
century. In the early modern period, the protestant reformation had
increased political control over ecclesiastical institutions in many parts
of Germany and Scandinavia, and catholic rulers had responded by
subordinating their churches over the ensuing two hundred years. In
both parts of Europe, an established ecclesia was seen as a essential
institution of state, and penal measures (highly reminiscent of English
legislation) were enforced against those who worshipped outside. For
example, Maria Theresa of Austria would not permit protestants in the
Austrian Netherlands to hold public office, or erect churches; and the
Polish constitution of 1791 – whilst granting some degree of toleration to
all faiths – also confirmed catholicism as the state religion.[35]

Admittedly, distinctive national *religions* (such as anglicanism) were
rarer; but Regalist Spain, Gallican France and Febronian Germany each
had a sense of autonomy from the international confessions to which
they belonged, and a very close parallel to England existed in Russia,
where Russian orthodoxy was a faith peculiar to one state. Indeed,
studying the role of the Orthodox church in Russian society, one is
easily reminded of Jonathan Clark's characterisation of the church of
England. Here too was an ecclesiastical organisation in league with the
government, which played an important part in upholding order and
obedience. For example, in 1720 Peter the Great's principal clerical
agent, Feofan Prokopovich, wrote a catechcetical *Russian primer* which
stated 'What doth God require in the fifth commandment? He commands us to honour and obey our parents, a name which includes our
Sovereign, our spiritual pastors and civil governors, our teachers, benefactors and elders.' In the same year, the established church was used as
an administrative agency of secular government, when Russian parish
priests were ordered to announce decrees about new taxes in all church
services.[36] Later, Catherine the Great was to show that she too saw
orthodoxy as a prime instrument of political and cultural influence
when financing the building of churches in Cossack areas. Given such
parallels between England and abroad, comparison with the continent

---

[35] For Maria Theresa's catholicism see Edward Crankshaw, *Maria Theresa* (1969),
pp. 300–2.
[36] J. Cracraft, *The church reforms of Peter the Great* (1971).

may well be valid, and consideration of the complexities of Europe may hold up valuable mirrors to the English situation.

Viewing Europe as a whole, the most remarkable feature was the complexity of the religious situation inside states. Whilst state-churches were the norm in the period, they were all less united, and less certain of themselves, than might be imagined from consideration of their self-image, and of the support they received from secular authorities. Across the continent, theological division, and concern about confessional heterodoxy, undermined any neat identity between faith and political loyalties. Even within the core territories of Russia, the unity of ortho-doxy was disrupted by the secession of the 'Old Believers' in the late seventeenth century.[37] This produced a diversity similar to that caused in England in the same period by the schisms of puritan dissenters and nonjurors in 1662 and 1689 respectively. More generally, three main factors seem to have produced ambiguity in the relationship between faith and identification with a state. Each derived from the prevailing conditions in the European continent in the eighteenth century, and each affected England (as part of Europe) as strongly as other countries.

The first reason for religious division within states was the simple fact that Europe was a small and diverse region, whose different parts were spatially close, and whose peoples were consequently able to interact and migrate to one other's territories. Eighteenth-century improvements in transport and communications, and the growth of trade, had the effect of shrinking the continent further, and of forcing its peoples into ever closer contact. Given this contiguity and ease of interchange of cultures, it was virtually impossible to police state borders so closely that religious influences from outside could be excluded. Examples of such infiltration were numerous. In Russia, for instance, both protestantism and catholicism spread into the core of Muscovy from the west as German, Swedish and even English settlements were established. In many ways, this infiltration was officially encouraged. From the time of Peter the Great onwards, the tzars may have seen the state religion as a bulwark of their regime, but they also wished to integrate their country into the European cultural mainstream, and this inevitably meant greater contact with people of other faiths.[38] Elsewhere in Europe, cross-border influences from contiguous or migrating peoples were as obvious. In the jumble of tiny states in Germany and Switzerland, for instance, the close packing of different confession's territories meant that people were able to live in areas officially hostile to them, and walk across a frontier on Sunday mornings to worship. Contemporary travel

---

[37] Nicholas V. Riasanovsky, *A history of Russia* (5th edn, Oxford, 1993), pp. 197–201.
[38] On this 'westernisation', see Riasanovsky, *History of Russia*, pp. 284–99.

literature commented on this phenomenon.[39] Similarly, the relative closeness of European cities and universities, and the increasingly effective means of communication between them, allowed scholars and academics of different faiths to maintain close contact through a self-defined 'Republic of Letters'.[40] Ironically, the importance of external influences may even have been encouraged by attempts to purge societies of religious heterodoxy. Early eighteenth-century persecution of protestants may have rendered France, Savoy and parts of the Habsburg empire more culturally homogenous; but the policy of intolerance forced victims to relocate, and added to the diverse religious mix of other parts of the continent, including Geneva, the Netherlands and the north German cities.[41]

England, of course, was no exception to this pattern of infiltration. The sea proved no barrier to foreign influences and the eighteenth century was marked by waves of settlers who did not share the national anglican faith. Partly these were encouraged by dynastic changes at the start of the period. William III's arrival from Holland in 1688, and the coming of George I from Hanover in 1714, imposed Calvinist and Lutheran monarchs on England, and opened the kingdom to Dutch people and Germans who followed in their wake. In the same decades, persecutions on the continental mainland introduced other adherents of foreign churches. People ejected from France and catholic parts of the Holy Roman empire sought sanctuary in London, but resisted integration into the English establishment and worshipped separately from their new hosts. Huguenots, Palatines and Moravians crossed the Channel and attracted the interest of religiously curious Englishmen. In the 1790s, French catholic refugees from the 'Terror' introduced another heterodox community. Even when not settled by foreigners, England's position as the leading protestant power, and its relative intellectual freedom, ensured that it would receive influences from its neighbours. The international republic of letters had important English branches, and reformed Christians from all over the continent (who looked to England as the leader of their cause) established contact with English politicians and English clerics. As a result, a network of

---

[39] See, for example, the description of the situation in Cologne in [François] Maximillion Misson, *A new voyage to Italy* (2 vols., 1695), I, p. 35, and the description of Metz, ibid., p. 49.

[40] Anne Goldgar, *Impolite learning: conduct and community in the republic of letters, 1680–1750* (New Haven, 1995).

[41] Again, travel writers commented. See, for example, the descriptions of Geneva and Holland respectively in [William Bromley], *Remarks made in travels through France and Italy* (1693), p. 365; [William Carr], *An accurate description of the United Netherlands* (1691), p. 6.

correspondence and lobbyists introduced forms of foreign spirituality into the country. A prime example was the fascination for the pietist experiment at Halle. The educative and social work undertaken by these German protestants became the inspiration for many British initiatives, gaining particular converts amongst enthusiasts for workhouses, charity schools and the SPCK.[42] Such contacts did not only open England to experiences beyond anglicanism. In certain circumstances, as in the birth of methodism, they could lead to direct challenges to the state religion. When the English followed models suggested by strangers, they could come to criticise the local established church for not living up to their ideals.[43]

A second reason for the internal religious diversity of European states was the very nature of these political entities. In an era before mass politics, and before the continent was remodelled by nineteenth-century nationalisms, states had not been established as political expressions of self-conscious cultural groups. Rather they had grown through the military conquests, marital alliances and accidental inheritances of their ruling families. This meant, of course, that they had incorporated peoples of very different ethnicities and beliefs, and that it would always be difficult to impose any religious or ideological uniformity on the diversity of subjects which resulted. Russia's westward expansion into Poland and the Baltic region, for example, brought many catholics and Lutherans within its borders in the eighteenth century. Similarly, Austrian Habsburg expansion into the northern Balkans brought that family into increasing contact with orthodoxy and islam; and Prussian expansion in northern Germany swept many catholics into protestant Brandenburg's fold – especially in Silesia.

In this pattern of dynastic expansion leading to religious diversity, England's empire was no exception. In the late Stuart and Hanoverian era, the anglican church faced challenges from Scotland, Ireland, Wales and even America. These were all areas brought into England's ambit by earlier conquest or royal succession; and all had cultures which the English establishment found it impossible to assimilate fully. Scotland, for example, though joined to England by the union of crowns in 1603 and the union of parliaments in 1707, had brought a wholly separate ecclesiastical tradition into the new state, in which Calvinism and presbyterianism had played a far more dominant role. This had meant

---

[42] For these international contacts, see Tim Hitchcock, 'Paupers and preachers: the SPCK and the parochial workhouse movement', in Lee Davison, Tim Hitchcock, Tim Keirns and Robert B. Shoemaker, eds., *Stilling the grumbling hive: the response to social and economic problems in England, 1689–1750* (Stroud, 1992).

[43] For the example of Moravian influence over early methodism, see Rack, *Reasonable enthusiast, passim* but especially p. 207.

that the early Stuart monarchs had failed to bring their northern realm to the English model in the decades before the British civil wars; that the episcopal church which was restored in both England and Scotland in 1660 had failed to suppress radical protestantism north of the border; and that the presbyterian church established in Scotland in 1689 had not been integrated with the church of England at the final assimilation of the two polities. This led to an extraordinary situation in which a new united kingdom had separate state churches in different parts of its territory. Wales was placed under anglican administration – but here language created a serious problem for what would otherwise have been a unifying ecclesiology. In the eighteenth century, Welsh-speaking anglican clergy tended to be denied preferment: a lack of cultural recognition which created a space into which methodism and later nonconformity could move.[44] Ireland posed another problem again, as an established anglican-style church failed to assimilate either the catholic majority, or the minority of Scots presbyterians in the north – despite the backing of harsh penal laws excluding the heterodox from basic areas of civilian life. Finally, America, which had been a refuge for dissidents from the church of England in the seventeenth century, continued its separate way in the next hundred years. Strong congregational, presbyterian and quaker churches prevented the establishment of an anglican hierarchy in the transatlantic colonies, and were eventually to form the core of the independence movement as they defended their autonomy from what they saw as an imperialistic English establishment.[45] None of this, of course, threatened anglican hold over England directly, but it produced an uncomfortable variety, and source of heterodox influence, within the English polity. England's European-style history as an expanding state and a dynastic power produced a host of problems for its ecclesiastical establishment.

The third, and perhaps most interesting, reason for Europeans rejecting a unified faith as the basis of national or political identity, was that it stood in the way of the main concern of most states: namely their international security, and Great Power status. To understand this, some background is needed. The most important context here is the chronic instability of Europe. The eighteenth century was one of tension between states, and struggle for dominance in the continent, as several broadly equal powers flexed their muscles against one another. Warfare

---

[44] Though the church had earlier avoided this problem through its active promotion of Welsh culture: see Philip Jenkins, 'The anglican church and the unity of Britain: the Welsh experience, 1560–1714', in Steven G. Ellis and Sarah Barber, eds., *Conquest and union: fashioning a British state, 1485–1725* (1995), pp. 115–38; and ch. 6 below.

[45] Clark, *Language of liberty*; Bernard Bailyn, *The intellectual origins of the American revolution* (Cambridge, MA, 1967), pp. 246–72.

was almost endemic, all states had to look to their military defences, and many were ambitious for territorial expansion. Of course, such international rivalry was not in itself new or peculiar. However, developments over the years before the eighteenth century had transformed the nature and conditions of conflict, and had had an important impact on the internal ordering of European realms. Since the late middle ages, a series of technological, strategic, social and infrastructural changes had altered the face of warfare: and although historians have argued over the precise timing and nature of this 'military revolution', its effects by the eighteenth century were fairly clear. They were to enlarge the scale of military conflict and to prolong its potential length, so that victory came far more through efficient and sustained mobilisation of a whole society's resources, than solely through brilliant operational command.[46]

The result of such changes was to alter ruler's political priorities, and in particular to alter their view of the religiously heterodox. Once it was clear that military security meant maximising the available resources of a society, concern that religious dissidents were being excluded from contributing to the national military and economic stock began to outweigh fears of the political instabilities brought by internal diversity. Where religious disabilities prevented groups serving the state (or might hinder the accumulation of materials and money) disabilities came to be seen as liabilities, and a wave of toleration swept the continent.

Examples here are particularly numerous from the late eighteenth century, and especially from realms ruled by the so called 'enlightened despots'. In the case of these rulers, concern about military security was joined by a related doctrine which saw religious persecution as an unproductive restriction on trade, and by the monarchs' own self-image as the modernisers and liberators of their societies. Thus Joseph II of Austria did much to reduce the dominance of the catholic church, viewing it as an obstacle to the interests of the state. He abolished the inquisition and the contemplative orders; he granted religious liberty to his non-catholic Christian subjects and sought to integrate Jews in Austrian society; and (against considerable clerical hostility) established the principle that marriage was essentially a civil contract. Also, following contemporary theories about the effects of intolerance on the economy, Joseph invited the heterodox to revive trade in depressed areas of his empire. At Ostend, protestants were allowed to worship freely inside the town as a means of regenerating the port.[47] This greater

---

[46] For a brief summary of these developments and debates see Jeremy Black, *A military revolution? Military change and European society, 1550–1800* (1991).

[47] The roots of Joseph's attitudes can be traced in Derek Beales, *Joseph II* (Cambridge, 1987), pp. 465–73.

religious tolerance on the part of the catholic emperor was matched by developments in protestant Prussia. There Frederick II, whilst continuing his father's policy of stirring up protestant unrest in Habsburg territories, respected catholic rights in his conquests of Silesia and west Prussia. He obliged protestant minorities to go on paying tithes to catholic priests in the new territories, gave refuge to Jesuits, and allowed a catholic church to be consecrated in Berlin.[48] Meanwhile Catherine the Great of Russia declared in 1773 that she would emulate God in tolerating all faiths and creeds, and ordered ecclesiastical authorities to leave matters concerning other faiths to civil regulation.[49]

Once again, trends which affected Europe also affected England. From at least the mid-eighteenth century, awareness of England's position as a great power (competing with others both in Europe and for expanding overseas empires) meant a re-evaluation of attitudes to the religiously heterodox. By the 1770s political elites were contemplating the emancipation of Roman catholics. Rebellion in the American colonies, and the prospect of a broad European alliance against England, forced consideration of ways to allow the mass of the Irish population and Scots Highlanders to be recruited into the armed forces, and directed attention to the penal religious legislation which prevented this. Relief acts in England and Ireland followed in 1778, and were proposed for Scotland before anti-catholic rioting caused the authorities to back off.[50] Therefore, in English possessions, as elsewhere, power rivalries were weakening the role of religion in defining and expressing political allegiance – even as old prejudices about the alien nature of heterodoxy demonstrated they would not be quick to die. Other parallels between England and the continent included moves against mortmain (the inalienable possession of land by the church) and against religious censorship. The former was prohibited in a number of states, including Bavaria (1704, 1764), France (1749), the Austrian Netherlands (1753), Austria (1767), Venice (1767) and Naples (1769–72), whilst the English regulations were tightened up in 1736. In England an attempt in 1702 by Archbishop Tenison to revive pre-publication censorship failed, whilst secular authorities took over control of censorship in a number of places including Tuscany (1743), Lombardy (1768) and Portugal

---

[48] Walther Hubatsch, *Frederick the Great: absolutism and administration* (1973), pp. 190–211.
[49] For Catherine's religious policy, see John T. Alexander, *Catherine the Great: life and legend* (Oxford, 1989), pp. 76–7.
[50] Nigel Abercrombie, 'The first relief act', in Duffy, *Challoner*, pp. 174–94; Robert Kent Donovan, 'The military origins of the Roman catholic relief programme of 1778', *HJ*, 28 (1985), 79–102; Robert Kent Donovan, *No popery and radicalism: opposition to Roman catholic relief in Scotland, 1778–1782* (New York, 1987).

(1768).[51] All these moves suggested a general relaxation on the part of governments towards religious diversity; and a determination to break the stranglehold of established churches on national life. Emotionally, rulers may still have been attracted by the ideal of subjects united beneath them in a faith which they shared. The practicalities of economic and military rivalry, however, dictated different policies.

IV

On the evidence above, considering England as part of Europe shows the same complex and ambiguous relationship between religion and nationality as was revealed in the diverse and disputed nature of English protestantism. England was not alone in lacking a simple, uncontested faith on which to base a simple, uncontested national identity. Having demonstrated this, however, it is perhaps time to be more constructive, and suggests some new directions for the burgeoning scholarship of religion and nationality. How should historians adopt their approaches in the light of the confusions uncovered?

The most basic and obvious point is that writers should beware of overly simplistic accounts of Hanoverian England. Whilst Clark alerted historians to the centrality of religion in eighteenth-century politics and society, and whilst there is much in Colley's suggestion that national identity was a artificial creation which needed some other emotion (such as anti-popery) around which to crystallise, it is necessary to build on these insights without suggesting that any neat pattern or elegant thesis can be advanced. Instead, it is more appropriate to emphasise the contingent and multiple nature of identities when looking at the relationship between faith and nationality. Monotype views of the church and national identity are unsatisfactory because they ignore the choices available to people. Men and women in the eighteenth century had a number of ways in which they could think of themselves; and they might adopt different – even contradictory – ones according to circumstance. To take just one example: a recent study of catholics and presbyterians in Hanoverian Lancashire suggests that stereotypical views of 'papists' and subversive dissenters may have created sectional divisions in society, but may simultaneously have allowed vertical cohesion between social strata. A *national* identity overlaid on top of these denominational and class identities would have added yet a further dimension, and permitted people to adopt ideas and values selectively from the range of ideologies on offer. In this situation, nobody would have identified themselves

[51] W. J. Callahan and D. Higgs, eds., *Church and society in catholic Europe in the eighteenth century* (Cambridge, 1979).

exclusively with denomination, class, or country. Their values and ideas would have been drawn from each, like a patchwork, and not come from one wholesale.[52] Future scholarship should recognise such possibilities, and treat identity as something flexible.

This diversity and fluidity is the main field of research suggested by a critical approach to eighteenth-century identities: but the evidence reviewed above also invites examination of two further areas. First, it becomes clear that there is a danger in concentrating on themes found in metropolitan print culture. In print, writers and legislators tended to describe or advocate ideals. Modern stress on such ideals can unnecessarily reify them, and can lead scholars to ignore the far less clear-cut conditions of actual life. In practice, regimes made messy compromises when trying to enforce national/religious allegiances; people implementing policy on the ground found the situation more complex than theorists at the cultural centre; and populations sought accommodations as they had to find ways of living with heterodox neighbours. Furthermore, it seems that such compromises became more widespread as the eighteenth century wore on. The tone of confessional life and politico-religious identities altered, and the contrast with discriminatory legislation became more apparent. As this happened, penal legislation became more of a problem for the state than a support of it; and much of the legal code may have become redundant before it was abolished. Given this, it is clear that assessment of the relationship between print culture and actual practice must become an urgent issue for historians in the field. Obviously this raises considerable methodological difficulties: but the problems must be tackled before scholars can make any solid claims about the true content of religious or national identities.

The final area for research suggested by this chapter is a comparative investigation of England and its European neighbours. Treating societies in isolation always has potential dangers. In the field of faith and nationality, where reaction to external cultures may have played such a central role in defining identities, ignorance of a European context is particularly hazardous. Partly this is because failure to compare denies students possible tools of analysis. Whatever may eventually be decided about the degree of English 'exceptionalism' within Europe, English polity, society and culture were not so far outside the continental mainstream that seeking parallels with conditions elsewhere would be futile. Examples provided in this chapter show that some insight can be gained from knowledge of rival nations. Perhaps more importantly, however, modern historians should take a continental view, because their

---

[52] Jan Albers, '"Papist traitors" and "presbyterian rogues": religious identities in eighteenth century Lancashire', in Walsh et al. eds., Church of England, pp. 317–33.

eighteenth-century subjects so often did so. For Hanoverian English people, foreigners were sometimes bogeymen (an 'other' to be feared and hated rather than met and understood) but they were also sometimes real human beings with whom one might have contact and sympathy. The European continent was too small, integrated and interdependent to reduce all aliens to cartoon monsters, and borders were too permeable to prevent the penetration of populations and ideas. In this situation, all nations were affected by influences from outside. A wider continental culture competed with more located religio-national identities, and all Europeans would have had a sense of themselves belonging to something broader than their polity, or confessional group. Recognising this degree of interchange should be an important step for historians of eighteenth-century England. Along with a more flexible conceptualisation of what identity is, and a greater concentration on real lives to balance print culture, the continental context should enrich and stimulate a field too long haunted by chimerical spirits of the age.

4 'To protect English liberties': the English nationalist revolution of 1688–1689

Steven Pincus

I

'A nation is composed of private men; all brought up very near in the same customs, and instructed much by the same sort of teachers: the Prince must take them as he finds them', explained one pamphleteer in the immediate wake of the revolution of 1688–9. 'He that would introduce monarchy into Holland, which will drown for liberty at any time, or settle a republic in France which will and does so eagerly fight for slavery, will have a task of no small performance.'[1] One of the earliest historians of the revolution began his account in a similar tone. 'Certain it is', the author of the *History of the late revolution* observed, 'that nothing more provokes and irritates a nation born to freedom, as the English nation is, than attempts to deprive them of the ancient constitutions of their liberty.'[2] What these commentators had in common was a concurrently local *and* European understanding of 1688. Whilst they celebrated developments within England, they saw recent events within the context of a Europe composed of nations like their own. For them, the revolution had preserved things the English nation held dear: but it had taken place in a continent composed of other peoples, each with their own characteristics and traditions to defend. In 1688, there was a widespread English nationalism, forged in a cosmopolitan context.

This simultaneously cosmopolitan and nationalist view of 1688–9 sits in uneasy tension both with traditional accounts of the origins of nationalism and with the historiography of the revolution itself. Those historians who are willing to allow for the existence of an early modern nationalism insist that it developed out of an antagonism to, not a constructive engagement with, European nations.[3] Linda Colley, whose

[1] *The character of a prince* (1689), pp. 3–4.
[2] *The history of the late revolution in England* (1689), p. 1.
[3] Jonathan Israel has recently asserted that even those who invited William to intervene in English politics looked 'at matters from a strictly insular point of view', Jonathan Israel, 'The Dutch republic and the "Glorious Revolution" in England', in Charles Wilson and David Protor, eds., *1688: The seabourne alliance and diplomatic revolution* (1989), p. 32.

pathbreaking *Britons* has done so much to return the study of nation-alism to British historiography, insists that Britons 'defined themselves
. . . in conscious opposition to the "Other" beyond their shores'; their
national identity was defined 'almost despite themselves, by a confronta-tion with the "Other"'.[4] For Colley, of course, this confrontation with
the 'other' occurred predominantly in the massive struggle with France
which occurred between 1689 and 1815. Since 'these were religious
wars, and perceived as such by both sides', Colley insists on 'the
absolute centrality of protestantism' in British nationalism.[5] For Tony
Claydon, whose work focuses more explicitly on the revolution and its
aftermath, the account of English nationalism begins with an assump-tion of 'English xenophobia'.[6] Claydon, like Colley, understands Eng-land's protestantism to be the fundamental issue which set it apart from
other European nations. William's polemicists, Claydon insists, under-stood the revolution 'as part of an international protestant crusade'.[7]
Protestant beliefs need to be 'returned to the centre stage' in our
understanding of the revolution and its attendant nationalism because
there can be no doubting 'the persisting influence of the early protestant
worldview'.[8] Annabel Patterson has similarly insisted that 'religion was
the central issue in the debates' defining English nationalism in the later
Stuart period.[9] Antipathy towards catholic Europe, then, defines
English nationalism for those willing to allow for its development in the
early modern period.

Most students of nationalism, by contrast, deny that England or
Britain expressed any nationalist sentiment in the early modern period.
Rogers Brubaker's claim that 'Europe was the birthplace of the nation-state and modern nationalism at the end of the eighteenth century' can
find innumerable echoes in the vast social scientific literature dealing
with nationalism.[10] There are at least three sorts of explanations as to
why this should be so. First, and most typically, it is claimed that
nationalism requires mass politics and mass politics can only happen
after the industrial revolution. While admitting that in exceptional cases

[4] Linda Colley, 'Britishness and otherness: an argument', *JBS*, 31:4 (1992), 316, 311.
[5] Linda Colley, *Britons: forging the nation* (New Haven, 1992), p. 3; Colley, 'Britishness',
p. 316.
[6] Tony Claydon, *William III and the godly revolution* (Cambridge, 1996), p. 17.
[7] Ibid., p.139.
[8] Ibid., pp. 5, 229.
[9] Annabel Patterson, '"Crouching at home and cruel while abroad": Restoration
constructions of national and international character', in R. Malcolm Smuts, ed., *The
Stuart court and Europe: essays in politics and political culture* (Cambridge, 1996), p. 218.
[10] Rogers Brubaker, *Nationalism reframed: nationhood and the national question in the new
Europe* (Cambridge, 1996), p. 1. See among many others, E. J. Hobsbawm, *Nations and
nationalism since 1780* (Cambridge, 1990).

agrarian societies could generate something like nationalism, Ernest
Gellner has suggested that 'the social organization of agrarian society
. . . is not at all favourable to the nationalist principle'. It was the
anomie and egalitarianism associated with stripping people away from
the hierarchical agrarian economy which made nationalism psychologically attractive and sociologically possible.[11] Second, it is often said that
'the dawn of the age of nationalism' requires 'the dusk of religious
modes of thought'. It was this which required, argues Benedict Anderson, 'a secular transformation of fatality into continuity, contingency
into meaning . . . few things were (are) better suited to this end than an
idea of nation'.[12] Third, nationalism necessitates a political theory
which allows the people's primary allegiance to be to the nation. Such
an allegiance was not possible until the late eighteenth century. 'The
concept of "nationalism" could not emerge before that of "nationality"',
argues Jonathan Clark, 'and nationality itself took a quite different form
in common law. Before 1776 . . . the relation of an individual to the
state was still as it had been legally defined in Calvin's case in terms of
the subjects' allegiance to a particular monarch.'[13] John Breuilly has
drawn upon all of these accounts to prove 'the absence of any distinctive
English nationalist ideology'.[14]

Both interpretations – that English nationalism was fundamentally
xenophobic and religious, on the one hand, and that early modern
England was insufficiently modern to have a nationalism, on the other –
dovetail perfectly with the image of 1688–9 as a fundamentally conservative event. John Morrill correctly captured the consensus of the
contemporary historiography when he declared that 'the "Sensible
Revolution" of 1688–89 was a conservative revolution'.[15] 'The "glorious revolution" of 1688', proclaims J. R. Western, 'was so called
precisely because so much of it was not in the modern sense revolutionary.'[16] Similarly, J. R. Jones has commented on the 'generally
conservative character of the constitutional settlement', whilst Stephen

---

[11] Ernest Gellner, *Nations and nationalism* (Ithaca, 1983), pp. 39–40. A similar argument
is implied by Ron Suny in *The revenge of the past: nationalism, revolution, and the collapse
of the Soviet Union* (Stanford, 1993), p. 14. See also Peter Alter, *Nationalism*, trans. by
Stuart McKinnon-Evans (1989), pp. 77–8.
[12] Benedict Anderson, *Imagined communities* (revd edn, 1983), p. 11. Gellner also argues
that 'an industrial high culture is no longer linked – whatever its history – to a faith and
a church'. Gellner, *Nations and nationalism*, pp. 141–2.
[13] J .C. D. Clark, *The language of liberty, 1660–1832* (Cambridge, 1994), pp. 46, 52.
[14] John Breuilly, *Nationalism and the state* (2nd edn, Chicago, 1993), pp. 86–7.
[15] John Morrill, 'The sensible revolution', in Jonathan Israel, ed., *The Anglo-Dutch moment*
(Cambridge, 1991), p. 103.
[16] J. R. Western, *Monarchy and revolution: the English state in the 1680s* (Totowa, NJ,
1972), p. 1.

Saunder Webb has portrayed the events as counter-revolutionary, and Malcolm Smuts has argued that from William's perspective 'the European wars of religion had never ended. The revolution's victory over popery and arbitrary government was but one chapter in an international struggle already more than a century old.'[17]

Against these views I will argue that 1668–9 constituted England's first nationalist revolution. While much of the rhetoric surrounding the event was indeed moderate in tone, reflecting the rapidity and totality of the revolutionaries' victory over their enemies, this should not mask the novel and remarkable nature of their achievement. Despite the wide range of political and religious beliefs espoused by the revolutionaries, the vast majority justified their actions in nationalist terms: terms which had both civic and ethnic aspects. The revolutionaries of 1688–9 believed they had saved the English nation – its liberties, its religion, and its culture – from an impending French tyranny.

Nationalism, as I understand it, has a very specific meaning. Following Anthony Smith, I take nationalism to be 'an ideological movement for attaining and maintaining autonomy, unity and identity on behalf of a population deemed by some of its members to constitute an actual or potential nation'.[18] Nation in this context means (and here I follow David Miller) 'a community (1) constituted by shared belief and mutual commitment, (2) extended in history, (3) active in character, (4) connected by a particular territory, and (5) marked off from other communities by its distinct public culture'.[19] Nationalism, however, does not insist on the absolute priority of national identity over all other kinds of identity. 'We typically regard our nationality as a constituent of our identity on a par with other constituents', observes Dr Miller, 'and the obligations that flow from it as competing with obligations arising from other sources'.[20]

The year 1688–9 was a nationalist revolution in this sense of the term. The public culture espoused in the revolution, however, was much more varied and rich than a purely protestant nationalism would allow. Scholars have given an insufficiently nuanced account of the role

---

[17] J. R. Jones, 'The revolution in context', in J. R. Jones, ed., *Liberty secured? Before and after 1688* (Stanford, 1992), pp. 29, 12; Stephen Saunders Webb, *Lord Churchill's coup* (New York, 1995), p. 165; R. Malcolm Smuts, 'Introduction', in Smuts, ed., *Stuart court and Europe*, p. 18.

[18] Anthony Smith, *National identity* (Reno, 1991), p. 73.

[19] David Miller, *On nationality* (Oxford, 1995), p. 27. I should acknowledge here how influential Dr Miller's book has been on my thinking. Smith offers a similar definition in *National identity*, p. 14.

[20] Miller, *On nationality*, pp. 45–6. Here I disagree with Suny who holds that for nationalists 'loyalty to nations overrides all other loyalties', Suny, *Revenge of the past*, p. 13. Breuilly insists on a similar view, *Nationalism*, p. 2.

played by religion in the revolution because they have been so concerned to show that early modern England was a religious rather than a secular society. Protestantism did play a vital role in the revolution of 1688–9, but this role was clearly distinguishable from an early protestant world-view. For the revolutionaries of 1688–9, protestantism was but one aspect of the national identity threatened by James II's French style of government. The nationalist ideology espoused in 1688–9 was not one of undifferentiated antagonism to catholic Europe, but a subtle and sophisticated ideology based on economic, political and cultural engagement.

This sort of nationalism was possible and attractive in early modern England because it had experienced a series of significant social, political and cultural transformations. Indeed, it was in the seventeenth century that nationalism, for the first time, became a plausible way of organising and understanding politics. England had made a transition to a market economy, a phase of social and economic development which can be placed between Gellner's idealised agrarian and industrial societies.[21] Not only was print capitalism firmly established in late seventeenth-century England, but social spaces for discussing politics, religion and culture such as coffee houses, taverns, marketplaces and business exchanges were also well ensconced.[22] While late seventeenth-century England remained a deeply religious society, religion's place within that society had changed. In the wake of almost two centuries of inconclusive religious struggles (wars fought in defence of universalist religious principles) many in England, as in the rest of Europe, began to take a more sceptical view of religion's relationship to politics. The crusading spirit was coming to be replaced by a notion that Christ's kingdom was not of this world.[23] Nationalism, in this context, was one particularist solution to a problem generated by reformation and counter-reformation commitments to ineluctably conflicting universalisms. Finally, the events of 1688–9 constituted a nationalist revolution in the sense that it was largely understood as a moment of mass popular political activity, a moment in which the primary allegiance of most English men and

---

[21] I follow Anthony Smith's suggestion that this was a sufficient social precondition for the development of nationalism, *National identity*, p. 60.

[22] See my discussion of coffee houses and the possibilities for public discussion in '"Coffee politicians does create": coffee houses and Restoration political culture', *JMH*, 67:4 (1995), 807–34.

[23] For one account of this retreat in England, see my 'From holy cause to economic interest', in Steve Pincus and Alan Houston, eds., *A nation transformed: reinterpreting later Stuart Britain* (Cambridge, forthcoming); see also my discussion of this phenomenon, along with the other authorities there cited in *Protestantism and patriotism: ideologies and the making of English foreign policy, 1650–1668* (Cambridge, 1996), pp. 450–1.

women was to the nation, not to a particular monarch. What, according to David Miller, distinguishes earlier notions of national character from 'modern ideas of nation and nationality, is the idea of a body of people capable of acting collectively and in particular of conferring authority on political institutions'.[24] Claire McEachern has recently shown that a well-developed and sophisticated sense of English national identity long predated the late Stuart period, but it was only in 1688–9 that the majority of the English people appealed to the nation as authorising their political actions against the established regime.[25]

English nationalists endorsed and promoted the revolution of 1688–9 because they were committed to opposing the aspiring French universal monarch Louis XIV. They loathed the political and religious style of Louis and feared that James II was attempting to mimic him at home and appease him abroad. But they also had a deep attachment to English political and religious culture. For these people a nationalist understanding of politics – a commitment to particularist cultural and political groupings – seemed the only viable principle both for organising domestic political life and for coexistence in a Europe composed of many cultures, religions and types of polity. The successful nationalism of 1688–89 was a revolutionary achievement: a 'Glorious Revolution' indeed.

II

In February 1685, James II ascended the throne of England in a flush of popular enthusiasm. The new king's enemies as well as his friends all commented on the political nation's unanimous support for the catholic monarch. Sir John Lowther, hardly one of James' closest political allies, thought him 'the most popular prince that had been known in England of a long time'.[26] James II, recalled Charles Caesar, 'was saluted King by an universal acclamation; welcomed by the addresses and congratulations of all his subjects'.[27] This enthusiasm, it soon become clear, turned in part on the popular expectation that James II would turn his long military and naval experience to good use against France. Throughout 1685 and 1686 the nation's poets called for the king to check Louis XIV's 'vast design', and to let France feel 'just punishment for pride'.[28] These were not just the sentiments of radical whigs, or airy

---

[24] Miller, *On nationality*, p. 30.
[25] Claire McEachern, *The poetics of English nationhood, 1590–1612* (Cambridge, 1996), *passim*, especially p. 5.
[26] John Lowther, Viscount Lonsdale, *Memoir of the reign of James II* (1857), p. 450.
[27] Charles Caesar, *Numerus infaustus* (1689), p. 100.
[28] *To the king: a congratulatory poem* (1685), pp. 5–6; Thomas Durfey, *An elegy upon the*

flights of poetic fancy. According to the West India merchant Christopher Jeaffreson the 'generality of the people, are desirous of war with France'.[29] Similarly, the tory John Nalson advised parliament that it was 'the true interest of the nation' to aid James in securing them 'from the danger of France',[30] and, in 1685, the extremely loyal House of Commons drew up an address to the monarch calling for him 'to declare, proclaim and enter into an actual war' against Louis XIV.[31]

This English loathing of Louis XIV stemmed from his perceived universalism. English calls for war were based on fears (growing steadily since France's entry into the second Anglo-Dutch conflict in 1666) that Louis intended to crush the independence of all other nations and become a universal monarch.[32] Despite attempts to limit the extent and ferocity of anti-French sentiment, England was saturated with Francophobia by the reign of James, and the populace had become convinced that Louis posed a threat to the national integrity not only of themselves but of all Europe. 'It is agreed at all hands', asserted one commentator uncontroversially, 'that the French set up for an Universal Commerce as well as for an Universal Monarchy.'[33] 'Does not all Christendom in general, and the English nation in particular, look upon the great man of France as a common enemy?' asked Richard Booker, the rector of Icklingham.[34] William Lawrence summed up English sentiment perfectly when he explained 'the French King thinks that for men to obey other Princes is to taste of the forbidden fruit, and therefore . . . drives whole nations from the paradise of peace and plenty'.[35]

Unfortunately for James, in the face of such deep English desire for a war to end Louis' universalism, he did nothing. In the minds of many, he did less than nothing. Not only did most people in England feel their king was appeasing France, many were sure that James had signed an alliance with Louis. Newsletters, which were carefully scrutinised by the

---

late blessed monarch King Charles II (1685), p. 10. See also, *A poem on the present assembly of parliament, November 9th 1685* (1686), p. 4.

[29] Christopher Jeaffreson to Col. Hill, 19 February 1685, in John Cordy Jeaffreson, ed., *A young squire of the seventeenth century: from the papers (A. D. 1676–1686) of Christopher Jeaffreson of Dullingham House, Cambridgeshire II* (1878), pp. 167–8.

[30] John Nalson, *The present interest of England* (2nd edn, 1685), p. 44.

[31] 'Address to James II', 1685, BL, Add. MSS 63773, f. 25r.

[32] See my *Protestantism and patriotism*, pp. 350–68; '"From butterboxes to wooden shoes": the shift in English popular sentiment from anti-Dutch to anti-French in the 1670s', *HJ*, 38 (1995), 37–62; 'The English debate on universal monarchy', in John Robertson, ed., *A union for empire: the union of 1707 in the history of British political thought* (Cambridge, 1995).

[33] *A short discourse upon the designs, practices & counsels of France* (1688), p. 8.

[34] Richard Booker, *Satisfaction tendred to all that pretend conscience* (1689), p. 5.

[35] William Lawrence to William Paulett, 27 Oct. 1693, India Office Library, Eur E 3871B, f. 46r.

government during James II's reign, frequently reported rumours of an impending Anglo-French alliance.[36] Court gossips circulated rumours of a 'league offensive and defensive', insisting always that James was keeping 'close to the French'.[37] One illegally published pamphlet warned cryptically that the king's eyes were 'fast closed with the enchanted slumbers of the French Delilah',[38] whilst Sir William Trumbull, who was James' ambassador successively in Paris and in Constantinople, gradually became convinced of 'a secret league between the two kings'.[39] By the decisive summer and autumn of 1688, the English nation was obsessed with fears of their monarch's friendship with Louis XIV. In August the anglican divine Dr. William Denton was 'certain the King expects a squadron of French ships to be at his command',[40] whilst in the following month, the Londoner William Westby averred that 'everybody speaks of a holy league' between James II and Louis XIV.[41] So pervasive were the fears of an Anglo-French alliance, that Dr William Sherlock thought 'this did more to drive the King out of the nation, than the Prince's army'.[42]

Fears of French influence over James went even deeper than concern about possible international alliances, however. The king, most came to believe, sought to replace the English national political culture with that of France and to replace an English with a French government. One pamphleteer explained that the nation had looked to William of Orange because 'the three kingdoms of England, Scotland, and Ireland' were being 'reduced into the pattern of the French King in government and religion'.[43] Similarly, one poet thought James II was following his French cousin's 'perfect pattern . . . of governing all by one sovereign will',[44] whilst another was sure that England's 'oppressors' were 'fleshed with the barbarous precedent in France'.[45] This English sense that their

---

[36] London newsletter, 11 Mar. 1686, Folger Lc 1635; 7 July 1687, Folger Lc 1830; 29 Dec. 1687, Folger Lc 1901.

[37] ? to John Ellis, 27 Feb. 1686, BL Add. 4194, f. 40r; J. Fr. to John Ellis, 21 July 1686, BL Add. 4194, f. 81v.

[38] *The design of France against England and Holland* (1686), p. 2.

[39] Sir William Trumbull's diary, 18 Jan. 1686, BL Add. 52279, f. 27r. See also Sir William Trumbull to William of Orange, 4/14 Jan. 1686, BL, Trumbull MSS Misc. XXIV, unfoliated.

[40] Dr William Denton to Sir Ralph Verney, 29 Aug. 1688, Bucks RO, Verney MSS, Reel 43, unfoliated.

[41] William Westby, Memoirs, 24 Sept. 1688, Folger V.a. 469, f. [36ar]. See also Westby, Memoirs, 22 Nov. 1688, Folger V.a. 469, f. 48r.

[42] William Sherlock, *A letter to a member of the convention* [1689], p. 4.

[43] *An account of the reasons of the nobility and gentry's invitation* (1688), p. 8.

[44] *A discourse to the king* [Amsterdam, 1688], p. 1.

[45] *The deliverance, a poem to the prince of Orange* (1689), p. 3. See also, *A congratulatory poem to his highness* (1688, broadside).

political culture was being Frenchified was both well developed and
quite sophisticated. Since the early 1680s many English wits had
complained of 'French councillors and whores', and the 'French education' which had 'changed our natures, and enslaved our nation'.[46] At
the same time, the French presence at court (manifest in Francophilic
privy councilors and Jesuit advisors) had driven many to blame all
England's 'misfortunes these many years unto French councils'.[47]
Within this set of suspicions, the policies pursued by James and his
Frenchified ministers were naturally perceived as French policies, and
England was thought to be headed for the blend of tyranny, poverty and
misery which France was believed to exemplify. For instance, the
enlarged standing army (whose very camp at Hounslow Heath was
explicitly modelled on Louis XIV's military installations)[48] was thought
to turn 'the civil government into a military; and that is not the
government of England'.[49] English law too, was turned into a French
mockery under its catholic king. In subverting 'the civil government and
established laws', one angry English controversialist proclaimed, 'the
French precedent was too exactly followed'. 'The methods here observed were the same with those which had been taken in France.'[50]

Most significantly, perhaps, James' attempts to overturn the test act
by declaration, and to pack parliament to have the penal laws statutorily
reversed, were also interpreted in a French context. It was 'the doings in
France' which taught the English to beware 'what feeble things edicts,
coronation-oaths, laws and promises repeated over and over again prove
to be'.[51] By first closeting privy councillors and MPs, and then by
submitting the entire country to his notorious three questions regarding
the test act and penal laws, James II had threatened 'the freedom and
being of our Parliaments, just as the French King first invaded the
supreme legal authority of France, which was vested in the Assembly of
Estates'.[52] 'The King, by this dispensing power', thundered Sir George
Treby in the convention, 'might have packed members of Parliament,
like the Parliament of Paris, which is in the nature of registers, only to

---

[46] 'The impartial trimmer', c.1682, NLS, Adv. 19.1.12, f. 15r. See also 'England's
congratulation', 1690, Folger M.b. 12, f. 153v; 'England's present state', in W. G. Day,
ed., *The Pepys ballads* (5 vols., Cambridge, 1987), III, p. 163; 'Satyr on the affairs of the
camp', 1686, NLS, Adv. 19.1.12, f. 159r; *Present state of France* (1687), p. 17.
[47] *Modern history, or the monthly account*, II:3 (Dec. 1688), p. 98.
[48] William Blathwayt to Sir William Trumbull, 25 Jan. 1686, BL, Trumbull MSS Misc
XXIV, unfoliated.
[49] *A friendly debate* (1689), p. 37.
[50] *An account of the pretended prince of Wales* (1688), p. 6.
[51] 'Reasons against repealing the acts of parliament concerning the test', 1687, BL, Add
69955, fs. 1–2.
[52] *Account of the reasons*, pp. 7–8.

record the King's will and pleasure by his dragoons.'[53] Within this context, and given the fears that James II had allied with a monarch who had brutally ended religious diversity in his own kingdom through his revocation of the edict of Nantes, it was almost impossible for James' subjects to trust his professed commitment to religious toleration. For them, the repeal of the test acts and the penal laws was merely a prelude to forced conversions. Gilbert Burnet sneered that James II's promises of toleration 'are no other way to be kept, than the assurances which the Great Lewis gave to his Protestant subjects'.[54] 'The method they have taken', the dissenter Roger Morrice wrote of James II's declaration of indulgence, 'is perfectly like that of France, for that King issued out an edict at first to confirm the Edict of Nantes' only later to eat away at its privileges and finally revoke it.[55] It was the example of Louis XIV, according to *The Dilucidator*, which 'made those of England fear that the King, after having rendered his religion powerful and ruling, would undertake to make them Catholics after the dragoon mode, as has been done to those of France'.[56] On this evidence, it seems the English turned against James II's toleration, not because they opposed religious leniency, but because they feared the king was following the pattern of his cousin Louis XIV.

The choice available to the English in 1688–9 was, therefore, one between two distinct national political cultures. Sir Richard Cocks later summarised the perceived options in the starkest of all possible terms. 'That government that is settled upon the biased designing will and pleasure of one frail man is that despotical tyrannical government the thinking Englishman abhors', he lectured in 1694. 'It is French government where the will of the prince is the law, reason and religion of the people.'[57] Similarly, the episcopalian cleric Robert Kirk recalled that it had been James II's 'intimacy with the French King and learning his methods' which had 'cooled the hearts of many who wished well to King James'.[58] Thus, far from being unaware of European developments before the revolution, the English were obsessed with Louis XIV's drive to achieve universal dominion. They were obsessed not because of some innate little Englandism or xenophobia, but because they were certain that France's universal aspirations posed a threat to their own national

---

[53] Anchitel Grey, *Debates of the House of Commons* (10 vols, 1689), IX, p. 14.

[54] Gilbert Burnet, *Some reflections on his majesty's proclamation . . . in Scotland* [1687], p. 3.

[55] Roger Morrice, entering book, 9 Apr. 1687, Dr Williams Library 31Q, p. 89.

[56] James Johnston to ?, 8 Dec. 1687, Nottingham University Library, Pw A 2112g.

[57] Sir Richard Cocks, 'Charge spoke at midsummer sessions 1694', Bod. Eng. Hist. b. 209, f. 28v. See the similar comments in James Wellwood, *Memoirs* (3rd edn, 1700), p. 242.

[58] Robert Kirk, 'Sermons, Occurrences . . .', Mar. 1690, EUL, La. III 545, f. 98v.

identity as well as to the national identities of every other state. Although the English initially had high hopes for James II, their optimism about his intentions waned as he failed to engage Louis XIV in war while flirting with French envoys and ambassadors, and attempting to impose a French political culture on England. By the summer of 1688 a wide range of the English political nation was convinced that James II had become completely dependent on Louis XIV. For them England's national independence was very much in jeopardy.

III

The popular English perception that James II had replaced the English with the French style of government, coupled with the belief that he was relying on political advice from allies and servants of the French king, created the classic nationalist problem. A situation in which 'the rulers of the political unit belong to a nation other than that of the majority of the ruled' or in which politics is dominated by 'an alien group', constitutes for nationalists, according to Gellner, a 'quite outstandingly intolerable breach of political propriety'.[59] It is unsurprising, in this context, that the English people turned overwhelmingly against their ostensibly Frenchified monarch.

The recent scholarly attention on the vast and complicated preparations for the invasion made by William of Orange and the Dutch States General has done much to obscure the depth and significance of the popular support the prince of Orange had within England.[60] In fact, however, there is considerable evidence that a mass popular opinion turned against James in the months before the revolution, and that the English people played an active part in bringing William to the throne. There was, after all, a national culture of public political discussion (described in the burgeoning scholarship of the late Stuart 'public sphere') which informed the English of James' policies, and according to the marquis of Halifax meant the royal programme had no chance of success.[61] Moreover, the controversial nature of James' actions ensured they would become flashpoints of popular opinion; whilst the comprehensiveness of the king's campaign did much to politicise the nation and unite it against him. For example, the king's campaign to query potential electors as to their intentions regarding the penal laws rapidly backfired. This campaign was truly national in the sense that agents were sent into

[59] Gellner, *Nations and nationalism*, p. 1.
[60] See, in particular, Jonathan I. Israel, 'The Dutch role in the Glorious Revolution', in Israel, *Anglo-Dutch Moment*, pp. 105–62.
[61] Halifax to William of Orange, 25 Aug. 1687, PRO, SP 8/1/Part II, fs.143–4.

the localities to ascertain the views not only of those already qualified to vote in parliamentary elections, but also those who might be so qualified as well. However, instead of paving the way for a compliant parliament, the quaker William Penn, who was one of the king's advisors in the affair, thought 'the method of questions has angered and united the nation'.[62] 'The universality of this business', Sir John Lowther remembered, made it 'the action of the kingdom.'[63]

By the late 1680s, then, the English were an extremely well-informed and agitated political nation, whose sense of the ideological issues at stake had only been deepened by James's attempts to alter the national political culture. As each new manoeuvre by James and his advisors seemed to transform England into another France, nationalist sensibilities were increasingly irritated. As early as November 1687, Roger Morrice thought that should the Dutch invade 'the kingdom generally would stand well affected to them, and great numbers from about London were very likely to go meet them where they land'.[64] By the summer of 1688, the famous set of seven whig and tory gentlemen reported that the English were 'so generally dissatisfied with the present conduct of the government [that] there are nineteen parts of twenty of the people throughout the kingdom, who are desirous of a change'.[65] When William finally did arrive, English men and women of all social ranks throughout the country rose in support. Important garrisons in Devon and Cornwall defected, and almost immediately after the prince landed his ranks were swelled by 'a multitude of common people'.[66] Meanwhile, in Yorkshire and Derbyshire, risings occurred whose importance in dividing James' attention, and in preventing him from securing help from Scotland or Ireland, have been underplayed in recent scholarship. 'All the Northern country' quickly declared for the prince of Orange, reported the Dutch ambassador.[67] Similarly, in traditionally loyalist Oxford the town 'unanimously rose' for William,[68] whilst Londoners 'showed no other concern for this revolution but what might express their satisfaction and approbation and in a word all things conspired to testify their joy on this occasion'.[69] Gilbert Burnet, who had come over with William's armada,

[62] James Johnston to ?, 25 Nov. 1687, Nottingham University Library, Pw A2103.
[63] Lowther, *Memoir*, p. 459.
[64] Roger Morrice, entering book, 26 Nov. 1687, Dr Williams Library 31 Q, p. 207.
[65] Shrewbury, Devonshire, Danby, Lumley, Compton, Sidney and Russell to William of Orange, 30 June 1688, PRO, SP 8/1/Part II, f. 224v.
[66] Earl of Nottingham to Viscount Hatton, 15 Nov. 1688, BL Add 29594, f. 131v.
[67] Van Citters to States General, 27 Nov. / 7 Dec. 1688, BL, Add 34510, f. 190r.
[68] John Evelyn Jr. to John Evelyn, 15 Dec. 1688, BL, Evelyn MSS, vol. III, Letter 646.
[69] R. D. to ?, BL Egerton 2717, f. 417r.

could not but marvel at 'the concurrence of all in the nation, and especially of the great body from which the chief opposition was expected', and given the surprisingly small numbers, and almost total ineffectiveness, of committed Jacobites, his astonishment is understandable.[70] In terms of popular participation, William's accession was at least as much a national revolution as a Dutch invasion: Sir Charles Sedley was not exaggerating much when he told William the English people 'all cried out, as with one voice, save us, heroic prince, or we are lost'.[71]

Not only did the English *act* as a nation to promote a revolution in 1688–9, they also *understood* their actions as a national revolution. While there was a broad range of interpretations available to the supporters of the revolution, the vast majority of those interpretations were nationalist ones. Although as recently as 1685 the English had apparently endorsed a theory of indefeasible hereditary right (an idea which upheld the universal superiority of monarchy as the divinely instituted form of government), by 1688–9 they were understanding their politics in much more nuanced and particularist terms.

The first sign of this realignment of political assumptions came in a remarkable consensus about the underlying principles of political theory. Supporters of the revolution, wherever they stood on the broad political spectrum, all concurred that forms of government were *national* not divine creations. They rejected the universalism of patriarchalism (and some forms of republican political thought) in favour of the idea that government varied according to the political characters of different peoples. The essence of the argument was laid out most clearly by the author of *A brief vindication*. He pointed out that particular forms of government could not be 'determined by God or nature, as government in general is . . . for then they should be all one in all nations . . . seeing God and nature are all one to all'. In his view it was left 'to every nation and country to choose that form of government which they shall like best'.[72] Commentators across the political and ecclesiastical spectrum found the logic of this inescapable, and the point was repeated with great frequency throughout the revolutionary period. On the anglican side, Richard Claridge, the rector of Peopleton in Worcestershire, announced that 'almighty God has no where determined in his word a model for our civil government, but has left us, as all other nations, to

[70] Gilbert Burnet, *A sermon preached in the chapel of St. James, 23 December 1688* (2nd edn, 1689), p. 14.
[71] Sir Charles Sedley, 'To the king on his birthday', in Sir Charles Sedley, *Works* (1702), p. 91.
[72] *A brief vindication of the parliamentary proceedings against the late King James II* (1689), pp. 5–6.

such a form as shall be agreed upon by the people'.[73] Similarly, the high church cleric Thomas Long insisted 'the ordinance of government is from God and nature, but the species of it, whether by one or more, is from man'.[74] Those with more radical and with dissenting pedigrees made similar statements about the national basis of political power. In a speech reprinted in 1689, Algernon Sidney proclaimed that 'God hath left nations unto the liberty of setting up such governments as best pleased themselves'[75], whilst the whig divine Daniel Whitby thought that because God had only given 'general appointment or ordinance, that all nations shall have some government placed over them', no one could claim to rule by divine right.[76] *The Dilucidator* was therefore reporting on a virtual consensus when it declared that 'all government has ever been susceptible of different forms, according to the interests and dispositions of different nations'.[77]

Of course, whilst acceptance that nations determined their own constitutions might pave the way for more 'nationalist' accounts of politics, it still left great scope for disagreement about the particular nature of English government. Indeed, supporters of the revolution did enunciate a wide variety of arguments in defence of their cause. Moreover, in the revolutionary moment, ideas were quite fluid, and some individuals advanced different sorts of arguments at different circumstances, or even expressed different types of argument within the same statement. Nevertheless, despite this variety and fluidity, two types of interpretation – both insisting on the national nature of the revolution – tended to dominate.[78] First, there were those who argued that the nation had risen up in resistance to a tyrannical monarch who had tried to impose a French government on the English people. Second, more moderate supporters of the revolution (and this included many who had preached passive obedience since 1660) claimed that English loyalty was to English law rather than to any particular monarch, and that any ruler who ceased to govern by English law effectively unkinged himself.

What these theories had in common was that they placed the national constitution and the national community above loyalty to the abstract principle of hereditary monarchy. By putting the welfare and rights of

---

[73] Richard Claridge, *A defence of the present government* (1689), p. 2.

[74] Thomas Long, *A resolution of certain queries* (1689), p. 4.

[75] Algernon Sidney, in *The dying speeches of several excellent persons who suffred for their zeal against popery and arbitrary government* (1689), p. 19.

[76] Daniel Whitby, *Considerations humbly offered for taking the oath of allegiance* (1689), p. 35.

[77] *The Dilucidator*, IV (February 1689), p. 86.

[78] I have found a slightly different range of theoretical positions from those described by Robert Beddard, 'The unexpected whig revolution of 1688', in Beddard, ed., *The revolutions of 1688* (Oxford, 1991), pp. 66–7.

the English people at the centre of their concerns, they explained 1688 in nationalist terms.

Perhaps unsurprisingly, there was a great efflorescence of resistance theorising in the era of the revolution. An extraordinarily large number of writers, politicians and preachers (perhaps far more than recent scholarship has recognised) advanced stages of the argument that the English people were essentially free; that the community had made a contract with their rulers to allow the exercise of power; and that resistance to rulers was justified if ever they broke the contract. What this vast wealth of treatises shared was their treatment of the English people as the source of authority, and their belief that the nation could take action to protect its rights and liberties, even against its own monarch. They thus all accepted *nationalist* interpretations of the revolution. This aspect of their thought is most clearly demonstrated in their common use of languages of defence and invasion. Resistance theorists tended to talk about 1688 as if it were an international war. They described the revolution as the recourse of an independent nation which had legally and justly defended its liberty against an alien aggressor. James II was, therefore, treated as if he were attempting a *foreign* conquest: nobody could doubt a nation's right to take up arms against such a man. 'We own it rebellion to resist a king that governs by law', announced the nobility gathered at Nottingham in November 1688, 'but he was always accounted a tyrant that made his will the law; and to resist such an one, we justly esteem no rebellion, but a necessary defence.'[79] Another commentator spoke of the English being provoked into arms by James II's 'encroachments'[80] and Richard Claridge (having previously argued that when rulers 'degenerate into bloody murderers of their country . . . resistance is not rebellion, but a just and lawful defence') also used the language of aggression against the nation. He argued that the English should be governed by law, and that 'when contrary to this law we are invaded (as we were in the late King's time in everything that was near and dear to us) we may justly defend ourselves against such illegal doings'.[81] Again, according to the author of *A brief account of the nullity of King James's title*, the king's subversion of the English constitution was so complete, his principles so inimitable to the English political nation, that it was just for the English to oppose him 'in all such hostile enterprises no less than any other open invader'.[82]

---

[79] 'The declaration of the nobility . . . at Nottingham', in *A second collection of papers relating to the present juncture of affairs in England* (1688), p. 30.
[80] 'Proposals humbly offered in behalf of the princess of Orange', in *A seventh collection of papers relating to the present juncture of affairs in England* (1689), p. 1.
[81] Claridge, *A defence*, pp. 4–5.
[82] *A brief account of the nullity of King James's title* (1689), p. 8.

Not all, or perhaps even most, of the defenders of the revolution suggested that there had been active resistance to James II. Many were content to take the second line that by violating English law, by ceasing to rule in an English manner, James II had in effect unkinged himself. The English people remained loyal; their king had merely ceased to exist through his own actions. While this view allowed its proponents to circumscribe more severely the grounds for active resistance, it was no less of a nationalist argument since it insisted on the primacy of English traditions, culture, law and faith. For all their conservationist rhetoric, the proponents of this view had revolutionised their understanding of English society. What bound their community together was no longer their unswerving loyalty to their divinely appointed monarch, but their profound and unbending commitment to their national religion and their national constitution.

This process of social redefinition began for many loyalists early in James II's reign. Under unrelenting pressure from the court, both lay and clerical defenders of the church of England were compelled to redefine their commitment to loyalty. In 1686 Bishop Compton of London was brought before the ecclesiastical commissioners for his refusal to suspend Dr John Sharp for his anti-papist sermons. The case quickly became a *cause célèbre*, and was 'the talk all over England'.[83] It was therefore extremely significant that Compton (who came from a 'family who were always loyal and desirous to be serviceable to the crown') announced that 'for his own part it should be a matter of sorrow for him to disobey the King's commands', but that what he did was 'not so much his own sense as the sense of his friends and the law'.[84] Compton's preference for his friends and the law of the land as against the king marked a real turning point in anglican theories of obedience, and the bishop soon had many ideological fellow travellers. For example, the tory Edmund Bohun thought James 'was bound to govern us according to law, and we were not bound to submit to any other than a legal government',[85] whilst Elizabeth Eyre, a loyal devotee of the church, gave allegiance to the constitution priority over allegiance to the monarch. 'Although in my single private capacity I ought to submit to, and suffer the greatest injustice rather than disobey the lawful magistrate', she explained, 'yet as I am an Englishman, I think I am as much obliged, by all ties both civil and sacred, to defend the government and constitution of which I am a member, as I am to obey the king; and that

[83] Sir Ralph Verney to Edmund Verney, 15 Aug. 1686, Bucks RO, Verney MSS, Reel 41, unfoliated.
[84] London newsletter, 10 Aug. 1686, Folger Shakespeare Library, L.c. 1693.
[85] Edmund Bohun, *The history of the desertion* (1689), sig. [A4r].

being the primary obligation, ought to be discharged in the first place.'[86] In the light of such comment, Mark Goldie is surely right to insist that 'churchmen' had developed 'a considered case for resistance' during the reign of James.[87]

By 1688, then, anglicans had come to argue that their primary allegiance was to their national community, and had come to define their monarch as the protector of that community. The next stage of tory conversion came during the revolution itself, when the position they had reached allowed them to argue that James had ceased to be king when he failed to uphold English law. Examples of such argument were numerous. For example, one moderate pamphleteer reasoned that, because 'government according to law is essential to our government', a ruler who 'leaves the proper government, and assumes another kind of government abhorred by our constitution . . . plainly ceaseth to be our governor in any sense'.[88] Similarly the conservative churchman Thomas Long insisted, 'the King, even before leaving his kingdom had deserted the government. He that is not willing to hold the government of England, as constituted with certain limitations and conditions annexed, doth constructively renounce it.'[89] Again, and pithily, Sergeant Maynard told the Commons, 'the question is not, whether we can depose the King; but whether the King has not deposed himself'.[90] By themselves, such statements illustrate how far anglicans had gone in accepting defence of the national constitution as their prime obligation. However, the full nationalist implications of this line of thought were made clearest by those who went a step further and maintained that the government had been dissolved when the king had abdicated. Writers who argued this way were prepared to suggest that, with the collapse of legitimate authority, power had returned to a national community which was able to remodel the monarchy in these special circumstances. Thus the Suffolk anglican Richard Booker was certain that 'the late King did abdicate, and that the government did devolve upon the people'. It was on this basis that the constitutional convention, 'a full representative of the whole nation', met in Westminster.[91] Similarly, one paper purportedly circulated by the marquis of Halifax reminded its audience that 'the

[86] Elizabeth Eyre, *A letter from a person of quality in the north* (1689), p. 8.
[87] Mark Goldie, 'The political thought of the anglican revolution', in Beddard, ed., *The revolutions of 1688*, p. 112. I am not absolutely convinced by Goldie's claim that 'those who resisted James regularly claimed to be standing upon conscience, upon the law of God rather than the law of the land', p. 117.
[88] *Agreement betwixt the present and preceeding government: or a discourse of this monarchy, whether elective or hereditary* (1689), pp. 33–4.
[89] Long, *Resolution of certain queries*, pp. 27–8.
[90] John Maynard, 28 Jan. 1689, in Grey, *Debates*, IX, pp. 11–12.
[91] Richard Booker, *Satisfaction tendered to all that pretend conscience* (1689), p. 4.

government being dissolved, we are in such a state at present as a people where no government is yet set up' and that in 'such a state the people are to meet in their representatives and agree upon their constitution'.[92] Again, Sir John Evelyn thought that 'a Parliament of brave and worthy patriots', had the opportunity 'to produce a kind of new creation amongst us' after the English had descended into 'chaos'.[93] Since James II was no longer king, the author of *Four questions debated* posited, 'there must be a sort of reverter to the people'.[94]

Thus the revolution of 1688–9 was defended in a variety of innovative ways, ways which redefined allegiance in nationalist terms. A broad spectrum of Englishmen and women thought that the form of government, the nature of political culture, was nationally specific. Most came to believe that James had sought to replace England's national political culture with that of France. Some suggested that since the king's innovative governmental style was tantamount to a foreign invasion, resistance was justified to defend English national integrity. Others, including many who had defended passive obedience at the moment of James' accession, thought that English loyalty was primarily to English law and English customs rather than to a particular monarch. Since James had violated that law, he ceased to be an English king and was no longer owed obedience. While these different scenarios represent real and tangible ideological differences, they were both nationalist scenarios. Both groups had replaced the monarchical allegiance associated with Calvin's case with a nationalist allegiance.

IV

What role did protestantism play in the nationalist revolution of 1688–9? Recently scholars have placed a great deal of emphasis on the backward-looking religious nature of the revolution, reacting against a previous generation who accorded religion very little explanatory power. This new generation of scholars has interpreted William's invasion and the war which followed it as confessional crusades. This has left students of nationalism with two interpretative options. Either they could argue, along with Colley and Claydon, that protestantism was constitutive of English nationalism; or, they could argue, along with many social scientists, that because of the fundamentally religious nature of English society there could be no nationalism. These options, I suggest, are too

---

[92] 'A brief account concerning matters of fact', 28 Jan. 1689, Bod. Rawl. D1079, f. 4v.
[93] Sir John Evelyn to John Evelyn Jr., 18 Dec. 1688, BL, Evelyn MSS, vol. XIV, letter 1555.
[94] *Four questions debated* (1689), p. 6.

constrictive. By limiting the debate to the binary options of secular or religious society, historians have denied that late seventeenth-century English men and women were committed protestants with a worldview remarkably different from that of the early protestants. The protestantism defended and enunciated by the revolutionaries, I contend, was not a crusading protestantism, but one which understood protestantism to be a constituent in, though not constitutive of, English national identity. Other nations, they claimed, legitimately held other religious beliefs. James lost his throne not because he was a catholic, but because he was a catholic ruling in a catholic style over a protestant nation. His policies – not his beliefs – lost him the crown. Similarly, most in England denied that the war begun in 1689 against France was a war of religion. For them it was a war to protect national integrities against the aspiring universal monarch: Louis XIV.

There was a religious – even providentialist – element to contemporary understanding of the events of 1688. However, since God was acknowledged to act through nations as well as individuals, this did not contradict a nationalist conception of the revolution. Nor was the protestantism involved the crusading protestantism of the early reformation. Because so many believed along with Sarah Cowper that 'Antichrist is the philosopher's stone in divinity', few in England thought wars of religion legitimate; and they were consequently reluctant to interpret 1688 as part of an evangelical drive to promote a true faith.[95] Rather, the political attachment which the English showed to their religion at the time of the revolution was because protestantism was the religion by law established. They defended the protestant church because it was the national church. They valued it as something ensconced in English culture and society by the English constitution. Thus one revolutionary pamphleteer argued, 'if by the laws of any government, the Christian religion, or any form of it, is become a part of the subjects' property, then [it] falls under another consideration'. In these circumstances (the circumstances which obtained in England) one must view the national religion, 'not as it is a religion, but as it is become one of the principal rights of the subjects to believe and profess it'. 'Then we must judge on the invasions made on that, as we do of any other invasion that is made on our other rights.'[96] Charles Caesar concurred by stating that, in England, 'the religion of the nation is the law of the nation', and by insisting that that alone justified forcible defence of it.[97] One particularly precise observer argued that England, had 'a national church political'.

[95] Sarah Cowper, commonplace book, c. 1673–1710, Herts RO, D/EP F 37, p. 202.
[96] 'Enquiry into the means of submission', in *Second collection*, pp. 5–6.
[97] Caesar, *Numerus infaustus*, pp. 101–2.

'There is this difference between a church national, the Church Catholic, and particular churches', recounted this theorist. 'The two latter are of divine right and essential consideration, but the former is and can be only a humane institution, for it is manifestly accidental to the Church of Christ that the chief magistrate and the whole people should be Christian.'[98] For these writers, protestantism was merely one part of the national identity of England. Faith was to be defended, but only as part of the citizen's rights and property, and as a constitutional religion protected by law.

More widely, few English people saw the change of regime in 1688 in a crusading context. James' policies, not his religious beliefs, did him in. 'The late King's religion did not hinder his possessing himself of the throne, neither was that the cause of his leaving it', averred one polemicist. 'He might have enjoyed it and made the best of it, as to himself, in all freedom.' Unfortunately, however, he had 'thought it beneath him to stop here' and had destroyed the basis of his position as he trampled 'all the laws of the kingdom under his feet'.[99] 'No body sure will say that our hate was more to the Papist than to the King for his mal-administrations', reasoned the author of *A justification of the whole proceedings*, 'for 'tis evident the whole nation gave him a respect suitable to the greatest love for the first years, and if we altered after, 'twas for actions whereof he had not been guilty during those years'.[100] 'The expedition of the Prince cannot pass for a war on the account of religion in the judgement of any reasonable person', insisted another contemporary who stated that the prince of Orange had come to save English laws rather than faith;[101] and the 'Trimmer' in *A Friendly debate* argued, James 'was not deposed, nor molested . . . for his religion'.[102] In fact, so far was the revolution from being a religious crusade, that one pamphleteer suggested James might have enjoyed his personal religion without offending protestant Englishmen, and might even have been able to favour his catholic subjects, if only he had not attempted to pursue his aims unconstitutionally.[103]

It is true, of course, that the convention of 1689 forever excluded catholics from being kings of England. This stipulation, however, was

---

[98] *The amicable reconciliation of the dissenters to the church of England* (1689) [p. 1]. Richard Baxter apparently also made the same claim, see Robert Kirk, 'Sermons, occurrences', 10 Nov. 1689, EUL, La. III 545, f. 39.

[99] 'Some short notes on a pamphlet', in *Tenth collection of papers relating to the present juncture of affairs in England* (1689), p. 16.

[100] *Justification of the whole proceedings* (1689), p. 12.

[101] *View of the true interest of the several states of Europe* (1689), pp. 53–4.

[102] *Friendly debate*, pp. 3, 35.

[103] *View of the true interest*, p. 37.

not evidence of a protestant crusading spirit. It did not stem from an eschatological worldview, but merely from a pragmatic recognition that catholic rulers had proved incompatible with this protestant nation. It was 'too dear experience' (and *not* some early protestant conception of universal truth) which convinced the author of one memorandum that 'popery' was 'inconsistent with the office of an English King'. This wording was echoed in the resolution adopted by Commons and Lords.[104] 'There is nothing in statute nor common law against a Popish Prince', agreed the civil lawyer Gilbert Dolben, 'but it is against the interest of the nation',[105] whilst Sir Richard Temple boomed 'that we have found by experience, that a Popish King is inconsistent with the government of a Protestant nation'.[106] For these men, 1688 was a successful act by the English political nation to replace an increasingly Frenchified government with an English one. It was a protestant revolution only in the sense that the English national religion was defended as one of the elements (albeit an important element) of English national identity threatened by James.

V

Because of the centrality of opposition to perceived French universalism for the revolutionaries, Colley, Claydon and others are right to point to the conflict with France which followed 1688 as an important testing ground for English nationalism. War against the aspiring French universal monarch was one of the central goals of the English revolutionary nationalists, so it was in proclaiming and defending that war that the nationalists were able to give their ideology more precise definition. Yet for the English, and this includes William's own propagandists, the war was an attempt to protect national integrities against an aspiring universal monarch, not a confessional conflict. Indeed, English polemicists constantly pointed out that it was only French propagandists who were raising a religious crusading banner in a desperate, but mendacious, attempt to garner allies. For the rest of Europe, and especially for England, the war pitted the entire community of European nations against the supreme violator of national identity, Louis XIV.

Evidence for these attitudes can be seen in parliament within a week of William and Mary's coronation. Then, a committee of the House of Commons drafted an address to their new monarchs calling for war

104 'Reflections upon the most proper way of regulating the succession', Jan. 1689, Bod. Rawl. A326 (Halifax's Papers), f. 79v. See above p.1 for the convention resolution.
105 Gilbert Dolben, 29 Jan. 1689, in Grey, *Debates*, IX, p. 28.
106 Sir Richard Temple, 29 Jan. 1689, in Grey, *Debates*, IX, p. 27.

against France. 'We have examined the mischiefs brought upon Christendom in late years by the French King', they reported, and accused him of attempting to 'subject it to an arbitrary and universal monarchy'.[107] Far from concentrating upon protestantism, and rejecting arguments 'about the strategic and commercial dangers of allowing France to dominate Europe', the Commons address (like all other Williamite publications) emphasised just those claims.[108] The report claimed that Louis had used 'a variety of means' to weaken European rivals, and keep them in a perpetual state of alarm. He had threatened them with his fleets and armies, corrupting their ministers, and even descended to 'intrigues by women' who were sent as wives or seductresses to lie as 'snakes in their bosoms to eat out their bowels'. In addition, the committee reported, Louis XIV had attacked the commerce of his rivals. His policy was 'never to admit an equal balance of trade, nor consent to any just treaty or settlement of commerce', so that others paid for their own ruin. The addressers concluded with a call for arms which made their horror of France's strategic domination clear. They hoped that William would fight so that 'a stop may be put to that growing greatness of the French King, which threatens all Christendom with no less than absolute slavery'. Such a war would protect the 'justice and liberty' of 'all Europe in general, and this nation in particular'.[109]

A month later William enthusiastically accepted the Commons' call to arms, and declared war against France. The declaration made it clear that William, too, rejected wars of religion. The document opened by recounting Louis XIV's crimes against the catholic Holy Roman emperor, who was William's ally. These perfidious actions made it clear that the French monarch was no religious crusader, but the 'disturber of the peace, and the common enemy of the Christian world'. Commerce too came to the fore as Louis XIV was accused of devastating the property of Englishmen in Hudson's Bay, New York and the Caribbean. These acts, coupled with France's protectionist measures, were 'sufficient evidences of . . . designs to destroy the trade, and consequently to ruin the navigation upon which the wealth and safety of this nation very much depends'. When the new monarchs did come to discuss French hostility to protestants, they made no mention of Louis' religious zeal, of his desire to recatholicise Europe, or even of his persecution of Huguenots. They merely complained that Louis' attacks on 'our English Protestant subjects in France' was 'contrary to the law of nations, and express treaties'.[110]

---

[107] *An address agreed upon at the committee for the French war* (1689), p. 1.
[108] Claydon, *William III*, p. 142.   [109] *An address*, pp. 3–6.
[110] *Their majesties declaration against the French king* (1689). I read this document rather differently than Claydon, *William III*, p. 143.

Louis had violated the rights of Englishmen and women: consequently William and Mary raise a nationalist, not a crusading, sword.

The first official fast sermons, the genre in which the English were most likely to emphasise the religious aspects of the war against France, also re-enforced the nationalist and anti-universalist nature of the war. Before the House of Commons on 5 June 1689, Thomas Tenison emphasised that the English were going to war against Louis, 'who is reputed, even by the head of the Roman Church' to be 'the common enemy of West-Europe'. Highlighting the well-known ecumenical nature of the struggle, Tenison preached that 'we are at war with one who (how unlike soever he is to be governor of the world) hath set himself in the seat of God, by making his personal glory his ultimate end'.[111] That same day, William Wake, one of the new monarchs' chaplains, rehearsed many of the same themes before the Commons. Wake called on his countrymen to become 'the scourge and terror of the universal enemy of truth, peace, religion, nature; in short, of all the common laws and rights of God and of all mankind'.[112] This war against France, he made clear, was neither a religious crusade nor a war of secular aggrandisement. It was a war to be fought 'not of your nation only, but of all the nations round about us'; nor were the fortunes 'of your own country and religion only' at stake. 'This is the fatal crisis', Wake thundered, 'that must secure or ruin both them and us forever.'[113]

The extraordinarily large public discussion of the war against France (discussion which took place in provincial parish churches, in coffee houses, in newsletters, in periodicals and in hundreds of pamphlets) confirmed that the English populace concurred with their governors about the novel nature of the conflict. In all this open comment, the fight was not a war of religion, but a war to protect the national integrities of all Europe. While the English repeatedly emphasised that protestantism was an essential part of their own national identity, they agreed with the works of European writers (both catholic and protestant) which were broadcast by the regime, and which made clear that France threatened all national identities.

A first example of English refusal to explain the world in terms of an apocalyptic struggle between religions can be seen in the almost total rejection of Louis' claim to be fighting a holy war. While French

---

[111] Thomas Tenison, *A sermon against self-love. Preached before the House of Commons, 5 June 1689* (1689), p. 25. I obviously have a radically different reading of this sermon and this passage than Claydon, *William III*, p. 144.

[112] William Wake, *A sermon preached before the House of Commons, 5 June 1689* (1689), p. 32.

[113] Ibid., p. 31.

propagandists feverishly scribbled tracts, treatises and sermons proclaiming that their monarch was engaged in a war of religion against the
protestant fanatic William III, only English Jacobites upheld their views.
Most commentators echoed Spanish and imperial tracts which denounced the hypocrisy of French claims. 'It is a matter of astonishment',
scowled one pamphleteer, 'that the French who have been the authors
of so much mischief, and damage to the Catholic Princes, and to the
Catholic religion, should go about to persuade the world, that the
present revolution in England is a war on the score of religion.'[114]
Another writer, the author of the *Happy union*, explained Louis' claims
by the French king's discovery that his old means of seduction and
subversion were failing. Facing disaster, Louis tried desperately to
persuade 'the Catholic potentates' that 'this is a war for the sake of
religion'. However, it was the ruin of 'his Machiavellian politics which
he dreads more than the establishment of the reformation'.[115] 'It is not
religion that pushes the French King', but fear that the tide had turned
against him, insisted the English author of *The means to free Europe*. If
the 'Grand Monarch' ever got the upper hand, 'after he had pulled
down William [and] overcome the Protestant Princes, he would do the
like to all the Roman Catholics, one after another, and thus become
Master of Europe'.[116]

In such a context, none of Louis' claims to zealous catholicism rang
true for English audiences. For example, his religious persecution could
not make him a *devôt*. 'All the wise men of the world were at a loss' to
explain Louis XIV's persecution of the Huguenots, Sir John Lowther
recalled, 'for nobody could conceive it to be a motive of conscience. His
morals and politics had ever been a sufficient confutation of that
notion.'[117] 'If the King did exterminate the Huguenots and heresy out of
his kingdom', concluded one English catholic writer, 'he did not do it
out of any principle of religion; but that religion was only a pretence to
aggrandize himself, and to attain to the Universal Monarchy.'[118] Similarly, the French king's notoriously bad relations with the pope made a
mockery of his catholic crusading credentials. Before the revolution of
1688–9 the pope and his envoy in England were well known to be
opponents of Louis XIV. Diplomats, newsletter writers and political
gossips busily circulated accounts of the most recent squabbles between
the Holy See and the Most Christian King.[119] 'The pope is well known

---

[114] *View of the true interest*, p. 54.
[115] *The happy union of England and Holland* (1689), p. 46.
[116] P. B., *The means to free Europe from the French usurpation* (1689), pp. 153, 160–1.
[117] Lowther, *Memoir*, p. 473.   [118] *A letter from a Roman catholick* (1689), p. 2.
[119] London newsletter, 17 Nov. 1687, Folger Lc 1884; 29 Nov. 1687, Folger Lc 1888;
Bevil Skelton to Sunderland, 10/20 Dec. 1687, PRO, SP 78/151, f. 123r; James Fraser

to be of the anti-Jesuitical faction, and to be implacably maligned by them', noted the great recorder of political gossip, Roger Morrice. Consequently he was opposed to the French king, 'who is now the patron general to the Jesuits, as formerly the King of Spain was'.[120] Louis XIV's 'ambition knows no difference between Catholics and Protestants', commented one participant in a popular dialogue just after the revolution, 'else he would never have fallen out with his Holy Father the Pope'.[121]

If the English were unconvinced by Louis' claim to be fighting a religious crusade, they were as insistent that their own side was not engaged in one. For example, they were aware of, and reassured by, William's alliances with rulers of very different faiths. Most extraordinarily, they seized on evidence of the rift between Paris and Rome, and were happy to accept the pope as a full member of their international alliance. It was clear to the vast majority of people in England both during and after the revolution that Innocent XI did not understand politics in confessional terms. In 1688, Sir Robert Southwell heard that 'the Emperor and some other Popish Princes and even the Pope himself' were well informed of William's intended invasion, and far from joining in a confessional alliance against the revolution they 'wished well to it' hoping it would lead England 'to join with the confederates against France'.[122] After the revolution, the pope and England's new governors made common cause in insisting that the European war now on foot was no war of religion. One papal polemic was republished in England denouncing Louis XIV as 'the Christian Turk, and as great an enemy to Europe as the Mahometan one'.[123] Papal support for the war against France and Innocent's refusal 'to send anything to King James' was well advertised in London.[124] 'The Pope is not so fond of his old Mumpsimus, or of the decrees of the Council of Trent it self, as to suffer France to conquer Italy, Spain, or Germany, no nor England, nor Holland neither, how much soever it might seem to facilitate their reduction to the See of Rome', concluded Edmund Bohun. The pope understood very well, thought Bohun, that once Louis 'shall make himself the Universal Monarch of Europe' he 'will certainly put an end to the sovereignty, wealth, grandeur and independency of

to Sir Robert Southwell, 15 Dec. 1687, Folger Vb287(39); J. Fr. to John Ellis, 16 Oct. 1688, BL, Add 4194, f. 382v.

120 Roger Morrice, entering book, 6 Nov. 1686, Dr. Williams Library, 31 P, p. 650.
121 *A dialogue between Dick and Tom* (1689), p. 10.
122 Sir Robert Southwell, 'A short account of the revolution', Folger, V.b. 150, vol. I, f. lv.
123 *The intreigues of the French king at Constantinople* (1689), sig B1 (for papal provenance of the pamphlet), pp. 23–4.
124 London newsletter, 25 Apr. 1689, Folger, L.c. 2007.

the Court of Rome and the pope will become as subject to him (notwithstanding his infallibility) as the Mufty is to the Grand Signior'.[125] Roger Morrice heard in London that the pope was proclaiming throughout Italy that 'the French King makes not . . . war upon the account of religion, but only to tyrannize over his neighbours and to increase his own dominions'.[126]

The English were equally well informed about their alliance with the Holy Roman Emperor, and that catholic monarch's insistence that the war against France was no war of religion. France, they knew, had done everything possible to alienate the emperor. While insisting on the extirpation of heresy at home, Louis XIV had covertly aided a protestant rebellion in Hungary.[127] He had encouraged the Ottomans to refuse a negotiated peace with the Austrian Habsburgs, prompting Sir John Lowther to comment that 'religion' is 'insignificant' in cases 'where interest comes in competition'.[128] Soon after the revolution, one English newspaper could report that both the emperor and the catholic states of Bavaria announced that 'Christendom does not at present suffer for religion, but for ambition': the ambition of France.[129] Edmund Bohun thought that the emperor's support of William against the catholic James II made perfect sense. James, the Habsburgs knew, had 'embraced a design' which 'would raise France to such an height of power as could never be retrieved'. 'The Emperor of Germany is as religious and as zealous a Prince for the Roman Catholic religion as ever sprung out of that family', Bohun continued, 'but he has to mind, after all, to lose his life, his empire, and his liberty; he had rather there should be some heretics in Germany, than to suffer the French King to send his apostolic dragoons to convert them, and drive him into exile.'[130]

Most people in England were thus well aware that the alliance against Louis XIV was a multiconfessional one; and most consequently concluded that they were not engaged in a confessional crusade. 'It is certain that the diversity of religion has always been as a large and vast abyss betwixt the Catholic and the Protestant Princes', conceded one pamphleteer, 'but the cruelty and perfidiousness of the French has filled up that abyss, and levelled the way between them, and all difficulties are

125 Bohun, *History of the desertion*, pp. 4–5.
126 Roger Morrice, entering book, 8 June 1689, Dr. Williams Library, 31 Q, p. 569.
127 *Letter from a Roman catholick*, p. 2; *An appendix to the translation of Tully's* Panegyrick *on Julius Caesar* (1689), pp. 16–17; *The detestable designs of France expos'd, or, the true sentiments of the Spanish Netherlands* (1689), p. 15.
128 Lowther, *Memoir*, pp. 470–1. See the similar comment in *The Dilucidator*, II ([19/29 Jan.]1689), pp. 48–9.
129 *The Dilucidator*, I (5/15 Jan. 1689), p. 9; IV (Feb. 1689), p. 91.
130 Bohun, *History of the desertion*, p. 5.

at present laid aside.'[131] 'Who will be so silly as to fall into that trap' of thinking the current conflict a war of religion, asked one journalist incredulously. 'Can it be well imagined that this war should be a war of religion, and that these three Potentates [the Pope, the Emperor, and the King of Spain] should, with the Protestant Princes, have conspired the ruin of the Church of Rome?'[132] 'This war', explained Sir Richard Cox to a grand jury, 'is for the defence of the laws, liberties, customs, and religion as well papist and protestant from the barbarous and avaricious tyranny and invasion of the French King. The Emperor, the King of Spain, the confederate Princes, the supporters of the Roman See help us and assist.'[133] There was, of course, a league of protestant princes. But they were interested in preventing, not promoting, a war of religion. 'Nor does it appear that the Protestant states, the English and Hollanders, either have or can have any prospect of conquest, nor any other interest than that of the public safety and the preservation of the liberty of Europe', wrote one pragmatic commentator.[134] The memorial issued by the elector of Brandenburg 'tends to prove', concurred another, 'that the Union of Protestant Princes has in no wise for its scope a war of religion, as France would fain persuade the world, but that it only exerts the interests which they have in common with other Catholic Princes'.[135] The protestant princes 'rest satisfied with maintaining themselves in the possession of their rights, and their religion', *The Dilucidator* asserted, 'neither their genius nor their interests, prompt them to think of invading or oppressing the Catholic States'.[136]

Behind this rejection of the idea of religious war was a widespread agreement that religious diversity was inevitable, and that therefore international relations should be, and indeed were, organised around principles of interest. Alliance against France should be entered into 'without having respect for the diversity of religions of which they make profession; neither ought any differences therein to stand in competition with their interest', posited one thinker, 'since there have been and always will be diverse opinions amongst Christians concerning matters of religion'.[137] 'The difference of [religious] sentiments ought never to prevail against the common notions which the whole world is agreed upon', advised one Dutch writer serialised in England, 'since it is impossible to reunite all peoples' minds in one and the same belief.'[138]

[131] P. B., *Means to free Europe*, p. 154.   [132] *Monthly Account*, II:4 (Jan. 1689), 124.
[133] Sir Richard Cox, 'A charge', Michaelmas 1695, Bod. Eng. Hist. b. 209, f. 30r.
[134] *Detestable designs of France*, p. 18.   [135] *The Dilucidator*, I (5/15 Jan. 1689), p. 9.
[136] Ibid., II ([19/29 Jan.] 1689), 44.   [137] *View of the true interests*, 35–6.
[138] *The Dilucidator*, I (5/15 Jan. 1689), 22–3.

'Interest', insisted the *Dilucidator*, 'is the mover of states among themselves; and especially of those that by their reciprocal commerce and neighbourhood, stand in need of mutually aiding and defending each other.'[139] Within this set of assumptions, the struggle against France, the struggle which did so much to define the thinking of the revolutionaries in 1688–9, had to be a struggle to protect European national liberties against an aspiring universal monarch, not a war of religion. The Anglo-Dutch alliance made possible by the revolution allowed both nations to be 'the restorers of Europe to her liberties'.[140] The 1688 revolution, and the international alliance against France made possible by it, proclaimed another commentator, made it certain that 'the project of France concerning the Universal Monarchy of Christendom will fall to the ground'.[141] The alliances resulting from the revolution, chimed in another, 'tends to the glorious end, which is the safety and repose of Europe, of which the most Christian King has been the disturber for several years'.[142]

Thus whilst the English, along with most Europeans, had not lost their profound religious beliefs over the course of the seventeenth century, they had ceased to call for wars of religion. The zeal of the early reformation and counter-reformation had not been lost; but it had been tempered. The experience of almost two centuries of unending bloody and devastating religious wars made all Europeans more sceptical in analysing crusading calls. Instead, inhabitants of the continent struggled to find a basis of political relationships that would avoid ineluctable and insoluble conflicts. Nationalism offered just such a solution. Goaded into action by Louis XIV's universalist political and cultural aspirations, people called for multiconfessional alliances based on mutual national interest, to oppose the French European menace. The English political nation, which had long hoped to enter the fray against France, embraced the revolution and the opportunity which it gave them. They did so, because they understood their revolution and its consequences in nationalist terms.

VI

England's 1688 revolution was a nationalist revolution. Europeans did not have to wait for industrialisation or events in France in the late eighteenth century to witness a mass political movement in defence of a bounded community sharing a public culture. The commercial nature

---

[139] Ibid., II ([19/29 Jan.] 1689), 38.   [140] *Happy union*, p. 4.
[141] *View of the true interest*, p. 45; see also, P. B., *Means to free Europe*, pp. 11–12, 50.
[142] *Detestable designs of France*, p. 18.

of English society meant that information and ideas spread remarkably rapidly throughout the community, allowing Englishmen and women to imagine themselves as sharing in common national characteristics.

These shared national characteristics, centring on an English self-image as a free, commercial and legally protestant people, had been profoundly threatened by the growing power of Louis XIV and by James II's adoption of French political style. It was not hatred of France, but love of their own nation which so agitated Englishmen and women. By the 1680s, the English had come to share a deep nationalist sensibility which was so profoundly challenged by the policies and actions of James II that it led them to insist that ultimate political authority lay in the nation. They claimed that their allegiance was to English tradition, English custom, English religion and English law, rather than to a particular king – and English people of all social classes took political action based on those beliefs. Those who were more whiggish in their outlook claimed a right to resist James II in defence of their nation. Unlike earlier protestants who had rebelled against their governments, the English in 1688 did not claim to resist James because he was an un-godly king but because he was an un-English king. Others, who were moderate or tory in political persuasion, argued that James II had unkinged himself, had abdicated, by governing in a French rather than an English fashion. Absolute obedience was due, they claimed, not to the monarch but to the legal monarch, the monarch who governed according to the laws of England. These two groups of men and women were revolutionaries not in the sense that they believed they were creating a new nation in 1689 (only some of them thought that) but in the sense that they appealed to the nation, rather than scripture or the monarch, as they source of political authority. Nationalist revolution-aries often claim to be recovering national traditions when they are in fact inventing them.

Protestantism did play a large role in the revolution of 1688–9; but this is not the same as saying that the revolution was a war of religion, or that the English continued to display an early protestant worldview. The English worshipped at protestant churches because they believed protes-tantism to be the true primitive Christian religion. Yet they fought to defend English protestantism because it was the religion established by law. The English, like most Europeans, no longer fought in defence of universalist principles; they fought for national ones. Protestantism was one part of the English national identity defended in the revolution, but it did not constitute that identity.

It was precisely because the English recognised and valued national diversity in early modern Europe, that they could insist that the desired war against France (a desire which was as much cause as consequence of the revolution) was not a religious war. The English supported the Austrian emperor, the king of Spain and the pope himself because they knew they were engaged in a desperate struggle to protect national integrities against the aspiring universal monarch, Louis XIV. Since different nations had different religious cultures, no nation had the right to impose its beliefs on others. Government propaganda and national sentiment were in full agreement: the age of religious wars was over. It was the interest of all European nations, whatever their confessional practices, to unite against France.

The revolution, one journalist explained, set 'England at liberty to act according to its true interests', its national interests.[143] James II lost his crown not simply because he was a catholic, but because he was a catholic who failed to follow English laws, govern in an English style or pursue English national interests. By insisting that authority lay in the nation, the revolutionaries of 1688–9 made sure they could never again be ruled by a king who 'blindly embraced' the policies and methods of foreign countries.[144] It was because the English understood their revolution in these nationalist terms that it proved to be both bloodless and innovative. It was in this sense, at least, a 'Glorious Revolution'.

[143] *The Dilucidator*, II ([19/29 Jan.] 1689), p. 41–2.
[144] *True interest of the princes of Europe*, pp. 37–8.

5   A history of variations: the identity of the eighteenth-century church of England

Brian Young

> In the profession of Christianity, the variety of national characters may
> be clearly distinguished.   Gibbon, *The decline and fall of the Roman empire*[1]

In 1753, in a typically audacious act of intellectual precocity, the
sixteen-year-old Edward Gibbon, who came to possess one of the most
cosmopolitan of English intellects, converted to catholicism.[2] Though
Edward Gibbon senior had been tutored by the notably pious nonjuror
William Law, he was a casualty of his own half-hearted worldliness, and
quickly set about rescuing his wayward son from the clutches of
continental 'superstition': an error to which he himself was so allergic as
to condone the attempted inculcation in his child of the scepticism of
David Mallet, Bolingbroke's publisher. When this remarkable venture
failed, it was to Switzerland that the son was dispatched in order to be
reclaimed for the greater protestant fold.[3] After the apparent success of
his Swiss cure, Gibbon continued to develop in his un-English manner.
Scottish scepticism seeped into his soul from readings of Hume, and the
infidelities of the *philosophes* continued both to attract and to repel his
scholarly sensibility through his subsequent intellectual life.[4]
    A number of lessons can be learned from Gibbon's early experience
and subsequent career, some of which are more typical of his contemporaries than the actual details of his conversion, reconversion and

---

[1] David Womersley, ed. (1994), III, p. 423. I am grateful to Mishtooni Bose, Nigel Aston,
John Burrow, Colin Kidd, William Lamont, Isabel Rivers, John Robertson, John Walsh
and Donald Winch for reading and commenting on an earlier draft of this chapter.
[2] As Leslie Stephen economically paraphrased Gibbon's account of his reading cure from
catholicism, 'Gibbon had ceased, as he tells us to be an Englishman . . . [He] had,
however, become not a Swiss or a Frenchman, but a cosmopolitan', 'Gibbon's
autobiography', *Studies of a biographer* (1898–1902), I, p. 152.
[3] The best source for this experience remains John Murray, ed., Gibbon's *Autobiographies*
(1896). For a sympathetic study, see D. J. Womersley, 'Gibbon's apostasy', *British
Journal for Eighteenth-century Studies*, 11 (1988), 51–70.
[4] J. G. A. Pocock, 'Superstition and enthusiasm in Gibbon's history of religion',
Eighteenth-century Life, 8 (1982), 83–94; J. G. A. Pocock, 'Gibbon's *Decline and fall* and
the world view of the late enlightenment', in his *Virtue, commerce and history: essays on
political thought and history* (Cambridge, 1985), pp. 143–56.

ultimate, if tacit, apostasy. For example, his father's hearty detestation of most things catholic was a principal *leitmotif* of English self-identity in the eighteenth century, whether acquired in contradistinction to the French, the Irish or any number of continental nations.[5] Likewise, the desire to hold 'priestcraft' at bay (a legacy of the civil war period which anti-clericals had developed into a blunt instrument of political ideology) was so strong as to attract the occasional clergyman to its cause, let alone an apparently obedient son of the church of England such as Gibbon's father.[6] More importantly for our current purposes, Gibbon's life demonstrates two themes which will be central to this chapter. The first is the fundamental division of the anglican church on basic issues of doctrine and ecclesiology. As recounted by his *Autobiographies*, it was the depth and persistence of such disagreements which shook Gibbon's faith in the English establishment, and led to him to seek what he thought was the greater authority and certainty of Roman catholicism.[7] Much later, these disputes were to become important to Gibbon again, feeding the famous treatment of Christianity in *The decline and fall*. The second theme illustrated by the historian's progress was the international context of Hanoverian anglicanism. In seeking help from abroad, Gibbon's father was mirroring the practice of many English protestants who looked for continental allies in their spiritual struggles. Specifically, a sense of fraternity had grown up between the Swiss clergy and their anglican counterparts at the end of the Stuart age, and, more widely, the bonds between protestants in Europe had tightened as confessional loyalties reasserted themselves in fields as diverse as diplomacy, warfare, scholarship and devotion.[8] Throughout the

[5] Linda Colley, *Britons: forging the nation, 1707–1837* (New Haven, 1992), ch. 1. For a detailed study, see Colin Haydon, *Anti-catholicism in eighteenth-century England, c. 1714–80* (Manchester, 1993).

[6] Mark Goldie, 'The civil religion of James Harrington', in Anthony Pagden, ed., *The languages of political theory in early modern Europe* (Cambridge, 1987), pp. 97–122; Mark Goldie, 'Priestcraft and whiggism', in Quentin Skinner and Nicholas Phillipson, eds., *Political discourse in early modern Britain* (Cambridge, 1993), pp. 209–31; Peter Harrison, *"Religion" and the religions in the English enlightenment* (Cambridge, 1990); J. A. I. Champion, *The pillars of priestcraft shaken: the church of England and its enemies, 1660–1730* (Cambridge, 1992).

[7] Edward Gibbon, *Autobiographies*, p. 88.

[8] For contacts with the Swiss see Eamon Duffy, '*Correspondence fraternelle*: the SPCK, the SPG and the churches of Switzerland in the war of the Spanish succession', in Derek Baker, ed., *Reform and reformation: England and the continent c.1500–c.1750, SCH* (Subsidia 2, Oxford, 1979), pp. 251–80. For wider confessional solidarity, see especially, the work of W. R. Ward: *The protestant evangelical awakening* (Cambridge, 1993); 'Power and piety: the origins of religious revival in the early eighteenth century', *Bulletin of the John Rylands Library of Manchester*, 63 (1981), 231–52; 'Orthodoxy, enlightenment and religious revival', in Keith Robbins, ed., *Religion and humanism, SCH*, 17 (Oxford, 1981), pp. 275–96; 'The eighteenth-century church: a European

eighteenth century, therefore, English clerics appealed to Europeans to legitimate and support their particular theological positions. They stressed their connections with protestants on the continent, and were keenly concerned about their church's reputation with Christians overseas. Taken together, this internal division within the establishment, and its tendency to set itself within an international context, suggest that the church of England could provide only a problematic foundation for any sense of English nationality. Its confusion about its own position, and its membership's insistence on identifying themselves with continental movements, questioned the establishment's role as a solidly or solely *national* institution.

This chapter will explore this problem by examining several contested issues among the eighteenth-century clergy. In particular it will concentrate on the interlinked fields of ecclesiology, of doctrinal debates over the trinity, of the disputed status of dogma itself, and of the growth of anti-clericalism both within and outside religious circles. As these areas are closely entangled, and as the main themes emerge repeatedly at different points in the story, no exhaustively chronological or rigidly categorised coverage will be attempted. Rather, the history of the church will be treated thematically, and by association, taking the issues raised by Gibbon's biography as starting points. Once the flavour of such debates has been experienced, the uncomfortable variety and supranational sensitivity of the English clergy will be clear. In the end the surprise may be, not that the church had problems providing a focus for the nation, but that the idea of a national church survived at all.

II

At the very start of the eighteenth century, Gilbert Burnet, the bishop of Salisbury and noted historian of his times, emphasised his fears about anglican divisions, and his worries about the impact they had on his church's European audience. The closing passage of his preface to his *Exposition of the thirty-nine articles* (1699) merits citation in full:

I shall conclude this Preface with a Reply that a very Eminent Divine among the Lutherans in Germany made to me when I was pressing this matter of Union with the Calvinists upon him, with all the Topicks with which I could urge it, as necessary upon many accounts, and more particularly with relation to the present State of Affairs. He said, He wonder'd much to see a Divine of the Church of England press that so much upon him, when We, notwithstanding the Dangers we were then in (it was in the Year 1686) could not agree our

view', in John Walsh, Colin Haydon and Stephen Taylor, eds., *The church of England c. 1689–c. 1833: from toleration to Tractarianism* (Cambridge, 1993), pp. 285–98.

Differences. They differed about Important Matters, concerning the Attributes of God, and his Providence; concerning the Guilt of Sin, whether it was to be charged on God, or on the Sinner; and whether men ought to make good use of their Faculties, or if they ought to trust entirely to an Irresistible Grace? These were matters of great Moment: But, he said, We in England differed only about Forms of Government and Worship, and about things that were of their own nature indifferent; and yet we had been quarrelling about them for above an Hundred Years, and we were not yet grown wiser by all the Mischiefs that this had done us, and by the Imminent Danger we were then in. He concluded, let the Church of England heal her own Breaches, and then all the rest of the Reformed Churches will with great Respect admit of her Mediation to heal theirs. I will not presume to tell how I answered this: But I pray God to enlighten and direct all men, that they may consider well how it ought to be answered.[9]

As the experience of the young Gibbon demonstrates, the situation lamented by Burnet did not improve in the rest of the century. Indeed, far from being confined to disputes over things indifferent, larger doctrinal issues were later to loom in anglican controversies – an apologetic embarrassment of which Gibbon took full advantage in his later, anti-doctrinal, writings. As persistent in Georgian ecclesiology was Burnet's concern for the anglican identity as part of a protestant international. This would become obvious, for instance, in the unitarians' desire to establish themselves as a specifically international religious grouping, just as their intellectual forebears, the clerical critics of rigidly dogmatic high churchmanship, had been anxious to associate themselves with the attack on Calvinistic dogmatism which had been undertaken by their Swiss colleagues. Yet whilst such Alpine, sceptical and protestant dimensions would be integral to many eighteenth-century clerics, the initial perspective provided by Gibbon's brief conversion was decidedly French and catholic in character.

Indeed, as Gibbon's primary guide to matters religious was the French divine Bossuet, it is Gallicanism, which preserved a confessional resemblance to the established church of England, which acts as a first means of examining the identity, or identities, of anglicanism as a national religion in the eighteenth century.[10] Since Gallicans insisted on the peculiarly *French* nature of their branch of catholicism, a significant number of anglicans had seen in the Gallican church an attractive analogy with their own ecclesiology, compromisingly unprotestant and unEnglish though this affinity was in the eyes of many of their fellow clergy. Joseph Bingham, the distinguished author of a major work of

9　Gilbert Burnet, *An exposition of the thirty-nine articles of the church of England* (1699), pp. ix-x.
10　For useful discussion, see Aime-Georges Martimort, *La Gallicanisme de Bossuet* (Paris, 1953), esp pp. 13–16. Gilbert Burnet made similar observations on Gallican Erastianism in *A letter to Mr. Thevenot* (1689), pp. 5, 33–5.

ecclesiastical history, the *Origines ecclesiasticae*, produced a book in 1706 which extracted Gallican principles from French sources as a means of making an effective apology for the otherwise unique nature of the church of England.[11] Similarly, Archbishop Wake had been attracted to Gallicanism in his initiatives towards a rapprochement between the churches in England and France in 1717.[12] It has to be acknowledged that for many English clerics Gallicanism was a step too far (in 1712, White Kennett, the future bishop of Peterborough, called the French 'the next Church in the Way to Rome'), but the wide desire to associate with French theology amongst other commentators demonstrated that the English looked to Europe even as they tried to define their own peculiar establishment.[13]

Unfortunately, the French response to such ecumenical thinking was not always welcoming. Rather than celebrating anglicanism as a sister communion, many Gallicans – especially Bossuet in his influential *Histoire des variations des églises protestantes* (1688) – used a battery of arguments to try to unchurch the English establishment.[14] Thus Bossuet's was a history of heresy, focusing on Calvinism and Lutheranism, the twin sources of what he called a pretended reformation, the illegitimate perversion of what the primitive fathers and doctors of the church had called for under the rubric of reform.[15] History, whose authority Bossuet constantly invoked, was supposedly his only source in his indictment of the protestant reformation.[16] The religion of protestants was, he asserted, riddled from its very beginning with variations, being merely the product of intellectual and moral subtleties and equivocations. Accordingly, had its later adherents but known of these historical origins, it would have made them realise that their faith was a matter for contempt.[17] Hence the open accusation of protestantism as heresy; and the comparisons drawn between the modern Roman church with its ancient trinitarian orthodoxy (resolutely opposing Arianism) and the

---

[11] Joseph Bingham, *The French church's apology for the church of England* (1706)

[12] Norman Sykes, *William Wake: archbishop of Canterbury, 1657–1737* (2 vols., Cambridge, 1957), I, ch. iv.

[13] Cited in G. V. Bennett, *White Kennett, 1660–1728, bishop of Peterborough* (1957), p. 83.

[14] Though Wake had experienced hope as well as regret in his relations with Bossuet and his controversial writings: Sykes, *William Wake*, I, pp. 255, 325; II, pp. 2, 23 On Bossuet and his theological significance, especially as it developed in England, see Owen Chadwick, *From Bossuet to Newman* (2nd edn, Cambridge, 1987).

[15] Since Gibbon owned the English translation made by Levinius Brown in 1742, references in the main text will be to that version, with the original following in the notes. Thus for this first reference, see Bossuet, *The history of the variations of the protestant churches* (Antwerp, 1742), I, p. 4; *Histoire des variations des eglises protestantes* (Paris, 1688), I, pp. 4–6.

[16] *History*, I, pp. xxi–xxii; *Histoire*, I, pp. xx–xxii.

[17] *History*, I, pp. iii–iv; *Histoire*, I, pp. v–viii.

many variations, among them anglicanism, which had betrayed such falsehoods in doctrine.[18] Dispassionate history was Bossuet's alleged witness, so that the doctrinal variations of the reformers, 'like those of the Arians, will discover, what they would fain have excused, have supplied, have disguised in their belief'.[19]

Bossuet's interpretation of the English reformation was naturally of a piece with these general observations, but added to it were biting charges of political opportunism and religious hypocrisy. Henry VIII was the conventional villain of the piece, the lamentably sexual origins of the church of England early exposing it to ridicule, detested equally by catholics and Lutherans.[20] Taking as his main source Gilbert Burnet's *History of the reformation (1679–81)*, a popular piece of anglican historical apologetic, Bossuet satirised Cranmer's deception of Henry VIII regarding his secret second marriage, thereby undermining, to his satisfaction, one of Burnet's proto-anglican heroes.[21] Central to the indictment was the charge of anti-papal erastianism, a matter of horror even for a Gallican bishop. That Jesus Christ supposedly instituted a priesthood dependent on the prince for its authority was, Bossuet declared, ' the most scandalous flattery that ever enter'd into the heart of man'.[22] In his view, it was more agreeable for the apostate English to acknowledge the monarch's authority on religious matters than to accept in the papacy a principle established by God for Christian unity. All of this was to ignore, Bossuet contended, the foundation of the church in England by Pope Gregory the Great, so that in renouncing the papal power England's divines both weakened their origins and severely compromised the authority of their ancient traditions.[23]

Despite these attacks, Bossuet remained hopeful that England's academic strengths, especially its distinguished tradition of patristic scholarship, would help to bring it back to the fold. He wrote:

So learned a Nation, 'tis to be hoped, will not always remain under this seduction: the respect they retain for the Fathers, and their curious and

---

[18] *History*, I, pp. iv–vi; *Histoire*, I, pp. iv–viii.

[19] *History*, I, pp. xxviii–xxix; *Histoire*, I, pp. xxvii–xxx: 'comme celles des Ariens, découvriront ce qu'ils ont voulu excuser, ce qu'ils ont voulu suppléer, ce qu'ils ont voulu déguiser dans leur croyance'.

[20] *History*, I, pp. 294–5; *Histoire*, I, pp. 357–8.

[21] *History*, I, pp. 321–4; *Histoire*, I, pp. 359–63. On Bossuet's dependence on Burnet, see Alfred Rebelliau, *Bossuet historien du protestantisme: étude sur l'*Histoire des variations *et sur la controverse au dix-septième siècle* (3rd edn, Paris, 1909), pp. 178–9, 186–7, 219–20. Cf. Gilbert Burnet, *A censure of Mr. de Meaux's history of the variations of the protestant churches*, appended to *A letter to Mr. Thevenot*, pp. 19–57.

[22] *History*, I, p. 325; *Histoire*, I, pp. 392–4: 'la plus scandaleuse flaterie qui soit jamais tombée dans l'esprit des hommes'. Henry VIII's hatred of the papacy was, Bossuet asserted, 'la règle de sa foi', *Histoire*, I, p. 398.

[23] *History*, I, pp. 341–2; *Histoire*, I, pp. 414–16.

continual researches into antiquity, will bring them back to the doctrine of the first ages. I cannot believe the Chair of St Peter, whence they received Christianity, will always be the object of their hatred.[24]

Yet such optimism was, in reality, a somewhat feeble attempt to qualify the reservations Bossuet voiced about divisive elements in English protestantism, elements which were destined to grow rather than to diminish in the eighteenth century. Anglicans were to be rent asunder by arguments on the status of patristic authority, anti-dogmatics suspecting it of preserving within protestantism suspiciously Roman catholic elements, while more orthodox divines emphasised the centrality of the early fathers for the anglican claim to be part of a truly catholic tradition. Patristic study undoubtedly aided those who saw in the church of England a catholic communion analogous with Gallicanism, but it alienated those who saw in anglicanism a branch of a wider protestant community.

Leaving aside, then, Bossuet's scattered remarks on the desirability of clerical celibacy (which found few anglican adherents – excepting William Law and a handful of others)[25] one should concentrate on his attacks upon trinitarian heresy as that which most compromised the theology of English sectarianism. So central was this accusation that it found a place in a seemingly more crucial dismissal of the twin protestant notions of *sola scriptura* and the right to private judgement as found in Burnet's *History of the reformation*. Reformation preachers, Bossuet alleged, persuaded their hearers, with varying degrees of disingenuousness, of what they would find in the bible, but only so far as this conformed to their own principles. They might as well have persuaded them that the scriptures contained an explicitly Arian conception of the trinity as that they supported any of the claims of Lutherans or Calvinists.[26] Unsuitable sects like the Socinians and anabaptists, therefore, all too naturally originated in the very nature of reformation debate. A contrast was drawn with ancient and medieval heretical divisions: the early unorthodox sects had drawn their strength from the inherent depravity of the human species, while protestant heresies

---

[24] *History*, I, p. 374; *Histoire*, I, pp. 454–5: 'Mais une nation si savante ne demeurera pas long-temps dans cet éblouissement: le respect qu'elle conserve pour les pères, & ses curieuses & continuelles recherches sur l'antiquité, la rameneront à la doctrine des premiers siècles. Je ne puis croire qu'elle persiste dans la haine qu'elle a conçue contre la chaire de saint Pierre d'ou elle a récu le Christianisme.' On the broader questions raised by such study, both in France and England, see Bruno Neveu, 'L'érudition ecclésiastique de XVIIe siècle et la nostalgie de l'antiquité Chrétienne', in Robbins, ed., *Religion and humanism*, pp. 195–225.

[25] B. W. Young, 'The anglican origins of Newman's celibacy', *Church History*, 65 (1996), 15–27.

[26] *History*, I, p. 337; *Histoire*, I, pp. 408–9.

were the very result of their new and particular conception of the church itself.[27]

In such writing, Bossuet used the divisions of the English to undermine their claims to be participating in a European catholicity. The English response to this, however, was to insist more deeply upon that participation: particularly by emphasising English claims to the common heritage of orthodox Christianity – the primitive fathers and councils of the church. William Wake, replying to a previous attack by Bossuet in 1686, couched his reply in the eirenic language of the early church, assigning anglicanism the status of orthodoxy by implication:

We fairly believe the Holy Scriptures, and what soever they teach or command, we receive and submit to, as to the Word of God. We embrace all the ancient creeds, and in them all that Faith which the Religious Emperors, by their Advice, decreed should be sufficient to intitle them to the common name of Catholicks.

What new Donatists, Gentlemen, are you, to presume to exclude us from this Character?[28]

Similarly, while George Bull's patristically grounded defence of orthodox trinitarianism in his *Judicium ecclesiae catholicae* (1694) had secured Bossuet's admiration, when the French prelate asked why this anglican priest, who had ably secured the authority of early church teachings, remained in a schismatic communion, Bull replied that the church of England, and not the 'corrupt' one of Rome, was actually closer to the primitive ideal of the church catholic.[29] The language and imagery of the early church were absolutely central to such exchanges, both between the church of England and continental Christians, and between the various parties which made up eighteenth-century anglicanism. This ought not to be surprising, since such identification with primitive purity is a legitimation exercise common to Christian debate in the early modern period, with a notable variant in the apologetic struggle between Jansenists and Gallicans.[30] It provided the dominant

---

[27] *History*, II, pp. 441–3; *Histoire*, II, pp. 609–15.

[28] William Wake, *An exposition of the doctrine of the church of England* (1686), p 82. The controversy with Wake was conducted during the highpoint of Gallican discussion, that is between 1688 and 1696. This largely concerned the primitive and pastoral ideal of the prerogatives of the episcopate: Martimort, *La Gallicanisme de Bossuet*, pp. 645–6.

[29] George Bull, *The corruptions of the church of Rome in relation to ecclesiastical government* (2nd edn, 1707), pp. 3–5, 6–9, 101–2.

[30] Gallicanism, however, had long defended itself through self-identification with the early rather than with the primitive church: J. H. M. Salmon, 'Clovis and Constantine: the uses of history in sixteenth-century Gallicanism', *JEH*, 41 (1990), 584–605. For a useful statement regarding such divisions in the eighteenth century, see Dale van Kley, *The Jansenists and the expulsion of the Jesuits from France, 1757–1765* (New Haven, 1975). Gallican–Jansenist disputes had all but died out by the late 1770s, and problems for the French church began to centre on enlightenment criticisms of Christianity:

motif for the intellectual taxonomy of Christianity which informs much of the argument of Gibbon's *Decline and fall* (a work which began within the orbit of a protestant enlightenment, but which was constantly alert to the contribution of catholic scholars) and it served to underline arguments concerning ascriptions of orthodoxy and heresy throughout the eighteenth century. As a result, the English continued to refer to European traditions, even as they turned inwards to debate the proper doctrine and government of their own national church.[31]

This is certainly true of the single most important, and disruptive, centre of disunion within the eighteenth-century church of England, to which Bossuet significantly alluded: the nature of the trinity. Disputes over the trinity were endemic to the church. As Gibbon mischievously noted in his memoirs, William Chillingworth, a fellow ex-convert to catholicism whose return to the anglican fold had occasioned an apologetic masterpiece in *The religion of protestants* (1638), probably died an Arian or a Socinian.[32] Similarly, the two ornaments of England's very particular experience of an anti-dogmatic, Christian enlightenment, John Locke and Isaac Newton, were respectively and correctly suspected of inclinations towards the trinitarian heresies of Socinianism and Arianism. Locke's concern for the acceptance of no more than a dogmatically minimal Christianity led to a defence of religious toleration which left him suspect to many of his anglican contemporaries,[33] while Newton preferred the adoption of a Nicodemite stance, allowing his

---

Nigel Aston, *The end of an elite: the French bishops and the coming of the French revolution, 1786–1790* (Oxford, 1992), pp. 26, 28.

[31] J. G. A. Pocock, 'Gibbon's *Decline and fall*'. On Gibbon's use of Pascal and Tillemont see David P. Jordan, *Gibbon and his Roman empire* (Urbana, IL, 1971), pp. 125–41, 157–8.

[32] *The autobiographies of Edward Gibbon*, p. 129.

[33] On which subject see the important work of Mark Goldie: 'The theory of religious intolerance in Restoration England', in O. P. Grell, Jonathan I. Israel and Nicholas Tyacke, eds., *From persecution to toleration: the Glorious Revolution and religion in England* (Oxford, 1991), pp. 331–68; 'John Locke, Jonas Proast and religious toleration 1688–1692', in Walsh and Taylor, *Church of England*, pp. 143–71; 'John Locke and anglican royalism', *Political Studies*, 31 (1983), 61–85. On the Socinian identity of Locke's religion and its consequences for his thinking, see John Marshall, *John Locke: resistance, religion and responsibility* (Cambridge, 1994), chs. 8–10. On England's peculiar experience of enlightenment, see Roy Porter, 'The enlightenment in England', in Porter and Mikulas Teich, eds., *The enlightenment in national context* (Cambridge, 1981), pp. 1–18; J. G. A. Pocock, 'Post-puritan England and the problem of the enlightenment', in Perez Zagorin, ed., *Culture and politics from puritanism to the enlightenment* (Berkeley, 1980), pp. 91–112; J. G. A. Pocock, 'Clergy and commerce: the conservative enlightenment in England', in Raffaele Ajello, E. Cortese and Vincenzo Piano Mortari, eds., *L'eta dei lumi: studi storici sui settecento Europeo in onore di Franco Venturi* (Naples, 1985), I, pp. 523–62; B. W. Young, *Religion and enlightenment in eighteenth-century England: theological debate from Locke to Burke* (Oxford, 1998).

theological and ecclesiological beliefs to be both subtly adumbrated by Samuel Clarke (once aptly described by Leslie Stephen as 'Newton's theological lieutenant'),[34] and eccentrically and dangerously elaborated by his Cambridge successor, William Whiston.

Whiston's emphatically open Arianism exposed him to derision, not least as he defended it as the purest form of Christianity. He gained few if any followers, and personal idiosyncracies did not help his case. His adoption of other fringe beliefs, notably a highly individual form of millenarianism, further undermined his religious and academic authority.[35] What is of more immediate interest is that Whiston appealed to antiquity in justifying his position, and in this he was at one with many of his co-religionists in the opening decades of the eighteenth century.[36] At the other end of the theological spectrum, William Law, in common with his fellow nonjurors, drew on the primitive age of the faith in delineating the ideals of Christian life in his influential devotional writings, *A practical treatise upon Christian perfection* (1726) and *A serious call to a devout and holy life* (1729).[37] Neither Arians nor nonjurors were typical of the religious frame of mind in the early eighteenth century, but they do signal the nature of the divisions that would grow within it over the century, leading one to wonder what was 'typical' at any given moment over such a long swathe of time.

Arianism and Socinianism, whatever the numerical paucity of their consistent adherents, were both decidedly influential amongst the anglican intelligentsia, while dissenters, both as inheritors of what was left of the latitude of speculation available during the mid-Stuart interregnum and as extremely conscientious students of philosophy and theology, had already begun to move in such a direction during the opening decades of the century.[38] Dissenting divines debated the need

---

[34] Leslie Stephen, *History of English thought in the eighteenth century* (2 vols., 1876), I, pp. 119–31.

[35] James E. Force, *William Whiston: honest Newtonian* (Cambridge, 1984).

[36] Eamon Duffy, ' "Whiston's affair": the trials of a primitive Christian, 1709–1714', *JEH*, 27 (1976), 129–50; Duffy, 'Primitive Christianity revived: religious renewal in Augustan England', in Derek Baker, ed., *Renaissance and renewal in Christian history*, *SCH*, 14 (Oxford, 1977), pp. 287–300.

[37] B. W. Young, 'William Law and the Christian economy of salvation', *EHR*, 109 (1994), 308–22.

[38] There is a need for more work on the links between the theologies of the Interregnum and those which were to develop in eighteenth-century dissent For an unexpected survival within anglicanism, see B. W. Young, ' "The soul-sleeping system": politics and heresy in eighteenth-century England', *JEH*, 45 (1994), 64–81. John Milton is plainly central to the question, not least as his poetic reputation was to rise so high, albeit his general reputation as a prose writer experienced a notable decline: cf. Dustin Griffin, *Regaining paradise: Milton in the eighteenth century* (Cambridge, 1986). Isabel Rivers, *Reason, grace, and sentiment: a study of the language of religion and ethics in England,*

for subscription to articles of faith at Salters' Hall in 1719, publicly dividing themselves into parties of orthodox and Arian theologians in the process.[39] Such an open procedure was not then available in the church of England, but anglicans had only recently been at war, as 'high' churchmen' crying 'The Church in Danger!' had attempted to turn convocation into an instrument of heresy-hunting against latitudinarians, some of whom were as prominent as Gilbert Burnet, Bossuet's historiographical whipping-boy.[40] These divisions between a tradition-driven 'high church' and a latitudinarian and occasionally anti-dogmatic 'low church' are well known, and although this is not the place to discuss them, it is important to bear in mind that a divided communion was not an obvious means of eirenic nationality when the question of its own very identity was at stake.

However, whilst the division between 'high' and 'low' churchmanship was, to a considerable extent, the ecclesiastical analogue of the 'rage of party' in the reign of Queen Anne,[41] one must bear in mind that church 'parties' are not political parties, and that aside from the affiliations between nonjurors and Jacobites, patterns of political partisanship and ecclesiastical identity were not automatically obvious.[42] In fact, studying the complexity of political and theological divisions between clerics, still further doubts arise about the coherence of the communion. Not only

1660–1780, I, Whichcote to Wesley (Cambridge, 1991), also provides an interesting route to the resolution of such questions.

[39] Roger Thomas, 'Presbyterians in transition', in C. G. Bolam, Jeremy Goring, H. L. Short and Roger Thomas, eds., *The English presbyterians: from Elizabethan puritanism to modern unitarianism* (1968), pp. 113–74, esp. pp. 151–74; J. T. Spivey, 'Middle way men: Edmund Calamy, and the crises of moderate nonconformity, 1688–1732' (unpublished D. Phil. dissertation, Oxford, 1986), chs. 11–12.

[40] Geoffrey Holmes, *The trial of Doctor Sacheverell* (London, 1973); Holmes, 'The Sacheverell riots: the crowd and the church in early eighteenth-century London', *P&P*, 72 (1976), 55–85; G. V. Bennett, *The tory crisis in church and state, 1688–1730: the career of Francis Atterbury, bishop of Rochester* (Oxford, 1975); Mark Goldie, 'The nonjurors, episcopacy, and the origins of the convocation controversy', in Eveline Cruickshanks, ed., *Ideology and conspiracy: aspects of Jacobitism, 1689–1759* (Edinburgh, 1982), pp. 15–35; Martin Greig, 'Heresy hunt: Gilbert Burnet and the convocation controversy of 1701', *HJ*, 37 (1994), 569–92. On the survival of such views, see Paul Langford, 'Convocation and the tory clergy, 1717–61', in Eveline Cruickshanks and Jeremy Black, eds., *The Jacobite challenge* (Edinburgh, 1988), pp. 107–99.

[41] Cf. J. P. Kenyon, *Revolution principles: the rage of party, 1689–1720* (Cambridge, 1977); Nicholas Phillipson, 'Politeness and politics in the reigns of Anne and the early Hanoverians', in J. G. A. Pocock, ed., *The varieties of British political thought, 1500–1800* (Cambridge, 1993), pp. 211–45.

[42] There were even Jacobite dissenters, on whom see Paul Kleber Monod, *Jacobitism and the English people, 1688–1788* (Cambridge, 1989), pp. 154–7. On the nature of church 'parties' in the period, see Walsh and Taylor, 'Introduction: the church and anglicanism in the "long" eighteenth century', in *Church of England*, pp. 1–64, at 29–45. For a study which closely relates political and religious identity, see J. C. D. Clark, *English society, 1688–1832* (Cambridge, 1985).

was the church divided, it was fractured along a bewildering variety of faults, all cutting across each other. Thus, some Hutchinsonians in Sussex, decided 'high' churchmen to a man, and conventionally described as ultra-tories, were actually whigs, not least as the politics of patronage made that a pragmatic position to hold.[43] Similarly, a glance at many ecclesiastical biographies of the period reveals disparities between political partisanship and ecclesiastical commitments.[44] Joseph Butler, whose 'high' church sensibilities made him the object of much anti-clerical prejudice, was none the less a loyal supporter in the House of Lords of the whig administration of his day.[45] Again, whilst the court whiggery of Benjamin Hoadly (whose notorious 1717 sermon delivered before George I on the invisible church of Christ cast doubt on the ultimate authority of any church, national or otherwise) has its echoes in the princess of Wales' support for Samuel Clarke, any neat identification of anti-dogmatism with whiggery was spoilt by the variety of responses to such arguments.[46] Two of Hoadly's most vociferous opponents, William Law and Joseph Trapp, were respectively a Jacobite and a Bolingbrokean tory, but others who replied to him were sincere whigs of various sorts.[47] Samuel Clarke's most effective critic, Daniel Waterland, who attacked Clarke's Arian apologetic with weapons drawn from the credal formularies of the early church, was a fairly typical Cambridge whig, but his somewhat unlikely protégé, Edmund Law, became the centre of a rather more radical interest within the church of England. It was this group that was to move anti-dogmatism beyond its previously courtly ambit into a

---

[43] Jeffrey S Chamberlain, '"The changes and chances of this mortal life": the vicissitudes of high churchmanship and politics among the clergy of Sussex, 1700–1745', (Ph.D. dissertation, Chicago, 1992), ch. 9; Chamberlain, 'Portrait of a high church clerical dynasty in Georgian England: the Frewens and their world', in Walsh and Taylor, *Church of England*, pp. 299–316. On the 'tory' image of Hutchinsonians see C. B. Wilde, 'Hutchinsonians, natural philosophy and religious controversy in eighteenth-century England', *History of Science*, 18 (1980), 1–24.

[44] Cf. Norman Sykes, *Edmund Gibson, bishop of London, 1669–1748* (1926), and Bennett, *White Kennett.*

[45] Christopher Cunliffe, 'The "spiritual sovereign": Butler's episcopate', in Cunliffe, ed, *Joseph Butler's moral and religious thought: tercentenary essays* (Oxford, 1992), pp. 37–61, at 45–7.

[46] Benjamin Hoadly, *The nature of the kingdom or church of Christ* (1717) On the ensuing 'Bangorian controversy', see Norman Sykes, 'Benjamin Hoadly, bishop of Bangor', in F. J. Hearnshaw, ed., *The social and political thought of some English thinkers of the Augustan age, 1650–1750* (1928), pp. 112–56, and Reed Browning, *Political and constitutional ideas of the court whigs* (Baton Rouge, 1982), ch. 3.

[47] William Law, *The bishop of Bangor's late sermon and his letter to Dr Snape in defence of it, answered* (1717); Law, *A second letter to the bishop of Bangor* (1717); Joseph Trapp, *The real nature of the church or kingdom of Christ* (1717); Henry D. Rack, '"Christ's kingdom not of this world": the case of Benjamin Hoadly versus William Law reconsidered', in Derek Baker, ed., *Church, society and politics*, SCH, 12 (1975), pp. 275–91.

commonwealthman tradition.[48] Law's greatest friend, Francis Blackburne, the rabidly anti-catholic archdeacon of Cleveland, even abandoned writing a biography of Luther in favour of compiling the life of Thomas Hollis, the chief promoter of commonwealthman politics in eighteenth-century England and America, a work which is effectively a repository of the English republican tradition as it memorialised itself in the closing decades of the eighteenth century.[49]

Aside from their mutual suspicion of catholicism, leading to extreme fears of its growth in Ireland, Blackburne and Hollis were also critics of 'priestcraft'. They thus introduce another source of division within anglicanism which ranked alongside, and further complicated, the disunity over secular politics, relations with foreign churches, and the trinity. As an anti-dogmatic theologian, Blackburne felt able to lambast the sacerdotal pretensions of fellow clergy, such as Butler, whom he suspected of being crypto-catholics; hence also his lifelong enmity with Archbishop Secker.[50] Widely differing conceptions of the role of the priesthood were thus to be found within the church of England. It is worth noting in this respect the anti-clerical apologies for their not attending divine worship which Blackburne concocted on behalf both of Hollis and, replying to Johnson's notoriously critical account of the poet's life, of Milton, a patron saint of the commonwealth tradition.[51] All of this was in keeping with a desire for 'further reformation', as Blackburne and his followers exhorted the cause of continuous reform

[48] Daniel Waterland, *The case of Arian subscription considered* (Cambridge, 1721). On Cambridge as a centre of various whig interests see John Gascoigne, *Cambridge in the age of the enlightenment: science, religion and politics from the restoration to the French revolution* (Cambridge, 1989); Gascoigne, 'Anglican latitudinarianism and political radicalism in the late eighteenth century', *History*, 71 (1986), 22–38.

[49] Francis Blackburne, 'Some account of the author', prefixed to *The works theological and miscellaneous of Francis Blackburne MA* (Cambridge, 1805), pp. liii–liv. The author, the archdeacon's son, dedicated the edition to Christopher Wyvill, 'the disinterested and intrepid assertor of civil and religious liberty, the zealous advocate of constitutional reformation in the state'. On the fears of 'popery' endemic to this circle, see Haydon, *Anti-catholicism*, pp. 184–91.

[50] Cf. Francis Blackburne, 'A serious enquiry into the use and importance of external religion', in *Works*, I, pp. 91–171; 'Erasmus's preface to his paraphrase', ibid., I, pp. 25–89; 'Considerations on the present state of the controversy between the protestants and papists of Great Britain and Ireland', ibid. I, pp. 91–171. For differing perspectives regarding Ireland, see Jacqueline R. Hill, 'Popery and protestantism, civil and religious liberty: the disputed lessons of Irish history, 1690–1812', *P&P*, 118 (1988), 96–129.

[51] Francis Blackburne, *Memoirs of Thomas Hollis, esq* (1780), I, pp. 472–3; Blackburne, *Remarks on Johnson's Life of Milton* (1780), pp. 95, 104, 107, 111. For a definitive appreciation of such thought, see the classic study by Caroline Robbins, *The eighteenth-century commonwealthman* (Cambridge, MA, 1959). A yet broader treatment of these and allied questions is provided by Peter N. Miller, *Defining the common good: empire, religion and philosophy in eighteenth-century Britain* (Cambridge, 1994).

as the means of religious preservation between the twin evils of 'super-stition' (catholicism) and 'enthusiasm' (methodism). The latter was the subject of a letter sent by Blackburne to Archbishop Herring in 1754, and published in 1771 as a contribution to the campaign to repeal subscription to the thirty-nine articles, the central objective of mid- and late-century anglican anti-dogmatism.[52] The failure of their petition to parliament, significantly defended in the House of Commons by Sir George Savile, soon to become a hero of the Yorkshire Association, was symptomatic of the ecclesiastical crises of the 1770s, as defections from the church of England into the new denomination of unitarianism began to make themselves felt.[53] For the younger generation, by this stage, the national church had failed, and loyalties lay with the promotion of what they perceived to be religious truth rather than with established apolo-getic.[54]

Interestingly, this conclusion, born of the inability of anglicanism to comprehend its battling traditions, led to renewed emphasis on an international context, and again revealed the confusions extra-British dimensions could produce within English protestant identity. Among the patrons of Theophilus Lindsey's newly formed Essex Street uni-tarian chapel at its foundation in 1774 was Benjamin Franklin. The radical component of anti-dogmatic protestantism thus looked, at least with one eye, across the Atlantic.[55] Nor did unitarians feel bound by the

[52] Francis Blackburne, 'A letter written by a country clergyman, to Archbishop Herring, in the year MDCCLIV', *Works*, II, pp. 101–34. A similar public missive was published by John Disney, *A letter to the most reverend the archbishop of Canterbury, on the present opposition to any farther reformation* (1774). On the campaign to repeal subscription, see Martin Fitzpatrick, 'Latitudinarianism at the parting of the ways: a suggestion', in Walsh and Taylor, *Church of England*, pp. 209–27.

[53] The leader of the association, the former clergyman Christopher Wyvill, had also contributed to the earlier debate in his clerical incarnation: *Thoughts on our articles of religion* (1771). More thought ought to be given regarding the specifically Yorkshire provenance of so much reform debate in the late eighteenth century. Localist differences plainly affect the notion of a 'national identity'. In the meantime, see Ian R. Christie, *Wilkes, Wyvill and reform: the parliamentary reform movement in British politics, 1760–1785* (1962); Christie, 'The Yorkshire association, 1780–4: a study in political organisation', in his *Myth and reality in late eighteenth-century British politics* (1970), pp. 261–83.

[54] See especially the important work of G. M. Ditchfield: 'Ecclesiastical policy under Lord North', in Walsh and Taylor, *Church of England*, pp. 228–46; 'The subscription issue in British parliamentary politics, 1772–79', *Parliamentary History*, 7 (1988), 45–80.

[55] Alfred Owen Aldridge, *Benjamin Franklin and nature's God* (Durham, NC, 1967), pp. 208–11. Across the Atlantic in 1774, two of Edmund Law's Virginia-bound charges were to be accused of arianism, on which see Rhys Isaac, *The transformation of Virginia, 1740–1790* (Chapel Hill, 1982), ch. 10. J. C. D. Clark sees this as confirmation of his conspiratorial reading of anti-dogmatism: *English society*, pp. 307–15, 422–3. Francis Blackburne was a strong opponent of an American episcopate, on which see 'A critical commentary on Archbishop Secker's letter to the

English Channel and any constricting sense of francophobic national identity, even when England faced its most pressing challenge from the French. This group's vehement sense of their own distinct religious identity encouraged them to petition parliament for repeal of the blasphemy act and the trinitarian clause of the Toleration Act in 1792, not necessarily the best of times for such an campaign.[56]

However, for all their commonwealthman patriotism, it was to Switzerland that appeal was most frequently made by anti-dogmatic divines in their call for a relaxation of subscription. Many decades earlier, Gilbert Burnet, who wrote as a consciously reformed theologian, and whose contacts with Europeans had been stronger than the vast majority of his clerical contemporaries, had been in touch with Swiss divines, and he had been particularly close to the 'Helvetic Trio' – Jean Alphonse Turrettini, Samuel Werenfels and Jean Frederick Osterwald – the architects of a repudiation of the Calvinist *Formulae consensus*, hitherto subscribed to by Swiss reformed pastors.[57] In the later eighteenth century, Francis Blackburne defended both Burnet and his Swiss colleagues in his attack on dogmatic religion, *The confessional* (1767), helping to create an atmosphere conducive to the translation into English of an allied work by a Swiss theologian, Herport, in 1768. In this enterprise Hollis, the internationally minded promoter of republican thought, was predictably involved.[58] As late as 1785, Richard Watson re-printed Osterwald's pro-reform tract, *A treatise concerning the present corruption of Christians, and the remedies thereof*, in his multi-volume aid for students of divinity, *A collection of theological tracts*. The subtleties of Switzerland, a congeries of cantons with differing confessional identities,

---

right honourable Horatio Walpole' [1770], in *Works*, II, pp. 1–99. Cf. Stephen Taylor, 'Whigs, bishops and America: the politics of church reform in mid-eighteenth-century England', *HJ*, 36 (1993), 331–56. Thomas Jefferson was then at work on a statute which would transform religious life in Virginia in ways at least congruent with the legacy of anti-dogmatism: cf. J. G. A. Pocock, 'Religious freedom and the desacralization of politics: from the English civil wars to the Virginia statute', in Merrill D. Peterson and Robert C. Vaughan, eds., *The Virginia statute for religious freedom* (Cambridge, 1988), pp. 43–73.

[56] G. M. Ditchfield, 'Anti-trinitarianism and toleration in late eighteenth-century British politics: the unitarian petition of 1792', *JEH*, 42 (1991), 39–67. On the tergiversations of toleration in eighteenth-century England, see Hugh Trevor-Roper, 'Toleration and religion after 1688', in Grell, Israel and Tyacke, *From persecution to toleration*, pp. 389–408.

[57] On these Swiss reformers, see Linda Kirk, 'Eighteenth-century Geneva and a changing Calvinism', in Stuart Mews, ed., *Religion and national identity*, SCH, 18 (1982), pp. 367–80.

[58] Francis Blackburne, *The confessional: or a full and free inquiry* (3rd edn, 1770), pp. 83–5, 153–7, 214; B. Herport, *An essay on truths of importance to the happiness of mankind* (English translation, 1768); Francis Blackburne, *Memoirs of Thomas Hollis esq.* (1780), I, pp. 302–3, 375.

plainly appealed as much as its clean-limbed protestantism to those of an anti-dogmatic persuasion, whether they were divines or apparent sceptics. The young Gibbon, in this instance very much the father of the man, reflected on the resulting ironies in a letter sent to his aunt, Catherine Porten, in February 1755:

> I have at length good news to tell you; I am now good protestant & am extremely glad of it. I have in all my letters taken notice of the different mouvements of my mind, entirely catholic when I came to Lausanne, wavering between the two Systems & at last fixed for the protestant, when that conflict was over I had still another difficulty; brought up with all the ideas of the Church of England, I could scarce resolve to communion-with Presbyterians as all the people of this country are. I at last got over it in considering that whatever difference there may be between their churches and ours, in the government & discipline they still regard us as brethren & profess the same faith as us.[59]

The difficulties caused by the European dimension in English theological discussion were also illustrated in the career of William Wake, who had sought protestant unity in tones sufficiently troubled to resemble Gibbon's. Emphasising that episcopacy be properly instituted as the prime desideratum on the part of anglican proponents of union with the reformed, the archbishop highlighted one of the key problems with any such union.[60] Wake, in common with Burnet, had enjoyed extremely friendly relations with the Swiss refomers. He had aided them with suitable memoranda in their liberal contentions with the imposition of the *Formulae consensus*. This, however, was an extremely sensitive position which left Wake open to accusations of injudicious flirtation with the tenets of anti-dogmatism by orthodox Swiss pastors.[61] Here, indeed, was something of an embarrassing paradox for the orthodox if 'latitudinarian' Wake, whose aspirations to be an ecumenical reconciler belied his difficult relations with anti-dogmatists in a church of England then given over to the Bangorian controversy and to incessant wrangling over the nature of the trinity. Norman Sykes portrayed Wake's personal crisis in the 1710s and 1720s with admirable economy, noting that 'the spectacle of a divided church, torn by internal dissension and vexed by controversy concerning the fundamentals of the faith, was particularly distressing to Wake in his efforts to heal the divisions of European Christendom'.[62] Such efforts were nevertheless maintained by Wake, who devoted particular energy to the formation of good relations with the Lutherans, as befitted a loyal servant of the new Hanoverian dynasty. Relations were especially cordial with Daniel Ernst Jablonski, counsellor to the king of Prussia, although matters became much more

[59] J. E. Norton, ed., *The letters of Edward Gibbon* (3 vols., 1956), I, p. 3.
[60] Sykes, *Wake*, II, pp. 3, 6–7, 14.   [61] Ibid., II, pp. 24–60.   [62] Ibid., II, p. 3.

complicated by the interference of the princess of Wales, the future Queen Caroline (the theologically informed consort of George II), whose occasional promotion of anti-dogmatic theologians such as the divisive Samuel Clarke failed to reassure her archbishop of the possibility of doctrinal peace within the church of England.[63] European protestants would continue to complicate anglican apologetic, as the vivid religious experience of Huguenots, Moravians and pietists began to influence the internal developments that would shortly lead to the work of Whitefield and Wesley in evangelical revival, both in England and in America.[64] William Law, an early confidant of Wesley, with whom he eventually broke in 1739, also fell in with German theology, albeit in this instance it was the obscure writings of Jacob Boehme, the Silesian mystic, which dictated the course of the remainder of his literary career.[65]

Alongside the origins of the evangelical impetus – a matter of immediate and long-term concern for the internal discipline of the church of England – the 1730s was a decade rife with yet another brand of English religious feeling: anti-clericalism. This was a largely indigenous development, but it plainly has similarities and links with the growing secularism of much continental sentiment and thought over the eighteenth century. Robert Walpole himself was reconciled to the loss of his chief clerical ally, Bishop Gibson, through his support of the quakers' tithe bill in 1736, which was denounced as an anti-clerical initiative by the man once known as 'Walpole's pope'.[66] Gibson and others had been obliged to answer a tendentiously sceptical appraisal of revealed religion, Matthew Tindal's *Christianity as old as the creation* (1730), a confident tract by an opportunistic fellow of All Souls College (a sort of secular

---

[63] Ibid., II, pp. 60–88, 154–60.

[64] In addition to the work of W. R. Ward cited in footnote 8 above, see John Walsh, 'Origins of the evangelical revival', in Walsh and G. V. Bennett, eds., *Essays in modern church history* (1966), pp. 132–62; Jean Orcibal, 'The theological originality of John Wesley and continental spirituality', in Rupert Davies and Gordon Rupp, eds., *A history of the methodist church in Great Britain* (1965), I, pp. 81–111; C. J. Podmore, 'The bishops and the brethren: anglican attitudes to the Moravians in the mid eighteenth-century', *JEH*, 41 (1990), 622–46. For a particularly vituperative response to the Moravians see George Lavington, *The Moravians compared and detected* (1755).

[65] J Brazier Green, *John Wesley and William Law* (1945); Eric W. Baker, *A herald of the evangelical revival: a critical inquiry into the relation of William Law to John Wesley and the beginnings of methodism* (1948); John Sitter, *Literary loneliness in eighteenth-century England* (Ithaca, 1982), pp. 60–73; Caroline F. E. Spurgeon, 'William Law and the mystics', in *The Cambridge history of English literature* (Cambridge, 1912), IX, pp. 305–28; Patrick Grant, 'William Law's spirit of love: rationalistic argument and Behmenist myth', in his *Literature and the discovery of method in the English renaissance* (1984), pp. 124–45.

[66] Stephen Taylor, 'Sir Robert Walpole, the church of England, and the Quakers' tithe bill of 1736', *HJ*, 28 (1985), 51–77.

vicar of Bray). Tindal's book was held by its clerical critics, mindful of the recent influence of Bernard Mandeville, to be potentially subversive of the moral order.[67] Answering freethinkers was one of the few occasions on which otherwise disparately aligned clergy could be reconciled: Tindal faced replies from Gibson, the nonjuror Law, and from arguably the most learned of English divines, Daniel Waterland, as well as a host of minor clerical scribblers, both anglicans and dissenters.[68] It was in this frequently religiously indifferent atmosphere that an anonymous poet, glorying in the alias of *Philopatriae*, celebrated the history of South Britain in 1731 with a notably anti-clerical accent. The pretensions of ecclesiastics are cut down, not only rhetorically but even in the relatively small space allotted them in a poem which devotes more time to detailing the varieties of fish to be found in England's rivers and around its shores than it does to the claims of the fishers of men. Its anti-catholicism, albeit seemingly couched in *via media* anglican tones, readily contracts into a clear suspicion of the catholic claims of an established episcopal church, replete with the obligatory reference to Archbishop Laud:

> The State review'd, a little let us try,
> And touch her Ecclesiastick Polity:
> In Doctrine sound, in Discipline severe,
> But little this pursue, or that revere.
> Whose high Pretence to Decency and Form,
> Have brought the very Gospel into Scorn;
> Learned they are, but yet alas we see
> They miss our Souls and strike our Property
> For whilst they seek to force, and not persuade,
> They seem to act the old coercive Trade,
> And lose the Substance to embrace the Shade.
> Away with all Religion which commence
> A War with Scripture, Reason, or with Sense,
> Nothing more hurtful unto any State,
> Than when Ecclesiastics are too great.

[67] On Mandeville, see E. J. Hundert, *The enlightenment's fable: Bernard Mandeville and the discovery of society* (Cambridge, 1994); M. M. Goldsmith, *Private vices, public benefits: Bernard Mandeville's social and political thought* (Cambridge, 1985); Goldsmith, 'Liberty, luxury and the pursuit of happiness', in Pagden, *Languages of political thought*, pp. 225–51; Dario Castiglione, 'Considering things minutely: reflections on Mandeville and the eighteenth-century science of man', *History of Political Thought*, 7 (1986), 463–88. William Law assayed an interesting response prior to formulating the arguments of his 'holy living' books: *Remarks upon a late book, entituled* The fable of the bees (1724).

[68] Edmund Gibson, *The bishop of London's third pastoral letter to the people of his diocese* (1731); William Law, *The case of reason or natural religion* (1731); Daniel Waterland, *Scripture vindicated: in answer to a book intituled*, Christianity as old as the creation (1731).

> Hail Persecution, thou infernal Spark,
> Bred in the horrid Regions of the Dark,
> Nourish'd by Superstition and false Zeal,
> The worst of Plagues into a Common-weal;
> Rampant in Rome, and Absolute in Spain,
> Whose bloody Kalenders record thy Reign.
> Thy sanguine Robes are lin'd with Force or Fraud,
> And first Rate Villains all thy Acts applaud,
> From Beaton, Bonner, down to little Laud.
> Thou Mass of Ills, that glories in thy Crimes,
> Spreading thy Venom into frozen Climes;
> And now thou Imp, avant, be doom'd to dwell
> Within thy native proper Sphere, Hell;
> And may that Villain meet deserved Pain,
> Who dare attempt to bring thee here again.[69]

Such anti-clericalism was not to disappear with the 'Robinocracy'. It remained a constant in eighteenth-century English life, as the legacy of freethinking calcified into a prejudice inherited by men of the ilk of Horace Walpole, although it had also been transformed into new levels of sophistication by Gibbon, who had learned in his turn from Hume, intellectually the most damaging of eighteenth-century Christianity's opponents.

Gibbon's own relations with Christianity are decidedly complex, and his deployment of mordant irony often obscures more than it reveals. The clearest and most constant element in his religious thought, however, was a suspicion of clerical claims to authority, which, curiously, owed much to the Gallican criticism of the English establishment which he had absorbed in his youth. Gibbon's reaction to the defeat of the anti-subscriptionists, as revealed in a letter to John Baker Holroyd, of February 1772, is as typical as anything he would later evince in the *Decline and fall* of his quizzically amused attitude towards organised religion:

Though it is very late, and the bell tells me that I have not above ten minutes left, I employ them with pleasure in congratulating you on the late Victory of our Dear Mamma the Church of England. She had last Thursday 71 rebellious sons who pretended to set aside her will on account of insanity: but 217 Worthy Champions headed by Lord North, Burke, Hans Stanley, Charles Fox, Godfrey Clarke &c, though they allowed the thirty nine clauses of her Testament were absurd and unreasonable supported the validity of it with infinite humour. By the bye C F prepared himself for that holy War by passing twenty two hours in the pious exercise of Hazard. His devotions cost him only about £500 an hour in all £11000.[70]

[69] Philopatriae, *South-Britain: a poem* (1731), pp. 22–3.
[70] *Letters of Edward Gibbon*, I, p. 305.

Although Thomas Cadell, Gibbon's publisher, was a worshipper at Lindsey's chapel, Lindsey himself had little love for Gibbon, as is revealed in a letter of 1781: 'There never was a more industrious or more artful adversary to Divine Revelation than our Historian, and not many of more ability.'[71] Gibbon had as little time for unitarians as he had for trinitarians, and the analogous squabbles in the early church over the nature of the Godhead provided a large element of his critique of religion in the early volumes of the *Decline and fall*. The divisions of Christianity were seen to be endemic to its various theologies, and the reader of Bossuet adeptly absorbed some of his early mentor's methods in turning history against philosophical and denominational claims. His vision of the religion of Jesus and his immediate followers radically undermined the case made by consciously orthodox opponents of heresy:

> It has been remarked with more ingenuity than truth, that the virgin purity of the church was never violated by schism or heresy before the reign of Trajan or Hadrian, about one hundred years after the death of Christ. We may observe with much more propriety, that, during that period, the disciples of the Messiah were indulged in a freer latitude both of faith and practice, than has ever been allowed in succeeding ages.[72]

It does not take too much imagination to appreciate the ironies of this claim, especially as it touched the catholic, patristically grounded claims of members of the church of England. Bossuet had been unexpectedly allied with the logic of the protestant right of private judgement in a devastatingly corrosive account of Christian origins. If the early church could be undermined with such weaponry, how much more perilous was the state of a doctrinally divided church of England? This was the challenge made by Gibbon, and in so doing he managed to provoke differing interests within the church in a union reminiscent of the attacks on Tindal, the infinitely more crude freethinker of the 1730s. Gibbon faced replies from a multiplicity of divines, including such otherwise inveterate enemies as the liberal Richard Watson and Joseph Milner, master of Hull Grammar School and one of the architects of evangelical revival within the church of England.[73]

The latter phenomenon is still relatively unexplored – but it provides one final example of the endless variety of eighteenth-

---

[71] H McLachlan, ed., *Letters of Theophilus Lindsey* (Manchester, 1920), pp. 6–7, 18.

[72] Gibbon, *Decline and fall*, I, 457.

[73] Richard Watson, *An apology for Christianity, in a series of letters to Edward Gibbon, esq* (Cambridge, 1776); Joseph Milner, *Gibbon's account of Christianity considered* (York, 1781); J. D. Walsh, 'Joseph Milner's evangelical church history', *JEH*, 10 (1959), 174–87.

century anglicanism.[74] Reaction to the anti-subscription petition of 1771 provided a major focus for revivified Calvinism, making one further wonder at the apparent irony of Blackburne's claim that he himself was a Calvinist 'of the largest and most liberal sort'.[75] Augustus Toplady was especially prominent in this revival, defending the thirty-nine articles from what he considered to be the Arminianising perversions read into them by Gilbert Burnet and Daniel Waterland, and from the wholesale opposition to such firmly Calvinist formulae voiced by the anti-dogmatic petition against subscription.[76] Likewise, Toplady's fellow Calvinist James Hervey, author of two mid-century favourites of popular religious apologetic, *Meditations among the tombs* (1746) and *Theron and Aspasio* (1755), had been an evangelical from very early years, and in 1758 enjoyed an exemplary evangelical death, sure of salvation purely through the merits of Christ.[77] The evangelical conversion of the previously sceptical Arthur Young on the death of a pre-cociously pious daughter in 1797 was a significant herald of Calvinist revival among the devout laity, a process which accelerated in the opening decades of the nineteenth century.[78] This was the world reconstructed by Boyd Hilton, in which Calvinism, both sectarian and established, helped to create an age of political, social and economic 'atonement'.[79]

From what has been said, it is clear that the familiar divisions of the nineteenth-century church of England had many of their origins in the religious debates of the eighteenth century. The growth of unitarianism into near respectability, the prevalence of evangelical attitudes, the Coleridgean inheritance of a 'broad church', all could claim descent from earlier movements within anglicanism. As the important work of Peter Nockles has recently demonstrated, much the same can be said of

[74] Cf. Walsh and Taylor, 'Introduction', *Church of England*, at pp. 43–5. John Walsh is at work on a study of the revival of Calvinist anglicanism.

[75] Blackburne, *Works*, I, p. lxxviii.

[76] Augustus Toplady, *The church of England vindicated from the charge of arminianism* (1769); Toplady, *Clerical subscription no grievance: or, the doctrines of the church of England proved to be the doctrines of Christ* (1772).

[77] 'The life of the reverend James Hervey, AM.', prefixed to, *A collection of the letters of the late reverend James Hervey. A.M.* (2 vols., 1760), I, pp. v-lx, at pp. xxi-xxiii. For analysis of the context of Hervey's work, see Isabel Rivers, 'Shaftesburian enthusiasm and the evangelical revival', in Jane Garnett and Colin Matthew, eds., *Revival and religion since 1700: essays for John Walsh* (1993), pp. 21–39.

[78] M. Betham-Edwards, ed., *The autobiography of Arthur Young* (1898), ch. 12. On the wider evangelical movement of which Young was an early enthusiast, see Ford K. Brown, *Fathers of the Victorians: the age of Wilberforce* (Cambridge, 1961). Interestingly, Young regretted that 'the young theologians of Geneva are at this day instructed much more in Osterwald's *Catechism* than in Calvin's books', *Autobiography*, p. 307.

[79] Boyd Hilton, *The age of atonement: the influence of evangelicalism on social and economic thought, 1785–1865* (Oxford, 1988).

the 'catholic' wings of the church of England, themselves subject to internal contention as they argued over the self-ascription of 'orthodoxy'.[80] The legacy of the nonjurors was plainly a matter of some moment to the Oxford movement, while the ultra-orthodoxy of the Hutchinsonians informed that of the 'Hackney Phalanx'. Traditions of patristic scholarship continued to develop within such Oxford circles as those presided over by Palmer of Worcester and Routh of Magdalen.[81] How concerned were such groups with national identity, as opposed to their identity as members of a church whose catholicism they considered purer than that of ultramontane Rome? Plainly, the church of England, as Coleridge emphasised in *On the constitution of the church and state* (1829), was an idea of supreme importance in an England which was still coming to terms with the French revolution and the legacies of its wars with Napoleonic France – but the specifically 'catholic' identity of that church considerably complicated the notion of a protestant nation as the unifying agent in English, let alone 'British' self-construction.[82] It is indeed ironic that one of the most reflective works on the question of the relationship between England and its specifically national church was written by Robert Southey, whose theology was decidedly (if covertly) unitarian in character.[83] Loyalty to the church of England and fidelity to England were usually linked in extremely subtle and delicate ways, but it would seem that for many churchmen, and for equally devout laymen, theology and religion somehow dictated their relationship with the state.[84]

[80] Peter Nockles, 'Church parties in the pre-Tractarian church of England 1750–1833: the "Orthodox" – some problems of definition and identity', in Walsh and Taylor, *Church of England*, pp. 334–59.

[81] Peter Nockles, *The Oxford movement in context: anglican high churchmanship, 1760–1857* (Cambridge, 1994)

[82] On the possibly Baxterian and essentially protestant nature of Coleridge's enterprise, see William Lamont, 'The two "national churches" of 1691 and 1829', in Anthony Fletcher and Peter Roberts, eds., *Religion, culture and society in early modern Britain: essays in honour of Patrick Collinson* (Cambridge, 1994), pp. 335–52. Coleridge was very critical of fringe dissent, as can be appreciated in his considerations concerning Lavington on the Moravians (see footnote 64 above): Samuel Taylor Coleridge, *Marginalia*, ed. H. J. Jackson and George Whalley (3 vols., Princeton, 1992), III, pp. 492–8.

[83] Sheridan Gilley, 'Nationality and liberty, protestant and catholic: Robert Southey's *Book of the church*', in Mews, *Religion and national identity*, pp. 409–32; David Eastwood, 'Robert Southey and the meanings of patriotism', *JBS*, 31 (1992), 265–87.

[84] This is to raise complicated Rankean and Actonian questions of the relationship between church and state, which there is simply not the space to address here It is at the least interesting that Acton, the cosmopolitan Victorian catholic, saw questions of the supremacy of liberty of conscience successfully emerging between the 1680s and the 1820s, years of great contention within the church of England. For a convenient collection of Acton's thoughts on this and allied questions, see George Watson, *Lord Acton's history of liberty: a study of his library* (Aldershot, 1994), ch. 5. Cf. 'The history of

To conclude with the bracingly sceptical thoughts of a Scot. In his essay 'Of national characters', which first appeared in the second edition of his moral, political and literary essays in 1748,[85] David Hume adverted to the universal nature of the clerical class, noting that 'it is a trite, but not altogether a false maxim, that priests of all religions are the same; and though the character of the profession will not, in every instance, prevail over the personal character, yet it is always to predominate with the greater number.'[86] With his frequently wounding experience of presbyterian Scotland, anglican England and Roman catholic France, Hume could well claim to have known what he was writing about. Such anti-clericalism did not leave him without an appreciation of the perceived benefits of the religious and social toleration of the English, as he reflected on the central paradox of their uniquely wide sense of an essentially protestant national identity. 'The genius of a particular sect of religion', he noted, was 'apt to mould the manners of a people', and, since 'all sects of religion are to be found among them', then 'the ENGLISH, of any people in the universe, have the least of a national character; unless this very singularity may pass for such.'[87]

Such a conclusion subtly and cunningly ignores the contentious nature of religious debate among the clergy and loyal churchmen of whatever hue. Hume's desire for what one might call de-Christianisation seemingly blinded him to the fact that the contest between 'enthusiasm' and 'superstition' continued within as well as without the church of England in the eighteenth century.[88] Edmund Burke, whose Christianity did not entirely divorce him from a degree of acceptance of the social criticism of Hume and Gibbon, may well have detected a new form of enthusiasm at work in the French revolution, but he had also attacked the opponents of subscription in 1772 as potential subverters of civil as much as of ecclesiastical peace.[89] The unitarianism of the 1780s and 1790s, which developed in large part from the

freedom in Christianity', in Acton's *The history of freedom and other essays*, ed. John Neville Figgis and Reginald Vere Laurence (1909), pp. 30–60.

[85] David Hume, *Essays moral, political and literary*, ed. Eugene F. Miller (Indianapolis, 1987), pp. 197–215.

[86] Ibid., p. 199.   [87] Ibid., p. 207.

[88] The classic distinction of an already established contrast was made by Hume in his essay 'Of superstition and enthusiasm', in his *Essays*, pp. 73–9, and applied in his *History of England*. On the political and historiographical consequences of which, see Duncan Forbes, *Hume's philosophical politics* (Cambridge, 1975), pp. 202, 214–15, and Victor G. Wexler, *David Hume and the history of England* (Philadelphia, 1979).

[89] J. G. A. Pocock, 'Edmund Burke and the redefinition of enthusiasm: the context as counter-revolution', in François Furet and Mona Ozouf, eds., *The French revolution and the creation of modern culture, III: The transformation of political culture, 1789–1848* (Oxford, 1989), pp. 19–36; Edmund Burke, 'Speech on clerical subscription', in Paul Langford, ed., *The writings and speeches of Edmund Burke, II, Party, parliament and the*

anti-subscriptionist wing of the church of England, was not to Burke's taste, or to that of many of his contemporaries, but it was a vivid testimony to the dissensions which characterised the religious life of the time, and to a sense of identity which transcended that of the nation alone. Unitarians were, after all, amongst the strongest of the Francophile 'friends of peace' in the 1790s and 1800s.[90] England may have been a protestant nation, but its national church harboured variations, both catholic and proto-unitarian, which led its members to identify with things and places other than and beyond England. It is, perhaps, a testimony to the strength of the idea of the church of England, and to the comparative weakness of dissent (including Roman catholicism), that it maintained the allegiance of so many disparate members.

American crisis, 1766–1774 (Oxford, 1981), pp. 359–64. The Burke–Paine controversy also contained strong theological elements, on which see Ian Harris, 'Paine and Burke: God, nature and politics', in Michael Bentley, ed., *Public and private doctrine: essays in British history presented to Maurice Cowling* (Cambridge, 1993), pp. 34–62.

[90] J. E. Cookson, *The friends of peace: anti-war liberalism in England, 1793–1815* (Cambridge, 1982), pp. 4, 9–10, 22, 33, 186–7, 191, 209. On the role of unitarian sentiments in domestic and international politics, see J. G. A. Pocock, 'Political thought in the English-speaking Atlantic, 1760–90, part 2: empire, revolution and the end of early modernity', in Pocock, *Varieties of British political thought*, pp. 283–317.

Britain and Ireland

6 The British dimension, religion, and the shaping of political identities during the reign of Charles II

Tim Harris

The later Stuart period has never been particularly sure of its own identity. Does it belong with the revolutionary upheavals of the first part of the seventeenth century; is it a distinct period in its own right; or is it the beginning of the long eighteenth century? Never quite certain, it tends to fall through the historiographical gaps. We see this confusion when we turn to the whole question of national identities and the writing of British history. There has been great interest in recent years in taking a 'three kingdoms' approach to the political upheavals under the early Stuarts.[1] It has even been suggested that we can detect a 'briticisation' of the nobility at this time.[2] Moving forward in time, the issue of protestantism and the emergence of a British national identity under the Hanoverians has attracted considerable attention.[3] Yet restoration historians have been slow to follow these trends. On the surface there are grounds for suspecting that a British approach might be worth pursuing for the reign of Charles II. After all, the words that came to be adopted during the exclusion crisis of c. 1678–83 to describe the partisan divide that emerged in England under the later Stuarts strongly suggest the importance of the British dimension to English political identities: whig meant Scottish presbyterian, tory an Irish-catholic cattle thief. With the

---

[1] Conrad Russell, *The causes of the English civil war* (Oxford, 1990); Conrad Russell, *The fall of the British monarchies 1637–1642* (Oxford, 1991); John Morrill, 'The Scottish national covenant of 1638 in its British context' and 'The causes of Britain's civil wars', in his *The nature of the English revolution* (1993), pp. 91–117 and pp. 252–72; Jane Ohlmeyer, *Civil war and restoration in three Stuart kingdoms: the career of Randall MacDonnell, marquis of Antrim* (Cambridge, 1993).

[2] John Morrill, 'The fashioning of Britain', in Steven G. Ellis and Sarah Barber, eds., *Conquest and union: fashioning a British state, 1485–1725* (1995), p. 26.

[3] See, in particular, Gerald Newman, *The rise of English nationalism: a cultural history 1740–1830* (1987); Linda Colley, *Britons: forging the nation, 1707–1837* (New Haven, 1992); Colin Kidd, *Subverting Scotland's past: Scottish whig historians and the creation of an Anglo-British identity, 1689–c. 1830* (Cambridge, 1993); Alexander Grant and Keith J. Stringer, eds., *Uniting the kingdom? The making of British history* (1995), chs. 11–13.

notable exceptions of Ronald Hutton, whose biography of Charles II provides parallel histories of the three kingdoms, and Richard Greaves, whose work on the radical fringe also takes in Scotland and Ireland, there has been very little interest in the possibilities of a British history for the later-Stuart period.[4] Indeed, it is highly revealing that a recent collection of essays on 'the making of British history', which spans from Anglo-Saxon times to the present, contains no contribution on the period between the Stuart restoration of 1660 and the Hanoverian succession of 1714.[5]

It remains far from clear, as yet, whether exploring the British dimension will prove particularly fruitful for the restoration period; maybe there is not much of an integrated story to be told. Besides, questions are already beginning to be raised at the more general level about the value of the three-kingdoms approach for the seventeenth century. How much sense does it make to attempt a British history for a period when there was as yet no British state, no British government and no sense of British identity? Are not those who seek to write a British history reduced to studying the relationships and interactions between England and two neighbouring foreign powers, Scotland and Ireland? If so, why stop there? Why not look also at France, Spain, the United Provinces or the American colonies, whose impact on England was arguably just as significant (and perhaps more so)? Furthermore, is it not the case that a British history makes sense only at the level of the political elite? John Morrill and Jane Ohlmeyer have pointed to prominent members of the ruling class who possessed a multi-kingdom identity, but surely the same could not be said for the vast majority of ordinary women and men who inhabited the Britannic archipelago. Might not a concentration on the British dimension be a retrogressive step, which carries with it an implicit call to old-fashioned, high political history, concentrating on the elite and abandoning recent trends towards a social history of politics in the seventeenth century?[6]

The point of this chapter is to examine the ways in which it makes

---

[4] Ronald Hutton, *Charles II: king of England, Scotland and Ireland* (Oxford, 1989); Richard L. Greaves: *Deliver us from evil: the radical underground in Britain, 1660–1663* (New York, 1986); *Enemies under his feet: radicals and nonconformists in Britain, 1664–1677* (Stanford, 1990); *Secrets of the kingdom: British radicals from the popish plot to the revolution of 1688–89* (Stanford, 1992); and *God's other children: protestant nonconformists and the emergence of denominational churches in Ireland, 1660–1700* (Stanford, 1997). See also the important article by Toby Barnard, 'Scotland and Ireland in the later Stewart monarchy', in Ellis and Barber, eds., *Conquest and union*, pp. 250–75.

[5] Grant and Stringer, eds., *Uniting the kingdom?*

[6] These questions were raised in discussion with Mark Kishlansky and David Underdown at the North-East Conference on British Studies at Bentley College on 1 October 1994, where an early version of this paper was presented.

sense to take a British or a three-kingdoms approach to the problems of the restoration period – to explore, in John Pocock's words, the ways in which 'the various peoples' that inhabited 'the area known as "Great Britain and Ireland" . . . interacted so as to modify the conditions of one another's existence'.[7] I shall begin by showing that certain major problems that faced the restoration polity operated on a British level (rather than on separate national ones), and were recognised to do so. In several crucial respects, political identities – at both the level of the elite and the subaltern classes – were conditioned by an awareness of being part of a larger Britain, rather than being merely inhabitants of the constituent, independent kingdoms; we even see the existence of cross-national allegiances. I shall then offer a detailed examination of the ways in which developments in Ireland and Scotland affected public opinion in England during the exclusion crisis. The British perspective, it will be argued, helps us make better sense of both the whig and tory responses at this time. The whig concern over popery and arbitrary government, we shall find, was not merely a reaction to the prospect of a popish successor – an imagined fear of what might happen in England in the future; it was also a reaction to a very real threat from popery and arbitrary government that existed at that moment in Charles's other kingdoms. On the other hand, the full power of the tory case against the whigs – that exclusion would lead to civil war, and that its proponents were radical nonconformists bent on destroying the existing establishment in church and state – can only be appreciated once we recognise that the tories were thinking in British, and not purely English, terms. Despite the importance of the British dimension, however, we cannot really talk about the existence of a British identity at this time – largely because of a lack of ideological cement. A shared sense of protestantism or fear of the catholic other, for reasons that will become apparent, failed to bond the disparate political and religious cultures of the British Isles together in the way that has been claimed for the eighteenth century.

I

At first sight, the prospects for writing a British history for the period after 1660 seem less promising than they do for the earlier seventeenth

---

[7] J. G. A. Pocock, 'The limits and divisions of British history: in search of the unknown subject', *AHR*, 87 (1982), 317. This paper limits itself to looking at England, Scotland and Ireland, since I am interested in studying the interaction between three different states that shared the same king; the principality of Wales, incorporated into the English realm since the act of union of 1536, provides a somewhat different case, which will not be addressed here, though this is not intended to minimise the significance of the Welsh experience.

century. Neither Charles II nor James II possessed the same imperial vision as James I, nor did they seem eager to promote a greater degree of harmonisation between their three kingdoms, as did both their grandfather and father. The trend towards the emergence of a British ruling class that some historians have detected under the early Stuarts was reversed after 1660.[8] Few Scots or Irishmen held important positions at court or in the government in England in Charles II's reign, with the notable exceptions of Lauderdale and Ormond. Both Charles II and James II saw themselves as kings of England first and foremost, with English interests paramount; the court in England during their reigns was very much an English court; and the various ethnic, religious and national identities in the constituent kingdoms showed no signs of weakening or becoming melded into a more unified British outlook.[9]

It would be wrong to conclude, however, that a British approach to the restoration period has no value. There were a number of significant ways in which English, Scottish and Irish affairs did interact with each other to produce historical developments that can be understood only in a British context. At the very basic level we have to return to the fact that England, Scotland and Ireland, whilst being separate kingdoms, shared the same king, and the policies that this man pursued in one of his realms often did have an important impact in the others. Indeed, it is arguable that the very fact that the later Stuarts lacked the imperial vision of James VI and I, and were perceived invariably to be putting English interests first, enhanced an awareness in Scotland and Ireland of the degree to which they were ruled by an imperial monarchy. If we restrict ourselves to Scotland and Ireland for the moment, it is certainly the case that the histories of these two countries cannot be understood solely in national terms, since developments in both these kingdoms

---

[8] Morrill, 'Fashioning of Britain'; N. Cuddy, 'The revival of the entourage: the bedchamber under James I, 1603–1625', in David Starkey, ed., *The English court: from the wars of the roses to the civil war* (1987), pp. 173–226; Keith Brown, 'Courtiers and cavaliers: service, anglicization and loyalty among the royalist nobility', in J. S. Morrill, ed., *The Scottish national covenant in its British context* (Edinburgh, 1990), pp. 155–92; Keith Brown, 'The Scottish aristocracy, anglicization and the court', *HJ*, 36 (1993), 543–76 (esp. 552–3); Conrad Russell, 'The Anglo-Scottish union 1603–1643: a success?', in Anthony Fletcher and Peter Roberts, eds., *Religion, culture and society in early modern Britain: essays in honour of Patrick Collinson* (Cambridge, 1994), pp. 240–3.

[9] Keith Brown, 'The origins of a British aristocracy: integration and its limitations before the treaty of union', in Ellis and Barber, eds., *Conquest and union*, pp. 222–49; Barnard, 'Scotland and Ireland in the later Stewart monarchy'. But cf. David Stevenson, 'The English devil of keeping state: elite manners and the downfall of Charles I in Scotland', in Roger Mason and Norman Macdougall, eds., *People and power in Scotland: essays in honour of T. C. Smout* (Edinburgh, 1992), pp. 141–2, who argues that, following the restoration, the Scottish nobility increasingly came to adopt the manners, attitudes and accents of their English counterparts, looking to the nobility south of the border as their cultural role-models.

were often crucially affected by decisions taken and policies pursued in England.

Many of the problems that developed in restoration Ireland and Scotland were related to the nature of the restoration settlement itself, a settlement that was an attempt by a restored monarch who was king in three kingdoms to deal with the legacy of the British crisis which had brought down the monarchy in the first place. In Ireland the most sensitive issue was land, and because of the operation of Poynings' law, the details of the land settlement were essentially worked out by the English Privy Council. Neither catholics nor parliamentarian or Cromwellian adventurers obtained the sort of compensation they expected under the act of settlement of 1662 (and subsequent act of explanation of 1665), whilst it was those with powerful connections to the English court who were best placed to do well. Disaffected interests in Ireland represented the land settlement as a betrayal by a corrupt English administration determined to promote the interests of royal favourites and courtiers. One author alleged that Clarendon refused to allow land to be given back to the Irish catholics under the justification that 'the Protestant English Interest . . . in Ireland' could not be maintained 'without extirpating the Natives'. 'This proud human', the tract went on, 'joyntly with some others, to get Money for themselves, and Estates for their Children, contrived the general extirpation of the whole Irish race.'[10]

In Scotland, by contrast, the most difficult problem facing the restoration regime concerned the settlement in the church. Here presbyterianism was overturned and an episcopalian and erastian church was restored. Although we need not agree with those presbyterian historians who argued that most Scottish people were naturally inclined to presbyterianism (in fact the civil war and interregnum probably bequeathed a substantial legacy of antagonism towards presbyterian clericalism), there was no spontaneous attempt north of the border to restore episcopalian governance and practices as there had been in England. The religious settlement in Scotland was very much one imposed from

---

[10] [Nicholas French], *A narrative of the settlement and sale of Ireland* (1668), quotes on pp. 16, 24. See also [Nicholas French], *The bleeding Iphigeneia* (1675) and *The unkinde desertor of loyall men and true friends* ([Paris], 1676); Dr Williams' Library, Roger Morrice, Ent'ring Book, Q, pp. 116–17; J. C. Beckett, *The making of modern Ireland 1603–1923* (1966), pp. 118–21; J. G. Simms, 'The restoration, 1660–85', in T. W. Moody, F. X. Martin and F. J. Byrne, eds., *A new history of Ireland: III, Early modern Ireland, 1534–1691* (Oxford, 1976), pp. 422–9; S. J. Connolly, *Religion, law and power: the making of protestant Ireland 1660–1760* (Oxford, 1992), pp. 13–17; Karl S. Bottigheimer, 'The restoration land settlement in Ireland: a structural view', *IHS*, 18 (1972), 1–21; L . J. Arnold, *The restoration land settlement in county Dublin, 1660–1688: the history of the administration of the acts of settlement and explanation* (Dublin, 1993).

above, and one which was designed to make the Scottish church most manageable by a king who was absent in England. Charles II himself loathed the Scottish presbyterians as a result of the part they had played in the wars against his father, and thought that presbyterianism was a religion not only unfit for gentlemen but unsuitable for a monarchy. In a royal proclamation issued on 6 September 1661 he announced the abolition of presbytery because of 'the unsuteablnes thereof to his Majestie's monarchical estate'. It was better to place the church in the hands of bishops who, as royal appointees, could be expected to do the king's bidding. Moreover, the restoration of episcopacy in Scotland, as Keith Brown has pointed out, was dictated by a desire to maintain conformity with his kingdoms of England and Ireland, where the limited support for presbyterianism made the restoration of episcopacy a necessity. The religious settlement in Scotland therefore restored the church to the position of 1633, outlawed the covenant and presbyterian conventicles, and by an act of 1669 established a royal supremacy 'in all causes ecclesiasticall within this kingdom'.[11]

If we turn from the restoration settlement to the economy, again we see that what happened in both Ireland and Scotland was crucially affected by the policies of those who ruled England. Ireland, which tended to be treated as a colonial dependency rather than an independent kingdom, had its economy subordinated to that of the mother country. The export of Irish wool to foreign countries, which had long been prohibited, was made a felony by an act of 1662. Two acts of 1663 and 1667 put a stop to the rapidly expanding and highly prosperous Irish cattle trade, in order to protect the interests of English cattle breeders. The Irish economy received a further blow from the navigation act of 1671, which undermined Irish overseas trade by insisting that all imports from the colonies had to be landed first in England.[12] As a *Letter from a gentleman in Ireland* put it in 1677, the jealous English 'interpret our industry as Theft': 'you prohibit our Cattel, you restrain our Wool; our Manufacture is intolerable; you forbid our Trading with any Forreign Commodities in your own Plantations . . . We are in all

---

[11] Keith M. Brown, *Kingdom or province? Scotland and the regal union, 1603–1715* (1992), pp. 148–50; Julia Buckroyd, 'Anti-clericalism in Scotland during the restoration', in Norman MacDougall, ed., *Church, politics and society: Scotland 1408–1929* (Edinburgh, 1983), pp. 167–85; I. B. Cowan, *The Scottish covenanters 1660–88* (1976), ch. 2; William Croft Dickinson and Gordon Donaldson, eds., *A source book of Scottish history: volume three, 1567 to 1707* (1954), pp. 152–60; Julia Buckroyd, *Church and state in Scotland, 1660–1681* (Edinburgh, 1980).

[12] Beckett, *Making of modern Ireland*, pp. 128–9, 131; Simms, 'The restoration', pp. 443–4.

things, indeed, treated by you like, or worse than Aliens.'[13] Since trade was predominantly in the hands of the protestants in Ireland, it was mainly the protestant interest which resented the lack of economic independence that the imperial relationship brought; there was no common sense of protestant British interest here.

Scotland enjoyed a degree of political and economic independence from England which Ireland did not. Nevertheless, the policies pursued by the English government necessarily had a significant impact north of the border. The English navigation act of 1660, designed primarily to hit the Dutch, also had deleterious effects on Scotland, which was a major trading partner of Holland, whilst the Anglo-Dutch war, which broke out in 1664, caused a further depression in Scotland's economy. Overseas trade was inevitably heavily affected by foreign policy. The problem was that, in both England and Scotland, the formation of foreign policy was acknowledged to be the undoubted prerogative of the king of the respective countries, and he was the same person; whatever was done in this area, therefore, inevitably had British implications. Foreign policy initiatives taken by the king of England also had ramifications for domestic politics in Scotland. The Scottish presbyterians, dispossessed at the restoration, held strong sympathies for their Calvinist brothers in Holland (some Scottish presbyterians, indeed, had been driven into exile in Holland), and there were repeated fears in the reign of Charles II that the republican Dutch might seek to assist the covenanters with arms and supplies to plot against the government and destabilise the restoration monarchy. In order to pay for the defence of his northern kingdom, Charles II had to summon a special convention of the estates to vote for new taxes, since the dislocation caused by the Dutch war had led to a drop in the revenues from customs and excise, even though asking for more money at a time of recession was a risky undertaking. The problem became a circular one, and was intrinsically British in the making.[14]

A similar picture emerges if we look at religion. Irish religious policy was also influenced to a significant degree by the exigencies of English domestic politics. Despite the existence of penal laws restricting their religious, political and economic freedoms, in practice Irish catholics enjoyed a considerable degree of *de facto* toleration, unless the situation in England dictated otherwise. For example, the failure of Charles's

---

[13] [Andrew Marvell], *A letter from a gentleman in Ireland to his brother in England, relating to the concerns of Ireland in matter of trade* (1677), pp. 8, 21. Cf. *A vindication of the present government of Ireland, under his excellency Richard Earl of Tirconnel* (1688), pp. 1–2.

[14] William Ferguson, *Scotland's relations with England: a survey to 1707* (Edinburgh, 1977), pp. 153–4; Hutton, *Charles II*, pp. 224–5.

attempted indulgence of 1672 provoked a severe anti-catholic backlash in the English parliament in 1673, and led in turn to a renewed bout of persecution in Ireland. Another drive against catholics in Ireland followed the revelations of the Rye House plot in 1683 (an alleged conspiracy by protestant nonconformists), since the English government could not be seen to be clamping down on protestant dissent at home while ignoring the problem of catholic dissent in Ireland (especially when government propagandists in England were trying to score debating points by arguing that dissenters and catholics were just as bad as each other).[15] Although domestic religious policies in Scotland and England took largely independent courses, the episcopalian establishment in Scotland realised the necessity of winning allies in the south in order to protect their church. Indeed, the very weakness of episcopalianism in Scotland meant that the Scottish bishops saw the fortunes of the two churches, north and south of the border, as intricately bound together.[16] During the exclusion crisis, the Scottish bishops were well aware that if the campaign of the English whigs had succeeded, the position of their church – which depended so much upon the support they got from the royal brothers and the English court – would have been seriously jeopardised.[17]

The issues raised by Charles II's style of government, and the concerns about the religious and political leanings of the royal court, which came to a head in England with the exclusion crisis, carried with them implications for all of Charles's kingdoms, and invite consideration in a British rather than a purely English context. The alleged popish plot had both Scottish and Irish dimensions. The initial revelations by Titus Oates predicted what was in essence a re-run of the earlier British crisis that led to the outbreak of the civil war: first Scotland was to rise in rebellion, then Ireland, before the English protestant establishment was to become the target of popish conspirators.[18] The attempt to exclude the duke of York from the succession – that is, to exclude the heir to the throne not only of England, but also of Scotland and Ireland – obviously had British ramifications. As such, the inhabitants of Scotland and Ireland felt themselves deeply concerned with what was going on in England during the exclusion crisis, aware that they were involved in a problem which was British in scale, rather than simply English. And

[15] Connolly, *Religion, law and power*, pp. 22–4.
[16] HMC, *Laing*, I, p. 396.
[17] William Nelson Clarke, ed., *A collection of letters addressed by prelates and individuals of high rank in Scotland and by two bishops of Sodor and Man to Sancroft archbishop of Canterbury* (Edinburgh, 1848), p. 26.
[18] Kalev Peekna, 'English views of Ireland, 1641–1691' (unpublished Brown University Honors Thesis, 1995), pp. 100–1.

these issues were of concern not just to the ruling elite – whether briticised or not; they were also of vital concern to a broader section of the Scottish and Irish populations.

This point can be illustrated by looking at how the struggle over the succession was carried on 'out-of-doors' in Scotland and Ireland: as in England there were demonstrations, effigy-burnings, petitions and addresses. On Christmas Day 1680 the students of the University of Edinburgh, together with the local apprentices and other tradesmen, decided to burn the pope in effigy – in self-conscious imitation of the London pope-burnings: the students got the idea from a copper-plate engraving 'representing the manner of burning the Pope at London', which they saw hanging on the wall of an Edinburgh tavern. The authorities suspected that English agitators might have put the students up to it, and two English youths (thought to have connections with the whig gentry) were amongst those arrested by the magistrates as ringleaders. The scholars wore blue ribbons in their hats with the words 'No Pope', 'No Priest', 'No Bishop', 'No Atheist' embroidered upon them. This practice of wearing blue ribbons was in turn soon to be copied by the English, as a way of proclaiming their support for the duke of Monmouth as an alternative successor to the catholic York.[19] Monmouth himself had a popular following in both Scotland and Ireland. When he visited Edinburgh in June 1679, he was greeted with 'loud Shouts and Acclamations' as he passed through the streets of the city.[20] In 1682 a group of Dublin apprentices planned to take advantage of a May Day demonstration against the threat posed to domestic artisans by the Huguenot refugees from France to seize upon the Guards and declare for Monmouth, although as it turned out the conspiracy was put down before it could come to anything.[21]

---

[19] Bod., MS Carte 228, fo. 169; *The Scots demonstration of their abhorrence of popery* [Edinburgh, 1681]; N. M., *A modest apology for the students of Edinburgh burning a pope December 25. 1680* (1681); L. L., *The history of the late proceedings of the students of the colledge at Edenborough* (1681); *True Protestant Mercury*, no. 3, 1–3 Jan. 1680/1; [Alexander Monro], *The spirit of calumny and slander, examin'd, chastis'd, and expos'd, in a letter to a malicious libeller* (1693), p. 64; *The register of the privy council of Scotland, 1681–2* (Edinburgh, 1915), pp. 4, 13, 23–4; Robert Wodrow, *History of the sufferings of the church of Scotland, from the restoration to the revolution* (2 vols., Edinburgh, 1721–2), II, pp. 217–19; *Historical selections from the manuscripts of Sir John Lauder of Fountainhall. Volume first, historical observations, 1680–1686* (Edinburgh, 1837) [hereafter Fountainhall, *Historical observations*], pp. 18–19, 25. According to Fountainhall, the practice of wearing blue ribbons was adopted because in Numbers 15, v. 38–9, God appointed the Israelites to wear blue ribbons so that they might remember and observe the Commandments. Since popery was condemned as idolatry under Scottish law, it was also therefore against the Ten Commandments.
[20] *A further account of the proceedings against the rebels in Scotland* (1679).
[21] *CSPD, 1682*, pp. 196, 198; HMC, *Ormond*, NS, VI, 359; Bod. MS Carte 168, pp. 1, 2.

There were also loyalist demonstrations in Scotland and Ireland. When the duke of York (or Albany, to use his Scottish title) and his duchess arrived in Edinburgh at the end of October 1680, they were met with 'the lowd and reiterated Acclamations of the People . . . the whole body of the People universally shouting with great joy and chearfulness, "Lord preserve His Majesty, and their Royal Highnesses"'.[22] In opposition to the activities of the students at Edinburgh on 25 December 1680, 'some of the Episcopall and Court party' took to sporting red ribbons, embroidered with the words 'I am no Phanatick.'[23] Charles II's birthday and anniversary of his restoration, 29 May, became the occasion for loyalist displays, as in England.[24] In Edinburgh in 1681 the day was commemorated with ringing of bells, 'discharging the great guns, trumpets sounding, bonfires, and all other expressions of joy'. The city constables were charged with supervising the construction of a series of bonfires along the High Street and for exacting contributions from the local inhabitants to defray the expense.[25] In both Dublin and Edinburgh in 1682, huge crowds of spectators gathered at large public bonfires and drank loyal toasts, acclaiming 'God Bless the King, and all the Royal Family.'[26] Many places and groups in Scotland and Ireland followed England and delivered loyal addresses to the crown during the years of the tory reaction and at the time of the accession of James VII and II in 1685, proclaiming their support for the hereditary succession (and by implication their opposition to the policy of exclusion promoted by the English whigs). In April 1682, for example, the sheriff, justices of the peace and grand jury of County Down, Ireland, drew up an address to Charles II stating that they were ready to 'serve and Defend your Majestye, your Heirs, and all lawfull Successors, and Religion as now Established by law amongst us', and praying that 'the Crowne of these Kingdomes, may for ever Continue in the same Royall Lyne'.[27] In April

---

[22] *A true narrative of the reception of their royal highnesses at their arrival in Scotland* (Edinburgh, 1680), p. 2.

[23] Fountainhall, *Historical observations*, p. 19.

[24] For 29 May in England, see Tim Harris, *London crowds in the reign of Charles II: propaganda and politics from the restoration until the exclusion crisis* (Cambridge, 1987), ch. 7; Harris, 'The parties and the people: the press, the crowd and politics "out-of-doors" in restoration England', in Lionel Glassey, ed., *The reigns of Charles II and James II and VII* (Basingstoke, 1997), pp. 125–51.

[25] Luttrell, *Brief historical relation*, I, p. 94; Marguerite Wood and Helen Armet, eds., *Extracts from the records of the borough of Edinburgh 1681 to 1689* (Edinburgh, 1954), pp. 15–16; R. A. Houston, *Social change in the age of enlightenment* (Oxford, 1994), p. 49.

[26] *Loyal Protestant Intelligence*, no. 165, 8 June 1682; no. 166, 10 June 1682. Contrary to the assertion in Houston, *Social change*, p. 292, the evidence of crowd agitation in Edinburgh during the exclusion crisis does point to divisions within the community.

[27] Huntington Library, HA 15010, 27 Apr. 1682, County of Down, Address to the King; National Library of Ireland, MS 11,960, pp. 140–1.

1685 the royal burghs of Scotland congratulated James VII on his
accession to the crown of Scotland, 'to which', they acknowledged,
'your Majesty has right by the unalterable Laws of this your ancient
Kingdom'.[28]

It is not my intention to imply that attitudes in Scotland and Ireland
were shaped solely or even mainly in response to developments that
were perceived to operate on a British level. I am certainly not trying to
posit the existence of something that might be called a British political
animal. There clearly were developments unique to Scotland and
Ireland which helped shape (in important ways) political identities in
those two kingdoms, and these require to be studied in their own right.
British history need not – indeed must not – become a way for historians
to exclude from the agenda those aspects of Scottish and Irish political
life which seem unimportant from a British (or English imperial)
perspective. Having said that, one might question whether there was
such a thing as a Scottish or Irish political animal either. The political
identities of the inhabitants of these kingdoms were never determined
solely by developments within their native realms. Moreover, both
countries were ethnically and religiously divided, and people's political
identities were shaped not only by these divisions, but also by their
alignments with various political and religious groupings in England.

In Scotland, for example, the Lowland, episcopalian Scots, in their
struggle against presbyterian nonconformists, naturally identified themselves with the episcopalian interest south of the border. They also used
the Gaelic Highland clans, many of whom were catholic, in their
campaign to suppress conventiclers in the south-west. The presbyterian
interest in Scotland, by contrast, identified more strongly with fellow
presbyterians and whig politicians south of the border than they did
with their fellow Scots. Their deepest antipathy was reserved for the
'barbarous Highlanders' that were used to suppress their meetings, who
were regarded as no more than a 'host of Savages . . . more terrible than
Turks or Tartars'.[29] In Ireland the situation was even more complicated.
The disempowered catholic majority (comprising at least 75 per cent of
the population) was split between the Anglo-Irish (or Old English), who
had had some success in recovering their lands at the restoration, and
the Gaelic Irish (the larger group) who remained predominantly dispossessed.[30] The protestant minority were divided between the ascendant

---

[28] *London Gazette*, no. 2030, 30 Apr.–4 May 1685.
[29] [Alexander Shields], *The hind let loose* (Edinburgh, 1687), p. 190; EUL, MS La. III,
350, no. 134. There was a long-standing tradition of cooperation across the border with
coreligionists. See Russell, 'Anglo-Scottish union', pp. 243–4.
[30] Bottigheimer, 'Restoration land settlement', pp. 19–21.

episcopalian (church of Ireland) interest and various nonconformist groups. The episcopalians naturally looked to Westminster for support in the maintenance of their position; the presbyterians by contrast, who were strongest in Ulster, felt a closer sense of common identity with their religious brethren in the Scottish south west.[31] The best the catholic Irish could hope for was that the sympathies the royal brothers held for catholics in England might rebound to their advantage, but the reign of James II and the Irish parliament of 1689 seemed to show that the Old English had little sense of common cause with their co-religionists amongst the native Irish.[32]

In short, the religious and political divisions that existed in restoration Britain tended to encourage the formation of cross-national allegiances. We see this most strikingly with regard to the radical fringe. The restoration governments were perpetually concerned – with some justification – that discontented elements in the three kingdoms might combine in an attempt to bring down the monarchy. Colonel Blood's Dublin plot of 1663, which grew out of the dissatisfaction with the liberality shown to Irish catholics by the court of claims in determining the land settlement, was supposed to be the trigger for similar risings in Scotland and England. The Rye House plot of 1683 involved plans for coordinated uprisings not just in various parts of England, but also in Scotland and Ireland. Both Scotland and England actually did rise in rebellion in 1685 following the accession of James II and VII, the former under the earl of Argyll, the latter under the duke of Monmouth, in what was intended to be (although it did not quite work out that way) a joint enterprise.[33] It was in the context of the existence of such cross-national allegiances that one Irish catholic could argue in the late 1660s that 'the true Interest of England (as relating to Ireland) consists in raising the Irish as a Bulwark, or ballance, against our English and Scotch Presbyterians'.[34]

II

Given the fact that Scotland and Ireland were ruled by an absentee king, it is understandable that these two countries should be affected in

---

[31] J. C. Beckett, 'Irish-Scottish relations in the seventeenth century', in his *Confrontations: studies in Irish history* (1972), pp. 26–46; James K. Hewison, *The covenanters* (2 vols., Glasgow, 1908), II, p. 175.

[32] J. G. Simms, *Jacobite Ireland 1685–91* (1969).

[33] For the various radical plots in restoration Britain, see Greaves: *Deliver us from evil*; *Enemies under his feet* and *Secrets of the kingdom*. See also Barnard, 'Scotland and Ireland', pp. 264–5.

[34] [French], *Narrative*, p. 25.

significant ways by developments in England.[35] In order to probe the extent to which there truly was a British dimension to the crisis that developed towards the end of Charles II's reign, we therefore need to return to England (where political developments could potentially have occurred in a greater degree of national isolation), and consider the extent to which events there were shaped by what was going on (or the perception of what was going on) in Charles's other two kingdoms. The remainder of this chapter will focus on the period of the exclusion crisis towards the end of Charles II's reign. Pamphlets, newsletters, speeches and correspondence at this time make it clear that English people were deeply concerned about Scotland and Ireland, and that these concerns shaped the way they reacted to the developing crisis in England.

Let us start by looking at the whigs. No one understood the nature of the British dimension to the crisis that developed in the aftermath of the popish plot more clearly than the earl of Shaftesbury. In a famous speech delivered in the House of Lords on 25 March 1679, Shaftesbury warned his fellow peers that in order to appreciate fully the danger from popery and arbitrary government under the present regime, they only need look at what was going on in Scotland and Ireland. 'Scotland and Ireland', Shaftesbury said, 'are two doors, either to let in good or mischief upon us; they are much weakened by the artifice of our cunning enemies, and we ought to inclose them with boards of cedar.'[36]

With regard to Ireland, Shaftesbury was worried about the security of the protestant establishment in the face of an aggressive catholic challenge: 'the Papists [had] their arms restored', few protestants were 'received to favour', 'the sea-towns, as well as the inland' were 'full of Papists', and the French were ready to invade to lend support to their co-religionists.[37] Shaftesbury's anxieties in this regard were made fully apparent a year later when he revealed to the English Privy Council that he had learned that the catholics in Ireland, with French assistance, were planning to rise in revolt and massacre protestants.[38] This was the 'Irish plot', usually seen as a fabrication by Shaftesbury to keep the political temperature at fever pitch when Oates' 'popish plot' was running out of steam. Yet the alleged Irish plot was nothing new; there had been recurrent reports in the 1660s and 1670s that the catholic powers of Europe, and especially the French, were preparing to make an

---

[35] Barnard, 'Scotland and Ireland', p. 250.
[36] Earl of Shaftesbury, 'Speech on the state of the nation', in William Cobbett, ed., *The parliamentary history of England* (36 vols., 1806–20), IV, cols. 1116–18.
[37] Ibid., col. 1118.
[38] Haley, *Shaftesbury*, pp. 569–99 *passim*, 617–18, 643–61 *passim*.

attempt on Britain through the back door of Ireland.[39] Fear of a foreign catholic invasion of Ireland persisted through the exclusion crisis. In December 1679, Charles II, in response to the demands of his parliament in England, issued a commission of array for raising the militia in Antrim, in order to prevent a foreign invasion and rebellion.[40] In February 1680, a London-based correspondent to the earl of Arran in Dublin reported that 'a great Lord' had told him how 'he much lamented poore Ireland as a Kingdome certainly lost', for 'what if the French should land 20 thousand men, fortifye at Kinsale, and send armes for the Irish?'[41] In early 1681 the whig newspaper, the *True Protestant Mercury*, carried a number of reports of how the protestants in Ireland lived in daily fear of an imminent French invasion.[42]

In addition to the foreign threat, the English were concerned that the protestant ascendancy in Ireland was being endangered by the lenient treatment afforded to catholics there. During the administration of the 'Cabal' (1667–73), Baron Berkeley, who became lord lieutenant of Ireland in 1670, had extended effective toleration to the catholic clergy in Ireland, and had been ordered to admit catholics to commissions of the peace and other minor offices, and to allow all subjects to hold property, engage in trade and be admitted as freemen of corporations.[43] Such moves provoked the English House of Commons to petition Charles II on 25 March 1673, asking him to 'maintain the Act of Settlement', order the catholic clergy to depart, suppress 'all Convents, Seminaries, and publick Popish Schools', dismiss all catholic judges, JPs, and other legal officials and prohibit 'Irish Papists' from being admitted to any of the corporations.[44] Although Charles acceded to these demands, and under Berkeley's successor, the earl of Essex, the protestant ascendancy seemed relatively secure, renewed fears emerged from the late 1670s. The duke of Ormond, who had succeeded Essex as lord lieutenant in 1677, was widely thought to be soft on the Irish catholics, sheltering them and their priests from the rigours of the penal laws.[45] In a debate in parliament on 26 October 1680 on the means of suppressing popery and preventing a popish successor, Sir Henry Capel complained about the dispensations given to catholics in Ireland to

---

[39] [French], *Narrative of the settlement*, p. 27; Connolly, *Religion, law and power*, p. 28; Huntington Library, HA 15394, information of John Moyre, 27 Dec. 1676.

[40] Huntington Library, HA 14176, Charles II to Lord Conway and others, 2 Dec. 1679.

[41] Bod., MS Carte 39, f. 107.

[42] *True Protestant Mercury*, no. 7, 15–18 Jan. 1680/1; no. 12, 1–5 Feb., 1680/1.

[43] Connolly, *Religion, law and power*, p. 21.

[44] *Commons Journal*, IX, pp. 276–7; Huntington Library, Hastings Parliament Box 4, no. 4; Grey, *Debates*, II, pp. 159–61.

[45] F. L., *Ireland's sad lamentation* [1681].

permit them to wear arms and live in corporations, a frightening prospect, Capel thought, since 'in Ireland, the Papists are at least five to one in number to the Protestants, and may probably derive from their cradle an inclination to massacre them again'.[46] When this second exclusion parliament was prorogued in January 1681, one English newspaper carried a report from Dublin of how 'The Papists here are much elevated at the News . . . insomuch that they Hector about the streets with Swords and other Arms: so that the Protestants even in this City are sensibly afraid, that they will execute some desperate Design upon them.'[47]

If the concern about Ireland was over the threat of popery, with regard to Scotland it was more about the threat of arbitrary government. As Shaftesbury pointed out in his speech of March 1679, 'slavery' was being introduced north of the border as a way of making room for 'popery'.[48] Attention was focused in particular on the policies of the duke of Lauderdale, Charles's secretary of state for Scotland from 1660 to 1680. Lauderdale had already been attacked by the House of Commons in April 1675 for seeking to promote 'an arbitrary form of government over us'. In part the Commons were worried about Lauderdale's support for Charles' English declaration of indulgence of 1672, which he had said ought to be obeyed because the king's edicts were 'equal with laws'. Yet they were also alarmed that Lauderdale had been able to establish a military force of some 20,000 foot and 2,000 horse north of the border, which was 'to be in a rediness to march into any part of this kingdom, for any service' wherein the king's 'honour or greatness may be concerned', creating the fear that an army from Scotland might be used to suppress political dissent in England.[49] Lauderdale was again attacked in the Commons in May 1679 for promoting 'arbitrary and destructive counsels, tending to the subversion of the Rights, Liberties and Properties of your subjects, and the alteration of the Protestant Religion established'.[50] He had dissolved the Scottish parliament in 1673, raised a sizeable standing army, and packed all judicatures so that 'Justice and Equity' was 'Administered according to his Pleasure'. On top of this, he was guilty of promoting

---

[46] *Parliamentary history*, IV, cols. 1166–7; J. S. Clarke, ed., *Life of James II* (2 vols., 1816), I, p. 602.

[47] *True Protestant Mercury*, no. 11, 29 Jan.–1 Feb. 1680/1.

[48] Shaftesbury, 'Speech on the state of the nation', col. 1116.

[49] *Parliamentary history*, IV, cols. 683–8; Grey, *Debates*, III, pp. 28–9; *A true and perfect collection of all messages, addresses etc. from the House of Commons, to the kings most excellent majestie, with his majesties gracious answers thereunto* (1680), pp. 25–6.

[50] *Parliamentary history*, IV, col. 1130; *True and perfect collection of all messages, addresses etc. from the House of Commons*, p. 48; Grey, *Debates*, VII, pp. 188–9.

popery. In 1669, having learned that the duke of York had changed his religion, he had procured an act in Scotland asserting the king's supremacy, placing the regulation of all ecclesiastical affairs 'absolutely in the King's Power', establishing the king essentially as a pope in his northern kingdom, and making it easier – it was alleged – for popery eventually to be brought in. In addition, he had specifically exempted catholics from the 1670 act against withdrawers from public worship, given papists in Scotland positions of command within the newly raised army, kept a correspondence with papists and priests, and accepted a pension from the French king.[51]

The most serious concern of the English opposition about the situation in Scotland related to the treatment of the presbyterians. With the re-establishment of episcopalianism north of the border at the restoration, a savage penal code had been enacted to deal with religious dissenters: harsh fines were imposed on those who attended nonconformist conventicles, some suffered transportation to places as dreadful as Barbados or New Jersey, whilst under an act of 1670 ministers who preached at field conventicles were punishable by death. Bonds were extracted from heritors and landlords for the allegiance of their tenantry, oaths of allegiance were imposed, and judicial torture was even employed in some proceedings against conventiclers. From 1663 the army began to be used to carry out arrests and impose fines, with troops being billeted, at free quarter, on those families who either would not or could not pay the excessive charges often levied. One contemporary complained how the presbyterians of the south-west were 'quartered upon till they be eaten up' and 'their goods . . . distrained and sold for a trifle', further alleging that the soldiers 'beat the poor people', bound and wounded them, and violently dragged them either to church or prison.[52] Lauderdale came to feel that this policy was counterproductive when the south-west rose in rebellion, largely against this military regime, in November 1666. Yet in 1678, when fears emerged again that this area was likely to rise in revolt, Lauderdale decided to repeat the tactic, and this time sent in the 'Highland Host'. One contemporary complained that they were quartered, free, 'in great numbers', that they 'cruellie abused the poor people when they had not satisfied them beyond their ability . . . killed and destroyed more bestiall

[51] *Some farther matter of fact relating to the administration of affairs in Scotland under the duke of Lauderdale* [1679]; *Some particular matter of fact, relating to the administration of affairs in Scotland under the duke of Lauderdale* [1679].
[52] James Kirkton, *The secret and true history of the church of Scotland from the restoration to the year 1678* (Edinburgh, 1817), p. 200; Cowan, *Scottish covenanters*, pp. 58–63; Hutton, *Charles II*, p. 225. Cf. HMC, *Laing*, p. 359; *Brief and true account of the sufferings of the church of Scotland* (1690), pp. 3–4.

then they needed for meat', and that they 'robbed on all roads', stripping people of clothes, shoes and money, 'wounding any who in the least refused to give what they had'.[53] Shaftesbury was to make the same complaint in the Lords in March 1679, protesting how the authorities in Scotland 'have lately plundered, and harrassed the richest and wealthiest counties of that kingdom, and brought down the barbarous Highlanders to devour them'.[54]

Developments in Ireland and Scotland, then, help us understand the intensity of the whig concern about the threat of 'popery and arbitrary government'. It was not a question of what might happen, one day, should the duke of York become king and rule in the tyrannical way that whiggish protestants expected from a catholic; the problem was already there, in England's own back yard (or back yards), and all the signs were that England was going the same way. In early January 1681, the Lords declared that they were 'fully satisfied' that 'for divers years . . . there hath been a horrid and treasonable Plot and Conspiracy, contrived and carried on by those of the Popish Religion in Ireland, for massacring the English, and subverting the Protestant Religion, and the ancient established Government of that Kingdom'. In the lower house Sir Henry Capel said that although some people 'smiled at' the popish plot in England, 'it is plain there was a Plot in Ireland', and 'the hopes of a Popish Successor' were 'the Grounds of all this'.[55] Sir Francis Winnington, in a debate in the House of Commons on 6 May 1679, maintained that 'Arbitrary power is the more ready to be exercised here, for being begun in Scotland.' That same day, Colonel Birch concluded that 'If there be any arbitrary power in the World, it is in Scotland.'[56] For many, indeed, it became particularly worrying that Charles, in order to save his brother from the attacks of the English opposition, chose to send the duke of York to head the government in Scotland during the exclusion crisis. In a speech made in the Lords following the rejection of the second exclusion bill in November 1680, Shaftesbury asked: 'In the mean while where's this Duke? . . . Why, he is in Scotland raising of Forces upon the Terra firma, that can enter dry foot upon us.'[57] Similar fears can be detected beyond parliament. Earlier that autumn one man had allegedly said that 'he believed it would not be long before the Duke came with an army out of Scotland to cut all the throats of the true

[53] Longleat House, Coventry MSS, XVI, f. 205. Cf. *A declaration of the rebels now in arms in the west of Scotland* [Edinburgh, 1679], p. 2; [John Gordon], *Plain dealing: being a moderate general review of the Scots prelatical clergies proceedings in the latter reigns* (1689), p. 11; Kirkton, *Secret and true history*, pp. 382–90; [Shields], *Hind let loose*, pp. 190–1.
[54] Shaftesbury, 'Speech on the state of the nation', col. 1118.
[55] Grey, *Debates*, VIII, pp. 251–2.   [56] Ibid., VII, pp. 194–5.
[57] [Earl of Shaftesbury], *A speech lately made by a noble peer of the realm* (1681).

Protestants and fire their houses and beat their children's brains out before their faces'.[58] We can find the same sentiments being expressed in Scotland, in language which confirms that people were thinking about these issues in British terms. For example, in early August 1680 a ship captain was sentenced to death for having said that the duke of York 'was on the Popish plot of taking away the King's life, and over-turning our religion and government; and that he was to consent to the bringing over the French king with an army into Britain; and that he had come himselfe to Scotland to make a Popish faction there'.[59]

III

So far we have been looking at the whig view. Those who had cavalier-anglican leanings were likely to see developments in Ireland and Scotland very differently. Let us now turn, therefore, to a consideration of how the British perspective helps us understand the tory opposition to the whig position and why they supported the catholic succession.

Opponents of exclusion were quick to point out that barring the duke of York from the succession to the English throne would create serious problems for a multiple kingdom. The English parliament had no right to determine the succession for Scotland or Ireland, and if the thrones of the three British kingdoms became separated, civil war was bound to follow. During the debates on the first exclusion bill in May 1679, supporters of the duke of York repeatedly insisted on 'the great prob-ability that Scotland, one of the antientest Monarchys in the world, would never joyn in changeing the Succession' but 'would catch at such an occasion to separate again from England'.[60] When the second exclusion bill was discussed in the Commons on 2 November 1680, Edward Seymour said: 'it cannot be imagined, that such a law will bind all here in England, or any in Scotland; and it is disputed whether it will be binding in Ireland: so that in all probability it will not only divide us amongst ourselves, but the three kingdoms one from the other, and occasion a miserable civil war'.[61] On 15 November, the earl of Halifax gave strong, pragmatic reasons in the debate in the Lords as to why

---

[58] *CSPD, 1682*, p. 506.

[59] Sir John Lauder of Fountainhall, *The decisions of the Lords of the Council and Session from June 6th, 1678, to July 30th, 1713* (2 vols., Edinburgh, 1759–61), I, p. 108. By 'Britain' the captain seems to have meant Ireland as well, since the rumours at this time were that the French would invade through Ireland. Fountainhall says the offence did not merit the death penalty, but 'this was done to fright England', the judges acting in the knowledge that the king was intending to convert the sentence to banishment.

[60] Clarke, ed., *Life of James II*, I, p. 550.

[61] *Parliamentary History*, IV, cols. 1185–6; Grey, *Debates*, VII, p. 408; Clarke, ed., *Life of James II*, I, p. 606.

exclusion was unfeasible: 'how imprudent it would be to declare the Duke an enemy to the State', he urged, when York 'was actually at the head of a powerfull Nation [Scotland], where there was an Army too', and when 'his power was no less considerable' in Ireland, 'where there was 10, or 15 Papists for one Protestant'.[62]

The British dimension further helps us to understand how the tories were able to construct their case against the whigs. As we have recently come to understand, tory propagandists sought to turn public opinion against the exclusionists by representing the whigs as republicans and nonconformists (in particular, presbyterians), who were bent on destroying the monarchy and the established church.[63] Within a purely English context, we may wonder how plausible such arguments might have seemed. Although there was a radical fringe within the English opposition movement, many English whigs were committed to preserving strong – albeit protestant – monarchy in England, and most nonconformists were moderate and peaceful (especially the presbyterians). The tories, of course, played on the public memory of the 1640s and 1650s, drawing parallels between the tactics of the parliamentary opposition to Charles II and that to Charles I, and warning that if the whigs were not stopped England was likely to travel down the same road again. Nevertheless, within a purely English context, there was little in terms of present political developments (at least before the revelations of the Rye House plot of 1683) to lend credence to such charges of political and religious extremism.

Yet the tories were not thinking in purely English terms; their propaganda makes more sense, and their arguments appear more powerful, when we recognise that they were thinking in British terms. In Scotland there did exist a radical strand of presbyterianism which continued to cause problems for the restoration regime throughout the 1660s, 1670s and 1680s (even if this radicalism was in part created by the stern measures the authorities took to try to suppress dissent). The field conventiclers in the south-west, in order to protect themselves against the actions of the military, began to arm themselves in the 1660s. On two occasions they actually rose in armed rebellion – in 1666 (Pentland Hills) and 1679 (Bothwell Bridge). In 1668 the covenanting minister James Mitchell and some associates hatched an unsuccessful plot to assassinate the archbishop of St Andrews, Dr Sharp, a leading advocate of the policy of repression; in 1679, shortly before Bothwell Bridge, Sharp actually was murdered by some radical covenanters. Nor

---

[62] Clarke, ed., *Life of James II*, I, p. 621.
[63] Harris, *London crowds*, ch. 6; Tim Harris, *Politics under the later Stuarts: party conflict in a divided society 1660–1715* (1993), pp. 94–102.

was this purely a Scottish problem; the south-west had close ties with Ulster, and there were continuing reports that presbyterians in Scotland were conspiring with their brethren in Ireland against the state.[64]

The radicals may not have been typical of Scottish presbyterianism as a whole, but the challenge they represented to the authorities was real enough, and the government was particularly concerned that it might lose control over the south-west corner of Scotland. After Bothwell Bridge a small, but highly aggressive, group of radical covenanters, the Cameronians, continued the campaign of subversive, political activism. In a manifesto posted at Sanquhar (Dumfriesshire), on 22 June 1680, they declared war on Charles II, condemning his 'Usurpation in Church-matters' and 'Tyranny in matters Civil', and maintaining that he had 'forfaulted' any right to the crown of Scotland. They further stated that they disowned the duke of York, that 'profest Papist', and protested 'against his succeeding to the Crown'.[65] In September of that year, at a great conventicle at Torwood in Stirlingshire, they excommunicated the king, and on 12 January 1682 they issued another declaration at Lanark, offering further reasons for their revolt from the government of Charles II and and explaining why they were endeavouring to extricate themselves 'from under a tyrants yocke'.[66]

The tory press frequently highlighted the danger posed by the radical presbyterians north of the border, and in that way sought to taint the English nonconformists by association. Hence, of course, why the English opposition came to be nicknamed 'whigs'. In a lengthy tract published in 1678, Roger L'Estrange compared 'the Platform of the Scottish Presbytery' with the position of the English presbyterians, in order 'to observe the Harmony betwixt Simeon and Levi; Their Consistorians, and Ours, in the Frame, and Scope of their Discipline'.[67] Significantly, L'Estrange accused the presbyterians of popery – as the 'popish' if not the catholic other – because they argued that ungodly kings could be deposed, and because of their alleged pretensions to absolute power and belief in their own infallibility.[68] Another pamphleteer, writing shortly after the dissolution of the Oxford parliament specifically against the tactics of the English whigs, posed the question

---

[64] The activities of the Scottish presbyterians between 1660 and 1688 can be traced in Cowan, *Scottish covenanters.*

[65] *A true and exact copy of a treasonable and bloody-paper, called, the fanaticks new-covenant* (Edinburgh, 1680), pp. 10–11; Dickinson and Donaldson, eds., *Source book,* III, pp. 177–9; *Edinburgh Gazette,* no. 2, 7–14 Dec. 1680.

[66] EUL, MS La. II, 89, no. 103, quote on f. 138; MS La. III, 344 I., no. 234; MS La. III, 350, no. 33; [Shields], *Hind let loose,* pp. 131–9, 143; *CSPD, 1682,* p. 39.

[67] Roger L'Estrange, *Tyranny and popery lording it over the consciences, lives, liberties and estates both of king and people* (1678), quote on p. 4.

[68] Ibid., pp. 23–4, 90–1.

whether the fanatics were the only persons truly zealous for the preservation of the present government: in Charles I's time, he asserted,
they had made 'the whole Kingdom a Bloody Theatre', and asking what
signs they had since given of their repentance for committing 'such
hellish Tragedies', replied, 'No other than that they have drawn the
Sword in Scotland.'[69] John Northleigh thought that Shaftesbury's
alleged plan for a protestant association to guard against a catholic
succession paralleled the Scottish covenant of 1643: 'Now there remains
nothing to do', he sarcastically remarked, 'but to drive the King out of
his Palace, Proclaim all his followers Delinquents; all his adherents
Enemies to King and Countrey; send post to Scotland, Messengers to
the Field-Conventicles, get another Army from the North, swallow a
second Solemn League; and then we shall have exactly a second 43.'[70]
Tory newspapers found there was much mileage simply in reporting the
activities of the radical covenanters north of the border. To give just one
example, in March 1682 Nathaniel Thompson published an account of
how about twenty fanatics in Lanark 'fell upon' a soldier whilst his party
were away getting provisions: 'having seized him', they 'first cut off his
Nose, Ears, and Privities, then pull'd out his Eyes and Tongue; and
having cut off every Finger and Toe one after another, left him in that
miserable condition, that he might be the longer dying, and then fled'.[71]

The political views of the radical covenanters raised questions about
their moral principles. In a tract condemning resistance theory, one
author complained that the Scots had been 'unhappily brought into
such a corruption of Morals, as has not been hitherto known among
Christians', for 'Are not Assassinations taught, as well as practis'd
among us?'[72] From here it was but a short step to a more wide-ranging
condemnation of the alleged social and moral principles of the Scottish
presbyterians. Some of the attacks on the radical sectarians in Scotland
bear a close resemblance to the anti-ranter literature in England in the
early 1650s. In a humorous tract of 1682, set as a dialogue between
'Anonymous' and 'Antipraelatus', the former reported that the covenanters in Scotland were complaining about how they were 'hunted from
their last and safest refuge, the Bed-chambers and Closets of . . .
Ladies', where they had 'oftimes given proof of their Manhood'.

---

[69] *A vindication of addresses in general, and of the middle-temple address and proceedings in particular* (1681), p. 7.

[70] [John Northleigh], *The parallel; or, the new specious association* (1682), pp. 5, 13.

[71] *Loyal Protestant Intelligence*, no. 128, 14 Mar. 1681/2. An account of this attack also appears in a manuscript London newsletter dated 11 Mar. 1682: *CSPD, 1682*, pp. 118–19.

[72] [J. Crauford], *A serious expostulation with that party in Scotland, commonly known by the name of whigs* (1682), p. 4.

Anonymous further maintained that he could give 'many instances' of sexual licentiousness: 'Yea Buggery, Bestiality, incest, Adultery.'[73] George Hickes's account of the covenanting preacher, James Mitchell, who was eventually executed in January 1678 for his part in the assassination plot against Archbishop Sharp, carried similar accusations, and even referred to the covenanters as 'Filthy, Cruel, Lying Ranters'. Hickes also discussed Mitchell's associate, Major Weir, who was indicted on 9 April 1670 on charges of incest, adultery and bestiality (with a mare and cow). Weir, who confessed to the charges, was sentenced to be strangled at the stake and his body burned. At his execution, Hickes tells us, 'the Body of this Unclean Beast gave manifest tokens of its impurity, by the erection of his Yard, and emission of Seed, as soon as it began to be heated by the Flames'.[74]

A British perspective can help us appreciate another seeming mystery, namely why the English tories believed the church of England would be safe under a catholic successor. Their faith in the duke of York in this respect appears naive with the vantage of hindsight, since as soon as York became king he did seek to break the anglican monopoly of worship and education. It is not necessary to assume that their belief in divine right and non-resistance, coupled with their implacable hostility towards the English whigs and nonconformists, led them to suspend their critical faculties when it came to assessing the reliability of the duke of York. Rather, tories and anglicans made an informed judgement based on the way the duke of York had behaved in the past. For two periods during the exclusion crisis – from November 1679 to February 1680, and again from October 1680 to March 1682 – York headed the royal administration in Scotland, where he had been sent by his brother to keep him out of the way whilst the crisis over the succession unfolded in England. York's hatred of the Scottish presbyterians led him to form a firm alliance with the episcopalian interest north of the border and to support a stern policy of repression. The Scottish bishops were duly impressed by York's efforts on their behalf, and repeatedly wrote to the English archbishop of Canterbury, William Sancroft, and his episcopal brethren, to tell them of this fact. Thus, in February 1680, shortly after

---

[73] *A letter from Scotland, with observations upon the anti-erastian, anti-praelatical, and phanatical presbyterian party there: by way of a dialogue between anonymous and antipraelatus* (1682).

[74] [George Hickes], *Ravillac redivivus: being a narrative of the late tryal of Mr James Mitchell a conventicle-preacher* (1678; 2nd edn, 1682), esp. pp. 35–44. See [Gilbert Crockart], *The Scotch presbyterian eloquence; or, the foolishness of their teaching discovered* (1692; 2nd edn, 1694), for a post-revolution attack on the sexual immorality of the Scottish presbyterians. Despite his crimes, Weir, who had lived in Edinburgh for many years prior to his trial and execution, 'had the reputation of being pious, devoted and strict in his way of life': Houston, *Social change*, pp. 161–2.

the end of York's first stay in Scotland, the Scottish bishops sent an 'Encyclical Letter' to the English bishops, asking them to 'assure his Royall Highness, that we are exceeding sensible of the infinite obligations we owe him for the great encouragement we received by his Highness gracious countenancing and assisting us in all our concerns while he was in this kingdome'.[75] In March 1682, on York's subsequent return to England, the Scottish bishops sent Sancroft another letter (which was also published separately and printed in the newspaper press) in which they told him 'what great Benefit the Church there hath received by the presence of His Royal Highness, who hath been a great Repairer of their Breaches, and put a stop to the growth of Schism . . . And that he did both privately and publickly demonstrate his Zeal to the Church of England.'[76] More generally, York's conduct in Scotland was held up as indicative of what an excellent ruler he would be if he came to the throne of England. As a tract of 1682 entitled *A plea for the succession* put it: 'View Him in His Conduct; and He hath, like a cheering Sun, thaw'd the Northern World, and overcome the Scottish Nation; not with Arms, but with Love, and Wisdom; where He is now become, next His Majesty, the Pride, and Darling of the Age.'[77]

IV

Before turning to conclusions, it would be wise to issue some caveats. This chapter is not arguing for the need to replace the national histories of the three British kingdoms by a sort of supra-British history. There were many developments in Ireland and Scotland in the restoration period that are best explored within their specific Irish and Scottish contexts – that would also be true of certain aspects of the various economic, political and religious issues explored here. It would be the worst sort of English imperialism to advocate the study of Scottish and Irish history purely through an English lens, or to suggest that the issues of Scottish and Irish history to be prioritised in our research should be those that were of concern to contemporaries in England. Likewise, it would be misleading to imply that every aspect of the exclusion crisis in England is best understood when set in a British context. Many publications from this time did not discuss developments in Ireland and Scotland, but instead focused solely on England: on what was happening

---

[75] Clarke, ed., *Collection of letters . . . to Sancroft*, pp. 8–9.
[76] *Loyal Protestant Intelligence*, no. 132, 23 March 1681/2; *The copy of a letter from Scotland, to his grace the lord archbishop of Canterbury* (Edinburgh, 1682); Fountainhall, *Historical observations*, p. 63.
[77] *A plea for succession in opposition to popular exclusion* (1682), p. 2.

there under the present king and what might happen should a popish successor inherit the English crown. When English publicists looked beyond their own kingdom, it was frequently to express alarm about developments on the continent, especially in France under Louis XIV. In exploring the Scottish and Irish dimensions to the exclusion crisis, we must not fall into the trap of arguing that Scotland and Ireland were the be-all and end-all, or lose sight of the fact that there were many, vitally important non-Scottish, non-Irish, and non-British dimensions to that crisis.

With this in mind, however, we need to recognise that there were important interactions between the three kingdoms which call for analysis on a British level. Many of the problems that developed in restoration Ireland and Scotland stemmed from the unsatisfactory nature of their respective restoration settlements in land and religion, settlements which were themselves attempts by a monarch recently restored to his three British crowns to resolve issues and conflicts that had emerged out of the British crisis that had precipitated the civil war. Moreover, whether in the area of economics, religion or politics, we have seen that there were crucial respects in which policies pursued and decisions taken in England had a vital impact on developments on Charles II's other two kingdoms. Many of these issues – the nature of the colonial relationship between Ireland and England, the question of the former's economic dependency upon the latter, the issue of catholic landownership, freedom of religion, and the nature of the religious establishment in Scotland and whether it could be different from that in England and Ireland – were to come to a head in the political crisis that emerged at the end of James II's reign, provoking a revolutionary upheaval which (in the Scottish and Irish contexts) can be described as neither 'bloodless' nor 'glorious'. Similarly, the attitudes of the English to the developing political crisis in England during Charles II's reign were conditioned in significant respects by an understanding of what was going on in Ireland and Scotland. When the whigs invoked fears about the threat of popery and arbitrary government, they were thinking in British terms; the danger seemed so imminent precisely because of what the royal brothers were up to in the other Stuart kingdoms. Yet the British dimension also enables us to understand how the tories were able to construct their case against the whigs and rally public opinion behind the crown. To bring home the threat posed by the whigs and their nonconformist allies they needed a bogey man, and that bogey man was provided by Scotland. It should also be apparent from what has been argued here that the quest for a British history need not be elitist. Indeed, much of this chapter has been concerned not with the ruling elite, but with how a wider population responded to political developments in Charles II's three kingdoms.

The ability of the English tories to exploit the Scottish situation to the advantage of the crown points to a further consideration. Existing scholarship on the British problem in the seventeenth century, by dint of the fact that it has been geared primarily towards explaining the crisis that emerged in the 1640s and 1650s, has tended to create the impression that the system of multiple kingdoms as it existed under the Stuarts was inherently unstable: hence (it might be inferred) the need for further revolutions in 1688–91, and for the redefinition of the political relationship between England and Scotland in 1707.[78] Yet multiple kingdoms could work to the advantage of a monarch, especially if he were skilful enough to play one off against another. Sir George Mackenzie, who was to become Charles II's Scottish lord advocate, realised this. This was why he opposed a proposed union between Scotland and England in 1669, believing it would be destructive to the king's interest. As he later recalled: 'whilst the Kingdoms stood divided, his Majesty had two Parliaments, whereof the one might always be exemplary to the other, and might, by loyal emulation, excite one another to an entire obedience; and, if either should invade the royal prerogative, or oppose unjustly their Prince's just commands, the one might prove a curb to the other's insolence'.[79]

Charles II was able to do exactly this in 1681: he dissolved the whig-dominated Oxford parliament in March, and called one in Scotland that summer, which was quick to prove its loyalty by passing an act making it 'high treason . . . to endeavour the alteration, suspension, or diversion of the said right of Succession, or the debarring the next laufull Successor'.[80] It is difficult to imagine how Charles II could have made a more effective political statement to the English whigs, warning them of the futility of pursuing exclusion. In fact, by the end of Charles II's reign, the situation of the British monarchy in all three kingdoms was relatively secure: the opposition challenge had been effectively overcome (the rebellions of Argyll and Monmouth in 1685 did not cause any series problems for the Stuart regime); the authority of the crown in both England and Scotland had been significantly bolstered; and in Ireland, the ascendant protestant interest was busy pledging its loyalty in a series of addresses (only amongst the presbyterians in the north can any disaffection be detected), whereas the catholic interest realised that its

---

[78] But see Russell, 'Anglo-Scottish union', for a refreshing counter-perspective.
[79] Sir George Mackenzie, *Memoirs of the affairs of Scotland, from the restoration of King Charles II*, ed. T. Thomson (Edinburgh, 1821), pp. 138–9.
[80] Dickinson and Donaldson, eds., *Source book*, III, pp. 185–6.

best hopes lay in supporting a royal administration that was committed to defending the succession of a catholic to the throne. That the situation was to change so dramatically in just three short years under James II and VII is more testimony to the failings of his own kingship than it is to the difficulties inherent in the management of the three British kingdoms in the later seventeenth century.

What all this reveals about national identities at this time, however, is somewhat complex. We have seen that political identities (whether in England, Scotland or Ireland) were shaped by an awareness of what was going on in Charles II's other kingdoms as a result of Charles II's style of government. Indeed, we can even detect the formation of cross-national political allegiances. Yet whilst it might be legitimate to talk about the existence of a British political awareness, we do not see the emergence of a British identity. This was partly because there was no integrated British state yet, which meant that the political identities of the English, Scots and Irish were also in significant respects shaped by developments which were unique to their own kingdoms and did not operate at a British level. It was also because Britain as a whole – like England – was a politically divided society. There was no unifying ideology that could bind the different peoples who inhabited the British realms together; neither protestantism nor anti-popery yet served this function. Some British protestants feared the foreign, catholic other and 'un-English' styles of absolutist rule: for them, a catholic successor would rule like Louis XIV in France, whilst what was going on in Ireland and Scotland confirmed that the Stuarts were bent on establishing popery and arbitrary government. Others, by contrast, defended a popish successor because they feared a greater threat to the security of the protestant church and state was posed by the exclusionists and their protestant nonconformist allies throughout the three kingdoms, who had learned their king-killing principles from the papists. The implications of this are worth pondering. When searching for the emergence of a British national identity in the eighteenth century, we cannot take a common sense of protestantism and shared antipathy towards catholicism for granted; we have to explain how these were transformed into unifying forces, something which they had certainly not been under the later Stuarts.

7   The bible and national identity in the British Isles, *c.* 1650–*c.* 1750

Scott Mandelbrote

[I]t can't be reasonably doubted, but the true Old *Britains,* or *Welch,* are Descendants of *Gomer.* And since it has been also observ'd above, that the *Germans* were likely Descendants of *Gomer,* particularly the *Cimbri,* to whom the *Saxons,* especially the *Angles* were near Neighbours: hence it follows, that our Ancestors likewise, who succeeded the Old *Britains* in these Parts of this Isle, were descended of the same son of *Japhet.*[1]

When they referred to the British church, English writers of the late seventeenth century did not mean their own church, the church of England, but rather the first Christian church ever to have been established in the British Isles. They believed that this church had been founded long before the Roman empire was converted to Christianity, and hundreds of years before St Augustine of Canterbury brought the Saxon invaders of Britain under the wing of a papacy which, they thought, had already been corrupted by that time.[2] For these authors, primitive Celtic, British Christianity was the original fire from which the torch of true religion, that was later kept burning by so-called heretics like John Wycliffe, had been lit. This was the historical true and apostolic church which propagandists of the English reformation, like John Foxe or John Beale, had claimed justified their assertion of

---

I wish to record my gratitude to the staff of the archives and libraries from whose holdings I have cited, and, in particular, to Muriel McCarthy and the late Gordon Huelin. I would also like to thank Ray Gillespie and Giles Mandelbrote, who provided helpful references; Clare Griffiths and Colin Kidd, for their encouragement and advice; and Rees Davies, for helping me with texts in Welsh.

[1] Edward Wells, *An historical geography of the old testament* (3 vols., 1721 [1st. 1711–12]), I, p. 131.

[2] William Camden, *Britannia*, ed. Edmund Gibson (2 vols., 1753 [1st. 1695]), I, cols. lxxxiii–v; John Inett, *Origines Anglicanae* (1704), p. 4; William Lloyd, *An historical account of church-government* (1684); Edward Stillingfleet, *Origines Britannicae* (new edn, 1840 [1st, 1685]); James Ussher, *Britannicarum ecclesiarum antiquitates* (Dublin, 1639); cf. Hugh Trevor-Roper, *Catholics, anglicans and puritans* (1987), pp. 144–9; Glanmor Williams, 'Some protestant views of early British church history', in his *Welsh reformation essays* (Cardiff, 1967), pp. 207–19.

157

independence from and superiority to Rome.[3] Thus, at the end of the seventeenth century, both Edward Stillingfleet, in his *Origines Britannicae*, and Edmund Gibson, in the new edition of William Camden's *Britannia* whose preparation he supervised, maintained that the Britons were converted to Christianity by St Paul.[4] Moreover, they discussed the opinion that the druids, the priests of the original inhabitants of the British Isles, had prepared the way for this conversion by maintaining belief in one god.[5] Other arguments for the antiquity and independence of England and its church drew on Geoffrey of Monmouth's account of the descent of the Britons from Trojan exiles, or stressed the independent, and almost protestant, stance of the Anglo-Saxon church, and its descent from an indigenous ecclesiastical tradition.[6] Aylett Sammes, in his *Britannia antiqua illustrata* of 1676, preferred a Phoenician origin for

[3] Katharine R. Firth, *The apocalyptic tradition in reformation Britain, 1530–1645* (Oxford, 1979), pp. 32–110; John Lewis, *The history of the life and sufferings of the reverend and learned John Wicliffe, D. D.* (1720); Margaret Aston, 'John Wycliffe's reformation reputation', in her *Lollards and reformers* (1984), pp. 243–71; cf. [Matthew Parker], *De antiquitate Britannicae ecclesiae* (Hanau, 1605 [1st. 1572]); May McKisack, *Medieval history in the Tudor age* (Oxford, 1971), pp. 1–49; see Anthony Milton, *Catholic and reformed* (Cambridge, 1995), pp. 270–321 for alternative views of church history.

[4] Stillingfleet, *Origines Britannicae*, pp. 38–49; Camden, *Britannia*, I, col. lxxxiii; on Gibson's editorship of Camden, see Stan A. E. Mendyk, *'Speculum Britanniae': regional study, antiquarianism, and science in Britain to 1700* (Toronto, 1989), pp. 212–28; Graham Parry, *The trophies of time: English antiquarians of the seventeenth century* (Oxford, 1995), pp. 331–57; Stuart Piggott, *Ruins in a landscape* (Edinburgh, 1976), pp. 33–53; cf. Richard Broughton, *A true memorial of the ancient, most holy and religious state of Great Britain* (n.p., 1650), a catholic work arguing for the original conversion of the British Isles by St Peter.

[5] Stillingfleet, *Origines Britannicae*, p. 58, which is, however, critical of Camden and others who cited Origen's testimony for druids' monotheistic practices; cf. Camden, *Britannia*, I, col. lxxxiv; Henry Rowlands, *Mona antiqua restaurata* (1766 [1st. 1723]), pp. 39–53; William Stukeley, *Stonehenge: a temple restor'd to the British druids* (1740), p. 2; Stukeley, *Abury: a temple of the British druids* (1743); A. L. Owen, *The famous druids* (Oxford, 1962), pp. 39–63. John Woodward, amongst others, ridiculed this high opinion of the druids, Bod., MS Ashmole 1817B, fs. 365–8.

[6] For example, William L'Isle, *Divers ancient monuments in the Saxon tongue* (1638 [1st. 1623]); Edward Thwaites, ed., *Heptateuchus, liber Job, et evangelium Nicodemi; Anglo-Saxonice* (Oxford, 1698); Elizabeth Elstob, *An English-Saxon homily on the birth-day of St Gregory* (1709); Aelfric *[The English Saxon homilies]*, ed. Elstob ([Oxford], ?1715); J. A. W. Bennett, 'The history of Old English and Old Norse studies in England from the time of Francis Junius till the end of the eighteenth century' (D.Phil thesis, Oxford, 1938), pp. 3–9; David C. Douglas, *English scholars* (1939), pp. 60–92; for Geoffrey, see *The historia regum Britanniae of Geoffrey of Monmouth*, ed. Acton Griscom (1929); *The British history, translated into English from the Latin of Jeffrey of Monmouth*, ed. and trans. Aaron Thompson (London, 1718); Camden, *Britannia*, I, cols. vi–x; Caradoc, *The history of Wales*, ed. William Wynne (1774 [1st. 1697]), Preface; Daniel Langhorne, *An introduction to the history of England* (1676), pp. 5–12; Robert Sheringham, *De Anglorum gentis origine disceptatio* (Cambridge, 1670), pp. 7–22; T. D. Kendrick, *British antiquity* (1950), pp. 101–2; Nicholas von Maltzahn, *Milton's* History of Britain: *republican historiography in the English revolution* (Oxford, 1991), pp. 91–117.

the British and their religion.[7] But the tradition which carried the manners and religion of the first inhabitants of the British Isles back closest to the original, pure religion of humanity was that sponsored both by Camden himself, and in a marginally different version which placed the Saxons in a better light, by the catholic apologist Richard Verstegen, whose *A restitution of decayed intelligence in antiquities* was reprinted frequently during the seventeenth century.[8]

According to this version of events, the British or Cymri were the direct descendants of Gomer, one of the children of Japhet, to whose progeny the Isles of the Gentiles had been promised when the earth was repeopled by the sons of Noah following the biblical flood.[9] A number of Welsh authors, such as Charles Edwards in the 1670s or Griffith Jones in the 1740s, stressed the supposed affinity of their language, which had descended from the tongue spoken by the original Britons who had taken sanctuary from Roman and barbarian invaders in the Welsh mountains, to the true speech of the ancient Hebrews.[10] They

---

[7] Aylett Sammes, *Britannia antiqua illustrata* (1676), pp. 38–73; on Sammes, see Parry, *Trophies of time*, pp. 308–24; cf. Samuel Bochart, *Geographia sacra* (Caen, 1646); Edmund Dickinson, *Delphi Phoenicizantes* (Oxford, 1655); and Theophilus Gale, *The court of the Gentiles* (2nd edn, 2 vols., Oxford, 1672–8), I, pp. 47–8.

[8] Camden, *Britannia*, I, cols. ii–v; R[ichard] V[erstegen] (or Rowlands), *A restitution of decayed intelligence in antiquities* (1655 [1st,1605]), pp. 1–43; there were at least six editions of this work published between 1605 and 1673. Cf. Parry, *Trophies of time*, pp. 49–69; Samuel Kliger, *The Goths in England* (New York, 1972 [1st. 1952]), pp. 115–19; Ethel Seaton, *Literary relations of England and Scandinavia in the seventeenth century* (Oxford, 1935), pp. 206, 245–6; Arthur B. Ferguson, *Utter antiquity* (Durham, NC, 1993) gives an excessively secularising account of Camden and others.

[9] See footnote 8 above. This became a very common idea: Arthur Bedford, *The scripture chronology demonstrated by astronomical calculations* (1730), pp. 194–5; *Camden's Britannia abridg'd* (2 vols., 1701), I, pp. 5–13; Langhorne, *Introduction*, pp. 12–22; John Milton, *The history of Britain* (1677[1st. 1670]), pp. 8–9; Sheringham, *De Anglorum gentis origine*, sig. b3v, p. 7; William Wotton, 'Dissertatio de confusione linguarum Babylonica', in John Chamberlayne, ed., *Oratio dominica* (Amsterdam, 1715), 2nd pagination, pp. 37–75. William Baxter, *A letter from Mr William Baxter to Dr Hans Sloane* [1707?] was a marginal dissenter – distinguishing the British from the Kimmerians. Authors like Joseph Mede (*Works*, ed. John Worthington (1672), pp. 271–84), Symon Patrick (*A commentary upon the historical books of the old testament* (2 vols., 1727), I, pp. 44–7), or Samuel Shuckford (*The sacred and prophane history of the world connected* (3 vols., 1731–40 [1st. 1728]), I, pp. 141–78) cautioned against the rapid spread of Noah's descendants out of Asia Minor. General discussions of the tradition of the diffusion of peoples and cultures in the early modern period include: Don Cameron Allen, *The legend of Noah* (Urbana, 1949), pp. 92–137; Margaret T. Hodgen, *Early anthropology in the sixteenth and seventeenth centuries* (Philadelphia, 1964), pp. 207–94; Stuart Piggott, *Ancient Britons and the antiquarian imagination* (1989), pp. 36–62; Paolo Rossi, *The dark abyss of time*, trans. Lydia G. Cochrane (Chicago, 1984), pp. 132–52; Arnold Williams, *The common expositor* (Chapel Hill, 1948), pp. 154–60; Sonia Brough, *The Goths and the concept of Gothic in Germany, 1500–1750* (Frankfurt, 1985); Daniel Droixhe, *La linguistique et l'appel de l'histoire, 1600–1800* (Geneva, 1978).

[10] Charles Edwards, *Hebraismorum Cambro-Britannicorum* (?1675); Edwards, *Y ffydd ddi-ffuant*, ed. G. J. Williams (Cardiff, 1936), pp. 186, 394–421; [Griffith Jones], *Welsh*

claimed that this, in turn, had been the language of humanity before the destruction of the tower of Babel, the confusion of tongues and the scattering of peoples.[11] Edward Lhuyd, in his *Archaeologia Britannica* of 1707, argued that all the languages of the British Isles, including Cornish, Irish and Scottish Gaelic, had their common source in Gaul.[12] Many of his contemporaries accepted that Lowland Scots and modern English had common Germanic ancestors.[13] Most authors, however,

piety (1740), p. 48; cf. [John Davies], *Antiquae linguae Britannicae dictionarium duplex* (1632), sig.**1r–3v; Theophilus Evans, *Drych y prif oesoedd*, ed. Garfield H. Hughes (Cardiff, 1961), pp. 19–21, 119; Evans, *History of the ancient Britons*, trans. George Roberts (Llanidloes and Rhayader [1865]), pp. 19–21, 130; John Lewis, *The history of Great-Britain* [ed. Hugh Thomas] (1729), 2nd pagination, pp. 1–4; John Wallis, *Grammar of the English language*, ed. and trans. J. A. Kemp (1972), pp. 80–5; cf. Bod., MS Eng. Misc. d. 447 (William Stukeley, 'On letters') and Thomas Llewelyn's more cautious remarks, NLW, MS 5285B (*Historical and critical remarks on the British tongue*). See also Piggott, *Ruins in a landscape*, p. 59; Geraint H. Jenkins, *Literature, religion and society in Wales, 1660–1730* (Cardiff, 1978); Jenkins, "'An Old and Much Honoured Soldier": Griffith Jones, Llanddowror', *WHR*, 11 (1982–3), 449–68; D. L. Morgan, 'A critical study of the works of Charles Edwards (1628–1691?)' (D.Phil thesis, Oxford, 1967), pp. 348–59. For the identification of Lewis' editor, see Hugh Thomas, *Proposals for publishing a manuscript, entituled, the history of Great-Britain* [1719]; Ffrancis G. Payne, 'John Lewis, Llynwene', *Y Llenor*, 14 (1935), 165–81. The anonymous *An owle at Athens* (Oxford, 1648) mocks this view of the affinity between Hebrew and Welsh. See also Nigel Smith, 'The uses of Hebrew in the English revolution', in Peter Burke and Roy Porter, eds., *Language, self, and society* (Cambridge, 1991), pp. 51–71.

[11] See footnote 10 above. William Baxter held the slightly different view that Welsh had an affinity with Armenian (he sited Eden as well as Ararat in Armenia), and that Hebrew had derived from that language: Bod., MS Ashmole 1814, fs. 147v, 171r–174v, 194r–195v, 236r–244v; Baxter, *Glossarium antiquitatum Britannicarum* (2nd edn, 1733), p. iv; Baxter, *Reliquiae Baxterianae* [ed. Moses Williams] (1726), pp. 2–6 (1st pagination), 278–81 (2nd pagination); the biblical references can be found in Genesis, 10:1–11:9. See also David S. Katz, 'The language of Adam in seventeenth-century England', in Hugh Lloyd-Jones, Valerie Pearl and Blair Worden, eds., *History and imagination* (1981), pp. 132–45; Howard D. Weinbrot, *Britannia's issue* (Cambridge, 1993), pp. 477–504.

[12] Edward Lhuyd, *Archaeologia Britannica* (Oxford, 1707), prefaces (cf. Lhuyd's earlier opinions in a letter of August 1698 in R. T. Gunther, ed., *Life and letters of Edward Lhwyd (Early science in Oxford*, vol. XIV) (Oxford, 1945), pp. 399–400); Frank Emery, *Edward Lhuyd F.R.S. 1660–1709* (Cardiff, 1971), pp. 87–9. Others agreed with him that the immediate origins of the British languages might have been in Gaul, see John Aubrey, 'Remaines of Gentilisme and Judiasme', in Aubrey, *Three prose works*, ed. John Buchanan-Brown (Fontwell, 1972), p. 132; *Camden abridg'd*, I, pp. 5–13; Langhorne, *Introduction*, p. 12; Wallis, *Grammar*, pp. 77–9, 89–95; and Philobiblicus Cantabrigiensis [John Chapman], *Remarks on a letter to Dr Waterland* (Cambridge, 1731), which also describes the various opinions of J. J. Scaliger, G. J. Vossius and Brian Walton. Cf. Edward Brerewood, *Enquiries touching the diversity of languages and religions* (1635 [1st. 1614]), pp. 21, 201, on Irish and Welsh as entirely separate mother tongues; Hugh Thomas opposed Lhuyd's views (which he translated out of Welsh), distinguishing between the Gomerian and Gallic British and Irish and the Milesian, Spanish Scots, see Lewis, *History of Great-Britain*, 1st pagination, pp. 59–71.

[13] Sheringham, *De Anglorum gentis origine*, pp. 128–42; Wallis, *Grammar*, pp. 103–5; Wells, *Historical geography*, I, pp. 108–75.

differed from Lhuyd in ascribing barbarous (often Scythian) ancestry to the Scots and the modern Irish, and in making them the enemies of the British.[14] In doing so, they stressed the common, Gothic inheritance of the Saxons who had peopled the British Isles following the withdrawal of the Romans, and of the Cymri. They were thus able to draw on traditions of the Scandinavian and Germanic descent of the line of Gomer, which embodied a history of political liberty and religious independence,[15] despite having rejected the consensus among continental scholars that the Goths and the Scythians were one people.[16] There was much common ground between this interpretation of ethnic and political history, and contemporary accounts of the nature of the Anglo-Saxon church, which stressed its freedom from Roman domination and its primitive simplicity. This church was the true heir to the ancient British church, and had been founded by relatives of the ancient Britons themselves.[17] Stillingfleet and others were critical about the veracity of the alternative mythographies provided by Scottish authors like George Buchanan or by the Irishman, Roderic O'Flaherty, which sought to assimilate their own national histories to the story of a common Gomerian or Scythian past for the peoples of the British

[14] Lewis, *History of Great-Britain*, 1st pagination, pp. 59–71; Sir William Petty, *The political anatomy of Ireland* (1691), pp. 103–6; Sheringham, *De Anglorum gentis origine*, pp. 128–42; Stillingfleet, *Origines Britannicae*, pp. 245–94. Some support for differing ancestries could be found in the work of Celtic historians themselves, see Roderic O'Flaherty, *Ogygia: seu rerum Hibernicarum chronologia* (1685); Geoffrey Keating, *The history of Ireland*, ed. and trans. David Comyn and P. S. Dinneen (4 vols., 1902–14), I, pp. 133–237 (cf. Keating, *The general history of Ireland*, ed. and trans. Dermod O'Connor (Dublin, 1723)), which suggests a Scythian descent, originating with Japhet's son Magog, rather than with Gomer, for the Irish and the Scots. Inett, *Origines Anglicanae*, pp. 11–15 and Lloyd, *Historical account*, pp. 5–10, 82–98, acknowledge the racial differences of British, Picts and Scots, but still argue for a common Christian past.

[15] See George Hickes, ed., *Institutiones grammaticae Anglo-Saxonicae, et Moeso-Gothicae* (Oxford, 1689), sig. b3v, for the common Gothic descent of 'Cimbric', Anglo-Saxon and the Scandinavian tongues; Brough, *Goths*; Kurt Johannesson, *The renaissance of the Goths in sixteenth-century Sweden*, ed. and trans. James Larson (Berkeley, 1982); Kliger, *Goths in England*; Hugh A. MacDougall, *Racial myth in English history* (Montreal, 1982); R. J. Smith, *The Gothic bequest* (Cambridge, 1987); cf. J. G. A. Pocock, *The ancient constitution and the feudal law* (2nd edn, Cambridge, 1987), pp. 56–8; Aaron Thompson criticised this interpretation, see Geoffrey of Monmouth, *The British history*, p. lxxiv.

[16] Confusingly, Sheringham, *De Anglorum gentis origine*, pp. 155–88, tried to identify Goths and Scythians, whilst differentiating British and Scottish; others who concurred with continental authors included Sir Thomas Browne, 'Of languages and particularly of the Saxon tongue', in *The works of Sir Thomas Browne*, ed. Geoffrey Keynes (4 vols., 1964 [1st. 1928]), III, pp. 70–83; for continental opinions, especially those of Marcus Zuerius Boxhorn, see Droixhe, *La linguistique*, pp. 72–144, and Joseph Theodoor Leerssen, *Mere Irish and Fíor-Ghael* (Amsterdam, 1986), pp. 334–5.

[17] See footnote 6 above; Inett, *Origines Anglicanae*, pp. 1–15; Stillingfleet, *Origines Britannicae*, pp. 90–374.

Isles.[18] They were wary of the story of common, Milesian origins to be found in the work of the catholic mythographer, Geoffrey Keating, whose writings legitimated the resistance of native Irish and Old English in Ireland, and their continued adherence to the church of Rome.[19] They distinguished between the different Celtic peoples, preferring the accounts of the Abbé Paul Pezron and of his disciple Theophilus Evans to those of Lhuyd, and stressing links between the Welsh and the English which tended to exclude the Scots and Irish.[20]

Thus, seventeenth-century English historiographers hinted at the existence of a common past for a pure, episcopal British church which embraced the Welsh and the English. Scottish authors at first expanded this heritage to include their own, presbyterian past, but later modified it to stress the affinities between the civilised peoples of England and the Lowlands, and a few of those who were sympathetic to the Irish past incorporated this into the story also.[21] Summing up views of the true church in ancient Britain and its remains, John Lewis wrote:

[18] See footnote 14 above; cf. George Buchanan, *Rerum Scoticarum historia* (Edinburgh 1582); O'Flaherty, *Ogygia*, pp. 63–73; Droixhe, *La linguistique*, pp. 86–92, provides the European intellectual context for belief in a common Scythian past for all the peoples of the British Isles; see also, Arthur H. Williamson, *Scottish national consciousness in the age of James VI* (Edinburgh, 1979), pp. 117–32. Unusually for an English work, Sammes, *Britannia antiqua illustrata*, argues for a common descent for all peoples of the British Isles, albeit from the Phoenicians.

[19] Keating, *History of Ireland*, I, pp. 187–237, II, pp. 2–117; cf. James Ussher, *A discourse of the religion anciently professed by the Irish and British* (1631), which argued that the modern Irish and Old English had abandoned the true, primitive faith they had once shared with the British; Brendan Bradshaw, 'Geoffrey Keating: apologist of Irish Ireland', in Bradshaw, Andrew Hadfield and Willy Maley, eds., *Representing Ireland* (Cambridge, 1993), pp. 166–90; Bernadette Cunningham, 'Seventeenth-century interpretations of the past: the case of Geoffrey Keating', *IHS*, 25 (1986–7), 116–28; Cunningham, 'Geoffrey Keating's *Eochair Sgiath an Aifrinn* and the catholic reformation in Ireland', *SCH*, 25 (1989), 133–43; Ute Lotz-Heumann, 'The protestant interpretation of history in Ireland: the case of James Ussher's *Discourse*', in Bruce Gordon, ed., *Protestant history and identity in sixteenth-century Europe* (2 vols., Aldershot 1996), II, pp. 107–20.

[20] Paul Pezron, *Antiquité de la nation, et de la langue des Celtes autrement appellez Gaulois* (Paris, 1703); cf. Pezron, *The antiquities of nations*, trans. David Jones (1706); Evans, *History of the ancient Britons*; P. T. J. Morgan, 'The Abbé Pezron and the Celts', *THSC* (1965), 286–95; Prys Morgan, 'From a death to a view: the hunt for the Welsh past in the Romantic period', in Eric Hobsbawm and Terence Ranger, eds., *The invention of tradition* (Cambridge, 1983), pp. 43–100; Among those who praised Pezron were [Jones], *Welch piety*, p. 46; William Nicolson, 'Dissertatio de universis totius orbis linguis', in Chamberlayne, ed., *Oratio dominica*, 2nd pagination, pp. 1–21, esp. pp. 14–16; Rowlands, *Mona antiqua restaurata*, pp. 19, 42–3; and Martin Lister, *A journey to Paris in the year 1698* (1699 [1st. 1698]), pp. 98–9. See Gunther, ed., *Life and letters*, pp. 378–9, 412–13, 439–42, 489–90 for Lister's failure to set up a correspondence between Lhuyd and Pezron, and pp. 399–400 for Lhuyd's doubts about Pezron.

[21] See Colin Kidd, *Subverting Scotland's past* (Cambridge, 1993); Kidd, 'The canon of patriotic landmarks in Scottish history', *Scotlands*, 1 (1994), 1–17; Kidd, 'Gaelic antiquity and national identity in enlightenment Ireland and Scotland', *EHR*, 109

The Christians of *Brittain*, (who, very probably, were converted by St *Paul* the Apostle of the *Gentiles*) it's reasonable to suppose, had the Scriptures in their own language; tho' by the almost entire destruction which was made of that people, and of their memorials by the *Saxons*, and the obscurity of their language, it's no wonder, that we have no copy of this translation now remaining: especially when we consider how maimed and defective the few copies which are left of the old *English* [that is Saxon] and *Gothic* Translations.

Lewis himself made various contributions to the history of primitive British Christianity, editing the first printed version of Wycliffe's new testament, and also acted to spread the message of the church of England throughout the British Isles, as a correspondent of the SPCK, and as the author of a version of the church catechism which was to be translated into Irish.[22] Throughout the seventeenth century, hunters of Celtic manuscripts across the British Isles – such as James Ussher or Narcissus Marsh, both archbishops of Armagh; William Bedell, bishop of Kilmore; or Edward Lhuyd – hoped to stumble across the holy grail of the text of an original British translation of the scriptures.[23] In the minds of such men, the ancient Celtic churches of the British Isles were true apostolic churches, and possessed the marks of this special status. Thus, in addition to their primitive episcopacy and vernacular liturgies, it seemed self-evident to any anglican that they must have had their own vernacular translations of the bible. The events of the reformation had established public worship and the use of scripture in the vernacular as signs of a true church, which helped to

(1994), 1197–214; Kidd, 'Teutonist ethnology and the Scottish nationalist inhibition, 1780–1880', *SHR*, 74 (1995), 45–68; Kidd, 'Antiquarianism, religion and the Scottish enlightenment', *The Innes Review*, 46 (1995), 139–54; Kidd, 'The ideological significance of Robertson's *History of Scotland*', in Stewart J. Brown, ed., *William Robertson and the expansion of empire* (Cambridge, 1997), pp. 122–44.

[22] John Lewis, *A complete history of the several translations of the holy bible and new testament into English* (2nd edn, 1739), p. xiii (paraphrasing Stillingfleet, *Origines Britannicae*). See also Lewis, *Life and sufferings of Wicliffe;* John Lewis, *The church catechism explain'd*, translated into Irish by John Richardson (1712). NLW, MS 11,699B; John Rylands University Library, Manchester, MS 47; BL, MS Add. 28,651, Bod., MS Eng. Misc. c. 273.

[23] T. C. Barnard, 'Protestants and the Irish language, c. 1675–1725', *JEH*, 44 (1993), 243–72; Joep Leerssen, 'Archbishop Ussher and Gaelic culture', *Studia Hibernica*, 22–3 (1982–3), 50–8; Bernard Meehan, 'The manuscript collection of James Ussher', in Peter Fox, ed., *Treasures of the library: Trinity College, Dublin* (Dublin, 1986), pp. 97–110; Richard Parr, ed., *The life of the most reverend father in God, James Usher* (1686), p. 101; Vivian Salmon, 'Missionary linguistics in seventeenth-century Ireland and a North American analogy', *Historiographia Linguistica*, 12 (1985), 321–49. Despite his searches, Lhuyd doubted that there had ever been a complete British translation of the bible, see NLW, MS 427E, number 42. John Toland claimed to have found an Irish manuscript of the gospels, which he used to defend the antiquity of Scottish and Irish presbyterianism and to attack Stillingfleet's and Lloyd's arguments for an episcopal ancient Irish church; Toland, *Nazerenus* (1718), letter II; Alan Harrison, 'John Toland, 1670–1722, and Celtic studies', in Cyril J. Byrne, Margaret Harry and Pádraig Ó Siadhail, eds., *Celtic Languages and Celtic peoples* (Halifax, NS, 1992), pp. 555–76.

distinguish the pure, protestant churches from the supposedly anti-christian Rome. Access to scripture in the vernacular underwrote the most basic assertion of reformed theology – that true Christianity was a religion drawn from the bible, whose practices were conformable with those of Christ and of the primitive church. As William Chillingworth famously put it in 1638, 'the bible only . . . is the religion of Protestants'.[24] More recently, Linda Colley has argued that biblical language and imagery, which need not necessarily have been obtained from reading of the bible itself, remained crucial ingredients in the glue which held together the eighteenth-century British state.[25] She claims that the authorised version of the bible, and interpretations based on it, united English and Scots (as well as Britons and Americans), and supplied them with many common perceptions of the world – much as the Geneva bible had helped to draw together the original Scots reformers, led by John Knox, and their English allies.[26] In this chapter, I want to explore the extent to which the bible could be a common resource throughout the British Isles between 1650 and 1750. Was the English bible able to fulfil the role which contemporary authors ascribed to the scriptures of the ancient British church, and draw together some or all of the peoples of the British Isles in a primitive religious purity which emphasised their common national heritage? Or did a work of translation, carried out by the divines of the early-seventeenth-century church of England, help to reinforce linguistic and theological divisions within Britain and Ireland?

The ideal of a British church embraced not only England and Wales, but also parts of Scotland and Ireland. It was an ideal which some late seventeenth-century writers believed could not be achieved unless all British people had access to the bible in their own tongue, in the manner of protestants everywhere. Yet the English bible seemed to some an obstacle to this, which underlined the linguistic and ethnic differences of the British Isles. Writing in 1686, Robert Huntington, provost of Trinity College, Dublin, complained of the 'slavery' of the Irish people, who were denied access to the bible in Gaelic.[27] Failure to rescue such unfortunates from Romish domination and from superstition might be a

---

[24] William Chillingworth, *The religion of protestants* (1684 [1st. 1638]), p. 290.
[25] Linda Colley, *Britons: forging the nation 1707–1837* (New Haven, 1992).
[26] Ibid., pp. 11–54; cf. Christopher Hill, *The English bible and the seventeenth-century revolution* (1993); Maurice S. Betteridge, 'The bitter notes: the Geneva bible and its annotations', *Sixteenth Century Journal*, 14 (1983), 41–62; Jane Dawson, 'Anglo-Scottish protestant culture and integration in sixteenth-century Britain', in Steven G. Ellis and Sarah Barber, eds., *Conquest and union: fashioning a British state 1485–1725* (1995), pp. 87–114.
[27] Bod., MS Rawlinson B 497, f. 24r; cf. T. C. Barnard, 'Provost Huntington: injunctions to schoolmasters in 1684', *Hermathena*, 119 (1975), 71–3.

serious indictment of the Irish church, and of its English mother, casting doubt on their commitment to God's decrees and to reformation principles. By the late seventeenth or early eighteenth century, increasingly high standards were being set (although by no means always being fulfilled) for mass bible literacy in England and Lowland Scotland, both in terms of the numbers of bibles being produced and sold, and of the number of ordinary people who were learning to read them.[28] Such literacy was, however, confined almost exclusively to English speakers. In response to this, some divines, such as John Richardson, rector of Belturbet, in county Cavan, insisted that all protestant people needed to be able to read the bible for themselves.[29] The Gaelic-speaking populations of Ireland and of the Scottish Highlands, as well as the Welsh speakers of Wales, had to be brought into the community of readers of scripture within the British churches. It was not enough that many in Ireland or the Highlands of Scotland had to listen to extempore translations of readings from the English bible into Gaelic, given by the priest or minister as part of the service.[30] (A practice, incidentally, which Samuel Johnson encountered on his journey to the Western Islands of

[28] For editions of the bible, see T. H. Darlow and H. F. Moule, *Historical catalogue of printed editions of the English bible 1525–1961*, revised and expanded by A. S. Herbert (1968); for some production figures, see Robert L. Haig, 'New light on the King's Printing Office 1680–1730', *Studies in Bibliography*, 8 (1956), 157–67; Christ Church, Oxford, MS Wake Letters 27, numbers 162, 165–6; John Johnson and Strickland Gibson, *Print and privilege at Oxford to the year 1700* (1946), pp. 86, 116, 202. On the extent of readership, see Margaret Spufford, *Small books and pleasant histories* (1981); J. Crawford, 'Reading and book use in 18th-century Scotland', *The Bibliotheck*, 19 (1994), 23–43; T. C. Smout, 'Born again at Cambuslang: new evidence on popular religion and literacy in eighteenth-century Scotland', *P&P*, 97 (1982), 114–27 – but contrast R. A. Houston, *Scottish literacy and the Scottish identity* (Cambridge, 1985).

[29] [John Richardson], *A proposal for the conversion of the popish natives of Ireland to the established religion* (Dublin, 1711); Richardson, *A short history of the attempts that have been made to convert the popish natives of Ireland* (1713 [1st. 1712]); BL, MS Add. 4276, fs. 100r–10lv; Barnard, 'Protestants and the Irish language', pp. 254–65; S. J. Connolly, *Religion, law and power* (Oxford, 1992), pp. 299–301. Cf. Harold Williams, ed., *The correspondence of Jonathan Swift* (5 vols., Oxford, 1963–5), I, pp. 242–4; Swift, *Journal to Stella*, ed. Williams (2 vols., Oxford, 1948), I, pp. 207, 229.

[30] For the extent of the problem, see C. W. J. Withers, 'The Highland parishes in 1698', *Scottish Studies*, 24 (1980), 63–88; Withers, *Gaelic in Scotland 1698–1981* (Edinburgh, 1984); Victor Edward Durkacz, *The decline of the Celtic languages* (Edinburgh, 1983); cf. Jeremy Taylor, *A dissuasive from popery to the people of Ireland* (Dublin, 1664). On extempore translation, see [Christopher Anderson], *A brief sketch of various attempts which have been made to diffuse a knowledge of the holy scriptures through the medium of the Irish language* (Dublin, 1818); Bod., MS Carte 269, f. 24r–v; NLS, MS 821, fs. 89r–v, 108v–109v; *Acts of the general assembly of the church of Scotland MDCXXXVIII-MDCCCXLII* (2 vols., Edinburgh, 1843), I, pp. 82–3, 189; Jane Dawson, 'Calvinism and the Gaidhealtachd in Scotland', in Andrew Pettegree, Alastair Duke and Gillian Lewis, eds., *Calvinism in Europe 1540–1620* (Cambridge, 1994), pp. 231–53; Donald MacKinnon, 'Education in Argyll and the Isles (1638–1709)', *Records of the Scottish Church History Society*, 6 (1938), 46–54.

Scotland.)[31] Yet, although many shared the assumptions of Huntington and Richardson about the need for protestants to read the bible in their own tongue, translation into the vernaculars of the British Isles, other than English, seemed to threaten the cherished ideal of a single, united British church. The diffusion of protestant values had become linked, in Ireland and Scotland especially, with the spread of English, which was supposed to help to civilise the barbarian Scythian peoples of the north and west.[32]

The circumstances of the production of English bibles during the late seventeenth and early eighteenth centuries also placed certain constraints on the widespread diffusion of the scriptures. Throughout the period under consideration, except for a brief period in the 1640s and 1650s, the right to print the English bible in England was a monopoly belonging, in theory, to the king's printer.[33] The universities of Oxford and Cambridge were also allowed to print bibles, but they rarely did so independently of the king's printer, despite a serious attempt by the Oxford University Press to enter the market in the 1670s and 1680s, one part of which was a plan to print 40,000 copies of the new testament for distribution at very low cost in Ireland.[34] North of the border, the printing of bibles was the monopoly of the king's printer in Scotland, a situation which became clearer following the grant made to Andrew Anderson in 1671. Under the terms of the bible patents, only bibles printed in England could circulate in England, and only bibles printed in Scotland ought to have been sold in that country. In practice, the trade in bibles crossed the border frequently, although not without

---

[31] Samuel Johnson, *A journey to the Western Islands of Scotland*, ed. Mary Lascelles (New Haven, 1971 [1st. 1775]), pp. 121–2.

[32] *Acts of the general assembly*, I, p. 282; Duncan C. Mactavish, ed., *Minutes of the synod of Argyll, 1639–51* (Scottish History Society, 3rd ser., 37 (1943)), p. 193; NLS, MS 821, fs. 116v–186, cf. George P. Johnston, 'Notices of a collection of Mss. relating to the circulation of the Irish bibles of 1685 and 1690', *Papers of the Edinburgh Bibliographical Society*, 6 (1901–4), 1–18; Durkacz, *Decline of the Celtic languages*; David Hayton, 'Did protestantism fail in early eighteenth-century Ireland?', in Alan Ford, James McGuire and Kenneth Milne, eds., *As by law established: the church of Ireland since the reformation* (Dublin, 1995), pp. 166–86; John Mason, 'Scottish charity schools of the eighteenth century', *SHR*, 33 (1954), 1–13; Charles W. J. Withers, *A case study in historical geolinguistics: the decline of Gaelic in northern Scotland 1698–1901* (Stafford, 1982); Withers, 'Education and anglicisation: the policy of the SSPCK toward the education of the Highlander, 1709–1825', *Scottish Studies*, 26 (1982), 37–56.

[33] William M. Clyde, *The struggle for the freedom of the press from Caxton to Cromwell* (1934), pp. 281–3.

[34] Harry Carter, *A history of the Oxford University Press. Volume 1: To the year 1780* (Oxford, 1975), pp. 93–109; Bod., MS Ballard 49, esp. fs. 233–5; for the failure of the proposal which included books bound for Ireland, see Johnson and Gibson, *Print and privilege*, pp. 116–17.

disputes and occasional seizures of goods.[35] From 1712, the printing of the English bible was almost entirely in the control of one family, that of John Baskett and his heirs. Baskett defended his rights vigorously, and succeeded in obtaining not only the patent in England, but also a share in, and subsequently control of, the Scottish patent. In addition, he had secured a lease from Oxford of the university's right to print bibles, and benefited from Cambridge's decision to suspend its privilege for a fee of £210 per annum, paid by the Stationers' Company as part of a deal concerning the printing of schoolbooks and other steady sellers.[36] Baskett was frequently accused of printing poorly corrected editions of the bible, on cheap paper, with old and broken type, and of selling them far too dearly. This accusation circulated particularly during the 1710s and early 1720s, when he was in dispute with James Watson, an Edinburgh printer who claimed a share of the Scottish bible patent.[37] Nevertheless, the prices of many of Baskett's bibles were low (for example, he supplied duodecimo bibles to charities at 1s 9d, in quires, and sold octavo bibles, again in quires, for 3s), and he seems to have been generally capable of satisfying demand at the level generated by such prices.[38] However, periodic attempts were made to break his monopoly, particularly with a view to supplying large numbers of very

[35] Darlow and Moule, *Historical catalogue*, p. 213; [John Lee], *Memorial for the bible societies in Scotland* (Edinburgh, 1824), pp. 113–69; Joyce Helene Brodowski, 'Literary piracy in England from the restoration to the early eighteenth century' (doctoral thesis, Columbia University, 1973), pp. 166–206.

[36] Carter, *History of the Oxford University Press*, pp. 168–9; Haig, 'New light'; A. F. Johnson, *Selected essays on books and printing*, ed. Percy H. Muir (Amsterdam, 1970), pp. 381–5; Archives of the Stationer's Company, London, Court Book G, f. 204r; Bod., MS Gough Gen. Top. 28, fs. 305–6; [Lee], *Memorial*, pp.179–81, and appendix, pp. 67–9; S. C. Roberts, *A history of the Cambridge University Press, 1521–1921* (Cambridge, 1921), p. 95, cf. Cambridge University Archives, D.I. 2, pp. 14–16, and Lambeth Palace Library, MS 939, no. 9.

[37] For complaints about the quality of Baskett's productions, see Bod., MS Ballard 4, fs. 111–12, MS Ballard 32, f. 13, MS Ballard 34, fs. 109–10; B. J . McMullin, 'The "Vinegar Bible"', *The Book Collector*, 33 (1984), 53–65; Percy Simpson, *Proof-reading in the sixteenth, seventeenth, and eighteenth centuries* (Oxford, 1935; repr. 1970), pp. 194–7; Archives of the SPCK, A[bstract] L[etter] B[ook] 9, nos. 6151, 6171, ALB10, nos. 6298, 6421, 6615, ALB11, no. 7262, Society Letters, CS2/12, pp. 72–5. On the dispute with Watson, see Bod., MS Ballard 7, f. 64, MS Gough Gen. Top. 28, fs. 305–8, MS Top. Middlesex c. 1, fs. 23–34; *John Baskett His Majesty's printer in London, and the representatives of Andrew Anderson, printer to K. Charl. II. in Scotland, appellants; James Watson, one of His Majesty's printers, respondent* (n.p., n.d.); *A previous view of the case between John Baskett, esq; one of His Majesty's printers, plaintiff; and Henry Parson, stationer, defendant* (Edinburgh, 1720); John A. Fairley, *Agnes Campbell, Lady Roseburn* (Aberdeen, 1925); John S. Gibb, 'James Watson, printer: notes on his life and work', *Papers of the Edinburgh Bibliographical Society*, 1 (1890–5), 1–8; W. J. Couper, 'James Watson, King's Printer', *SHR*, 7 (1909–10), 244–62.

[38] For prices in the period around 1720, see Christ Church, Oxford, MS Wake Letters 27, no. 165; SPCK, Minute Books, vol. VIII (1717–19), pp. 124–5; Haig, 'New light'.

cheap bibles to Wales, Ireland and the English poor. Thus, between 1719 and 1722, Henry Newman, the secretary of the SPCK, collected information about the printing of bibles, and explored whether it would be possible to obtain better-quality bibles more cheaply either from the king's printer in Edinburgh (Watson) or from a group of booksellers in Dublin, who had themselves raised a charitable subscription, between 1718 and 1722, to pay for the printing of 20,000 octavo bibles to be distributed in Ireland.[39] Eventually, however, Newman's investigations proved fruitless, principally because of restrictions on imports and exports which worked in Baskett's favour. The exclusive terms of the monopoly exercised by Baskett almost certainly did result in the printing of fewer English bibles in the early eighteenth century, and in the maintenance of a cost which was perhaps higher than necessary for those bibles. But the investment involved in printing large numbers of copies of a complicated text, to a high standard of accuracy, was such that it is doubtful that Baskett would have had any long-term challengers, even if it had proved possible to break his monopoly.[40] The relatively unsuccessful attempt of the Oxford University Press to break the monopoly of the London bible patentees in the late seventeenth century illustrated the difficulty of raising sufficient capital to enable a challenger to weather the initial storm of undercutting whipped up by the monopolists in defence of their position.[41] Yet, within the limits of seventeenth and eighteenth-century printing technology, the English bible had still become a common and relatively cheap book.[42] But although it circulated effectively in areas of high literacy, such as most of England and Lowland Scotland, in particular in towns and cities, and especially, though not exclusively, among the upper and middling

[39] Bod., MS Rawlinson D 839, fs. 30r–31v; SPCK, Minute Books, vol. IX (1719–21), p. 62, vol. X (1722–4), pp. 19, 22, 46–7; for the Dublin booksellers' proposals, see Christ Church, Oxford, MS Wake Letters 13, fs. 280–1.

[40] See Baskett's defence of himself to William Wake in Christ Church, Oxford, MS Wake letters 22, no. 276, and as reported in *Previous view*. In 1731, William Fenner obtained the lease of the right of Cambridge University to print bibles, but did not use it to break Baskett's monopoly: see Cambridge University Archives, D.I. 2, pp. 37–50, and Pr. P. 8. Two editions of the bible were produced by other Edinburgh printers in the late 1720s, and Baskett's heirs had competition in the 1740s from George Grierson's revival of the patent of the king's printer in Dublin and his illegal export of bibles to Britain; Darlow and Moule, *Historical catalogue*, pp. 250–66; M. Pollard, *Dublin's trade in books* (Oxford, 1989), pp. 3, 11, 78–9.

[41] See footnote 34 above.

[42] Evidence for this would require extensive digression. [John Ballinger], *The bible in Wales* (1906), p. 33 cites contemporary claims that 30,000 bibles a year were being sold in English around 1670, and Haig 'New light' shows the efforts made by the king's printer to ensure supply in 1720. That said, the price of paper placed an absolute limit on the cheapness of bibles, and the cheapest editions of Baskett's bibles sold at a rate of only 500 to 600 a year. See SPCK, Minute Books, vol. VIII, pp. 124–5; vol. X, p. 202.

sorts, by definition the printed English bible could not meet the demand for access to the biblical text from those who could not read or who could not understand English.[43]

The principal constraint on the production of bibles in Welsh, and in Scottish and Irish Gaelic, was financial. The cost of cutting type for Welsh and Irish, and the additional time spent on composing and on the correction of the press in any unfamiliar language or script, made the initial investment in such ventures prohibitively expensive for printers and booksellers themselves. Instead, the production of vernacular bibles for the Celtic peoples of the British Isles depended on individual or collective charity, and, in the case of the later editions of the Welsh bible supervised by the SPCK, on the collection of subscriptions from local benefactors and prospective readers.[44] This financial constraint was of course worsened by the relative poverty of the Welsh, Irish and Highland Scots, which made it unlikely that many of the bibles produced could be sold at any profit, rather than distributed through charity.

As it turned out, the printing of Irish and Scottish Gaelic bibles in this period was much like the production using English materials of bibles and new testaments in Turkish or Algonquian – one-off ventures which were the products of the zeal of a handful of people.[45] In contrast, the comparative frequency and success of the printing of Welsh bibles suggest that there were important differences between the Celtic areas of the British Isles which impinged on the problem of protestantism and national identity. As in the cases of the Scottish and Irish Gaelic bibles, all the Welsh bibles published in the seventeenth and early eighteenth centuries were printed in London by English printers. However, they were corrected and to a large extent distributed by Welsh speakers.[46]

---

[43] For evidence of the extent of distribution, see G. D. Henderson, *Religious life in seventeenth-century Scotland* (Cambridge, 1937), pp. 1–30; Houston, *Scottish literacy*, pp. 165–73, 297–300.

[44] Thomas Llewelyn, *An historical account of the British or Welsh versions and editions of the bible* (1768); [Moses Williams], 'A chronological account of the sevl. editions of the holy scripture in Welsh', BL, MS Add. 14,952; [Ballinger], *Bible in Wales*, esp. p. 34; Mary Clement, *The SPCK and Wales 1699–1740* (1954); M. G. Jones, 'Two accounts of the Welsh Trust 1675 and 1678(?)', *Bulletin of the Board of Celtic Studies*, 9 (1939), 71–80; Dermot McGwinne, 'The Moxon Irish type of 1680', *Printing Historical Society Bulletin*, 37 (1994), 1–7; R. E. W. Maddison, 'Robert Boyle and the Irish bible', *Bulletin of the John Rylands Library*, 41 (1958–9), 81–101; Eiluned Rees, 'Wales and the London book trade before 1820', in Robin Myers and Michael Harris, eds., *Spreading the word: the distribution networks of print 1550–1850* (Winchester, 1990), pp. 1–20.

[45] William Seaman, trans., *Domini nostri Iesu Christi testamentum novum Turcice redditum* (Oxford, 1666); *The holy bible; containing the old testament and the new. Translated into the Indian language* (Cambridge, MA, 1663).

[46] See [Ballinger], *Bible in Wales*, 2nd pagination, pp. 10–14; Jones, 'Welsh Trust'; Jenkins, *Literature, religion and society*, pp. 55–66.

The text of the Welsh bible had already been established by 1650, although there were substantial changes made both in the edition of 1690, which was intended for use in churches, and that of 1717, intended for private use.[47] The new testament had been translated into Welsh and printed in 1567, and the whole bible had been translated by William Morgan and published in 1588. Further, revised editions appeared in 1620 and 1630.[48] This process of translation had been made possible by the support of the Elizabethan hierarchy for a Welsh vernacular bible, support which may have been generated, in part, by the conviction that Welsh had been the original language of the British scriptures.[49] Almost all the editions of the Welsh bible can be associated also with local gentry support, either technical or financial.[50] These two factors helped to guarantee that Welsh bibles were used as part of a complete Welsh liturgy in both public and private worship, despite the continuing hopes of some English bishops that this linguistic accommodation might one day cease to be necessary.[51] The survival of Welsh as a language of devotion also helped to maintain it in other ways, and in the late seventeenth and early eighteenth centuries, Welsh remained the language of family life and of local administration across much of the principality, and especially in the north and west.[52] This, in turn, helped

[47]   *Y bibl cyssergr-lan sef yr hen destament a'r newydd* (Oxford, 1690); *Y bibl cyssegr-lan sef yr hen destament a'r newydd* (1717); cf. [Ballinger], *Bible in Wales,* pp. 38–41; *Proposals for reprinting the holy bible and common prayer book in the British or Welsh tongue* (1714), NLW, MS 5285B; BL, MS Add. 14, 952.

[48]   [Ballinger], *Bible in Wales*; NLW, *Y beibl yng Nghymru* – the bible in Wales (Aberystwyth, 1988); Isaac Thomas, *William Salesbury and his testament* (Cardiff, 1967); J. Gwynfor Jones, 'William Morgan, translator of the bible and bishop of Llandaff', *Gwent Local History*, 66 (1989), 37–48; R. Geraint Gruffydd, 'Michael Robert o Fôn a beibl bach 1630', *Transactions of the Anglesey Antiquarian Society and Field Club* (1989), 25–41; NLW, MSS 13217–18.

[49]   Ceri Davies, 'The 1588 translation of the bible and the world of renaissance learning', *Ceredigion*, 11 (1988–92), 1–18; Glanmor Williams, 'William Morgan's bible and the Cambridge connection', *WHR*, 14 (1988–9), 363–79; W. Ogwen Williams, 'The survival of the Welsh language after the union of England and Wales: the first phase, 1536–1642', *WHR*, 2 (1964–5), 67–93. Cf. Isaac Thomas, 'The contribution of two Welshmen to the English bible', *NLW Journal*, 28 (1993), 107–26 for the influence which the Welsh translation may have had on the English authorised version.

[50]   [Ballinger], *Bible in Wales*; Clement, *SPCK and Wales*, pp. 29–36, 97–8; Llewelyn, *Historical account*, pp. 17–22, 38–9, 45–6, 48; Thomas Shankland, 'Sir John Philipps; the SPCK; and the charity-school movement in Wales, 1699–1737', *THSC* (1904–5), 74–216; Gareth Elwyn Jones, *Modern Wales* (Cambridge, 1984), p. 129; cf. the more pessimistic assessment of the cultural contribution of the gentry in Philip Jenkins, *The making of a ruling class* (Cambridge, 1983), pp. 213–16.

[51]   Jenkins, *Literature, religion and society*, pp. 55–84; W. P. Griffith, *Learning, law and religion* (Cardiff, 1996), pp. 278–326; William Fleetwood, bishop of St. Asaph, *Charge to the clergy of that diocese in 1710* (1712), pp. 11–12; cf. John R. Guy, 'The significance of indigenous clergy in the Welsh church at the restoration', *SCH*, 18 (1982), 335–43.

[52]   Griffith, *Learning, law and religion*, pp. 327–433; Jenkins, *Literature, religion and society*;

to stimulate a real and continuing demand for bibles in Welsh, which complemented the efforts of evangelists to spread the gospel to the dark corners of the land.[53]

In 1647, the Welsh saints, Walter Cradock and Vavasor Powell, had promoted a Welsh new testament, followed in 1654 by a complete bible. Together with Morgan Llwyd, Cradock and Powell had close links with the Commission for the Propagation of the Gospel in Wales, and Powell in particular shared the fifth monarchist aspirations of the head of the commission, Major-General Thomas Harrison. The collapse of Harrison's regime in Wales, however, led to the termination of Powell's hopes for a new mission and church order there.[54] Interest in Welsh-language evangelisation was perhaps fortunate to survive this episode, although thereafter much of the impetus for it came from individuals based in London, rather than from those in the principality itself. In the 1670s, at a time of concern about possible catholic proselytising in Wales, a number of priests of the church of England who were noted for their preaching ministries in London, notably Edward Stillingfleet, John Tillotson and Edward Fowler, assisted the low churchman Thomas Gouge in setting up the Welsh Trust.[55] A major financial contributor to this scheme was Thomas Firmin, a wealthy London Socinian merchant. As well as printing and distributing editions of the Welsh bible in 1677 and 1689, the Welsh Trust helped to re-establish Welsh language evangelism as an aim of young, and rising, members of the hierarchy of the church of England. Although there was initially opposition to the proposals, and particularly to Gouge's activities as an itinerant, notably from Humphrey Lloyd, bishop of Bangor, no legal sanctions were available to halt the scheme, which won support from both churchmen

G. Nesta Evans, *Religion and politics in mid-eighteenth century Anglesey* (Cardiff, 1953), p. 79; John Davies, *A history of Wales* (1993), pp. 242–5, argues that Welsh was secure as a spoken language, although he accepts that the survival of the language of the bards, and its metamorphosis into the language of Welsh printed literature, owed much to the translation of the bible.

53 For example, NLW, MS 21481E; MS 359B, fs. 1, 23, 53, 63, 143, 147, 197–9, 261, 273–5, 313–15.

54 [Ballinger], *Bible in Wales*, pp. 30–2; Walter Cradock, *The saints fulnesse of joy in their fellowship with God* (1646); Vavasor Powell, *The scriptures concord* (1646), sig. A3r; Powell, *The bird in the cage* (1662), sig. A7v–B5r; R. Tudur Jones, 'The life, work, and thought of Vavasor Powell, 1617–1670' (D.Phil. thesis, Oxford, 1947); NLW, MSS 11436D, 11437B, 11439D; Thomas Richards, *The puritan movement in Wales, 1639 to 1653* (1920), pp. 73–273; Richards, *Religious developments in Wales, 1654–1662* (1923), pp. 204–40; B. S. Capp, *The fifth monarchy men* (1972), pp. 54–8, 62, 109, 178; Anne Laurence, *Parliamentary army chaplains, 1642–1651* (Woodbridge, 1990), pp. 117, 148, 167; Geoffrey F. Nuttall, *The Welsh saints, 1640–1660* (Cardiff, 1957).

55 Thomas Gouge, *The works of the late reverend and pious Mr. Tho. Gouge* (1706); Jones, 'Welsh Trust'; Llewelyn, *Historical account*, pp. 42–7; [Ballinger], *Bible in Wales*, pp. 33–7.

and dissenters.[56] At the end of the period of the activities of the Welsh Trust in London, William Lloyd, whilst he was bishop of St Asaph, edited a further edition of the Welsh bible, which was published in Oxford, and, later, as bishop of Worcester, he encouraged the SPCK in its first Welsh projects.[57]

Whereas much of the activity of the Welsh Trust had been concentrated in north Wales, a number of gentlemen with close ties with south Wales were involved with the charitable and missionary work of the SPCK from its inception. The most important of these was Sir John Philipps, of Picton Castle in Pembrokeshire, whose father, Erasmus, had been associated with the work of the Commission for the Propagation of the Gospel in Wales during the 1650s.[58] Sir John Philipps was generous and enthusiastic in promoting the charity school movement in Wales, and, through it, the spread of literacy and practical piety among the Welsh poor. His influence also helped to secure the continued support of the Welsh bishops for the SPCK's activities. Furthermore, it was from among his clients that the most significant figure in Welsh-language education and evangelism of the eighteenth century, Griffith Jones of Llanddowror, the founder of the circulating schools, came.[59] The SPCK supervised the production and distribution of editions of the Welsh bible printed in 1717 and 1727, and on both occasions large subscriptions were made by Sir John Philipps himself.[60] The SPCK's original venture was also supported by a bequest from the will of Caleb D'Avenant, a Herefordshire gentleman, obtained for the society by a local priest of the church of England, Erasmus Saunders, who was already closely involved with the society's plans in Wales.[61] Subscriptions for the bible of 1717 were collected in north Wales on a tour by Moses Williams, who also corrected the bible for the press, and in south Wales by Philipps and his friends.[62] Once cheap editions of the Welsh

[56] On Firmin's activities, see H. John McLachlan, *Socinianism in seventeenth-century England* (Oxford, 1951); opposition to the Welsh Trust can be found in Bod., MS Tanner Letters 40, fs. 18r–19v.

[57] See footnote 47 above, also A. Tindal Hart, *William Lloyd 1627–1717* (1952); David Robertson, ed., *Diary of Francis Evans, secretary to Bishop Lloyd, 1699–1706* (Wiltshire Historical Society (1903)). Lacking any effective means of distribution, Lloyd's bible was not bought in large numbers: SPCK, ALB 5, no. 3860.

[58] Shankland, 'Sir John Philipps'; Clement, *SPCK and Wales*; Mary Clement, ed., *Correspondence and minutes of the SPCK relating to Wales, 1699–1740* (Cardiff, 1952).

[59] On Jones see footnote 10 above; Clement, ed., *Correspondence and minutes*; W. Moses Williams, 'The friends of Griffith Jones', *Y Cymmrodor*, 46 (1939).

[60] SPCK, Minute Books, vol. VII (1715–16), pp. 10, 15, 80, 96, 118, 121–2; BL, MS Add. 14, 952.

[61] Clement, ed., *Correspondence and minutes*, pp. 60–95, 277–87.

[62] The first of the SPCK's Welsh bibles appeared in two issues in 1717 and 1718; the prayer book which accompanied those copies not intended for use by dissenters was

bible were available, ministers like Griffith Jones had little difficulty in stimulating demand for them, although their charity school pupils could rarely afford the books unaided. After the establishment of the first of his circulating schools, Jones continued to agitate for further reprintings of the Welsh bible and other Welsh devotional literature, and the SPCK produced further editions of the Welsh bible in 1746 and 1752.[63]

Although the numbers of Welsh bibles printed were small compared with the total number of English bibles in circulation (the editions sponsored by the SPCK numbered 10,000 or 15,000 bibles each), they reached a disproportionately large readership through the charity schools, and especially through Jones' circulating schools.[64] There, it was not uncommon for many pupils to share access to a single bible at different times. Children, who had learned to read in Welsh, could understand the bible, and simple interpretations of its message, and were able in turn to teach these to their illiterate parents.[65] Jones was quick to point out the contrast between this situation and that which had pertained before the printing of further editions of the Welsh bible. In the past, he claimed, children had spent many years learning to read the English bible aloud, at the end of which they still had no understanding of the meaning of the sounds they were making.[66]

Despite continuing problems, including pluralism and absenteeism among the clergy, and a shortage of Welsh-speaking bishops, the established church was able to consolidate its strength in Wales between 1670 and 1750, whilst successfully evangelising large numbers of people. It prevented catholic incursion, and, to some extent, countered the message of the quakers and other radical dissenters. This was possible, despite the survival of Welsh as a vernacular language, because of the concerted involvement of the ecclesiastical hierarchy and the indigenous tory gentry in the work of evangelisation, and because of

not ready until 1718, when distribution began: see Clement, ed., *Correspondence and minutes*, pp. 71–95, 277–87; BL, MS Add. 14, 952; [Ballinger], *Bible in Wales*, 2nd pagination, p. 13. The SPCK were forced to use Baskett's presses for their Welsh bibles, but were surprisingly pleased with the results, see SPCK, Society Letters CS2/5, p. 28.

63 See Clement, ed., *Correspondence and minutes*; NLW, MS 359B; opposition to the use of Welsh in the teaching and publication programme of the SPCK was comparatively limited and short-lived, but see SPCK, ALB 3, no. 2843.

64 The SPCK printed 10,000 copies of the Welsh bible in 1717–18, and 15,000 in 1746 and 1752; the number printed in 1727 is unknown; Jones may have bought as many as 2,000 copies of the 1727 edition alone, see [Ballinger], *Bible in Wales*, pp. 40–3, 2nd pagination, pp. 13–14; Clement, ed., *Correspondence and minutes*, pp. 163–94. Jones' activities to stimulate demand can be traced in his *A further account of the progress of the circulating Welsh charity-schools* (1740), and *Welch piety continued* (1742).

65 [Jones], *Welch piety*, pp. 7, 65; Jones, *Welch piety continued*, part 1, p. 60.

66 [Jones], *Welch piety*, p. 44.

successful innovations in publication and in education carried out under their patronage. Attempts to extirpate the Welsh language and replace it by the use of English were largely abandoned as a result of the achievements of such alliances. There were limits to this success, not least because of the compromises, especially with moderate dissenters, and later methodists, which were made in order to achieve it.[67] But, in Wales, the idea that the local Celts were as much a part of the British nation, and the British church, as their English neighbours, had some truth to it. The protestant ideal of the use of vernacular scriptures and liturgy was borne out by the practice of the established church in Wales, the heir to the true, British church as it was envisaged by its own divines.[68]

The history of the bible in Welsh contrasts sharply with that of the Scottish and Irish Gaelic bibles. Scottish Calvinist ministers had made considerable progress towards the conversion of the Gaidhealtachd during the late sixteenth and early seventeenth centuries, through a policy of Gaelic teaching and preaching, centred on attempts to convert the Highland chiefs and aristocracy.[69] These efforts were frustrated by the opposition to the presbyterian covenanters of many Highland chiefs, led by Alasdair MacColla, and their support for Montrose during the civil wars.[70] Nevertheless, during the 1650s, the synod of Argyll, whose jurisdiction included a large Gaelic-speaking population, attempted, albeit unsuccessfully, to produce a Gaelic edition of the bible. However, its efforts were halted in the end by the restoration of the monarchy, and the subsequent episcopalian settlement of the church in Scotland.[71]

---

[67] For complaints about methodists selling the SPCK's bibles, meant for anglicans, see [George Eyre Evans], 'Selling bibles too cheaply, 1748', *Transactions of the Carmarthenshire Antiquarian Society and Field Club*, 17 (n.d.), 9–10.

[68] Cf. Philip Jenkins, 'The anglican church and the unity of Britain: the Welsh experience, 1560–1714', in Ellis and Barber, eds., *Conquest and union*, pp. 115–38; A. G. MacWilliam, 'Bishop William Beveridge and the church of England', *Journal of the Historical Society of the Church in Wales*, 6 (1956), 82–91.

[69] See Dawson, 'Calvinism and the Gaidhealtachd'.

[70] David Stevenson, *Highland warrior: Alasdair MacColla and the civil wars* (Edinburgh, 1980); Allan I. Macinnes, 'Scottish Gaeldom, 1638–1651: the vernacular response to the covenanting dynamic', in John Dwyer, Roger A. Mason and Alexander Murdoch, eds., *New perspectives on the politics and culture of early modern Scotland* (Edinburgh, n.d.), pp. 59–94; Macinnes, 'The impact of the civil wars and interregnum: political disruption and social change within Scottish Gaeldom', in Rosalind Mitchison and Peter Roebuck, eds., *Economy and society in Scotland and Ireland 1500–1939* (Edinburgh, 1988), pp. 58–69; Macinnes, 'Seventeenth-century Scotland: the undervalued Gaelic perspective', in Byrne, Harry and Ó Siadhail, eds., *Celtic languages and Celtic peoples*; Macinnes, 'Gaelic culture in the seventeenth century: polarization and assimilation', in Ellis and Barber, eds., *Conquest and union*, pp. 162–94.

[71] Mactavish, ed., *Minutes of the synod of Argyll, 1639–51*, pp. xix, 127; Duncan C. Mactavish, ed., *Minutes of the synod of Argyll, 1652–61* (Scottish History Society, 3rd ser., 38 (1944)), pp. xiii–xxxii, 146, 161, 185, 210–11, 224, 235–8; Thomas

Despite these efforts, however, most Lowland Scots remained hostile to Gaelic, and put into practice the early seventeenth-century legislation which sought to limit its use.[72] The efforts of James Kirkwood, a Scottish episcopalian minister who was resident in Bedfordshire, to persuade Robert Boyle to allow the distribution in Scotland of the residue of the edition of the Irish bible which Boyle had funded in the 1680s, and to pay for a separate Scottish edition, in Roman letter, were not sufficient to overcome these prejudices.[73] The bulk of the Irish and Scottish bibles arrived in Scotland only after the 1688–9 revolution, which restored presbyterian church government, so that Kirkwood's efforts were hampered by his inability, as an episcopalian, to serve on the general assembly of the kirk. However, he did succeed in interesting the general assembly in a number of schemes over the next twenty years. In particular, he was a leading advocate of the provision of parochial libraries, and was involved, just before his death, in the formal establishment of the Society in Scotland for Propagating Christian Knowledge.[74] However, this grew out of the existing Edinburgh movement for the reformation of manners and shared in its members' hostility to Scottish Gaelic culture.[75] Kirkwood failed to generate any real interest, either in the printing and distribution of the Gaelic bible, or in Gaelic-language education. The distribution of the existing copies of the Gaelic bible, which the general assembly had taken out of his hands, occupied more

---

Mackenzie Donn, 'The Scots Gaelic bible and its historical background', *Transactions of the Gaelic Society of Inverness*, 43 (1960–3), 335–56; Donald Meek, 'The Gaelic bible', in David F. Wright, ed., *The bible in Scottish life and literature* (Edinburgh, 1988), pp. 9–23; Donald MacKinnon, *The Gaelic bible and psalter* (Dingwall, 1930); MacKinnon, 'Education in Argyll'.

[72] Durkacz, *Decline of the Celtic languages*, p. 4; Houston, *Scottish literacy*, pp. 76–8; John Lorne Campbell, *Gaelic in Scottish education and life* (2nd edn, Edinburgh, 1950); Withers, *Gaelic in Scotland*, pp. 28–35.

[73] NLS, MS 821, fs. 76–186; Durkacz, *Decline of the Celtic languages*, pp. 17–30; Michael Hunter, ed., *Robert Boyle by himself and his friends* (1994), pp. 107–10; Maddison, 'Robert Boyle and the Irish bible'; Royal Society, London, MS Boyle Papers, vol. 4, f. 103; cf. *The books of the old testament translated into Irish* (1685) [normally bound with the new testament in Irish published in 1681]; *An biobla naomtha, iona bhfuil leabhair na seintiomna*, ed. R[obert] K[irk] (1690).

[74] See footnote 73 above. *Acts of the general assembly*, I, pp. 227, 282, 287–8, 322, 330–2; 388; *Rules about ordering some libraries in the Highlands* (Edinburgh, 1705); *Her Majestie's letters patent, erecting a society in Scotland, for propagating Christian knowledge* (Edinburgh, 1709); *An account of the rise, constitution and management of the Society in Scotland for Propagating Christian Knowledge* (Edinburgh, 1720); William Blades, ed., *Proposals made by Rev. James Kirkwood (minister of Minto) in 1699, to found public libraries in Scotland* (1889); D. Maclean, 'Highland libraries in the eighteenth century', *Transactions of the Gaelic Society of Inverness*, 31 (1922–4), 69–97; Tristram Clarke, 'The Williamite episcopalians and the glorious revolution in Scotland', *Records of the Scottish Church History Society*, 24 (1990), 33–51.

[75] Withers, 'Education and anglicisation'; and see footnote 72 above.

than a decade.[76] Despite Kirkwood's blandishments, the SSPCK banned the use of the Gaelic language from its schools entirely after a couple of years.[77] Unlike its partner in Wales, the Scottish charity school movement, at least for the first half-century of its existence, was dedicated to the eradication of the vernacular of many of the children that it sought to educate, and its replacement with the English language.

The failure of Kirkwood's scheme, and in particular of the Scottish Gaelic bible, which had been adapted from the original Irish translation by Kirkwood's friend Robert Kirk, has often been attributed to the incompatibility of Irish and Scottish Gaelic.[78] Although the spoken languages had diverged considerably by the late seventeenth century, and Scottish Gaelic speakers did not know the script in which the Irish bible of 1685 had been printed, both Irish and Scottish Gaelic speakers shared the classical language of the bards, used in the translation of the bible.[79] Although Kirkwood himself recognised that there were several hundred archaisms in the book, he pointed out that this was also true of the authorised version of the bible, which was based on the early-sixteenth-century English of William Tyndale.[80] These archaisms had indeed presented no obstacle to readership of the English bible in Scotland or elsewhere. In truth, a more serious problem for Kirkwood had been his failure to win sustained support within the kirk, owing largely to the extent of Lowland presbyterian hostility to the High-landers, and distrust of the episcopalians of the north-east, with whom Kirkwood was closely connected. Such animosity had been stoked by the armed opposition to the covenanting movements in the Highlands, and was confirmed by the apparent success of Jacobitism among the Highland clans.[81] Coupled with the inadequacies of the parochial

---

[76] NLS, MS 821, fs. 112r–116r; *Acts of the general assembly,* I, pp. 287–8; Royal Society, London, MS Boyle Letters, vol. 5, fs. 121–2.

[77] NLS, MS 821, fs. 138v–173v; Leah Leneman, 'The SSPCK and the question of Gaelic in Blair Atholl', *Scottish Studies,* 26 (1982), 57–9.

[78] For example, Donn, 'The Scots Gaelic bible', p. 350; Victor Durkacz, 'The source of the language problem in Scottish education, 1688–1709', *SHR,* 57 (1978), 28–39, at pp. 29, 33. On Kirk's work as a translator and overseer for the press, see David Baird Smith, 'Mr. Robert Kirk's note-book', *SHR,* 18 (1920–1), 237–48; D. Maclean, 'The life and literary labours of the Rev. Robert Kirk, of Aberfoyle', *Transactions of the Gaelic Society of Inverness,* 31 (1922–4), 328–66; and especially, EUL, MS Laing III 545.

[79] Meek, 'The Gaelic bible', pp. 13–14: Kirk's version of 1690 overcame the problems posed by the Irish Gaelic script and its scribal abbreviations, but still failed to be a genuinely Scots Gaelic work.

[80] SRO, CH 1/2/24/1/2, fs. 117–19 (Kirkwood to George Meldrum, 18 Jan. 1704). On Tyndale's language and the authorised version, see Gerald Hammond, *The making of the English bible* (Manchester, 1982), pp. 16–67.

[81] See footnote 70 above; William Ferguson, 'The problems of the established church in the west Highlands and islands in the eighteenth century', *Records of the Scottish Church History Society,* 17 (1969–72), 15–31; Colin Kidd, 'Religious realignment between the

system in the north and west, it could manifest itself in the exclusion of the Gaels both from the worship of the kirk, and, increasingly, from membership of the historical Scottish nation itself. Thus, as Colin Kidd has shown, presbyterian historiography after 1689 sought to stress links with England in order to establish a common civil identity, rather than to worry about the status or past of the Highland Scots.[82] Provision for education in the Highlands, despite the work of the SSPCK (Society in Scotland for Promoting Christian Knowledge), remained slight and schooling was often unpopular.[83] Nevertheless, although Lowland Scottish protestants had perhaps abandoned their Highland brethren to residual catholicism, ignorance of the scriptures, and the uncertain attentions of the few men who ministered to the Highland parishes, catholic missionaries made relatively little progress in Scotland in the early years of the eighteenth century. The exclusive and critical attitudes of the English and the Lowlanders were reinforced, however, by the desire of the Highland chiefs and clans to preserve a distinctive way of life, at odds with polite society and polite religion. This way of life, in itself, seemed to confirm the judgement of contemporary historians and mythographers that the Highland peoples were a different, perhaps barbarian, race.[84]

In Ireland during the seventeenth and eighteenth centuries, the problem of ignorance of Gaelic on the part of the church's hierarchy was initially far more acute than it was in Scotland. Despite the existence of a scholarship scheme at Trinity College, Dublin, intended to train young Gaelic scholars for the ministry, few priests of the church of Ireland were able to speak the language of the majority population.[85] In part because of the opposition which he faced from other Irish bishops, notably from John Bramhall, but mainly because of the dislocation caused by the Irish rebellion of 1641, William Bedell's translation of the bible into Irish, which completed the work begun with the publication of

restoration and union', in John Robertson, ed., *A union for empire* (Cambridge, 1995), pp. 145–68; John MacInnes, *The evangelical movement in the Highlands of Scotland 1688 to 1800* (Aberdeen, 1951).

[82] See footnote 21 above.

[83] Houston, *Scottish literacy*, pp. 70–83; Withers, *Gaelic in Scotland*, pp. 120–40.

[84] Donald Maclean, *The counter-reformation in Scotland, 1560–1930* [1931]; R. A. Dodgshon, "'Pretense of blude" and "place of thair dwelling": the nature of Highland clans, 1500–1745', in R. A. Houston and I. D. Whyte, eds., *Scottish society, 1500–1800* (Cambridge, 1989), pp. 169–98; Stevenson, *Highland warrior*, pp. 267–301; cf. Roger L. Emerson, 'Scottish cultural change 1660–1710 and the union of 1707', in Robertson, ed., *Union for empire*, pp. 121–44.

[85] Salmon, 'Missionary linguistics'; M. H. Risk, 'Charles Lynegar, professor of the Irish language 1712', *Hermathena*, 102 (1966), 16–25; Muriel McCarthy, *All graduates and gentlemen* (Dublin, 1980), pp. 13–15; Barnard, 'Provost Huntington'; [Anderson], *Brief sketch*.

the Irish new testament in 1602, remained unpublished at his death.[86] Interest in the surviving manuscript revived in the 1670s, particularly in the light of the conversion to protestantism, and return to Ireland, of the exile catholic scholar Andrew Sall. Although an Irish bible might have done little to establish protestantism among the largely illiterate Gaelic population of Ireland, it might have helped to encourage further conversions following the model provided by Sall himself. Both Narcissus Marsh, as provost of Trinity College, and Henry Jones, bishop of Meath, showed considerable interest in the project of printing the bible, and they helped to secure the backing of Robert Boyle for the venture. Despite high costs, and difficulties with the transcription, the bible was eventually completed in 1685. It made little impact on its arrival in Ireland, however, other than as a curiosity.[87] This may have been because of increasing hostility to the native Irish, which helped to ensure that no effective measures were taken to teach reading in Gaelic. Serious attempts to deal with this problem, and to persuade the church hierarchy to undertake the conversion of the Gaels, were made by John Richardson at the end of the first decade of the eighteenth century, but with little success. Richardson took up projects which had been advocated in the lower house of the Irish convocation, and obtained English money and support, notably from the SPCK. He intended to set up charity schools to catechise Irish children, as a first step in protestant evangelism and education. For various reasons, however, including a lack of support within the church of Ireland for his schemes (caused in part by divisions between members of the episcopate appointed from England and those chosen from among the Irish clergy), Richardson's plans achieved very little.[88] In Ireland, the problems of conversion and of bible literacy were secondary to the problem of vernacular literacy

---

[86] T. K. Abbott, 'On the history of the Irish bible', *Hermathena*, 17 (1913), 29–50; [Gilbert Burnet], *The life of William Bedell, D.D.* (1685); F. R. Bolton, *The Caroline tradition of the church of Ireland* (1958), pp. 1–30; Deasún Breatnach, *The best of the English: Bedell and the Irish version of the old testament* (Dublin, 1971); R. W. Jackson, *The bible and Ireland* (Dublin, 1950); John McCafferty, 'John Bramhall and the church of Ireland in the 1630s', in Ford, McGuire and Milne, eds., *As by law established*, pp. 100–11; Vivian Salmon, 'William Bedell and the universal language movement in seventeenth-century Ireland', *Essays and Studies*, new ser., 36 (1983), 27–39; E. S. Shuckburgh, ed., *Two biographies of William Bedell* (Cambridge, 1902), Bod., MS Rawlinson Letters 89, fs. 57r, 59r–v, 61r–v, 64–5, 70r, 74–5 (Bedell to Ussher).

[87] NLS, MS 821, fs. 1–73; Bod., MS Ashmole 1816, fs. 323–4, MS Rawlinson B 497, f. 24r, MS Smith 52, fs. 121–8; Archbishop Marsh's Library, Dublin, MS Z 4.4.8; Thomas Birch, ed., *The works of the honourable Robert Boyle* (5 vols., 1744), V, cols. 602b–14b, 618b–619b; Maddison, 'Robert Boyle and the Irish bible'. Despite the attempt to distribute unsold copies of the Irish bible in Scotland, the book was still on sale in London in 1700, see *Books sold by Edmund Rumball* (1700).

[88] See footnote 29 above; Henry Cotton, *Fasti ecclesiae Hibernicae* (5 vols., Dublin, 1845–60), IV, p. 204; Hayton, 'Did protestantism fail?'.

itself, which was not tackled seriously in the period.[89] No real attempts were made to teach reading either in Gaelic or in English to the bulk of the catholic population in order to further the spread of protestantism. Instead, there was a misplaced confidence that economic and social factors would force out both the Irish language and Irish catholicism.[90] Whilst to some extent this proved to be true for the use of the Gaelic language itself, it was not a successful strategy for building either religious unity or a sense of common national identity between the New English protestants, and Gaelic speakers or catholic Old English.

In the second decade of the eighteenth century, the Dublin SPCK encouraged the establishment of charity schools to increase literacy among the poor protestants of Ireland. They accompanied this venture with a plan to print and distribute by subscription up to 20,000 copies of the English bible. Although this experiment was a qualified success, its form underlines the nature of the limits which were set for bible literacy in Ireland.[91] Far from being a tool to unite the nation, through the provision of a common religious or linguistic heritage, the English bible remained a symbol of division, the totem of a minority, rather than a resource for all.[92] Its status had been established as early as the Irish rebellion of 1641, during which the symbolic destruction of copies of the bible in English came to represent both native Irish hatred of protestantism and the New English, and English fears of the savagery and irreligion of the Irish.[93] By accepting that the Irish were a separate people, with an independent genealogy, as was suggested to them by the Milesian history of native authors like Geoffrey Keating, English churchmen and antiquarians were able to marginalise the Gaelic

---

[89] L. M. Cullen, 'Patrons, teachers and literacy in Irish: 1700–1850', in Mary Daly and David Dickson, eds., *The origins of popular literacy in Ireland* (Dublin, 1990), pp. 15–44.

[90] See Alan Bliss, *Spoken English in Ireland, 1600–1740* (Dublin, 1979); Bliss, 'The English language in early modern Ireland', and Brian Ó Cuív, 'The Irish language in the early modern period', both in T. W. Moody, F. X. Martin and F. J. Byrne, eds., *A new history of Ireland: volume III, Early modern Ireland, 1534–1691* (3rd impression, Oxford, 1991), pp. 546–60 and 509–45 respectively; Ó Cuív, 'Irish language and literature, 1691–1845', in Moody and W. E. Vaughan, eds, *A new history of Ireland: volume IV, eighteenth-century Ireland, 1691–1800* (Oxford, 1986), pp. 374–423; Leerssen, *Mere Irish*.

[91] Christ Church, Oxford, MS Wake Letters 13, fs. 280–1, MS. Wake Letters 14, nos. 114, 195; Hayton, 'Did protestantism fail?'.

[92] Barnard, 'Protestants and the Irish language'.

[93] BL, MS Harley 5999, fs. 18v, 52v, 56r, 58v–62v; Trinity College, Dublin, MS 811, f. 47v, MS 812, f. 213v, MS 813, fs. 1, 306, MS 815, fs. 23, 70v, 370, MS 817, f. 160, MS 818, fs. 22, 25, 27, MS 820, f. 50, MS 824, f. 149, MS 834, f. 63, MS 832, f. 87, MS 835, f. 30, MS 836, fs. 49, 63v, 64v; Aidan Clarke, 'The 1641 depositions', in Fox, ed., *Treasures of the library*, pp. 111–22; Raymond Gillespie, 'Destabilizing Ulster, 1641–2', in Brian Mac Cuarta SJ, ed., *Ulster 1641: aspects of the rising* (Belfast, 1993), pp. 107–21.

inhabitants of Ireland, and to make them into a race whose past, as well as present, separated them from membership of the true British church. Although there might be debate over whether there had once been an original, true church in Ireland, with its own scriptures and liturgy, few doubted that the perfidious Irish had willingly denied it for the errors of Rome, just as they continued to spurn the true protestant church of Ireland in the seventeenth and eighteenth centuries.[94]

This chapter has provided a brief survey of schemes to print and distribute the bible outside those areas of the British Isles where English was routinely spoken during the late seventeenth and early eighteenth centuries. Constraints of time and space have prevented a more complete analysis of the motives and activities of the individuals involved in this story. Nor can there be a full explanation of the often complex reasons for the failure or success of each particular venture. Nevertheless, I hope that this survey does reveal certain common assumptions which acted to restrict the usefulness of the bible as a symbol of national identity, and to restrict bible literacy largely to those who could read English. Although it can be seen that illiteracy was a major limiting factor on the exercise and spread of protestantism, as defined by the church of England, by itself this does not explain the exclusion of Gaelic speakers from the religion of protestants, the apparently 'popish' denial of the vernacular to the Irish and the Highlander. In these cases, senses of national identity among the English-speaking peoples of the British Isles, and a desire to exclude the enemy within, triumphed over the stated religious aims of protestantism. The qualified success of attempts to evangelise Celtic language areas and to achieve biblical literacy in Wales, in contrast, demonstrated the extent to which the formation of such national identities themselves required more than the existence of a common scripture or ideology. British and Welsh identities, together with the protestantism which sustained them, needed complex personal and political alliances for their propagation. These alliances were however underpinned by a history which suggested that, of all the various Celtic peoples of the British Isles, the Welsh had most nearly preserved the true, original Christianity which had once flourished there.

Whereas the position of the Welsh in the eyes of contemporary English historians was relatively positive, seventeenth and eighteenth-century Scottish authors tended to be as critical of the heritage of the

---

[94] Cf. Nicholas Canny, 'The formation of the Irish mind', *P&P*, 95 (1982), 91–116; T. C. Barnard, 'Crises of identity among Irish protestants 641–1685', *P&P*, 127 (1990), 39–83; Raymond Gillespie, *Devoted people: belief and religion in early modern Ireland* (Manchester, 1997).

Gaels as their English neighbours. Thus, although the English bible did play a major role in uniting the language and aspirations of English people and Lowland Scots, the same attitudes which furthered this union prevented the spread of a British biblical culture in the far north and west. The campaigns to extirpate Gaelic in Scotland, although linguistically quite successful, did not ultimately result in the protestant evangelisation of the Highlands, nor did the indifference shown to Gaelic speakers in Ireland help to spread protestantism there. Such approaches to the problem of language difference, however, reinforced the view that the Highlanders and Irish were alien races permanently at war with the Gothic races of the English, Welsh and Lowland Scots. As such, they were to be excluded not only from the nation, but from the community of the godly which helped to give it its identity. In the final analysis, the grounds for this exclusion lay in the pages of the book of *Genesis*, in the bibles which defined the religion of protestants.

Protestantism, presbyterianism and
   national identity in eighteenth-century
   Scottish history

David Allan

The exact nature of the relationship between protestantism and Scottish national identity in the hundred years between the Glorious Revolution and the outbreak of the French revolution has been obscured by a number of factors. First, the already problematic identity of the Scots within the British monarchy was further complicated as a consequence of the act of union. After 1707, as numberless commentators have lamented, Scottishness took on a more attenuated meaning than in previous centuries, the country having been stripped of some of the trademark paraphernalia of the modern nation-state.[1] Second, the violently contested history of reformed religion within early modern Scotland, perhaps even more than in the rest of Britain, made protestantism a fiendishly difficult matrix within which to construct broad-ranging political or cultural identities. The familiar association of catholicism with treason was complicated by the continuing alienation of episcopalians from a presbyterian establishment and their simultaneous links with Jacobite subversion, preventing reformed religion from being a constituent of a putative national consciousness for the population as a whole. Third, the historiography of eighteenth-century Scotland has also been unkind to religion in general. As with conventional interpretations of the contemporary history of continental European states, the age of the enlightenment has been regarded widely as one in which primarily religious concerns were at best in retreat among the most influential sections of Scottish society. If not exactly relegated to an insignificant role, religion – protestant or otherwise – has thus been assigned a relatively minor part in the social, intellectual and political

---

[1] Tom Nairn, *The break-up of Britain* (1977) remains the foundation text of modern concern for the nation's evanescent identity. A good current overview is T. C. Smout, 'Perspectives on the Scottish identity', *Scottish Affairs*, 6 (1994), 101–13. Alexander Grant and Keith J. Stringer, eds., *Uniting the kingdom: the making of British history* (1995) contains a number of essays germane to this problem.

lives of the period. It is the collective consequence of these factors that protestantism and national identity in eighteenth-century Scotland have remained relatively unfamiliar and seemingly uncomfortable bedfellows.[2] This is still the case despite the 'absolute centrality of Protestantism to British religious experience in the 1700s', powerfully asserted for the archipelago as a whole by Linda Colley.[3] In assessing the relevance of some of Colley's insights by means of a discussion of contemporary attitudes towards the Scottish past, this chapter issues a mild rebuke to an historiography which has for too long permitted this situation to continue unchallenged.

I

By a marvellous irony, our inability fully to appreciate the significance of protestantism in the historical understanding of eighteenth-century Scotland, and so the complex question of national identity, owes much to the importance of specifically religious sensitivities in constructing the received account of the Scottish past. For lying behind many of the present-day assumptions about the character of early modern Scotland is the opinion-forming influence of opposing confessional and denominational perspectives originating in that period. The record of Anglo-Scottish relations presented in the medieval chronicles, for example, was largely the work of monastic and clerical authors, and needs to be understood as part of the struggle between Scotland's native churchmen and the aggrandising English archdioceses of Canterbury and York.[4] Equally, the notion of 'commonweal', with which the Scots armed themselves conceptually for the fifteenth-century defence of their nationhood from the English, contained significant elements of a specifically moral identity, grounded in the idea that the Scots were especially noble, loyal and courageous.[5] Above all, the birth of modern historical scholarship in Scotland during the sixteenth century is inextricably linked with the emergence of what Anne Smith nicely christened the national 'Knoxplex': the reformation.[6] Hector Boece's *Scotorum historiae*

---

[2] An exception is Joseph M. Bradley, *Ethnic and religious identity in modern Scotland: culture, politics and football* (Avebury, 1995) which is, however, a sociological study of contemporary Scotland. See also Willie Storrar, *Scottish identity: a Christian vision* (Edinburgh, 1990), which valorises Scottish piety as the basis for society in the 1990s. Neither work, inevitably, has much to say about the eighteenth century.

[3] Linda Colley, *Britons: forging the nation, 1707–1837* (1992), p. 18.

[4] G. W. S. Barrow, *Kingship and unity: Scotland 1000–1306* (1981), pp. 68–70.

[5] R. A. Mason, 'Chivalry and citizenship: aspects of national identity in renaissance Scotland', in R. A. Mason and N. Macdougall, eds., *People and power in Scotland* (Edinburgh, 1992), esp. pp. 58–9.

[6] Quoted in Iain Finlayson, *The Scots* (Oxford, 1988), p. 44.

(1527) had already rendered the national past in a ripe rhetoric of pervasive moral corruption suited to the mood of the coming religious crisis.[7] A similar analysis was favoured by early protestant authors who needed to develop a persuasive critique of existing social and political morality. Writers like Robert Lindsay of Pitscottie, whose *History and chronicles of Scotland* (1565?) included a strident criticism of contemporary manners, certainly illustrate the arrival of strongly reformist sentiment in mainstream historiography.[8] Likewise, the once popular works of Sir David Lindsay, written mainly in the 1530s and 1540s, betray the emergence of broadly protestant sensibilities within the canonical texts treating the condition and character of the Scottish nation.[9]

George Buchanan, the most famous and most controversial of Scotland's distinguished renaissance historians, also owes much of his notoriety to the sharply protestant edge to his work, written in the untidy aftermath of Knox's activities. The *Rerum Scoticarum historia* (1582) offers a truly radical vision of Scotland's status as a historical entity.[10] Strongly coloured by its author's commitment to the presbyterian revolution of 1560, by which the French-backed catholic Guise regime had been expelled, the work sets out to vindicate the deposition of Mary in 1567 in favour of her young and prospectively protestant son James VI, to whom Buchanan acted as tutor. In Buchanan's choleric mind the moral dissection of the nation's collective story, very much in the vein of Boece, sustained a startling further conviction which thereafter became integral to the justification of this notably revolutionary reformation: that Scotland had always been historically protestant in character. In terms of strict scholarly accuracy this claim was of course meretricious nonsense. Yet this fact should not blind us to its profound importance in shaping throughout the next few centuries protestant Scots' sense of their own distinctive place in the world. That the Scots had indeed been chosen by God for a singular role in the worldwide reformation of religion was to occupy a central place in many Scots' understanding of themselves, especially within the presbyterian community which had been chiefly responsible for effecting the reformation. As Arthur Williamson has convincingly argued, a potent blend of Calvinist doctrine and sustained historical analysis had produced by the end of the sixteenth century a remarkably evocative and durable concep-

---

[7] Hector Boece, *Scotorum historiae a prima gentis origine* (Paris, 1527).

[8] Robert Lindsay, *The history of Scotland from 21 February 1436, to March 1565*, ed. R. Freebairn (Edinburgh, 1728).

[9] See Carol Edington, *Court and culture in renaissance Scotland: Sir David Lindsay of the Mount* (Edinburgh, 1995).

[10] George Buchanan, *Rerum Scoticarum historia* (Edinburgh, 1582).

tion of Scottishness closely bound up with a dynamic tradition of fervently committed, eschatological protestantism.[11]

Up to and including the early part of the present century, Scottish historiography remained strongly influenced by this essentially presbyterian vision of the past. Asserting the country's special place in the militant vanguard of international protestantism down the ages, this interpretation has charted the lamentable decline and periodic resurgence of sincere religious piety as the unvarying barometer of Scotland's moral health. If in the sixteenth century it was a line of argument which had allowed Buchanan to valorise the achievements of the reformers, then it was also to be used by his immediate successors like John Row, to portray Scotland as a bulwark of the reformist cause since the earliest days of the Christian church. The Scots were a people in whose affairs divine providence had frequently intruded: Row himself, as a contributor to the reformation, was confidently described as 'a great observer of passages of providence in his tyme, and recording them, wes verie usefull and instrumentall at the ministers first meetings'.[12] Even that loyalist to James VI, Sir Thomas Craig, was little troubled by the potentially unsettling implications of this belief in the Scots' singularly radical protestant identity, proudly boasting in 1605 that the people were indeed 'the first to impugn the tyrannous dogmas of Rome and to resist them stoutly'.[13] Over the next century the same vision of matchless Scottish spiritual purity, always insidiously threatened but always heroically triumphant, frequently dominated public discussion of the national condition. At the end of the sixteenth century, for example, the church of Scotland was described by the presbyterian author David Calderwood as having 'now come to the greatest puritie that ever it attained unto'.[14] Knox's extravagantly self-justificatory text, subsequently published as *The Historie of the reformation of the church of Scotland* (1587), likewise insisted that the Scots were everywhere 'acknowledged to be among the first who embraced the Faith of Christ' and that they had instituted a doctrinally pure and strictly presbyterian system of church government.[15] Retailing a highly charged account of the nation's significance in world history, such works helped turn the past into a serious matter of contention between supporters and opponents of Stuart religious policy in the three seventeenth-century British kingdoms.

[11] A. H. Williamson, *Scottish national consciousness in the age of James VI: the apocalypse, the union and the shaping of Scotland's public culture* (Edinburgh, 1979).

[12] John Row, *The history of the kirk of Scotland* (Edinburgh, 1842), p. 479.

[13] Sir Thomas Craig, *De unione regnorum Britanniae tractatus*, ed. and trans. C. Sanford Terry, Scottish History Society, vol. 60 (Edinburgh, 1909), p. 381.

[14] David Calderwood, *The true history of the church of Scotland* (n.p., 1678), p. 311.

[15] John Knox, *The historie of the reformation of the church of Scotland* (1644), b1r.

This essentially religious account of Scotland's place in world history undoubtedly discomforted the Stuart monarchy. In the eyes of Charles I's covenanting opponents, it was clear that his regime threatened the nation's very integrity as it threatened also Scotland's supposedly ancient protestant traditions. Laudian innovations, from a presbyterian perspective, could be equated historically with alien Roman practices as well as with more recent and scarcely more welcome anglican influences. They represented a denial of a precious spiritual inheritance. This resonant historical analysis lent real credence to the claims of those who went on to subscribe to the national covenant in 1638 and to defend it on the battlefield: the wars of the covenant reveal starkly the importance of the sense that Scotland had been characterised historically, before Charles's ill-judged interventions, as a fundamentally protestant nation. Undoubtedly, the problems of the Stuart throne were exacerbated by the specifically presbyterian inflection with which that identity had usually been articulated. In 1638, for example, one writer, probably John Leslie, sixth earl of Rothes and soon to be a leading covenanting politician, produced *A short relation of the state of the kirk of Scotland*, in which he asserted in the strongest terms the pristine integrity of the church with which Charles I was meddling: 'The Kirk of Scotland after the reformation of Religion did by degrees attaine as great perfection both in doctrine & discipline as any other reformed kirk in Europe.'[16]

Samuel Rutherford of St Andrews was another prominent contributor to the radical chorus, insisting in *Lex, Rex* (1644) that the bishops' recent activities in Scotland amounted to national apostasy among a hitherto spiritual and historically convenanted people: John Maxwell, bishop of Ross, for example, had been guilty of 'Tyranny over mens conscience, and invading places of civill dignity, and deserting his calling, and the camp of Christ'.[17] Alexander Petrie, too, exiled in Amsterdam after the restoration and the inglorious return of the Scottish bishops, not only insisted that 'the Church was governed without Bishops', at least until the time of Hildebrand, but further argued that it was possible to mark 'the speciall providence of God in Reforming the Church of Scotland, as hath been declared'.[18] In this light, it is not difficult to understand the fury with which successive royal attempts to roll back the achievements of the protestant reformation in Scotland were greeted throughout the seventeenth century by its staunchest presbyterian defenders.

---

[16] Anon., *A short relation of the state of the kirk of Scotland* (Edinburgh, 1638), A2r.
[17] Samuel Rutherford, *Lex, Rex: the law and the prince* (1644), A4v.
[18] Alexander Petrie, *A compendious history of the catholick church* (Amsterdam, 1662), pp. 276, 352.

After the restoration, bitter conflict ensued between the episcopalian and presbyterian traditions, fuelled by the preference of the Stuart state for the former and by the refusal of the latter's upholders to abandon the obligations of the covenant.[19] Where it was still manifested in learned disputation rather than in summary executions and pitched battles, the dispute about the nation's religious identity was again conducted instinctively by reference to conflicting interpretations of the past. For the episcopalian party, spoke men like Alexander Monro, principal of the University of Edinburgh until 1689, who insisted that the institution of bishops in Scotland, the very essence of episcopalianism, was justified by sound historical precedent.[20] On the presbyterian side stood his post-revolution successor, Gilbert Rule, and Rule's fervent colleague, Thomas Forrester, who both maintained that episcopacy, so far from being consistent with native religious traditions, was in fact an alien and popish innovation of notably late foundation.[21] It had been foisted on the long-suffering Scottish people, they insisted, by encroachments from Rome pursued with the active collusion of craven governments in London and Edinburgh. In this view, a recognisable formulation of the presbyterian analysis developed in the sixteenth century, Scottish piety and spirituality had long been based on the presbyterian system of church government. This, its late seventeenth-century devotees claimed, had first been established in Scotland by the Culdees of the fifth century. Similar claims for antique Scottish protestantism were made by fanatical presbyterian writers such as Alexander Shields, exiled like Petrie in the Netherlands, and by the elder Robert Fleming, also exiled in Holland prior to 1690 because of his commitment to a radical form of the protestant vision.[22] As with Buchanan's special pleading on behalf of pre-reformation protestantism in Scotland, one reads such material with as much desperation as incomprehension. Culdeean presbyterianism must have been a strange creature indeed; and the notion that episcopacy, which had manifestly prospered in Scotland for a thousand years, was actually an unwarranted and unprecedented innovation, strains twentieth-century credulity, as it strained the eighteenth-century patience of the acute Thomas Innes, beyond breaking-

---

[19] On the later significance of the covenant on Scottish self-perceptions, see Christopher Harvie, 'The covenanting tradition', in G. Walker and T. Gallagher, eds., *Sermons and battle hymns: protestant popular culture in modern Scotland* (Edinburgh, 1990), pp. 8–23.

[20] Alexander Monro, *An apology for the clergy of Scotland* (1692).

[21] Gilbert Rule, *A vindication of the church of Scotland* (Edinburgh, 1691); Thomas Forrester, *The hierarchical bishops claim to a divine right* (Edinburgh, 1699).

[22] Alexander Shields, *A hind let loose: or, an historical representation of the testimonies of the church of Scotland* ([Amsterdam], 1687); Robert Fleming, *The fulfilling of the scripture*, (3rd edn, [n.p.], 1681), first published 1671.

point.[23] But anachronistic cavills about accuracy and reasonableness miss the point. It is the palpable sense of Scotland's unique historical destiny as a reformed nation, as the legitimate guardian and supreme embodiment of a distinctively protestant vision through history, which is important. This belief, developed in the sixteenth century and if anything only sharpened in intensity by the controversy and violence of the seventeenth, inevitably provided the dominant view of the Scottish past to which later ages, and not least the eighteenth century, would have most ready access.

Importantly, this interpretation of previous ages could be applied to the circumstances which confronted eighteenth-century commentators. By offering such a vivid contrast to the ostentatious tolerance and urbanity of those who directed the contemporary church, the presbyterian characterisation of earlier centuries in Scottish history only accentuated the growing sense that the Hanoverian age was marked by a sudden rise of secularisation in general and unbelief in particular. The disturbingly evangelical tinge to the traditional view was not wholly congenial to those liberal-minded souls who ran the solidly established church of the 1760s, but it was enormously influential in shaping attitudes towards the moderate faction and on the state of Scottish religion under their stewardship. Latter-day exponents like John Witherspoon, sometime minister of Paisley and later president of the College of New Jersey, developed a cutting critique of the moderate hegemony which was to prove influential in the next age, as criticism of the church's eighteenth-century direction reached crisis point.[24] From the evangelical perspective of the so-called popular party, led by Robert Dick, John Erskine and Witherspoon, the Scots' age-old religious identity as a pure and untainted reformist people had fallen suddenly into unworthy hands. The moderates, it seemed, were guilty of selling presbyterianism short, of squandering the nation's spiritual birthright. They were an unrepresentative and dilettante elite, bent on destroying the legacies built up by Scottish protestantism down the ages. In Witherspoon's famously forceful satire, the moderates now avoided 'all the high flights of evangelic enthusiasm, and the mysteries of grace, which the common people are so fond of'.[25] Instead, they supposed that 'a minister must endeavour to acquire as great a degree of politeness in his

---

[23] For the catholic critic Innes it was plain that there had been in early medieval Scotland 'no pretended primitive church government without bishops': *Civil and ecclesiastical history of Scotland* (Edinburgh, 1853), p. 43.

[24] John Witherspoon, *The history of a corporation of servants discovered a few years ago in the interior parts of South America* (Edinburgh, 1765).

[25] John Witherspoon, *Ecclesiastical characteristics; or the arcana of church policy* (Glasgow, 1753), p. 15.

carriage and behaviour, and to catch as much of the air and manner of a fine gentleman, as he possibly can'.[26] In acquiescing on lay patronage, in accommodating themselves to a distant and corrupt civil power in London, in elevating politeness above piety and in deliberately emasculating the parish pulpit and the presbyterian court system, they had made the worthless period of their dominance notorious, claimed the evangelicals, in the long and glorious annals of the Scottish church.

In the nineteenth century the same vivid presbyterian historical rhetoric, most stridently voiced by the popular party, took on a renewed usefulness as a consequence of the disruption in the church of Scotland. Indeed, the cataclysm of 1843 was itself caused in part by differing interpretations of the direction purportedly taken by Scottish protestantism in the preceding century.[27] Evangelical presbyterians of the nineteenth century followed Witherspoon and his high-flying ilk in assailing the allegedly secularising and despiritualising influences attributed to the establishmentarian moderate hegemony rooted in the age of the enlightenment. This, as much as anything else, led men like Thomas Chalmers and Thomas Guthrie to found a rival ecclesiastical structure which claimed to be the sole legitimate heir of the nation's protestant tradition. The free church thus embodied a potent historical critique of eighteenth-century theology and pastoral activity which, publicised by its many literary organs and vehemently upheld by its vociferous spokesmen, long retained considerable influence. James McCosh, Witherspoon's successor at Princeton by exactly a century, was a leading exponent of this view in the later Victorian period, arguing in his hugely influential *The Scottish philosophy* (1875) that moderatism had been an unwarranted and deeply harmful deviation from the linear tradition of pure Scottish protestantism. Eighteenth-century ministers of this bent had been responsible for the people becoming 'callous to all religion', whilst their secular friends had perpetrated impiety after impiety:

In the turmoil of opinions which sprang up in this new state of things, there are rumours of deism, and even of atheism, being secretly entertained or openly avowed, and of the establishment here and there, in town and country, of 'hell-fire clubs', where bold men met to discuss new opinions, and even, it is said, to act mock ceremonies, intended to ridicule the sacraments, and all that is awful in religion.[28]

McCosh's evangelically minded successors of the early twentieth century scarcely relented in this assault on what was staunchly believed

[26] Ibid., p. 23.
[27] S. J. Brown and M. Fry, eds., *Scotland in the age of the disruption* (Edinburgh, 1993).
[28] James McCosh, *The Scottish philosophy: biographical, expository, critical, from Hutcheson to Hamilton* (1875), p. 18.

to have been rampant eighteenth-century irreligion. William Law Mathieson described the period in distinctly unflattering terms: the 'noontide of moderatism' was marked, he claimed, by many novel 'ecclesiastical demerits'.[29] As late as the 1940s authors like the Free church historian James MacLeod agreed that the eighteenth century had indeed been marked by a widespread hostility to religion.[30] Even in 1994, that earnest contemporary sect, the Scottish Republican Forum, pursued their ceaseless struggle against an English-dominated British state by evoking, and once again reformulating, the protestant vision of history: 'The covenanters', they enthuse (in a present tense which is itself highly significant), 'trigger off the first revolution of the three kingdoms and bring forward new class forces.'[31] Small wonder, then, that historians have traditionally found it difficult to identify a clear relationship between a supposedly decadent eighteenth-century protes-tantism and the collective identity of a suddenly stateless nation. *moral, cultural decline*

II

It is true that the eighteenth-century church of Scotland was dominated, politically if not numerically, by the moderate clergy, men closely associated both with the Hanoverian state and with the surviving post-union national infrastructure of city, church and university, particularly in Edinburgh.[32] On this much modern scholarship has achieved a broad consensus. Individuals like William Robertson, John Home, Alexander Carlyle, Hugh Blair and Adam Ferguson are important not merely because they held major clerical posts. They were also employed as university professors, they achieved international eminence in scholar-ship and literature, and they successfully advanced the local political interests of the London government. More prosaically, it was their immediate duty to exercise a restraining influence over the conduct of their less-well-heeled clerical colleagues. The moderates, it is clear, sought to diminish the impact of conventional theological and ecclesio-

---

29 W. L. Mathieson, *The awakening of Scotland: a history from 1747 to 1797* (Glasgow, 1910), pp. 186–241.

30 J. MacLeod, *Scottish theology* (Edinburgh, 1943).

31 Anon., *Jacobite or covenanter: which tradition?* (Edinburgh, 1994), p. 15. Anyone doubting the authenticity of the radical presbyterian vision as the embodiment of popular Scottishness is warned: 'Middle class historians often judge people by their words and hence can be easily taken in, by smooth tongued, elegant dandies, like Charles and James' (p. 27).

32 See esp. I. D. L. Clark, 'From protest to reaction: the moderate regime in the church of Scotland, 1752–1805', in N. T. Phillipson and R. Mitchison, eds., *Scotland in the age of improvement* (Edinburgh, 1970), 200–24; also R. B. Sher, *Church and university in the Scottish enlightenment* (Edinburgh, 1985).

logical disputes on Scotland's wider public life. At the same time, they attempted to curb the church's traditional tendency towards the censorship of heterodox belief. Their opposition to evangelical moves against the emerging Scottish theatre, culminating in the celebrated failure of the church to prevent Home's *Douglas* from being performed in Edinburgh in 1757, is well known. Moderate influence has also been detected trying to limit the effectiveness of the ecclesiastical courts in their traditional pursuit of alleged heresy and impiety, as in the unsuccessful case brought against the eccentric philosopher and jurist Lord Kames in 1755–6 for supposed necessitarianism. A secular-minded leadership of the church seemed successfully to have made presbyterian Scottish protestantism, once the bane of the politically quiescent and orthodox throughout all of Britain, as respectable as it was now impotent.

Under their influence, then, conventional presbyterian priorities apparently deferred to a meek establishmentarian politics. Blithely committed to a brand of whig constitutionalism borrowed from England, the moderate ministers and their lay accomplices, as Colin Kidd has shown, effected a sea-change in Scottish political self-perceptions.[33] To this extent it might not seem unreasonable to conclude, as many historians have done in relation to eighteenth-century Britain as a whole, that religion had been effectively subordinated to politics. But there are reasons to doubt the appropriateness of this view in a Scottish context. If one accepts that the country's politics ceased in the Hanoverian period to be influenced by matters theological or ecclesiastical, then the unquestionably incestuous relationship between the church's moderate leadership and the London administration can be seen as evidence of the demise of properly religious concerns even among the leaders of the established church. But if one rejects the premise – as the work of Jonathan Clark and others has encouraged English historians to do – then the picture in Scotland begins to look somewhat different.[34] If, as Colley suggests, political life across Britain was powerfully influenced by protestantism, then the close relationship between the church of Scotland and Hanoverian political culture takes on a rather different significance.[35] It becomes less eccentric to see the concern of moderate presbyterian clerics with Scotland's fortunes within both Hanoverian Britain and the wider world as retaining a strongly religious dimension.

[33] Colin Kidd, *Subverting Scotland's past: Scottish whig historians and the creation of an Anglo-British identity, 1689–c.1830* (Cambridge, 1993).
[34] J. C. D. Clark, *English society, 1688–1832: ideology, social structure and political practice during the ancien régime* (Cambridge, 1985).
[35] Colley, *Britons*, p. 47.

It begins to seem possible that their theological and ecclesiological commitments, at which evangelical commentators have always tended to scoff, might have retained starkly political and ideological implications. It is time, therefore, to reconsider the wider significance of religious affiliation, both in terms of the political activities of the church's leaders and in terms of their contribution to the renovation of eighteenth-century Scottish culture.

It is relevant in this regard that among the leaders of local opposition to the armies of Charles Edward Stuart in 1745 were the Edinburgh clergy and professoriate, Home and the presbyterian natural philosopher Colin Maclaurin to the fore. As one contemporary, John Campbell, noted with some justification, the clergy, 'with the Sword of the Gospel, gained a greater Conquest over those hot-headed Gentry' than had been managed by Sir John Cope and the defeated Hanoverian army in the field at Prestonpans.[36] Home himself went into print, late in life, with the definitive contemporary record of this seminal event, *The history of the rebellion in the year 1745* (1802).[37] Andrew Henderson, a like-minded sympathiser with the moderates, further reinforced this point, claiming in 1747 that, from the Scottish pulpits, 'With Flows of Eloquence, and Streams of Perswasion, they recommended loyalty to their King, a Regard for their Country, Liberties and Laws.'[38]

In these writings, establishmentarian Scotsmen comfortably deployed the orthodox presbyterian historical critique of Jacobitism, characterising it, like its correlate catholicism, as backward, superstitious and irrational. It is also noteworthy that Ferguson, formerly chaplain to the Black Watch at the battle of Fontenoy, was among the leaders of loyal outrage against the unwillingness of London to permit the arming of the Scots in self-defence in the 1750s and 1760s. That presbyterian ministers like Carlyle fronted the popular campaign to secure permission for the raising of a local militia again emphasises the crucial importance, organisationally and individually, of the church and its supposedly

---

[36] John Campbell, *A full and particular description of the Highlands of Scotland* (1752), p. 41.

[37] John Home, *The history of the rebellion in the year 1745* (1802).

[38] [Andrew Henderson], *The history of the rebellion, 1745 and 1746* (Edinburgh, 1747), p. 108. The equation of moderatism with strong anti-Jacobite utterances is nowhere more clearly illustrated than in the memory of Samuel Kenrick, an English dissenter, recalling after the Scottish treason trials of the 1790s his days as a student at Glasgow under Francis Hutcheson's tutelage: 'I feel a glow overspreading my heart at the very name of Hutcheson – from whose lips, like those of old Nestor you will know, persuasion flowed sweeter than honey – when it recalls to my mind his last farewell, warm effusions poured forth in defence of British liberty in the critical years of 1745 etc.': Kenrick to James Wodrow, 28 June 1794, Dr Williams' Library, London, Kenrick/Wodrow Papers, MS 24.157, 192. I am grateful to Ian McBride for this reference.

apathetic leadership in the definition and pursuit of Hanoverian Scotland's presumed interests within the protestant British state.[39] Carlyle's anonymous squib, *The question relating to the Scots militia considered* (1760), no less than *Reflections previous to the establishment of a militia* (1756) and the anonymous *Peg* pamphlet (1760), both of them probably by Ferguson, espoused a consistent and powerful blend of Scottish patriotic sentiment and protestant self-righteousness among the most influential sections of the clergy.[40] Henderson, too, in the *Considerations on the question whether a militia ought to extend to Scotland* (1760), was prepared to argue publicly that the protestantism of much of Lowland Scotland, and events such as the recent conversion of the Gordons in the north-east to the reformed religion, lent the country a character which deserved the trust and co-operation of the British parliament. What Richard Sher, in the best study of moderatism yet available, has termed an ideology of 'whig-presbyterian conservatism' not only aligned the men who dominated the church of Scotland with the London government.[41] It led them instinctively to identify Scotland's national interests in terms which were emphatically protestant, indeed still authentically presbyterian. In other words, Scottishness was articulated in terms which could best be defended by close association with the Hanoverian state but which clearly amounted to rather more than mute acceptance or passive acquiescence. Given the importance of these perspectives in eighteenth-century public discourse, the conventional presumption that connections between protestant religion and Scottish national consciousness could not have amounted to much under an anglicising, liberal and irresolute moderate clique begins to look rather less tenable.

The other main area in which the denigration of eighteenth-century Scottish religion in national life has been strongest has been our understanding of contemporary cultural and intellectual life. For more than two centuries, the Scottish enlightenment has been associated with the moderate churchmen and characterised by the possession of an overwhelmingly secular agenda. In certain cases, it has even been suggested that a basic antithesis existed between Scottish religion on the one hand and emerging enlightened values on the other. Thus Henry Buckle, Victorian England's greatest student of this problem, was convinced that eighteenth-century Scottish civilisation was specifically an escape

---

[39] John Robertson, *The Scottish enlightenment and the militia issue* (Edinburgh, 1985).
[40] Alexander Carlyle, *The question relating to the Scots militia considered* (Edinburgh, 1760); Adam Ferguson, *Reflections previous to the establishment of a militia* (1756); also *The history of the proceedings in the case of Margaret, commonly called Peg, only lawful sister of John Bull, esq.* (1760).
[41] Sher, *Church and university.*

wania ?
reaction

from the clutches of presbyterian protestantism, 'one of the most detestable tyrannies ever seen on earth'.[42] In the present century, Hector Macpherson also claimed that moderatism was simply 'the reaction' to the excesses of seventeenth-century Scottish protestantism.[43] Ironically, then, modern scholarship has tended to reinforce the equation of polite learning with irreligion drawn by the earliest critics of the moderate regime, while simply inverting the moral of the story. Such perspectives, like those which carelessly elide religion and politics in eighteenth-century Scotland and so assume the neutering of the former by the latter, have begun to receive rather more sceptical treatment. But their impact is with us still, again leading too many to think that protestantism and nationhood could not be closely related in the age of the Scottish enlightenment precisely because religion, under constant intellectual pressure, had ceased to matter.

Traditionally the picture of the Scottish enlightenment painted by academic study has emphasised its rationalistic aspirations, its materialistic emphasis and its determinedly practical and empirical bent.[44] That one of the greatest and most widely known studies of European thought in this period basks beneath the misleading title *The rise of modern paganism* has scarcely helped to inject any balance into the historiography.[45] For good measure, we have been encouraged to see the movement in Scotland as being aimed at importing English and continental modes of thought which, it is argued, overlay and increasingly obliterated older, more typically Scottish, patterns of thinking.[46] Much has been made of the impact of the scientific and medical endeavours of men like James Watt, James Hutton and three successive Alexanders Monro on popular conceptions of the natural world.[47] The concern for 'reason' demonstrated by Francis Hutcheson and Adam Smith has attracted a great deal of attention. 'Politeness', that familiar Addisonian contribution to modern society, has been identified at the very heart of enlightened literary and cultural endeavour.[48] The inven-

---

[42] Henry Buckle, *On Scotland and the Scotch intellect*, ed. H. J. Hanham (Chicago, 1970), p. 234.

[43] Hector Macpherson, *A century of intellectual development* (Edinburgh, 1902), p. 6.

[44] H. R. Trevor-Roper, 'The Scottish enlightenment', *Studies in Voltaire and the Eighteenth Century*, 58 (1967), 1635–58; G. E. Davie, *The Scottish enlightenment* (1981).

[45] Peter Gay, *The enlightenment*, 2 vols., (New York, 1966–9). The offending phrase occurs in the sub-title to the first volume.

[46] N. T. Phillipson, 'Politics, politeness and the anglicisation of early eighteenth-century Scottish culture', in R. A. Mason, ed., *Scotland and England: 1286–1815* (Edinburgh, 1987), pp. 226–46.

[47] S. Shapin, 'The audience for science in eighteenth-century Edinburgh', *History of Science*, 12 (1974), 95–121.

[48] N. T. Phillipson, 'Politics and politeness in the reigns of Queen Anne and the early

tion of classical political economy by Smith and Millar, and its supposed relationship with the rapidly commercialising economy of the west coast of Scotland, has always occupied a central position in the story.[49] More widely, it was believed that materialism underlay the concerns of Ferguson in the analysis of civil society and of those historians – Ferguson, Smith and Robertson among them – who evolved the so-called 'stadial theory' of historical progress, by which successive and universal stages of social evolution were characterised by their typical mode of subsistence.[50] All of these preoccupations have made the Scottish enlightenment appear positively inimical to traditional religious priorities. Scottish intellectual life, on this reading, was not only highly innovative, it was, as the evangelicals had always alleged, antagonistic to significant elements in previous national life. Most particularly, and as in the French enlightenment, it was hostile to the formerly crucial role of religion, an orientation of which David Hume – 'le bon David', 'the Great Infidel' or simply, to the common folk of Edinburgh, 'the Atheist', – could be held up as the pre-eminent human example. Here indeed was a deeply unpropitious intellectual environment in which protestantism and a modern national identity for Scotland might maintain a close relationship.

Analysis of the sermons and writings of the presbyterian ministers who actually sustained the Edinburgh enlightenment, however, has recently begun to reveal the unsuspected extent to which they remained motivated by recognisably religious concerns familiar from the Scottish past. Their endeavours, it seems from the work of John Dwyer in particular, were aimed at the effective reconciliation of a presbyterian morality with fashionable enlightened values. Notions such as 'sympathy', 'sensibility', 'propriety' and 'community', dear to Scottish enlightenment ethical theorising and much studied by recent academic interpreters, were closely related, in the minds of the literati, to the mores of what remained still a predominantly protestant society.[51] It has

Hanoverians', in J. G. A. Pocock, ed., *Varieties of British political thought, 1500–1800* (Cambridge, 1993), pp. 211–45.

[49] R. Pascal, 'Property and society: the Scottish historical school of the eighteenth century', *Modern Quarterly*, 2 (1938), 167–79; T. M. Devine, 'The Scottish merchant community, 1680–1740', in R. H. Campbell and A. S. Skinner, eds., *Origins and nature of the Scottish enlightenment* (Edinburgh, 1982), pp. 26–41.

[50] R. L. Meek, *Social science and the ignoble savage* (Cambridge, 1976); H. Höpfl, 'From savage to Scotsman: conjectural history in the Scottish enlightenment', *JBS*, 17 (1978), 19–40.

[51] John Dwyer, *Virtuous discourse: sensibility and community in late eighteenth-century Scotland* (Edinburgh, 1987); also 'The imperative of sociability: moral culture in the late Scottish enlightenment', *British Journal for Eighteenth-Century Studies*, 13 (1990), 169–84. On relations between Dwyer's discussion and Scottish identity, see T. C. Smout, 'Problems of nationalism, identity and improvement in later eighteenth-century

also been suggested that the rhetorical styles and techniques emanating from Scottish educational circles during the enlightenment, which were of such prodigious importance among the American clergymen of the revolutionary period, have their origins in the distinctive preaching traditions of Scottish presbyterianism.[52]

Nor did religious precedent and intellectual culture in the eighteenth century interact merely at the level of vocabulary and style. Substance overlapped too. I have argued elsewhere that enlightenment historical writing and its derivative disciplines, notable for their emphasis upon the inculcation of moral precepts and an obsession with providential determinism, actually bear the indelible marks of much older traditions of Scottish scholarship established in the aftermath of the Calvinist reformation.[53] Another recent scholar, Mary Fearnley-Sander, has shown how the preoccupations of post-reformation historiography can be teased out of a close reading of some of the major texts of the Scottish enlightenment, including the best-selling works of William Robertson.[54] The jeremiad, that classically presbyterian mode of public address and admonition much used by seventeenth-century Scottish ministers, apparently prospered anew in the age of the eloquent Witherspoon and Erskine.[55] Perhaps not entirely playfully, one student of this subject has even had the temerity to suggest that David Hume's own distinctive scepticism is itself in part an outgrowth of identifiably Scottish religious traditions.[56] If it can now credibly be proposed that even the offensive thoughts of the eighteenth century's most notorious atheist are a reflection of the anti-rationalist inclinations of orthodox Calvinism, then the possibility that protestantism and national identity might also have maintained a reasonably close relationship within the historical vision of enlightened Scotland perhaps no longer seems quite so implausible. One might next appropriately ask, then, whether there are indeed substantive grounds for such optimism.

Scotland', in T. M. Devine, ed., *Improvement and enlightenment* (Edinburgh, 1992), esp. pp. 12–15.

[52] David Daiches, '*Style périodique* and *style coupé*: Hugh Blair and the Scottish rhetoric of American independence', in J. R. Smitten and R. B. Sher, eds., *Scotland and America in the age of the enlightenment* (Edinburgh, 1990), pp. 209–26.

[53] David Allan, *Virtue, learning and the Scottish enlightenment: ideas of scholarship in early modern history* (Edinburgh, 1993).

[54] Mary Fearnley-Sander, 'Philosophical history and the Scottish reformation: William Robertson and the Knoxian tradition', *HJ*, 33 (1990), 323–38.

[55] R. B. Sher, 'Witherspoon's *Dominion of providence* and the Scottish jeremiad tradition', in Smitten and Sher, eds., *Scotland and America*, pp. 46–64.

[56] Stewart R. Sutherland, 'The presbyterian inheritance of Hume and Reid', in Campbell and Skinner, eds., *Origins and nature of the Scottish enlightenment*, pp. 131–49.

III

Persuasive evidence for the function of protestantism in the construction of Scotland's historical identity in the eighteenth century is not difficult to find. Religion, as I have already argued, could never become in Hanoverian Scotland a straightforward basis for the identity of an entire nation. But protestantism nevertheless had considerable potential as a basis for national identification. It was closely associated with the dominant groups in Hanoverian Scotland: the military activities and unruffled social leadership of the moderate clergymen and their lay supporters should remind us that the church of Scotland was not merely the lame and mute apologist for London government. Most protestant aristocrats, most protestant politicians and most protestant churchmen, even if they insistently questioned some of its local implications, also stood four-square behind Scotland's incorporation within a British state whose very existence rested on the notion of an exclusively protestant succession under Queen Anne and the three Georges. Furthermore, protestantism may have become more rather than less important to Scottish unionists as the eighteenth century progressed, just as Colley's claims about the religious dimension to emergent Britishness would seem to imply. With Jacobitism declining as a serious political threat at home, the experience of worldwide warfare against catholic France served to re-emphasise the need for Scotland's role in an increasingly expansive Britain to be viewed in terms of the successful assertion of shared, historically protestant, values upon the global stage: James Thomson's triumphalist 'Rule Britannia' (1740), memorably the work of a mere 'minister's son from the Scottish Lowlands', nicely encapsulates the striking process described by Colley.[57] Certainly in the decades during and after the Seven Years War it became more tempting not only for aspiring poets but for casuists and commentators in search of a composite British identity to equate the interests of both Scotland and England with the triumph of what were held to be quintessential protestant values – including thrift, industry, tenaciousness and self-sacrifice. At the same time, it may be that, by the 1750s, the increasing influence of moderatism within the established presbyterian church had in any case begun to make an accommodation with episcopalianism more acceptable, and a broader protestant identity domestically more viable within Scotland. Despite the early prominence in political discourse of themes such as the revolution settlement and the confounding of Jacobitism, which inevitably tended to be divisive among protestants,

[57] Colley, *Britons*, p. 11.

there are still signs even during the first half of the eighteenth century of a determined reworking of elements of the historical vision of Scottish protestantism taking place, in particular among those close to the centre of public life.[58]

Fundamental to the historiography and public discourse of the early eighteenth century was the legitimation, one might reasonably say sanctification, of a complicated chain of events which appeared to link Knox's reformation of 1560 with the revolution of 1689–90. By the removal of the hapless James VII from the throne and the insertion of William and Mary in his stead, Scotland's protestant liberties had supposedly been guaranteed amid a happy combination of providential intervention and far-sighted political leadership. Indeed, a cornerstone of the revolution settlement which had followed was the formal re-establishment of the presbyterian church of Scotland. Though to an extent undermined by the passage of the patronage act in 1712 under Queen Anne, which reintroduced lay control of benefices to the fury of the more evangelical members of the church, Scotland's proud reformist tradition did remain in those early decades of the eighteenth century a bulwark of the protestant succession and, after 1707, a natural ally of the Hanoverian British state. A most interesting example is found in the writings of George Mackenzie, first earl of Cromarty, once the servant of James VII but latterly a man who exhibited little discomfort in accommodating himself to the changed post-revolution order. His *An historical account* (1713), ostensibly devoted to the Gowrie conspiracy against James VI, in practice afforded a timely opportunity to deploy the protestant vision of Scotland's past. Inclined towards a moderate interpretation, Cromarty had no truck with the excesses of the presbyterian evangelicals. What remained necessary in his view, however, was a defence of the fundamental achievements of the Scottish reformation and of James's kingship; in his own words, the task was 'to vindicate that primary reformation, from the subsequent Errors and Malignancy, of the pretending Pseudo-Reformers'.[59] Whilst 'always defeated by Divine Providence', the theocratic conspirators against the Jacobean state, said Cromarty, had damaged the national interest and the cause of prudent Scottish protestantism, serving only to assist international catholicism with its 'pretended Ecclesiastick Jurisdiction over Men's Consciences'.[60]

---

[58] A different account from my own, though one which shares a concern for the major enterprise that was the reconstruction of Scottishness and Britishness in the Hanoverian age, is Colin Kidd, 'North Britishness and the nature of eighteenth-century British patriotism', *HJ*, 39 (1996), 361–82.

[59] George Mackenzie, *An historical account of the conspiracies by the earls of Gowry and Robert Logan of Restalrig against King James VI* (Edinburgh, 1713), p. 15.

[60] Ibid., pp. 10–14.

Another early-eighteenth-century exponent of the protestant vision was Sir James Dalrymple, son of the great jurist Lord Stair and a presbyterian historian of some distinction. For Dalrymple, as for the covenanters of the seventeenth century, it was Scotland's fundamentally different religious traditions, specifically its protestantism and its supposedly ancient history of presbyterian church government, which justified the nation's continued claims to independence and formed the basis of his rebuttal of aggressive English counter-claims. Introducing the *Collections concerning the Scottish history* (1705), he explained that his would be a work 'wherein The Sovereignty of the Crown and Independency of the Church are cleared; And an Account given of the Antiquity and Purity of the Scottish-British Church, and the Noveltie of Popery in this Kingdom.'[61] In other words, like Buchanan, Knox and Rule before him, Dalrymple conceived of the nation's past as vindicating the presbyterianism recently re-established in the revolution settlement: the church of Scotland had 'continued free from the Intrigues and Domination of the Bishop of Rome, till about the Year 1100', he asserted.[62] This history argued persuasively for recognition of profound differences between Scotland and England which 'by the providence and Goodness of God' remained evident in the survival of the presbyterian system.[63] Others who shared Dalrymple's distaste for strident English imperialism within Britain did nevertheless feel obliged to emphasise instead the shared protestant character of the two kingdoms, in a way which in fact prefigured the rhetoric of later unionist polemic. James Anderson, for example, writing in the same year as Dalrymple, and in a work published by the same printer, Andrew Andersons of Edinburgh, spoke no less effusively of 'two Protestant Independent kingdoms, which I pray GOD may continue in Peace and Amity, while Sun and Moon endure'.[64] For such authors, the religious identity of Scotland, long advertised by presbyterian historiography, was essential to an understanding of the case against naked English dominion in the early eighteenth century. To Anderson, writers like Buchanan and Craig, who had always upheld the nation's distinctiveness, were 'worthy Patriots'.[65] His own audience, meanwhile, were 'all true SCOTS-MEN, yea all Sincere well-wishers, of the peace and quiet of Britain'.[66] Yet the need for 'a Good Understanding' with England was still clear, the countries being 'by the Blessing of Heaven already Engaged to one another, by the most

---

[61] Sir James Dalrymple, *Collections concerning the Scottish history* (Edinburgh, 1705), Preface.
[62] Ibid., A1v.   [63] Ibid., p. LI.
[64] James Anderson, *An historical essay shewing that the crown and kingdom of Scotland is imperial and independent* (Edinburgh, 1705), p. 280.
[65] Ibid., p. 148.   [66] Ibid., Preface.

Endearing Tye of Religion'.[67] As the century progressed, it became clear that the traditional emphasis on Scotland's historic protestantism would also, as Anderson's argument unintentionally illustrated, sustain a broad unionist consensus on which the Hanoverian British state could be securely constructed.

Significant signs of the integration of Scottish protestantism within Hanoverian Britishness can be seen in the work of another presbyterian controversialist, the Dutch-educated minister and son of the earlier-mentioned writer, Robert Fleming, who, as early as 1701, was arguing, on the basis of common protestantism, for the sinking of denominational differences and the development of a united front with episcopalians and other British co-religionists against Louis XIV's expansionist catholicism. Generously praising the 'parts and learning', the 'piety and moderation also' of non-presbyterians, in Fleming's judgement any further wrangling between the different kinds of Scottish and English protestants was senseless.[68] On the contrary, Fleming, who was known to William III and seems to have been close to Archbishop Tenison during his ministry in London, maintained that they needed now to 'learn a little Prudence, even from our Popish Adversaries, that we might unite in Love, and in design to promote a general Interest, though we attain not to an exact Uniformity in all things'.[69]

Such pragmatic ecumenism, stemming from a sense of shared protestantism within Scotland, did not prevent Fleming, whose title boasted of his describing the *Rise and fall of the papacy*, from voicing strident anti-catholic views. Indeed, as Colley argues, anti-catholicism was an effective anvil on which a united Britain could be shaped. Fleming's beguiling blend of generous eirenicism towards fellow protestants and rank hostility towards popery was, then, to represent an increasingly typical eighteenth-century approach to the question of Scotland's historical identity. Drawing on older traditions of public discussion, this now emphasised the existence of a broadly protestant majority within both Scotland and Britain. And it therefore opened up for Hanoverian commentators the possibility of justifying Anglo-Scottish union, a marriage quite literally made in heaven, in specifically religious terms.

John Bonar, minister at Cockpen in Midlothian and one of the evangelical clergymen involved in the unsuccessful prosecution of Lord Kames, is actually a fine example of more confident mid-century sentiment on the protestant status of the British people described by

---

[67] Ibid., p. 280.

[68] Robert Fleming, *Discourses on several subjects. The first containing a new account of the rise and fall of the papacy* (1701), p. xiii.

[69] Ibid., p. xiv.

Colley.[70] In an unpublished manuscript *History of Tyre* (c.1758), Bonar voiced a powerful sense of presbyterian moral outrage at the nation's current predicament, beset, as it then seemed, by defeat and disappointment at a crucial moment in the Seven Years War. Writing before the 'Year of Victories' in 1759, when Britain's salvation would be wrought by soldiers and sailors from Minden and Lagos to Quebec, Bonar offered an analysis of his nation's place in the world and of its special relationship with God which arose straight out of the presbyterian historical vision of the sixteenth century. The cause of Bonar's particular anxiety was his realisation, when meditating on a fast day declared by George II in February 1758, that the situations of ancient Tyre and modern Hanoverian Britain were actually so similar:

> Upon that occasion, the Author of the following Dissertation, persuaded that there was some resemblance in point of Character between the Inhabitants of Britain, & those of Tyre; in order to excite that particular Congregation among whom he ministered in holy things, to bear their part in the general repentance & reformation, took the opportunity of setting before them the fall of this people, the greatest trading nation of Antiquity, & whose total ruin is frequently in Scripture ascribed to her universal degeneracy, & corruption of manners.[71]

Bonar's analysis is strikingly similar to that of John Witherspoon issued in 1776 on the occasion of the American declaration of independence, and indeed stands squarely in the grand tradition of presbyterian jeremiad sermons. In Bonar's case, no less than Witherspoon's with regard to the Americans, the special status of the Scottish or British people as a covenanted protestant nation under God was plainly integral to his vision.[72]

Similar ideas, building a sense of national consciousness in Scotland through an unashamed appeal to local religious sensibilities, are to be found in a second contemporary tract, *A just complaint on mankind for injuring, killing and eating animals*, probably written by one John Williamson of Moffat around 1765.[73] Here again, as with Bonar, it was the voice of the traditional presbyterian which was heard demanding the moral and spiritual regeneration of Scottish society – symbolised by the adoption of vegetarianism – in the light of the late disasters which had

---

[70] Colley, *Britons*, pp. 30–2.
[71] John Bonar, *The history of Tyre* (Edinburgh, New College Library: X156, 1/5, Box 27), p. 2.
[72] See Sher, '*Dominion of providence*'; also Ann Matheson, *Theories of rhetoric in the eighteenth-century Scottish sermon* (Lewiston, NY, 1995), an outstanding new discussion of eighteenth-century pulpit oratory, emphasising the extent of evangelical ire directed against 'lukewarm Moderatism and its attendant moral ills'.
[73] [John Williamson], *A just complaint on mankind for injuring, killing and eating animals*, NLS, Adv. MS 23.6.3, f. 1r. I am indebted to the Trustees of the NLS, for their kind permission to cite this manuscript.

befallen the nation in the wars against catholic France. Failure to improve public morality in this way had, in the providential framework envisaged by presbyterian commentators like Witherspoon and Williamson, brought the nation the miseries which it had so clearly experienced:

Men are Justly punished for Animal murders for example the late War in America arose about fishing and the fur Trade of Deer & Beaver skins in place of which men sold one another scalps. There were also bloody Wars between the Dutch & the English about the Herring fishing & beside these general Judgments particular punishments come on murdering men while fishing by Shipwrecks, colds, wants & by many accidents which attend fishing.[74]

Williamson's biography is uncertain, although it appears that he was not a clergyman himself.[75] But it is clear that he belonged to a profoundly protestant tradition of moral thought. As Colley explains, much public discussion was governed by the inescapable reality that 'protestant Britons believed they were in God's special care'.[76] Just as the British state was emerging victorious from its enervating wars with catholic France, it was the protestant vision, dominated by the people's unique convenant with God and the divine retribution which inevitably followed departure from it, that for John Williamson, a minor voice in enlightened Scotland in the 1760s, still explained the condition of the nation.

From the later years of the century there is yet more evidence that protestantism was in specific ways still important to some historians' sense of Scottish and British nationhood. Indeed, it is worth remembering in this connection the particular difficulties in Scotland which prevented passage of the catholic relief act until as late as 1793 – the year, significantly, in which Fleming's uncomplimentary historical work on the papacy was again republished.[77] Some, like the episcopalian writer John Skinner, bishop of Aberdeen, were now prepared to cast serious aspersions on the traditional protestant vision of the past, remarking acidically that ancient Scottish presbyterianism, the suppositious cornerstone of national distinctiveness since the time of Buchanan, was nothing more than 'an unsupported hypothesis by some of our profest historians'.[78] But such doubts, inevitably voiced more easily by sceptical episcopalians, seem to have made little immediate impact on

[74] *A just complaint*, f. 6v.
[75] For a discussion of Williamson's obscure biography, see my unpublished paper 'Greeks, Indians and the Scottish presbyterian: dissident arguments for vegetarianism in Enlightenment Scotland', in a forthcoming issue of *1650–1850: ideas, aesthetics and inquiries in the early modern era.*
[76] Colley, *Britons*, p. 29.
[77] R. K. Donovan, *No popery and radicalism: opposition to Roman catholic relief in Scotland, 1778–1782* (New York, 1987).
[78] John Skinner, *An ecclesiastical history of Scotland* (2 vols., 1788), I, 38.

the sense of the nation's religious identity among the Scottish establishment. Thomas Somerville, for example, minister at Jedburgh and a vocal presbyterian conservative gloomily surveying the unpromising scene in revolutionary Europe, continued to purvey a version of the timeless protestant interpretation of history, in which by now no real distinction between Scotland and England needed to be drawn. In the *History of political transactions and parties* (1792), Somerville staunchly defended the constitutional *status quo* by reference to the protestant revolution of 1689–90. He would seek, he proudly claimed, to 'afford repeated opportunities of inculcating principles of genuine patriotism upon those who wish to understand and to pursue the true interests of their country'.[79] His analysis of the reigns of Charles II and James VII, moreover, gives vent to his conviction, of a piece with Row and Calderwood in an earlier age, that providence had intervened at crucial moments to guide the destiny of this most protestant of countries, the united Anglo-Scottish state, effectively ensuring what he called 'the deliverance of Britain'.[80] The contrary designs of Louis XIV and James VII, in fact, had been thwarted by God: 'While we trace the disappointment of these to the superintendency of Providence, it will be both instructive and entertaining, to attend to the external means, by which the designs of Providence were effected.'[81] Somerville's argument rested sure in the knowledge, provided by a historiographical tradition which could be traced back to the reformation, that Scotland, now securely incorporated within Britain, possessed a special protestant identity. Protestantism, he gushed proudly, in words which might well have come nearly a century earlier from the earl of Cromarty, was a religion 'which disclaims the usurpation of human authority . . . which holds the scriptures alone to be the rule of truth'.[82]

John Lawrie, too, an Edinburgh schoolmaster and military historian writing in the 1780s from a more strongly evangelical standpoint, found it relatively easy to attribute Scottish and British triumphs over France to the historically protestant character of their peoples. This move was perhaps natural in an author whose title spoke without embarrassment of providing, like the younger Fleming, 'a short view . . . of the rise . . . and decline of Popery'. The victories of the Seven Years War, he observed, had been ascribed too readily to 'invincible wooden walls, and mighty armies' when God alone had been truly responsible. In fact both Britain's successes and her failures, including the more recent disasters in the American colonies, owed everything to the moral and religious

---

[79] Thomas Somerville, *The history of political transactions and parties, from the restoration of King Charles II to the death of King William* (1792), p. xxii.
[80] Ibid., p. xvii.   [81] Ibid., p. 397.   [82] Ibid., p. 587.

tone of reformed protestant society. Indeed, renewed spiritual endeavours were now needed, as Britain struggled valiantly against Spain and France, the 'Popish powers, who have always been the greatest supports of Popish tyranny'.[83] Were such measures adopted, however, Britain's future might yet still be blessed: 'Should a general reformation take place, among all ranks of people, from the king on the throne to the meanest of the people; then we should soon behold Britain raising her drooping head, and her warlike sons resuming their native vigour.'[84] In other words, moral and spiritual regeneration, that oldest of protestant prescriptions for remedying the ills of civil society, remained the key, in the eyes of the late-eighteenth-century presbyterian, to the greater worldly glory of the Hanoverian British state, itself what Lawrie contentedly described as 'the darling of providence . . . favoured beyond many other nations'. Protestantism, for a confident Scottish commentator in the age of the American and French revolutions, continued to be the guarantee as well as the measure of national integrity.

IV

Protestantism, of course, could be a divisive as well as a unifying factor. As Somerville himself wrote, speaking of the 1680s but touching a truth still no less germane a century later, 'The state of religion in Scotland concurred . . . to propagate discordant affections and divided interests, and to prevent a possibility of uniting the whole force of the nation, upon the occurrence of any extraordinary political commotion.'[85] Yet, as in England, where the problems were perhaps less severe, religion did make a significant contribution to widely found Scottish self-perceptions. As Colley puts it, protestantism 'gave the majority of men and women a sense of their place in history and a sense of worth'.[86] Partly this was so because the presbyterian church of Scotland, for all its internal ferment and fissures, remained a force to be reckoned with: constant proponent of the revolution settlement, physical defender of the Hanoverian state against occasional Jacobite insurgency, eloquent mouthpiece of dynamic British imperialism as it found its voice after mid-century and, in the considerable persons of the moderates, the undisputed arbiter of intellectual life and polite letters, established protestantism was in fact central to the affairs of eighteenth-century Scotland within an increasingly expansive Great Britain, whatever a

[83] John Lawrie, *The completion of prophecy: the clearest evidence of the truth of Christianity* (Edinburgh, 1781), p. 220.
[84] Ibid., p. 222.   [85] Somerville, *History of political transactions*, p. 246.
[86] Colley, *Britons*, p. 53.

historiography skewed by longstanding evangelical distaste has tended to infer.

But it is the relentless historical undertow to Scottish protestantism which probably brought it closest to successful identification with the nation itself. The loss of legislative statehood in 1707, laid on top of the departure of the monarchy in 1603, had problematised Scotland's identity like that of few other nations. The resulting uncertainties in the present only forced Scottish minds back more determinedly upon strident assertions about the past. History, the arena in which the sixteenth-century reformation had itself originally been justified, retained a very special significance in the public discourse of the Hanoverian age. As a result, Hume's apothegm that his was 'the historical age and this the historical nation' had a quite unintended contemporary resonance, specifically (and ironically, given Hume's attitudes) by virtue of Scotland's distinctive religious traditions.[87] Whether situated within a traditional Scottish or a wider British context, presbyterian claims and the protestant vision had continued in the eighteenth century to make the past integral to the identity of the nation.[88]

[87] *Letters of David Hume*, ed. G. Birkbeck-Hill (Oxford, 1888), p. 155.
[88] An earlier version of this chapter was presented to the Ecclesiastical History Seminar at the University of Edinburgh, May 1997. I am grateful for the comments and criticisms offered by the audience on that occasion.

[handwritten note: He sees it very specific in texts as evidence. Yet more widely seen in choices & experiences of imperial adventure]

9 Protestantism, ethnicity and Irish identities, 1660–1760

Toby Barnard

In 1666, the first duke of Ormond, lord lieutenant of Ireland, regretted to see 'men of birth', many of them members of 'the ancient nobility' and some his own kinsmen, 'incapable as well by their religion as education of those advantages and employments that would better become them than many that have them'.[1] Ormond was a little premature in mourning the passing of old values such as lineage and personal fealty to the English king of Ireland. Only in 1704 under his grandson, the second duke, also viceroy, was a test act passed. Thereafter certificates of communion according to the rites of the established protestant church of Ireland were required for national and many local offices. The belated introduction of a sacramental qualification, thirty years after its English original, can be seen as another example of Ireland being made to conform to English ways. However, owing to the confessional imbalance in Ireland where probably no more than 10 per cent of its inhabitants adhered to the state church, the impact of the test was dramatic. If the measure was widely enforced – and there is evidence that it was, both against catholics and protestant dissenters – then it created the characteristic protestant ascendancy which subsisted until 1780.[2] In practice, as has often been emphasised, it was not an inclusive protestant, but a narrow church of Ireland, dominance. Moreover, the term 'ascendancy' came into currency only when the system was collapsing, so that some would regard it as anachronistic to talk of an 'ascendancy' in Ireland before contemporaries used the word.[3] Since, in

---

[1] Ormond to W. Legge, 12 Sept. 1666, Staffordshire County RO, Dartmouth MSS D (W) 1778/1/i, 201.

[2] D. W. Hayton, 'Exclusion and conformity: the impact of the sacramental test on Irish dissenting politics', in K. Herlihy, ed., *The politics of Irish dissent* (Dublin, 1997), pp. 52–73 (I am grateful to Dr Hayton for allowing me to read this in advance of publication); I. McBride, 'Presbyterians in the penal era', *Bullán*, 1: 2 (1994), 73–86. For compliance: J. Taaffe to W. Smythe, 1 Jan. 1713[4], N[ational] L[ibrary of] I[reland], PC 436; MS 1515, f. 83; MS 4653, 6, 7 Mar. 1714[5]; MS 14101, 1 Mar. 1740[1].

[3] J. R. Hill, 'The meaning and significance of "protestant ascendancy" 1787–1840', in *Ireland after the union: proceedings of the second joint meeting of the Royal Irish Academy and*

conception and practice, the equivalent of an ascendancy did exist before 1787, the use of the term can be justified.

The test of 1704 confirmed a tendency of the previous century. Ethnicity as hitherto encapsulated in the loose designation of 'the English of Ireland' gave way to confession as the vital guarantor of political tractability.[4] The English of Ireland, seed of those who had settled since the invasion of Henry II, commonly called the Old English by the seventeenth century, bruited their claims to be the best custodians of the political and cultural values essential to the good government of Ireland. Yet frequently – and occasionally spectacularly – their behaviour diverged from that of the English in England. In the 1640s and again in the late 1680s, many of the Old English sided with losers: first, Charles I; next, James II. Such repeated political miscalculations led those who ran the English state to question the credentials of the English in Ireland. Their professed loyalism vanished under scrutiny; so, too, did their 'Englishness'. Hybrid origins – from Normandy, Wales and Scotland as well as England – and the hybridisation which had set in as the immigrants adjusted to local Irish conditions encouraged a view that, while once the planters might have been recognisably English, they had so far degenerated that they could no longer be entrusted with authority over the island. By the seventeenth century this supposed degeneracy was immediately visible in religion, for the majority of the Old English remained catholic: a sign of intellectual and ethical debility and an alarming deviation from the norms of English society.

Accordingly, the New English – those who had emigrated to Ireland from England, Wales, Scotland and protestant Europe since Henry VIII's reign – recommended themselves as alternative rulers thanks to their prevalent protestantism. By breeding they too were mongrels, diversified alike by geographical origins and economic circumstances. Once in Ireland, although necessarily they adjusted to indigenous ways, they preserved a vivid sense of themselves as English, Scots, French Huguenots or Palatines from the Rhineland. However, as time passed, their attitudes diverged from, even conflicted with, those of their compatriots whom they had left behind. Yet notions of Irishness spread only haltingly and unevenly within these immigrant communities. Usages such as 'the English of Ireland', 'the gentlemen of Ireland',

the *British Academy, London 1986* (Oxford, 1989), pp. 1–22; J. Kelly, 'The genesis of "protestant ascendancy": the Rightboy disturbances of the 1780s and their impact on protestant opinion', in G. O'Brien, ed., *Parliament, politics and people: essays in eighteenth-century Irish history* (Dublin, 1989), pp. 93–127; W. J. McCormack, *The Dublin paper war of 1786–1788* (Dublin, 1993), esp. pp. 157–8.
4 A. Clarke, 'Colonial identity in early seventeenth-century Ireland', in T. W. Moody, ed., *Nationality and the pursuit of national independence* (Belfast, 1978), pp. 57–71.

'Hibernus ab Anglia' or 'Anglo-Hibernus' skirted the issue of an Irish identity.[5] The label 'Irish' conjured the backwardness, incivility and catholicism from which protestants in Ireland violently dissociated themselves. An obvious alternative, 'British', caught on only in the crises of 1641 and 1688–9, popular among officials trying to solve riddles of accurate nomenclature or, later in the eighteenth century, among those keen to elevate the Ulster Scots to equality of regard with their English and Welsh neighbours in Ireland.[6] The fact that 'British' failed to displace 'English' and 'Ulster Scot' suggested the continuing vitality of ethnically and confessionally discrete groups within protestant Ireland.

An alternative label which elided racial and denominational differences, 'the protestant interest', was promoted particularly at times of danger.[7] This concept accorded primacy to creed and divorced it from the contested and potentially divisive questions of ethnicity. It aimed at comprehensiveness across the protestant denominations. Yet this aim was defeated by the workings of the test act which left as many protestant dissenters outside, as conformists within, the circle of civic and legal privilege. The notion of 'the protestant interest' was current when in the 1740s and 1750s protestants in Ireland started more willingly to acknowledge their Irishness. Since the designations served separate functions, the religious did not necessarily wane as stress on nationality waxed. But, as yet, the fluctuating relationship between the two usages awaits exact mapping.

II

The fractured protestant interest in eighteenth-century Ireland dismayed those who believed that the potency and menace of catholics – probably about 75 per cent of Ireland's population – required unity. The prospect of knitting together the unravelling protestant remnant brightened when some older dissenting congregations dwindled. Material

---

[5] D. Muschamp to T. Fitzgerald, 20 Mar. 1696[7], Damer House, Roscrea, Co. Tipperary, de Vesci MSS, H/2; T. Fitzgerald to Sir Thomas Vesey, 13 May 1704, ibid., J/3; H. B., *The mantle thrown off* (1689), p. 5; *St John Brodrick's vindication of himself* (1690), p. 3; R. Bulkeley, *The proposal for sending back the nobility and gentry of Ireland* (1690), p. 4; D. W. Hayton, 'Anglo-Irish attitudes: perceptions of national identity in Ireland, ca. 1690–1750', *Studies in Eighteenth-Century Culture*, 17 (1987), pp. 145–57; C. Innes, *Munimenta alme universitatis Glaguensis* (Glasgow, 1854), III, pp. 115, 116, 119, 122–4, 127, 128, 147, 149, 157, 160, 171, 175, 182, 184, 189, 196, 199, 201, 217, 229, 232, 233.

[6] H. B., *The mantle thrown off*, pp. 4, 9; Hayton, 'Anglo-Irish attitudes', 150–1; N[ational] A[rchives], Dublin, M 2533, p. 344; W. Henry, *The necessity of unity* (Dublin [1761]).

[7] T. C. Barnard, 'The protestant interest', in J. H. Ohlmeyer, ed., *Ireland from independence to occupation 1641–1660* (Cambridge, 1995), pp. 233–6.

pressures embodied in the test, together with genetic attrition, went far towards explaining this trend. By the mid-eighteenth century, for example, the once thriving baptist church in Cork was reduced to a couple of cranky old women.[8] Emblematic of the losses were the two sons of a presbyterian minister in County Longford, one of whom by the 1770s had become a member of parliament and the other a church of Ireland dean.[9] Most hopeful to the long-term success of eradicating protestant divisions was the disappearance in the early eighteenth century of many of those aristocratic and genteel patrons who had earlier protected the vulnerable dissenting congregations.[10] Hopes of the eventual reunion of the competing protestant denominations within the church of Ireland were, nevertheless, confounded by the flourishing condition of the Scottish presbyterians, quakers and, from the 1740s, the methodists. The presbyterians in Ulster, in particular, notwithstanding doctrinal and material difficulties, exhibited continuing organisational and numerical dynamism. Observers within the church of Ireland were disheartened by a situation in which their own privileged institution still made slow headway. In the past, structural and financial weaknesses and problems of personnel had excused the failure. However, by the eighteenth century, these defects, if not eradicated, had been corrected. Apologists of the established church, at first cheered by the divine favour manifest in the deliverances after 1641 and 1688–9, were cast down by the clear evidence of catholic and presbyterian vitality. In the 1720s it was claimed that the catholics, so far from decreasing under the penal laws, were growing. Ireland's protestant rulers, uncertain just how many their opponents numbered, applied the methods of political arithmetic and counted them. Between 1731 and 1733, catholics were enumerated, county by county.[11] In contrast, no national census surveyed protestant dissenters. Only in a couple of Dublin parishes and in occasional returns in bishops' visitations, was the extent of protestant nonconformity gauged. Otherwise, estimates spoke more of guess- than field-work.[12]

[8] Cork Baptist church, church book.
[9] O. Tweedy, *The Dublin Tweedys* (1956), p. 86.
[10] T. C. Barnard, 'Identities, ethnicity and tradition among Irish dissenters, c. 1650–1750', in K. Herlihy, ed., *The Irish dissenting tradition* (Dublin, 1995), pp. 34–5.
[11] *An abstract of the number of protestant and popish families in Ireland* (Dublin, 1736); 'Report on the state of popery in Ireland, 1731', *Archivium Hibernicum*, 1–4 (1912–15); Census of diocese of Elphin, 1749, NA, M 2466; T. P. Cunningham, 'The 1766 religious census, Kilmore and Ardagh', *Breifne*, i (1961), 357–62.
[12] R[epresentative] C[hurch] B[ody Library, Dublin], GS 2/7/3/10 (Meath), pp. 3, 14, 18, 21–2, 40, 42, 51, 53, 58, 59, 63; GS 2/7/3/34 (Derry), p. 12; (Dromore), p. 6; Pearse St Public Library, Dublin, Gilbert MS 35, 389; MS 36, pp. 372–8; Cunningham, 'The 1766 religious census', p. 362; E. J. Young, 'Eighteenth-century

This situation, well known in outline if not always in detail, cried out for explanations. Introspection revealed the shortcomings and divisions of the church of Ireland, sometimes a consequence of ethnic tensions within that establishment. As in the past, so in the eighteenth century, diagnoses also employed ideas of ethnic determinism. A feeling persisted that the match between denomination and racial origin, though never exact, remained close. By and large, the Old Irish stayed catholics; the Scots settlers, presbyterians. Only the middle ground held by the English was battled over by the rival confessions. Also, antiquity of settlement in Ireland could be related directly to denomination: the Old English were usually catholic; the newer English tended to be protestants of some complexion. In 1701 a visitor expressed the prevalent and easy equation. After a brief tour of the seaports of Cork, he concluded, 'people born here are distinguished by Irish and English: the former are the Roman Catholics, and ancient natives; the latter, the Protestants, whose predecessors came out of England and Scotland; they are not pleased to be called Irish at home . . .'[13]

These crude analyses helped to make sense of the confessional disunity of eighteenth-century Ireland. However, contemporary notions of ethnicity and denomination were mutable and muddled. How much more so were the realities. Even among the small contingents of immigrants whose racial composition looked unambiguous, such as the Huguenots and Palatines, no one denomination monopolised their loyalties. Instead they split between conformists and dissenters.[14] In Ulster, the bulk of Scottish settlers remained presbyterians, but selected between competing brands: new and old light, seceders and covenanters.[15] In the larger towns where a variety of congregations thrived, it was easy to drift in and out of churches. But where the presbyterian session became coterminous with the civil parish, and where alternative worship was rare or inaccessible, Ulster Scots would have difficulty evading the pressures to continue as presbyterians. Then too defectors faced other more personal and painful sanctions. A presbyterian who

[13] B. S. Ingram, ed., *Three sea journals of Stuart times* (1936), p. 196.
[14] G. A. Forrest, 'Religious controversy within the French protestant community in Dublin, 1692–1716', in Herlihy, ed., *Irish dissenting tradition*, pp. 96–110; V. Hick, 'The Palatine settlement of Ireland: the early years', *Eighteenth-Century Ireland*, 4 (1989), 113–30; Hick, '"As nearly related as possible": solidarity amongst the Irish Palatines', in Herlihy, ed., *Irish dissenting tradition*, pp. 111–25; R. P. Hylton, 'Dublin's Huguenot community: trials, development and triumph, 1662–1701', *Proceedings of the Huguenot Society of London*, 24 (1985), 221–9; P. J. O'Connor, *People make places: the story of the Irish Palatines* (Coolanoran, 1989), pp. 18–80.
[15] P. Brooke, *Ulster presbyterianism: the historical perspective* (2nd edn., Belfast, 1994), pp. 46–95; P. Teich, 'Presbyterian radicalism', in D. Dickson, D. Keogh and K. Whelan, eds., *The United Irishmen* (Dublin, 1993), pp. 33–48.

baulked at subscription to the Westminster confession in the 1730s remembered ruefully that 'those who had known me from my earliest years . . . few of them would converse with me for some considerable time'.[16] This scrupulous dissenter, hurt by the hostility, removed himself from the scene of his upbringing.

A church of Ireland bishop in the 1730s understood how similar material and psychological factors impeded any considerable movement of Irish papists into protestantism. Even those tempted by the reformed creed were 'unwilling to forsake their old friendships and dependencies, but felt strongly the ties and charities and natural magic of relations'.[17] Isolation, ostracism and violence could await those who converted. The publicity, indeed theatre, which attended conversion easily deterred the timid. Errors had publicly to be recanted; clerics often narrated the inner and external promptings which had guided them into their new church.[18] Moreover, conversions were sensationally publicised because they were so psychologically, though not statistically, important in the confessional warfare which still raged in eighteenth-century Ireland. The defectors, despite the way in which they boosted the morale of the church of Ireland, were seldom generously rewarded. Neither they, nor those of Old Irish origins who joined the established church, rose high within it. Indeed, there are signs, for example in the diocese of Limerick, of their inferior position.[19] Such shabby treatment reflected lingering doubts about the motives behind, and so the efficacy of, conversions. Furthermore, native Irish who embraced protestantism, liable to be disowned by their kinsfolk and neighbours, might not be fully assimilated into the protestant interest. Those who most smoothly negotiated the shallows and rapids in the passage from dissent to conformity had begun either in the small and doctrinally ill-defined protestant sects or in the upper strata of society. As the test act and other penal laws intended, property-owners and aspirants to office gained more than they

[16] T[rinity] C[ollege] D[ublin], MS 6447.

[17] T. Rundle, *A sermon preach'd in Christ-Church, Dublin, on the 25th day of March 1736* (Dublin, 1736), pp. 25–7.

[18] NLI, PC 519, Dopping Heppenstall MSS, manuscript version of Neil Carolan 'Motives of conversion to the catholic faith as it is professed by the reformed Church of Ireland', 1688; J. Clayton, *The defence of a sermon* (Dublin, 1701); Clayton, *A sermon preach'd at St Michan's . . . February the 23d 1700 [1] upon the receiving into the communion of the Church of England, the honble. Sir Terence Mac-Mahon . . . and Christopher Dunn* (Dublin [1701]); Robert Fanning, *A lost sheep* (Dublin, 1705); Andrew Meagher, *The popish mass celebrated by heathen priests* (Limerick, 1771); *The recantation of Cornelius O'Donnel, prior of Trim* (1664); *The whole reasons and abjuration of the Romish religion by Father J. L. on Monday the 9th of this instant Decemb. 1728* [Dublin, 1728]; T. C. Barnard, 'Protestants and the Irish language, c. 1675–1725', *JEH*, 44 (1993), 249–50.

[19] RCB, D 13/1/9–15.

lost by conforming to the state religion.[20] The numbers of those making this transition were large enough to give a measure of ethnic heterogeneity to the aristocracy and gentry of protestant Ireland, but did little to dent the monoliths of English and Scottish protestantism and Irish catholicism which confronted each other throughout the period.[21]

III

The New English in Ireland, like the Old English earlier, were viewed askance from England. During the eighteenth century, in contrast to the seventeenth, the English in Ireland did not have to choose sides in English civil wars. Instead they plunged into the political partisanship of the Hanoverian state. In doing so they deployed language and tactics lifted from London, and further demonstrated their Englishness. Nevertheless, whatever Irish protestants contended, increasingly their behaviour deviated from English norms. As a result, within England the notion of an Irishness at variance with English interests, previously associated with the aboriginal Irish and catholic Old English, attached to the English protestants in Ireland. English critics may have stigmatised the troublesome English in Ireland as Irish before the latter so described themselves. When a feeling of Irishness did develop in this quarter during the 1740s and 1750s it owed much to the maladroitness of Ireland's English rulers.[22] However, it was not simply, or primarily, a reaction to the animus of outsiders. The thoughtful, as they confronted the conundrum, were further puzzled by upbringing, education and travel. The inhabitants of eighteenth-century Ireland agonised less about their own identities than do the rootless and perplexed enquirers of

---

[20] T. C. Barnard, 'The worlds of a Galway squire: Robert French of Monivae, 1716–79', in G. Moran and R. Gillespie, eds., *Galway: history and society* (Dublin, 1996), pp. 271–5; L. M. Cullen, 'Catholic social classes under the penal laws', in T. P. Power and K. Whelan, eds., *Endurance and emergence: catholicism in Ireland in the eighteenth century* (Dublin, 1990), pp. 57–84; T. P. Power, 'Converts', ibid., pp. 101–27.

[21] Among the most striking examples: Ormond, Kildare, Antrim and Clanricarde. See, Damer House, de Vesci MSS, G/6, 'Form of receiving Lord Clanricarde into the Church of Ireland', 1698; Clanricarde to Abp. J. Vesey, 29 Nov. 1698; F. Shaw to same, 4 Nov. 1698; Barnard, 'French of Monivae', pp. 286–7; Cullen, 'Catholic social classes', pp. 57–84; F. G. James, *Lords of the ascendancy: the Irish House of Lords and its members* (Dublin, 1994), p. 100; C. Kenny, 'The exclusion of catholics from the legal profession in Ireland, 1534–1829', *IHS*, 25 (1987), 337–57; T. P. Power, 'Conversions among the legal profession in Ireland in the eighteenth century', in D. Hogan and W. N. Osborough, eds., *Brehons, serjeants and attorneys* (Dublin, 1990), pp. 153–74.

[22] Hayton, 'Anglo-Irish attitudes', 153–5; Hayton, 'From barbarian to burlesque: English images of the Irish, c.1660–1750', *Irish Economic and Social History*, 15 (1988), 22–31; D. O'Donovan, 'The Money Bill Dispute of 1753', in T. Bartlett and D. W. Hayton, eds., *Penal era and golden age* (Belfast, 1979), pp. 55–87; *Faulkner's Dublin Journal*, 18–22 Oct. 1743.

the late twentieth century. Inevitably, the strident polemicists have drowned the diffident and obscure. However, by heeding what was let drop inadvertently and privately, it is possible to retrieve more of the complex relationship between perceptions of nationality and confessional alignments. In particular, the often linked experiences of education and travel encouraged, or forced, reconsideration of this relationship.

A new antiquarianism in the late seventeenth and eighteenth centuries fostered minute genealogical researches. Those who had previously traced the descent of Gaelic notables transferred their skills to incoming dynasties.[23] Such investigations clouded ideals of racial purity and so complicated the notions of Irish protestants about themselves, both individually and collectively. Late in the 1730s, Samuel Madden, a relentlessly projecting church of Ireland don, expressed the resultant confusion. Cosmopolitan Irish protestants of his ilk were looked on as amphibious sports, 'envied as Englishmen in Ireland, and maligned as Irish in England'.[24] Madden, it should be remembered, wrote for rhetorical effect and to challenge topical misapprehensions. He gazed witheringly at the cultural and moral shortcomings of his co-religionists and compatriots, and bored them with schemes of reformation. An Irish protestant of Madden's wealth and standing could select from a stock of roles: cosmopolitan, national or local; ethnic or confessional.[25] Paradoxically, he wanted his contemporaries to proclaim their Irishness by conforming better to the international or English fashions.

Something similar happened in a contemporary family of comparable status and income: the Molyneuxs. In 1735, Sir Daniel Molyneux, head of the house in Ireland, travelled to Paris. There, he and his party were greeted effusively by a venerated *savant*, because 'we were English, and from Ireland.'[26] This acknowledgement accorded well with the view of ethnicity taken by another member of the family. In 1698, William Molyneux had published his *Case* in order to assert Ireland's constitutional, historic and natural rights. In it Molyneux had contended brazenly, 'the present people of Ireland are progeny of the English and Britons that from time to time have come over into this kingdom, and there remains but a mere handful of the ancient Irish at this day'.[27] Molyneux wrote as a controversialist. The background of

---

[23] K. Simms, 'Charles Lynegar, the O Luinin family and the study of Seanchas', in T. Barnard, D. O Croinin and K. Simms, *'A miracle of learning'* (Aldershot, 1998), pp. 264–83.

[24] S. Madden, *Reflections and resolutions proper to the gentlemen of Ireland* (Dublin, 1738, reprinted 1816), p. 96.

[25] NA, M 2533, pp. 464–5; F. Madan, *The Madan family and Maddens in Ireland and England* (Oxford, 1933), pp. 232–5.

[26] D. Molyneux to R. Howard, 12 Apr. 1736, n.s., NLI, PC 227.

his own family confused rather than confuted his contentions. The Molyneuxs, French settlers in medieval England, returned to Calais in the mid-sixteenth century as colonists, only to be expelled. They then tried their luck in Ireland. By the early eighteenth century, like others of their vintage, they were flourishing in the official and intellectual worlds of protestant Dublin.[28] Moreover, their bifurcating lines enmeshed England, the continent and Ireland, equally easy within and beyond the Hanoverians' multiple possessions. The expanding empire centred on London enlarged the opportunities for advancement for the conformist Irish. In this spirit, one Molyneux grabbed an opening to serve the prince of Wales as secretary.

William Molyneux's account of the historical and ethnic ancestry of the protestants of Ireland echoed the views of his forebears who had congregated around Ormond, and reverberated into the eighteenth century.[29] In 1744, Dean Patrick Delany denied that Ireland boasted even ten families of note, 'not originally British'. He also updated a traditional, sentimental appeal for greater generosity when he described the Irish protestants as 'an aggregate of colonies from Great Britain: they are your brethren, bone of your bones, and flesh of your flesh'. In the case of Delany, both his names told of an ethnic Irishness which sat oddly with his rhetoric, though not with his toryism.[30]

During the early eighteenth century, other prominent members of the protestant interest traced their intricate pedigrees. Thereby they acquired for themselves, and bequeathed to their heirs, a complicated ancestry. In consequence, although their Englishness was not necessarily weakened or abandoned, an incipient Irishness might be cherished. Notable among these chronicles of an Irish protestant family was that compiled in the mid-eighteenth century by Richard Edgeworth. 'The black book of Edgeworthstown', utilitarian and minatory in its purposes, is difficult to read as an elaborate device to allay the chronic insecurity of this interloping tribe. Edgeworth located his family precisely in that stratum of prosperous squires from which most members of the Dublin parliament, justices of the peace, high sheriffs, grand jurors and turnpike

[27] W. Molyneux, *The case of Ireland's being bound by acts of parliament in England stated* (Dublin, 1698), p. 20.

[28] C. Molyneux, *An account of the family and descendants of Sir Thomas Molyneux* (Evesham, 1820); J. G. Simms, *William Molyneux of Dublin 1656–1698* (Dublin, 1982), pp. 10–17.

[29] For example, the attitudes of Molyneux's father-in-law, William Domville, for which: Domville to W. Legge [1664], Staffordshire County RO, D (W) 1778/v/1148.

[30] P. Delany, *A sermon preach'd before the society . . . March 13th 1743/4* (1744), p. 15; J. B. Leslie and H. B. Swanzy, *Biographical succession lists of the clergy of the diocese of Down* (Enniskillen, 1936), pp. 22–3; E. MacLysaght, *Irish families: their names, arms and origins* (4th edn, Dublin, 1985), pp. 71–2.

commissioners were recruited. He refuted the envious who derided the Edgeworths as 'of new growth or as upstart', and the vain who 'may possibly represent them as a more considerable family than they really ever were'. Instead he demonstrated that 'the family was a good private gentleman's family, never masters of great fortunes, nor ennobled by the crown, but still lived in credit and above want'.[31] Edgeworth measured reputation by conventional gauges, hardly specific to Ireland or hinging on confession or ethnicity. Only, perhaps, in his pride that his forebears were 'often favoured by the crown with honourable employments' did he hark back to those passing values of fidelity to the English monarch espoused by the Ormonds. In the eighteenth-century world where loyalty focused on the abstractions of the protestant interest and the British empire, such personalised allegiances were thought sometimes to denote the sentimental tory, if not the covert Jacobite.[32] Edgeworth's family pride, like that of other contemporaries within the ascendancy, was more inclusive than his political principles. He happily memorialised those ancestors who had remained presbyterian after 1660 and his kinship with 'that learned, ingenious and worthy patriot', Robert Molesworth, at the opposite political pole from the Ormonds.[33]

Another whose researches into his lineage uncovered a mixed background was Henry Ware. As grandson of the celebrated antiquary, Sir James Ware, and kinsman of the less scrupulous historians, Bishop Henry Jones, Robert Ware and Walter Harris, Ware was steeped in a virulent anti-popery. A little plaintively he concluded from his desultory delving that the first of his ancestors to arrive in Ireland, William Piers, 'must have been a very considerable person' and 'a gentleman of good family in Yorkshire'. Ware did not shy away from chronicling those who, during the seventeenth century, had converted to catholicism and even entered the priesthood. Others he followed in their mercantile careers and to their Dutch domiciles.[34]

This private awareness of the variegations of kinship, well developed among the literate and leisured, remains to be connected with the public postures of the Irish protestants. The tangled lines patiently unknotted by an Edgeworth or a Ware need not have weakened their belief in their role as the English of Ireland. Nor, although catholics and dissenters were numbered among their kindred, did these facts reduce the importance of protecting their own property and privileges by upholding the test and other penal laws. Such personal histories and affinities further diversified attitudes which arose from objective and subjective assessments of the local danger from catholics and dissenters. The

[31] NLI, MS 7361, p. 171.   [32] Ibid., p. 171.   [33] NLI, MS 7361, pp. 181–2.
[34] Ibid., MS 2563.

interplay of these often hidden and contrary impulses can be sensed better than measured. Such is the situation with the commanding figure in the politics of early eighteenth-century Ireland. William Conolly, apparently quixotically, wanted to abrogate the test.[35] Much about Conolly is murky, but not his place among the native Irish of Donegal or his early and extensive alliances with families in north-west Ulster which spanned dissent and conformity.[36]

Education and travel, often dictated by ethnicity, might nevertheless modify its effects. A choice between study inside or outside Ireland accentuated the divisions among the protestants of Ireland. If schooling strained as well as stretched minds, at least the bruised were better equipped to muse on what they had endured. An Edgeworth testified to the tensions which resulted from tuition divided between Ireland and England. Enrolment at Dr Lydiat's school in Warwick wrenched the pampered Richard Lovell Edgeworth from his strict but enlightened parents. Distressed enough by the roughness with which he was now treated, he was mocked for his Irish accent and idioms. Despite adopting what he took to be a provincial English accent, young Richard was teased as 'little Irish'. None too soon his parents returned to Edgeworthstown and placed their son at Drogheda Grammar School. There, too, he was taunted for his speech: a mixture of what he had learnt at Warwick and from 'the English pronounciation' current in his father's house in the Irish midlands. Sometimes he was accused of coming from Cumberland; at other times, from Germany. Worry over the brogue and the disdain which it provoked within English society beset other Irish protestant parents.[37] It continued to remind how the English of Ireland did differ from the metropolitan English. By the same token, though, visitors to London from Scotland, Wales, East Anglia, northern and south-western England encountered similar contempt. Moreover, if all but the grandest and most anglicised Irish protestants were recognisable and comic to smart Londoners, idiom and dialect as well as dress and manners rendered the rustics of Connacht, Ulster and Cork absurd to Dublin sophisticates. In addition, it was hard to match the horror with

---

[35] J. Bulkeley to J. Bonnell, 18 & 25 July 1719, ibid., PC 435.

[36] T. C. Barnard, 'The government and Irish dissent', in Herlihy, ed., *The politics of Irish dissent*, pp. 9–27; L. Boylan, 'The Conollys of Castletown', *Quarterly Bulletin of the Irish Georgian Society*, 11: 4 (1968), 1–19.

[37] *Memoirs of Richard Lovell Edgeworth, esq.* (1820), I, pp. 47–50, 62–3; J. Smythe to W. Smythe, 24 May 1728, NLI, PC 449; TCD, MS 1121, p. 10; Hayton, 'Barbarian to burlesque', pp. 17–20, 23; H. Huth, ed., *Narrative of the journey of an Irish gentleman through England in the year 1752* (1869), pp. 30, 103, 156; M. L. Legg, ed., *The Synge letters* (Dublin, 1996), pp. 122, 198, 254.

which the cultivated traveller from Ireland regarded both the natives and the terrain which they faced after disembarking at Holyhead.[38]

Through the careful work of David Hannigan we know better how a relatively cheap and efficient Trinity College in Dublin catered to the embryonic protestant ascendancy.[39] However, the role of the institution in underpinning that system, both ideologically and materially, together with its contribution to the development of a distinctive Irish protestant identity, still await exact delineation. Moreover, the small number of those elected to the Dublin parliament who had graduated from a university, no more than 26 per cent between 1727 and 1760 – a target for Dean Swift's ridicule – suggested important cultural differences within the squirearchy, and between much of the landed interest and the better-educated urban and professional groupings. Oxford and Cambridge, owing to the anglican monopoly and the higher costs, attracted only those from Ireland with aristocratic incomes to equal their aspirations.[40] Apparently cheaper and therefore more favoured were the Scottish and Dutch universities and continental academies. They were also recommended by their freedom from denominational tests. Quickening travel enabled protestants from Ireland to share what others from Britain and catholic Ireland enjoyed. Except during the 1640s and the late 1680s, the overseas travel of protestants from Ireland was voluntary rather than enforced. It generally differed, in destination, duration and effect, from that of the defeated and displaced catholics. The Irish when in Europe, as in Scotland and England, gravitated first to kinsfolk and acquaintances. Yet few limited themselves to Irish company.[41] In consequence, the experience could soften ethnic rigidities.

The perambulations of grandees speeded their integration into the internationalised aristocracy of Britain and Europe.[42] Since

[38] D. Chaloner, 'The Rev. John Chaloner', *The Irish Ancestor*, 17 (1985), 60; *The down-fall of the counts: a new ballad* (Dublin, 1746/7); *The north country ordinary opened* (Dublin, 1739); Hayton, 'Barbarian to burlesque', 26–31.

[39] D. Hannigan, 'The University of Dublin, 1685–1750: a study of matriculation records' (M.A. dissertation, St Patrick's College Maynooth, 1995), pp. 23–70.

[40] J. L. McCracken, 'Central and local administration in Ireland under George II' (Ph.D. dissertation, Queen's University Belfast, 1948), p. 112; R. Molesworth, *Some considerations for the promoting of agriculture* (Dublin, 1723), p. 29; *The correspondence of Jonathan Swift*, ed. H. Williams (5 vols. Oxford, 1963–5), iv, 556. An address to Ormond from nineteen members of Oxford University with Irish connections in 1683 suggests a larger presence there: Bod. Library, Oxford, Carte MS 69, f. 165v; Hannigan, 'University of Dublin', pp. 58–9.

[41] R. French to W. Smythe, 29 May 1712, NLI, PC 447; ibid., MS 1508, pp. 148 [185]; Huth, *Narrative of the journey*, pp. 82, 125; Barnard, 'French of Monivae', p. 284.

[42] Barnard, 'The second earl of Cork and first earl of Burlington (1612–1698)', in T. Barnard and J. Clark, eds., *Lord Burlington: architecture, art and life* (1995), pp. 195–6; H. F. Brown, *Inglesi e Scozzesi all' Universita di Padova dell' Anno 1618 sino al 1765* (Venice, 1921), pp. 167–213.

concurrently economic and material forces were loosening Irish ties, too much should not be attributed to travel. Nevertheless, the heirs of modest Irish estates were introduced to sights and ideas which jolted them from inherited attitudes. The adolescent Robert Southwell, having studied in Oxford, was despatched to Italy in 1659. In Rome he haunted the salons and noted what he heard. Early he picked up those skills of self-effacement and dissimulation which would soon advance his career as ambassador and secretary of state under Charles II. In Italy he noted the table talk of cardinals and the exiled English republican, Algernon Sidney. He also encountered exiles from Ireland, usually catholics. Far from their homeland, they voiced strong sentiments of attachment. Lord Creagh, for example, confided that he would prefer to be buried on the highest mountain in Ireland than in St Peter's basilica, 'such is his country's love'.[43]

Jaunting through Ireland, Britain and western Europe quickly established itself as essential to the training of successive generations of Southwells.[44] It groomed them to serve both Stuarts and Hanoverians. Thanks to the extent of the English king of Ireland's possessions, families such as the Southwells were given a wide stage on which to strut. When eighteenth-century Southwells twitched the strings, their puppets in Downpatrick and Kinsale did not automatically respond. Cultural as well as physical distance impeded control. The thoroughly anglicised Southwells resorted to a vocabulary of honour, obligation and deference, not of crude confession or ethnicity.[45] These values evoked the ambience of the courtly Ormonds in which the Southwells had first flourished. However, even in 1754, a moment of inflamed Irish patriotism, when the burgesses of Kinsale resisted the tory Southwells, they did not oppose their own Irishness to the Southwells' Englishness. Quite the reverse: a leading spirit among the Irish protestants of Kinsale declared, 'I am an English tenant and will endeavour to support the same spirit of independency which distinguishes every peasant in our mother country. What are we that we should not be as free as they?'[46]

The tortuous path by which the Southwells ascended from small-town provincials on the Cork coast to be the Angarano of the age ensconced in a Vanbrugh mansion outside Bristol exemplifies one route

[43] BL, Add. MS 1632, f. 7v; T. Birch, ed., *The works of the honourable Robert Boyle* (5 vols. 1745), pp. 403–5.
[44] Journals of Edward Southwell, 1684–1716, Yale University, Beinecke Library.
[45] E. Southwell to A. Stawell, 7 Feb. 1735[6], University College Cork, U/55, Kinsale manorial papers 1698–1764; BL, Add. MS 20131, f. 103v.
[46] *A few words of brotherly advice to the free and independent electors of the town of Kinsale* (n.p., 1754), p. 6.

of the New English towards an unequivocal Englishness.[47] Yet, another line which stemmed from the first Southwell to arrive in Ireland in the early seventeenth century might equally well be chosen to typify such progress. The Southwells had to efface the taint of recusancy emanating from their most famous son, the poet and Jesuit. By 1688 the branch in Limerick had certainly succeeded. Thomas Southwell emerged as a precocious opponent of James II and, having narrowly escaped execution, garnered the rewards of a protestant hero. Adorned first with a baronetcy and then with a peerage, the Limerick Southwells continued as powers in national and local affairs until the 1770s when all was jeopardised. The second viscount converted to catholicism and retired first to the continent and then to England.[48] These vicissitudes, tedious to reconstruct and to recount, singly possess at best a parochial significance. Cumulatively, they suggest a protestant interest fabricated from miscellaneous materials rather than hewn from flawless English freestone, and therefore liable to shatter in adverse conditions.

Two further examples confirm how foreign travel varied the angles from which protestants from Ireland contemplated their country. Samuel Waring, heir to a County Down estate close in annual yield to that of the Kinsale Southwells, also toured Europe between 1687 and 1689. He did so after he had graduated from Dublin and in the company of Charles Butler, future earl of Arran, grandson of the quondam viceroy Ormond.[49] On his return, Waring devoted himself to the improvement of his patrimony and those public duties, including a seat in parliament, customarily entailed with such an inheritance. Earlier, in Italy, Waring was periodically reminded of home. In particular, as he was conducted around the Jesuit College in Rome, he saw images which depicted the several elements in the Stuarts' composite monarchy. A figure of Hibernia personified Ireland. Hibernia, although equipped with sceptre and harp, was crowned only with a ducal coronet. When asked why, since the pope had recognised Ireland as a separate kingdom, the Jesuit guide replied that, whatever the pope had decreed earlier, the title assumed by Henry VIII in 1541 lacked papal approval. The Jesuits in Rome, in common with many contemporaries, eulogised

---

[47] C. Campbell, *Vitruvius Britannicus* (3 vols., 1715–25), I, pp. 47–8. R. Loeber, 'Arnold Quellin's and Grinling Gibbons's monuments for Anglo-Irish patrons', *Studies*, lxxii (1983), 84–101; E. McParland, 'Edward Lovett Pearce and the new junta for architecture', in Barnard and Clark, *Lord Burlington*, pp. 158–9.

[48] G. E. C[ockayne], *The complete peerage* (13 vols., 1910–53), 12, pt. 1, 148–50; P. J. O'Connor, *All Ireland is in and around Rathkeale* (Coolanoran, 1996) pp. 107–10; BL, Add. MS 21122, f. 63.

[49] PRONI, D 695/225. These tourists are not noticed in L. Schudt, *Italienreisen im 17 und 18 Jahrhunderts* (Vienna and Munich, 1959).

the catholic James II as king of England or Great Britain, 'without mentioning Ireland'. Waring hardly needed to trudge as far as Rome to be reminded of the ambiguous status of his homeland. Nevertheless, hearing the views of others in this unexpected setting may have sharpened or altered his perceptions.[50]

In the records of Waring's foreign sojourn, his Irishness hardly obtruded. It is true that he noted among the useful addresses those of a 'smuddling' Irish priest and another who acted as agent of the Irish clergy in Rome. However their names were written alongside those of English and Scottish contacts. Also, although Waring had bought himself an Irish grammar before departing (Irish presumably being of more use to him outside than inside Ireland), his well-chosen library included architectural treatises, protestant theology and guide-books.[51] Inquisitive about what he encountered, and wishing to systematise his impressions, he frequently compared the sights with what he already knew. The comparisons were always with England, not with Ireland. On reaching Rome, he, like other good protestants including some from Ireland, utilised his best-placed contact, Cardinal Howard. The cardinal, renowned for his 'generous care and concern for his countrymen', carried Waring to the Dominican monastery at Monte Coelio.[52] There the dietary stereotyping of the meal – ribs of beef and plum puddings early in May – suggested that his hosts either did not differentiate between Irish and English or regarded Waring as English.[53]

How easily spells away from Ireland might be incorporated into the experience of landed protestants is revealed by the Cosbys of Stradbally. Again, though, the consequences in regard to notions of ethnicity and confession are complicated. Adversaries of the Ormonds who aspired to office found their progress blocked. One such was Dudley Cosby. Political opposition to Ormond led to Cosby's being posted as a captain to Spain, where he remained rather than be put to 'hard duty' elsewhere by Ormond. Imprisoned by the French during the War of the Spanish Succession and taken to Dijon, he returned to Ireland only in 1709, and promptly departed anew in order to retrench in England. This itinerant life ceased only in 1714, when the Hanoverian succession improved Cosby's prospects. However, his son was soon travelling: first, to complete his education in the Low Countries; then, after he had inherited, to economise by removing his family to Bristol.[54]

---

[50] M. Misson, *A new voyage to Italy* (4th edn, 1714), II, part 1, 177.
[51] PRONI, D 695/228.   [52] G. Burnet, *Burnet's travels* (new edn, 1737), p. 191.
[53] PRONI, D 695/226, pp. 26–7.
[54] 'Autobiography of Pole Cosby of Stradbally, Queen's County, 1705–1737(?)', *Journal of the County Kildare Archaeological Society*, 5 (1906), 84–7.

When first despatched to Leyden he moved along tracks which survived from his father's continental wanderings and which were kept in good repair between the Dublin presbyterians and Dutch congregations. If we can trust Cosby's later recollections, a multiplicity of often contradictory impressions crowded in on him. At Leyden he dined first at 'the English ordinary', where none but English, Scottish and Irish students ate. Disliking this segregation he quickly took himself to the public ordinary. Now he benefited from 'conversing with people of all nations'. During the vacations he penetrated deep into Germany and central Europe. Armed with letters of introduction 'to some top people at Hanover', he kissed the hands of George I and the prince of Wales. In Berlin he was presented to George I's daughter, the queen of Prussia, and again kissed her hand, 'being subjects of England'. Elsewhere, it was Cosby's Irishness not his Englishness which opened doors. In Munich, for example, he met several Irish priests 'who were joyful to see a countryman'. Similarly, in the Irish monastery at Prague, the inmates 'were as glad and full of joy to see us as if we were their own kin'. Cosby gratefully accepted this hospitality, but did not forget his own feelings of difference. Thus, while impressed by the magnificence of the monastic church in Prague, he dismissed the other conventional buildings as 'but ordinary and Irish all over, very dirty'. Moreover, he thought the amiable priests 'most extremely ignorant and very zealous of their superstitious religion'.[55]

Religion, then, caused dissension. Throughout his years abroad Cosby attended punctiliously to his religious duties. He went regularly to the English church at Leyden, 'which was the Established Church, that is Calvinist, alias Presbyterian'. Essentially this church belonged to the Scottish not the English or Irish establishment.[56] When Cosby took communion – never fewer than four times a year – he rode the 10 miles to Rotterdam to the newly built episcopal church.[57] On arriving in Leyden, Cosby's principal contact, supplied by the members of the Wood Street presbyterian church in Dublin, was with the minister of the English church. Some of the immediate predecessors of the latter were intimately connected with the Dublin dissenters.[58] The English church in Leyden was favoured by Cosby, but he also tasted sermons at rival establishments. Sometimes he frequented the French Calvinist temple and also the French catholic church. Later he insisted that he went to the popish services solely to improve his French. The experience

---

[55] Ibid., pp. 94, 97–8.
[56] Ibid., pp. 95, 166; W. Steven, *The history of the Scottish Church, Rotterdam* (Edinburgh, 1832), p. 313.
[57] Steven, *Scottish Church*, pp. 327–36.
[58] Ibid., p. 315; F. Iredell, *A funeral sermon preach'd . . . on the occasion of the death of the Rev. John Milling* (Dublin, 1705), p. 8.

deepened his antipathy towards 'the ridiculous worship of the mass'. Such confessional and cultural experimentation was unlikely in Ireland. There Cosby, although he showed some sympathy with individual presbyterians, conformed as the state demanded. Catholics lived outside his social ambit; even curiosity would hardly entice him into Irish catholic chapels. His formative years away from Ireland had seen Cosby switch backwards and forwards between Englishness and Irishness, his own self-definition sometimes at odds with what others took him to be. Thereafter he frequently measured himself against neighbours and rivals. He discriminated between them according to highly idiosyncratic and sometimes erroneous notions of ethnicity, denomination, lineage, gentility and honour.[59]

IV

One effect of European travel was to strengthen the sense in some Irish protestants that they belonged to an international community not bound by the domains of the English sovereign or of English-speaking. Irish protestants, themselves a beleaguered minority and with their own providential history of persecution, identified strongly with similar groups in France, the Low Countries and Germany. The Wood Street pastor, Joseph Boyse, remembered how the outlook of two conspicuous supporters of Irish dissent, Sir Arthur Langford and Dr Duncan Cumyng, had been coloured by direct contact with their suffering continental colleagues.[60] Foreign travel, often in pursuit of a fitting education, the monopoly of men, accentuated the sense of a distinctive dissenting ethos. The need to escape the anglican enclaves of Dublin, Cambridge and Oxford universities drew nonconformists further afield: particularly to Scotland and the United Provinces. With the constant traffic between Ulster and Scotland, training in Glasgow was easy. Between 1700 and 1709, nearly a quarter of the entrants to Glasgow University came from Ireland, mainly from Ulster.[61] During nearly ninety years after 1690, 65 per cent of the presbyterian clergy licensed to officiate in Ireland had been educated at Glasgow.[62]

---

[59] 'Autobiography of Cosby', pp. 172, 174, 253–9, 429, 432.

[60] J. Boyse, *The works* (2 vols., 1728), I, pp. 309, 315–16; R. W. Innes Smith, *English-speaking students of medicine at the University of Leyden* (Edinburgh and London, 1932), p. 60.

[61] I. M. Bishop, 'The education of Ulster students at the University of Glasgow in the eighteenth century' (MA dissertation, Queen's University Belfast, 1987); R. Gillespie, 'Church, state and education in early modern Ireland', in M. R. O'Connell, ed., *O'Connell: education, church and state* (Dublin, 1992), pp. 51–2.

[62] Hannigan, 'University of Dublin', p. 73.

These separate systems of training did not preclude contact when overseas between conforming and non-conforming protestants from Ireland. Nevertheless, these distinctive regimens fused the ethnicity of the Ulster Scots with a specific denomination. Other forces had kept alive this special sense, notably the humiliating exclusions embodied in the test. Moreover, the common history of the protestants in seventeenth-century Ireland, which should have united, tended to separate the different denominations. The dissenters felt that their sufferings as prime victims of catholic malevolence in 1641 and 1688–90 and as doughty champions of the protestant interest throughout the 1640s and more recently in besieged Derry and Enniskillen deserved better rewards than they had received.[63] Cooperation across the denominational frontiers could occur.[64] However, even an episode which paraded the presbyterians' loyalty to the protestant state and so seconded their claims to civic and legal equality, such as rallying to repel the pretender in 1715, simply exacerbated animosities. Supporters of the test belittled, once again, what the dissenters had done. Maybe some presbyterians, empowered temporarily as militia officers, revenged themselves on the churchmen who so lately had harried them. In turn, zealots of the established church expatiated on the low condition and indiscipline of the presbyterians.[65] Furthermore, the assimilation to episcopalian orthodoxy of the heirs of those aristocrats and gentlemen who had protected dissent after the restoration left Ulster presbyterianism with a social structure – urban, professional and artisanal – which discouraged casual contacts between the champions of the rival confessions.[66] In 1719 an optimist, probably informed by Waring, averred that the Scots in Ulster, while living 'according to the fashion of their country' and totally separated from the native Irish, subsisted 'in friendship, commerce and alliance with the English'.[67] Others, however, stressed how each ethnic group turned inwards and, organised around

[63] *A memorial by William Hamill* (1714); W. Hamill, *A view of the danger and folly of being publick-spirited* (1721); J. Kearney, *A sermon preached at the Church of St Werburgh's, Dublin, on Sunday the first day of March 1746–7* (Dublin, 1747); H. C. Lawlor, *A history of the family of Cairnes or Cairns* (1906), p. 173; I. McBride, *The siege of Derry in Ulster protestant mythology* (Dublin, 1997).

[64] T. C. Barnard, 'Reforming Irish manners: the religious societies in Dublin during the 1690s', *HJ*, 35 (1992), 805–38; Barnard, 'Identities, ethnicity and tradition', pp. 38–41.

[65] J. Smythe to W. Smythe, 6 Feb., 15 Mar. 1715[16], 14 Sept. 1716, NLI, PC 449; PRONI, D 2092/1/3, 30; *The report of the judges of assize for the north-east circuit of Ulster* (n.p., 1716).

[66] Royal Irish Academy, MS 24 K 19; Lambeth Palace Library, MS 1742, ffs. 49–56 (I am most grateful to David Hayton for a copy of the latter); Barnard, 'Identities, ethnicity and tradition', pp. 34–5.

[67] H. Misson, *Memoirs and observations on his travels over England, with some account of*

its distinct church, regarded rivals with incomprehension and fear. Such continuing mistrust helped to explain why the test act stayed on the statute book for so long.[68]

Theories of ethnic determinism readily accounted for the vitality of presbyterianism among the Scots of Ulster. Notwithstanding a succession of schisms and serious emigration from the province to North America, the grip of presbyterianism did not relax. Yet, whatever determinists might argue, in the eighteenth century and since, the denominational configurations were neither inevitable nor fixed. This we can sense through two autobiographies, which, despite their elisions and omissions, tell something of the internal dynamics and values of the alternative world of Ulster presbyterians existing alongside that of the local ascendancy.

The life of James Traill of Killyleagh, on the banks of Strangford Lough, as told by himself, displayed a chanciness rather than a purposefulness which he attributed to the workings of an inscrutable providence.[69] Raised in the church of Ireland, he nevertheless spent time as a pupil in the Belfast house of his kinsman, John McBride, the leading presbyterian minister of the town. Traill listened appreciatively to McBride's sermons, moved next to the famous dissenting academy in Killyleagh,[70] but then prepared to matriculate at the exclusively anglican Trinity College. This personal and denominational indecisiveness paralleled his uncertainty over a career. Either trade or the army appealed. In the event he opted for neither. Instead, he married, and with his wife he acquired a new religious allegiance: presbyterianism. Immediately he discovered sound theological reasons for his choice. Closer inspection showed that presbyterianism accorded better with reason and divine revelation. He also regretted that the church of Ireland, at least in its Dublin foundations, stopped non-communicants from witnessing the administration of the sacraments. These niceties of doctrine and liturgical practice justified a denominational affiliation for which Traill might have been thought destined by kinship and background.

Settled at Killyleagh, he devoted himself to his inheritance (worth more than £100 p.a.)[71] and sought the company of the devout. Still he

---

Scotland and Ireland (1719), p. 149; E. Smythe to W. Smythe, 7 Jan. 1749[50], NLI, PC 444.

[68] Barnard, 'The government and Irish dissent'; *A new ballad supposed to be wrote by a Reverend D-n in the north* ([Dublin], 1733).

[69] PRONI, D 1460/1.

[70] J. C. Beckett, *Protestant dissent in Ireland, 1687–1780* (1948), p. 41; J. S. Reid, *History of the presbyterian church in Ireland* (3 vols., Belfast, 1867), II, p. 519.

[71] Although he is listed in about 1720 (RIA, MS 24 K 19) he does not appear a few years later in a similar list (Lambeth, MS 1742, f. 50). It is possible but unlikely that during a decade he had dropped out of the economic elite of County Down.

remained an independent spirit. The divisions within Ulster presbyterianism saddened him, as did the low standards among some neighbours and ministers. Dissatisfied with the local pastor, he clubbed together with relations and friends to educate their children and instruct their families at home. His own collection of exegetical and devotional manuals included anglican as well as dissenters' classics. Also, he counted the local bishop and dean among the pious who were straining 'for the Church triumphant in heaven on earth'. Indeed he took a more favourable view of their labours than did some of their subordinates among the anglican clergy.[72] Moreover, his apparently amicable relationships with conformists seem to have been reciprocated by local adherents of the church of Ireland.

Protestants around Killyleagh agreed on the basics of faith and practical divinity and co-operated over the provision of decent buildings for corporate worship. Yet differences survived strong enough to drive some landowners of Traill's standing to sacrifice full civic rights and social acceptance. Traill inveighed against the test act as 'unchristian, inhuman, unnatural and undeserved', and backed the fruitless campaign to repeal it in 1733.[73] Moving in a circle of the educated and modestly prosperous fit to fill a range of local posts, he knew well how they were disabled by the law. As David Hayton has shown conclusively, the most damaging and dramatic exclusions through the operation of the test were in the boroughs of Derry, Belfast, Coleraine and Carrickfergus.[74] Even outside these municipalities there existed a range of profitable and prestigious offices from which the scrupulous dissenter was debarred. In some measure, Traill was insulated from the worst consequences of discrimination by his property and status. However, these same assets rendered his disqualification the more galling.

Traill traversed a network composed of kinsfolk and the like-minded which stretched across Ulster. It was linked by correspondents and acquaintances to Dublin and England, whither he occasionally went. Inevitably his world also embraced Scotland, but as one rather than the dominant element. Cousins from County Down trained there. One indeed ministered in Scotland before returning to the charge of Killyleagh.[75] In addition, one of Traill's own sons decided to study medicine at Glasgow. He persevered for two years, watched over by Traill's famous cousin, Francis Hutcheson, a professor there, before throwing it

---

[72] PRONI, D 1460/1; J. Smythe to W. Smythe, 5 Dec. 1729, NLI, PC 449.
[73] PRONI, D 1460/1, p. 43. On this campaign, see the forthcoming paper by J. G. McCoy, 'Ascendancy Ireland and the repeal of the sacramental test, 1731–1733' (I am very grateful to Dr McCoy for allowing me to read his paper).
[74] Hayton, 'Exclusion and conformity'.
[75] H. Scott, *Fasti ecclesiae Scoticanae* (5 vols., Edinburgh, 1920), III, p. 142.

up for country life in Ulster.[76] Traill's personal history suggested how the thoughtful balanced the competing pressures of conviction, careerism, kinship and neighbourliness. If Traill established some sort of equilibrium, it was not without agonising struggles. A contemporary, Adam Blair, responded differently to comparable problems.

Blair, born in County Antrim, was educated first in the locality and then at Glasgow University.[77] In 1739 he returned to Ballymoney, his birthplace, to be ordained. Because he scrupled to subscribe to the Westminster confession, he broke with the local session and was licensed by the Presbytery of Antrim. This sundered numerous ties with the neighbourhood. Rather than face the enduring hostility, he accepted a call to the congregation at Horse-Leap in King's County in 1748.[78] During a long ministry there he was sustained by ministers and lay people outside Ulster. Yet, early in the 1770s when the moment came to organise his sons' futures, Scotland reasserted its pull. The father himself took his two eldest sons to Glasgow, and arranged their tuition and board with a professor of anatomy.[79] One son succeeded in his chosen profession and, after doctoring at Athy, Bideford and in the British army, took over a practice in the Huguenot settlement of Portarlington. Meanwhile, Adam Blair, having retired from his ministry, returned to live with relations at Lisburn. In all this, Blair, like other committed presbyterians, operated in a world not defined by the structures of ascendancy Ireland. It remained a world in which, notwithstanding the rapid fall in numbers of the landed sympathetic to protestant dissent, a friendly squire, John Darby, had engineered Blair's settlement at Leap.[80] Furthermore, as the circle of gentry patrons of nonconformity contracted, that of prospering townspeople and genteel professionals expanded. Indeed, the changing social geography of Ireland, with the growth of the towns and of the middling sort within them, helped dissent.

V

The patterns of intertwining ancestry and confession varied. As ideas of Englishness, Scottishness, Irishness and Britishness developed, the sense of a powerful Ulster-Scots identity may have been threatened or

[76] W. Innes Addison, *The matriculation albums of the University of Glasgow from 1728–1858* (Glasgow, 1913), p. 17; PRONI, D 1460/1, p. 67.

[77] TCD, MS 6447; Addison, *Matriculation albums of Glasgow*, p. 14.

[78] C. H. Irwin, *A history of presbyterianism in Dublin and the south and west of Ireland* (1890), p. 332.

[79] TCD, MS 6447; Addison, *Matriculation albums of Glasgow*, p. 98.

[80] Irwin, *Presbyterianism in Dublin*, pp. 95, 332.

reinforced. Certainly the presbyterian churches, although disunited, maintained the idea and actuality of a community which straddled the North Channel. Thus, if much of detail remains to be uncovered, the central place of dissenting congregations in preserving Ulster Scottish- ness seems assured. If this was the case, it invites comparison with the English in Ireland, and how far the church of Ireland satisfied, or may indeed have created, ideas of Englishness and Irishness.

During the early seventeenth century, Charles I, Archbishop Laud and Bishop Bramhall of Derry had striven for greater uniformity, or at least congruity, in the public worship of the three kingdoms.[81] The liturgy and doctrines of the church of Ireland were modified, but their distinctiveness was not ended. Later changes, notably the Irish act of uniformity in 1666, surrendered much which had made it plausible to regard the church of Ireland as in communion with, but independent of and anterior in time to, the church of England. As the peculiarities of the Irish establishment faded, some commentators slipped unthinkingly between calling it still 'the church of Ireland' or 'the Church of England'.[82] Semantic confusion mirrored apparent fusion. By 1708, the English academic sent to rule the church of Ireland as primate could announce boldly, 'the Church of England and Ireland is one and the same Church'.[83] Such a conclusion came easily in Dublin, still predomi- nantly a protestant and even a conformist city, and a bastion of the English interest in Ireland. Elsewhere, local practices may have diverged more sharply from metropolitan standards. For the same reasons, optimists who acclaimed the eighteenth-century church as an agent of anglicisation as well as anglicanism often confounded aspiration with reality.

The church of Ireland, its liturgy modelled after that of the church of England and its appeal primarily anglophone, promoted the English as much as protestant interest. Its religious mission was still hampered by the institutional and financial weaknesses which had afflicted it since

[81] A. Ford, 'Dependent or independent? The church of Ireland and its colonial context, 1536–1649', *The Seventeenth Century*, 10 (1995), 163–81; J. MacCafferty, ' "God bless your free Church of Ireland": Wentworth, Laud, Bramhall and the Irish convocation of 1634', in J. F. Merritt, ed., *The political world of Thomas Wentworth, earl of Strafford 1621–1641* (Cambridge, 1995), pp. 187–207; J. Morrill, 'A British patriarchy? Ecclesiastical imperialism under the Early Stuarts', in A. Fletcher and P. R. Roberts, eds., *Religion, culture and society in early Modern Britain* (Cambridge, 1994), pp. 209–37.

[82] Sermon of T. Vesey, 20 Aug. 1658, Abbey Leix, Co Laois, de Vesci MSS, G/1; exchanges of Dr A. Dopping and Capt. Foley, 1673–4, NLI, PC 515; ibid., MS 4653, s.d. 28 May 1715; E. J. A. Impey, *A Roberts family, quondam quakers of Queen's County* (Birmingham, 1939), p. 85.

[83] Abp. Narcissus Marsh, 16 Feb. 1707[8], Bod., Smith MS 52, p. 151.

(and before) the reformation. It suffered also from serious ideological and ethnic divisions. By the eighteenth century, in so far as the church of Ireland had been conformed and subordinated to its English counterpart it was through the intrusion into its leadership of English-bred and educated clergy. This strategy continued, indeed was intensified, in the eighteenth century. It was disliked. In the 1720s, for example, the presence of a growing number of English bishops on the Irish bench provoked numerous incidents, some petty, others grave, in which their Irish brethren distinguished themselves.[84] The governments in London and Dublin attended closely to the choice of appropriate bishops. By 1727 the Irish sees were divided equally between English and Irish occupants; this situation still prevailed in 1760.[85] However, it was noticed that now the two senior archbishoprics, together with the most remunerative dioceses, went to English interlopers. These appointments personalised an issue which, in its cruder formulations, revolved around the supposed emasculation of the independent church of Ireland: a process which unhappily paralleled the English invasion into lay offices and the curbing of Ireland's legislative independence. Thus, the government, or at least the governors of the established church, were added to the grievances which obsessed patriots and incubated Irishness.

The bishops, undoubtedly important, especially to the business of the House of Lords, have perhaps been given too much attention as symbols and symptoms of what was wrong with the church of Ireland. Often the cathedral and parochial clergy enjoyed greater contact with the laity. These functionaries, from 500 to 800 of them, are less easily subjected to minute prosopographical analysis.[86] By the late seventeenth century, they could be recruited principally from the protestants born and reared within Ireland. Even in the leadership of dioceses, while the summer residence of dutiful bishops lengthened, deans, archdeacons and rectors lived there more continuously. Deaneries and other lucrative dignities attracted the sons of Irish protestant dynasties. Thus, at Limerick, Story, historian of the Williamite wars, was succeeded by a Bindon, a Massy and a Crosbie; in Lismore, the deans included a Jephson and an Alcock; and at Waterford, Bolton was succeeded by Harman. Each either belonged to a family prominent in the vicinity or threw himself

---

[84] P. McNally, '"Irish and English interests": national conflict within the church of Ireland episcopate in the reign of George I', *IHS*, 29 (1995), 295–314.

[85] J. Falvey, 'The church of Ireland episcopate in the eighteenth-century: an over-view', *Eighteenth-Century Ireland*, 8 (1993), 103–14; Falvey, 'The church of Ireland episcopate in the eighteenth century' (M.A. dissertation, University College Cork, 1995), pp. 40–4, 63; F. G. James, *Ireland in the empire 1688–1770* (Cambridge, MA 1973), p. 131.

[86] Barnard, 'Improving clergymen', pp. 136–8.

into the public affairs of the protestant nation. Throughout the eighteenth century, a puny contingent of English bishops struggled to direct a church in which most of the parochial clergy were more intimate with the oddities of provincial Irish life. This situation may have worsened the ideological and ethnic schizophrenia from which the church of Ireland had long suffered. It also increases the suspicion that, for all the nominal congruence between the established churches of the two kingdoms, that of Ireland followed its own inclinations, as betrayed by its clergy in country pulpits or over the dinner tables in their deaneries and parsonages.

This local coloration did not automatically beguile the protestant laity. On several issues, notoriously over tithes, church leases and property, self-interested lay people defeated reforming churchmen. Lay patrons and impropriators admired deferential and undemanding clerics. Nevertheless, eighteenth-century Ireland still lacked the proportions of the educated and professionals in contemporary England. In these circumstances, incumbents of the church of Ireland emerged as publicists for the protestant interest and, in the 1780s, a bishop (albeit of English background) first defined and defended 'the protestant ascendancy'.[87] Earlier, the high renown which Archbishop William King, Dean Swift and Archbishop Edward Synge earned by their writing and preaching cast some reflected lustre on the church which they served. The degree to which the clergy of the established church, and particularly those of unimpeachable Irish pedigree, prefigured rather than simply adopted the patriotism of the times has yet to be ascertained. Provincial clergymen, in most other matters servile towards their kinsfolk and patrons among the squirearchy, may simply have limped along in a movement which was gathering momentum already. Undoubtedly some incumbents, alert to their functions as exemplars and guides, and in some cases enjoying ample estates and emoluments, distinguished themselves by identifying and then attending to local problems. Alongside exertions for the material betterment of Ireland went a zeal for moral improvement. Vigilant clerics alternately belaboured their contemporaries for backsliding and defended Ireland and its people from the scorn of outsiders. Men of the cloth were among the earliest to contemplate their surroundings and past fondly.[88] Illustrative

---

[87] R. Woodward, *The present state of the church of Ireland* (Dublin, 1787).
[88] T. C. Barnard, 'The Hartlib circle and the cult and culture of improvement in Ireland', in M. Greengrass, M. Leslie and T. Raylor, eds., *Samuel Hartlib and universal reformation* (Cambridge, 1994), pp. 294–7; Barnard, 'Improving clergymen', pp. 136–51; H. F. Berry, *A history of the Royal Dublin Society* (1915), pp. 24–7.

of this responsiveness, and its part in awakening a livelier sense of Irishness, was the protestant annexation of St Patrick.

The English in Ireland, from the sixteenth-century earls of Kildare, the citizens of Dublin to the duke of Ormond, looked to George as a tutelary saint.[89] In the early eighteenth century, Andrew's cult was also promoted since his name day was close to the birthday of Dean Swift.[90] But seventeenth-century scholars of the church of Ireland, led by the redoubtable Archbishop Ussher, enlisted that 'most adaptable of saints' to prove that the church of Ireland had existed independent of England and uncorrupted by Rome.[91] The versatile Patrick was adopted both by Tridentine catholicism and Irish protestantism.[92] Already viewed as Ireland's special protector, by the 1750s Patrick was promoted by irenicists wanting to merge the skirmishing English and Scots in Ireland under a 'British' saint.[93] Moralists invoked his aid in bids to reform the manners of the protestant elite. Only in 1783, with the institution of the knights of St Patrick did the protestant state in Ireland formally accord him a special position. Long before that the 17th of March had been marked by festivities of which protestants approved even if they did not always themselves partake.[94] The spread and diversification of the protestant cult of Patrick, including the use of his name at baptism, offer one index of the stronger protestant identification with Ireland. Another is the development of Hibernia as a personification of an Ireland linked with but separate from the England of Britannia.

Two conformist protestants living in the rural hinterlands of Limerick

89 M. Clark and R. Refaussé, *Directory of historic Dublin guilds* (Dublin, 1993), pp. 41–2; S. G. Ellis, *Tudor Ireland* (1985), p. 58; T. C. Barnard, 'The uses of 23 October 1641 and Irish protestant celebrations', *EHR*, 106 (1991), 893.

90 NLI, MS 1522, p. 63; H. F. Berry, 'Notes from the diary of a Dublin lady in the reign of George II', *Journal of the Royal Society of Antiquaries of Ireland*, 5th ser., 8 (1898), 147; *Faulkner's Dublin Journal*, 29 Nov.–3 Dec. 1726.

91 A. Ford, ' "Standing one's ground" ', in Ford, McGuire and Milne, eds., *As by law established*, pp. 7–10.

92 B. Cunningham and R. Gillespie, ' "The most adaptable of saints": the cult of St Patrick in the seventeenth century', *Archivium Hibernicum*, 49 (1995), 82–104; M. K. Walsh, *"Destruction by peace": Hugh O'Neill after Kinsale* (Monaghan, 1986), p. 75.

93 J. R. Hill, 'National festivals, the state and "protestant ascendancy" in Ireland 1790–1829', *IHS*, 24 (1984–5), 30–2; Hill, 'Popery and protestantism, civil and religious liberty: the disputed lessons of Irish history 1690–1812', *P&P*, 118 (1988), 114–16.

94 Christ Church, Oxford, Wake MSS, xiii, ff. 51, 119; song of John Fleming, 1766, NLI, MS 25432; MS 1522, p. 108; MS 1524, p. 246; MS 1527, p. 84; MS 1528, 17 Mar. 1765; Barnard, 'The uses of 23 October 1641', p. 919; Hayton, 'Anglo-Irish attitudes', pp. 150–1; *An elegy on the much lamented death of those excellent patriots and lovers of their country the family of the potatoes* (Dublin, 1739/40); A. K. Longfield, *The Shapland Carew papers* (Dublin, 1946), p. 189.

city during the 1740s anchor these speculations to the prosaic routines of provincial Irish life. St Patrick's Day featured in the calendar of one, but so did numerous other secular and parochial events.[95] Nicholas Peacock was the shadowy cadet of a Yorkshire family which settled in county Limerick in the mid-seventeenth century.[96] Peacock acted as agent to local families only intermittently resident, and farmed on his own account. He enjoyed easy social relations with his employers from the squirearchy, dining frequently and sometimes staying with them overnight. Twice in a decade he rode up to Dublin, but only for a few days. Once he served as a juror but never as a magistrate. A beneficiary of the emergent protestant ascendancy, he lived largely outside the circles of privileged office-holders whose activities and attitudes still predominate in characterisations of eighteenth-century protestant Ireland.

Peacock's customary circuit was bounded by the River Shannon, the hilly frontier between Counties Limerick and Cork and the city of Limerick. Thanks to his own and his servants' frequent sorties into the city, and through the newspapers, he learnt of dangers. So, in March 1744, he noted preventative measures against the priests and, a couple of days later, 'an alarm of wars'.[97] As the ripples from the young pretender's descent lapped around the western seaboard of Ireland, Peacock obeyed his orders as a cornet in the militia and hastened to an array at Kilmallock, only to find no one there.[98] Peacock worshipped in the church of Ireland. However, he mentioned going to church only five or six times a year, probably because the country cures were served irregularly. Once he arrived, but the incumbent did not. On another occasion he was turned away from the church.[99] He also participated in the work of the vestry. Its main tasks, the applotment of rates and tithes, in both of which he was involved as a collector, generated dissension, On the evidence of his terse diary, he followed the prescribed forms of worship. But the ritual year invented by the protestant church and state in Ireland exerted only a feeble grip on him. None of the red-letter days – Charles I's martyrdom, Charles II's restoration, the birth, accession and coronation of the sovereign or the anniversaries of Guy Fawkes's plot and the Irish rebellion of 1641 – elicited comment or church

[95] NLI, MS 16091, 16, 17 Mar. 1740[1], 17 Mar. 1741[2], 16, 17 Mar. 1744[5], 17 Mar. 1746[7], 17 Mar. 1748[9], 17 Mar. 1749[50], 17 Mar. 1750[1].

[96] J. B. Burke, *A genealogical and heraldic history of the landed gentry of Ireland*, ed. A. C. Fox-Davies (1912), p. 552; S. Lewis, *A topographical dictionary of Ireland* (1837), II, p. 87.

[97] NLI, MS 16091, 6, 8 Mar. 1743[4]; ibid., MS 2714, p. 114; J. Brady, *Catholics and catholicism in the eighteenth-century press* (Maynooth, 1965), p. 74.

[98] NLI, MS 16091, 24 Nov. 1745.   [99] Ibid., 9 June 1745, 26 Mar. 1749.

attendance. Instead he commemorated the personal and local. He attended the intermittent weddings and burials of patrons, neighbours and kinsfolk. Each year the birthday of his principal employer, Hartstonge, was marked: sometimes with an assembly of the 'quality'; less acceptably (to Peacock) by 'rag, tag and bobtail'.[100]

Until he married in 1747 Peacock lived with a household of domestic and farm servants whose names suggest strongly ethnic and confessional differences from him. He knew the festivals in their alternative calendar, and allowed, even encouraged, their celebration, while himself abstaining. Like other protestant employers he regularly noticed St Patrick's Day.[101] Thus, in 1742 he recorded, 'I gave the servants 2s 8d and sent them to drink their Patrick's Pots.' Five years later he again noted, 'I gave my family leave to go to see St Patrick and bade them drink 3s 3d.'[102] Living close to a well sacred to Patrick, his cult may have been particularly powerful in the locality.[103] On other occasions, Peacock let his servants go to patterns, with money in their pockets from him. He, meanwhile, stayed at home, often reading.[104] His absence from these local holidays may have reflected, and widened, the differences in creed and race between Peacock and his household. But it may tell more of the distance created by increasing social and economic differentiation, which caused prospering and 'respectable' catholics also to withdraw from the demotic revels associated with patronal festivals and patterns.[105]

Peacock not only indulged his own employees (his designation of them as his 'family' is suggestive), but enjoyed intimacies with catholic neighbours. Isolated, and dependent as agent and farmer on the good will of the populace, such relationships may have betokened more calculation than spontaneity. Whatever were his motives, on 27 December 1743 he mentioned how the priest and others 'came to see me for their share of Christmas and went away in good order'.[106] The catholic religious were useful to him, not just to control potentially unruly

---

[100] Ibid., 25 July 1744.
[101] Ibid., MS 1552, p. 108; MS 1524, p. 246; MS 1527, p. 84; MS 1528, 17 Mar. 1765.
[102] Ibid., MS 16091, 17 Mar. 1741[2], 17 Mar. 1746[7].
[103] Lewis, *Topographical dictionary*, II, p. 249.
[104] NLI, MS 16091, 11 July, 15 Aug. 1741, 14 Feb. 1741[2], 11 July 1742, 24 Feb. 1742[3], 15 Aug. 1745, 8, 29 Sept. 1747.
[105] S. J. Connolly. *Priests and people in pre-famine Ireland* (Dublin, 1982), 148–74; Connolly, 'Approaches to the history of Irish popular culture', *Bullán*, 2: 2 (1996), 83–100; Connolly, 'Popular culture: patterns of change and adaptation', in S. J. Connolly, R. A. Houston and R. J. Morris, eds., *Conflict, identity and economic development: Ireland and Scotland 1600–1939* (Preston, 1995), pp. 103–13; K. Whelan, 'An underground gentry?', reprinted in Whelan, *The tree of liberty* (Cork, 1996), pp. 34–7.
[106] NLI, MS 16091, 27 Dec. 1743.

parishioners, but as customers. Peacock sold them linen towels, presumably for liturgical rituals, but disapproved of one priest who commandeered a neighbour's horse and paid only 5s 5d for it.[107] Once or twice these contacts clearly went beyond the merely politic. He attended a catholic wedding, contributing towards the cleric's dues, and had a priest to dine and stay overnight.[108] Elsewhere, at Agher in County Meath during the 1760s, a squire, higher in social status than Peacock, regularly entertained the parish priest at table.[109] Earlier, during the 1740s, another landowner in the same county had the priest to dine on St Patrick's Day.[110] As new standards of education, polite conduct and dress permeated sections of the priesthood, as well as of the protestant squirearchy, such instances of sociability multiplied. Even so, much depended on the local situation and the temperament of individual clergy and gentlemen. Moreover, as sectarianism revived in the later 1760s and as more catholics were caught up in political mobilisation, the tendency for sociability to ignore traditional confessional boundaries may have been arrested. In the 1770s, when a catholic gentleman took tea with a quaker neighbour, the event was rare enough to merit notice.[111]

Peacock's laconic diurnal obeys conventions and omits or distorts occurrences now otherwise lost to us. It would be presumptuous to deduce much about his motives and inner thoughts from it, let alone use it to construct a theory applicable to his similarly situated contemporaries. He jogged along harmoniously with neighbours, including the recently settled Palatines, the lately converted Quins of Adare as well as catholics.[112] He went through the outward forms of anglican religion, without any urgent religious impulse agitating his record. Occasionally he entered religious apothegms culled from scripture. These were volunteered at the year's end, when he promised to amend his life, and as he was about to marry.[113] Otherwise, in an act which appears to confirm the crudest equations of protestantism with capitalist success, he prefaced his periodic inventories of livestock and linen with imprecations. So, early in 1744, he beseeched, 'the Lord make me thankful, I have 8 table clothes, 5 napkins, 7 new shirts, 7 a year old and 12 old

[107] Ibid., 21 Feb. 1743[4]; 23 Aug. 1744.   [108] Ibid., 1 May 1750, 8, 9 July 1751.

[109] Ibid., MS 3855, 13 June, 26 Sept., 21 Nov. 1762; 13 Mar., 22 Apr., 26 June 1763.

[110] Cloverhill, Co. Cavan, Purdon MSS, diary of John Pratt, 17 Mar. 1745 [6].

[111] James More of Balyna, manuscript account of the O'More family, c. 1774, f. 34, private collection, Co. Kildare.

[112] O'Connor, *Rathkeale*, pp. 82–114; R. C. B. Oliver, 'The Hartstonges and Radnorshire, part 1', *Transactions of the Radnorshire Society* (1973) table 3; C. Wyndham-Quin, Countess of Dunraven, *Memorials of Adare manor* (Oxford, 1865), pp. 187–9.

[113] NLI, MS 16091, 5 Jan. 1739[40], 31 Dec. 1741, 18 July 1743, 14 Dec. 1745, 5 May, 1747.

shirts, 24 stocks, 6 towels, 5 pair of new sheets, a fine pair, a coarse pair and an old pair, 11 pair of yarn stockings, 7 pair of worsted, 3 of cotton, 3 of thread, 2 of silk, 2 old, 3 new handkerchiefs'. In similar mode he would later bless God for his numerous beasts and even for his copious supply of handkerchiefs.[114]

An equally brief and formalised record kept for a shorter spell by a contemporary of Peacock varies the impression of how the modestly comfortable protestants lived.[115] Lucas, a young farmer, dwelt still with his parents to the north of Limerick near Corofin. He occupied a similar level in society to Peacock, and followed many of the same pursuits. He mingled with the protestant farmers of the district. When the harvest put coin in his pocket he jaunted a little further afield and kept the company of squires. Lucas went more often than Peacock to church of Ireland worship, almost every fortnight in 1741. This may mean no more than that his parish was better served than Peacock's, or that his own way to the church was shorter and easier. The harsh winter of 1741, the culmination of two severe seasons, left little trace in Peacock's annals, situated as he was in the lush plain at the confluence of the Rivers Shannon and Maigue. In contrast, it took Lucas regularly to burials and a day of fast and humiliation decreed by the government to deflect the divine wrath from Ireland.[116]

The worlds of these dim provincials were not sealed against outside influences. From time to time the distant Dublin government and even the remote Hanoverian state impinged. Yet, notwithstanding the occasional flurries when wars or invasions were rumoured, the everyday and elemental preoccupied these protestants, as it did their catholic employees and neighbours. The random survival of their testimonies, and these even more random reflections on them, caution against elaborate theories of identity and ethnicity. In accounts of eighteenth-century Ireland, raucous patriots have frequently drowned the introspective. The private reflections of the latter, like Cosby, Traill, Blair or Peacock, soften the stark polarities. But they offer little assistance in reconstructing collective identities. Even if they did not remain wilfully individualistic, a simple aggregation of such examples constitutes little more than the historical equivalent of *pointillisme*. In place of the broad expressionism which has often characterised the canvas of ascendancy Ireland, we may be confronted with one speckled with a few isolated dots, which, no matter how imaginative the beholder, cannot be composed into any comprehensible scene. Moreover, the private annalists, if they veil their prejudices more discreetly than the polemicists, are not

[114] Ibid., 25 Jan. 1743[4], 17 Dec. 1744, 3 Aug. 1745, 1 May 1747.
[115] Ibid., MS 14101.   [116] Ibid., 18, 19 Jan. 1740[1], 3, 4 Feb. 1740[1].

innocent of prejudice and presuppositions. As a result, though the testimony assembled here confirms that each of the confessions was permeable, and that attitudes towards and within the separate denominations varied, it does not weaken the image of an island in which sectarian and ethnic divisions were accentuated rather than moderated. Certainly some of those who have been paraded here chose to think of themselves as Irish not because of any clear lineage but through personal idiosyncrasy and cultural conditioning. Nor were these identities always consistently and continuously maintained. Changed company and conditions elicited fresh postures. The same individuals at different moments and places, therefore, adopted or were accorded the standing of English, Scots, Ulster Scots and (occasionally) Britons; labelled according to the province, region or town where they lived; or classified either as townspeople or rustics, civil, polite and anglophone rather than uncouth, primitive and Irish, protestant not papist. Incongruous juxtapositions resulted. The upper reaches of the church of Ireland ascendancy embraced those whose names – Butler, Conolly, Delany, Duigenan, Fitzgerald, O'Brien – confute any notion of racial exclusivity among the elite. However, striking as these examples of movement across the confessional frontiers are, the expectation persisted that ethnicity match denominational affiliation. Little that can be retrieved from eighteenth-century Ireland suggests that this contemporary assumption was fundamentally wrong.

10 'The common name of Irishman': protestantism and patriotism in eighteenth-century Ireland

Ian McBride

Although Linda Colley's *Britons* does not deal explicitly with John Bull's other island, its central thesis is of great importance for Irish historians. Neither the protestant triumphalism nor the cult of the British constitution which she describes were confined to Great Britain: they constituted the ideological co-ordinates of the protestant ascendancy in Ireland between 1690 and 1800, and of the various forms of settler 'nationalism' which challenged the imperial administration during that period. This common British heritage was transformed by the peculiarities of the Irish situation, however, producing a different pattern from that found in England or Scotland. Whig political culture was skewed by the inferior status of the Dublin parliament, while the anti-catholicism of the ascendancy was sharpened by the close proximity and numerical strength of 'the other'.

Until recently, scholars of eighteenth-century Ireland have largely ignored British and imperial perspectives, operating instead within an insular context. In the last century a canon of patriotic writings was constructed which began with William Molyneux and skipped forwards to Jonathan Swift, Charles Lucas, Henry Grattan, before culminating in Wolfe Tone. The period of legislative autonomy between 1782 and 1801 – popularly known as 'Grattan's parliament' – served as an inspiration for repealers and home rulers, while the more radical form of patriotism which surfaced in the 1790s was used to legitimise republican separatism.[1] Over the last twenty-five years the nationalist interpretation has come under heavy fire, but revisionists have failed to generate an alternative set of organising principles.[2] Indeed a residual teleology can

---

[1] Gerard O'Brien, 'The Grattan mystique', *Eighteenth-Century Ireland*, 1 (1986), 177–94; Robert Mahony, *Jonathan Swift: the Irish identity* (New Haven, 1995), chs. 4–6.

[2] The most important exception is J. T. Leersen, 'Anglo-Irish patriotism and its European context: notes towards a reassessment', *Eighteenth-Century Ireland*, 3 (1988), 7–24. For a broader discussion of patriotism, see Maurizio Viroli, *For love of country: an essay on patriotism and nationalism* (Oxford, 1995), esp. the introduction.

be detected in the continuing preoccupation of historians with the cultural origins of national consciousness. It is still often assumed that the central dynamic in this period is supplied by the divergence of Irish political culture from its British roots: that patriotic writers, from Molyneux to Tone, were actively engaged in the business of becoming *more Irish* than their predecessors.

This chapter employs an alternative framework for the study of eighteenth-century Irish patriotism. Its basic premise is that national identities in the early modern period were primarily defined not in terms of linguistic or cultural differences but in terms of polity (the myth of an ancestral constitution) and religion (a sense of chosenness). With regard to the first of these, my approach is indebted to the 'British' or three-kingdoms perspective which has become increasingly popular among early modern historians of this archipelago. Following the lead of J. G. A. Pocock, scholars have begun to uncover a diversity of cultures in the British empire, all engaged in the appropriation, interpretation and criticism of political discourses and institutions which had been imported from England.[3] This is as true of the Anglo-Irish elite of Dublin and, to a lesser extent, the provincial culture of presbyterian Ulster, and even of the middle-class spokesmen of the Catholic Committee, as it is of Lowland Scots or American colonists.[4] Far from drawing on Gaelic sources, Irish patriotism was anglocentric and, arguably, it was increasingly so.[5]

At the same time, we have learned much from Linda Colley, Colin Haydon and others about the religious basis of collective identities during the early modern period.[6] Of course it has long been recognised that the patriot conception of the Irish nation was an exclusively protestant one, and that even Wolfe Tone retained enlightenment

---

[3] For examples of this approach, see J. G. A. Pocock, *Virtue, commerce and history: essays on political thought and history, chiefly in the eighteenth century* (Cambridge, 1985), esp. chs. 4, 11; Colin Kidd, *Subverting Scotland's past: Scottish whig historians and the creation of an Anglo-British identity, 1689–c. 1830* (Cambridge, 1993); Kidd, 'North Britishness and the nature of eighteenth-century patriotisms', *HJ*, 39 (1996), 362–82; John Robertson, ed., *A union for empire: political thought and the British union of 1707* (Cambridge, 1995); J. P. Greene, *Peripheries and center: constitutional development in the extended polities of the British Empire and the United States 1607–1788* (1986). It must be stressed that the adoption of a British approach is not meant to deny the validity of alternative histories based on national, regional or local perspectives.

[4] 'Anglo-Irish', like 'anglican', is an anachronistic term, but I have retained it here as a convenient shorthand term for those who in the 1690s thought of themselves as the English in Ireland.

[5] See, for example, Michael Ryder, 'The Bank of Ireland 1721: land, credit and dependency', *HJ*, 25 (1982), 557–82, which describes the adoption of 'country' rhetoric by opposition politicians in Ireland.

[6] For a discussion of this literature see the essays by Haydon and Black in this volume.

prejudices against the church of Rome, but little research has been carried out on the subject. This essay will suggest that such prejudices were not just a regrettable hangover from the seventeenth century, but were central to the mainstream tradition of Irish patriotism in the eighteenth century, and even to the republican project of the United Irishmen in the 1790s. The example of Ireland thus alerts us to the ambiguous and contested nature of anti-popery, highlighted throughout in this volume. If, on one level, the reformed faith promoted an ideological consensus which united Britons against the catholic powers of Europe, on others it acted to underpin separate identities, particularly where these could attach themselves to surviving 'national' institutions.

I

'Protestantism', Linda Colley has written, 'was the foundation that made the invention of Great Britain possible.'[7] It was the primary cultural resource which united the peoples of England, Scotland and Wales throughout a century of conflict with France, despite the persistence of national, regional and local differences. In the decades after the battle of the Boyne, protestants across the Irish Sea subscribed to the same reformation rhetoric, its tone rendered all the more strident by their precarious position as an embattled minority in a popish land. Anti-catholicism, institutionalised in the penal code, tirelessly promoted in sermons, pamphlets and newspapers, and embodied in both public rituals and plebeian celebrations, was the single most salient feature in the cluster of attitudes and assumptions which constituted the mental world of the protestant ascendancy. While the Britons of the larger island defined themselves against the despotic monarchies of the continent, however, their Irish brethren were more concerned with the internal threat represented by the native Irish population, obdurately attached to a bloodthirsty creed which had apparently inspired a series of conspiracies, rebellions and massacres.[8] A protestant sense of chosenness thus interacted with memories of the religious and ethnic conflicts of the seventeenth century to form a distinctive garrison mentality.

In reconstructing the self-image of *Hibernia Anglicana* after the Williamite wars, the most useful sources are the anglican sermons preached on official holy days.[9] In addition to 30 January (the martyrdom of

---

[7] Linda Colley, *Britons: forging the nation 1707–1837* (1992), p. 54.

[8] But see Gerard O'Brien, 'Francophobia in later eighteenth-century Irish history', in David Dickson and Hugh Gough, eds., *Ireland and the French Revolution* (Dublin, 1990), pp. 40–51.

[9] T. C. Barnard, 'The uses of 23 October and Irish protestant celebrations', *EHR*, 106 (1991), 889–920; Robert Eccleshall, 'Anglican political thought in the century after the

Charles I), 29 May (the restoration) and 5 November (the discovery of the 'gunpowder plot', 1605, and William III's landing at Torbay, 1688), the church of Ireland had set aside 23 October for the commemoration of the rising of 1641. On such occasions preachers drew upon old testament texts to make sense of the sufferings and triumphs they had experienced in what one bishop described as 'our *Protestant Canaan*'.[10] Their deliverance from catholic Ireland, like the liberation of the children of Israel from Egypt, was interpreted as a providential blessing bestowed by the deity upon his favoured people.[11] It was this sense of collective destiny, welded together in the heat of religious and racial conflict, that bound together the protestant nation of the eighteenth century.

The stereotyped images of protestantism and popery employed by Anglo-Irish writers utilised a familiar set of polarities – freedom/slavery, reason/superstition, civility/barbarity, industry/idleness – to demonstrate that Roman catholicism was the absolute inversion of true Christianity. The defining characteristic of the Roman church, however, was the use of savagely violent forms of persecution to maintain and extend its tyrannical reign. The votaries of Rome, it was believed, were bound by their religion to root out heresy; they were released from fulfilling oaths made with heretics; and they owed an absolute allegiance to the papacy which nullified their civil obligations to temporal rulers. The inevitable result was the frequently recited litany of plots and insurrections dominated by 1641. Anglican sermons, often drawing on Sir John Temple's *The Irish rebellion* (1646), recycled stories of the atrocities committed at Portadown and elsewhere. Their congregations learned how the papists, inflamed by their malevolent priests, had turned the whole kingdom into a field of blood, committing barbarities 'that cannot be paralleled in the History of any other Nation from the beginning of the World to this Day'.[12]

If popery was 'a complicated System, mixed up with many Doctrines

revolution of 1688', in D. George Boyce, Robert Eccleshall and Vincent Geoghegan, eds., *Political thought in Ireland since the seventeenth century* (1993), pp. 38–41.

[10] Francis Hutchinson, *A sermon preached in Christ-Church, Dublin, on Friday, November 5th, 1731* (3rd edn, Dublin, 1731), p. 5.

[11] Edward Walkinton, *A sermon preached Octob. 23. 1692 in St Andrew's Church, Dublin* (Dublin, 1692), p. 7. Other examples of the genre are Edward Wetenhall, *A sermon preached Octob. 23. 1692* (Dublin, 1699); Henry Maule, *A sermon preached in Christ-Church, Dublin . . . the twenty-third day of October, 1733* (Dublin, 1733); John Travers, *A sermon preach'd at Christ-Church in Dublin . . . the fifth of November, 1711* (Dublin, 1711); Edward Synge, *Thankfulness to almighty God for his more ancient and later mercies and deliverances vouchsafed to the British and protestants, within the kingdom of Ireland* (1711).

[12] William Henry, *The necessity of unity: a sermon preached in St Andrew's Church, Dublin . . . on the twenty-third day of October, 1761* (Dublin, 1761), p. 11.

of a political Nature', the central charge remained that catholics were bound by their religious principles to dethrone heretical princes and to murder their subjects.[13] It was repeatedly emphasised that papists were punished not because of their beliefs regarding transubstantiation, purgatory or the worship of images, absurd and anti-christian though these might be. Rather, attention came to focus increasingly on the threat posed to civil government, as it was argued that the legal tolera-tion of catholicism was simply incompatible with the preservation of a protestant establishment.[14] Defined in this loose way – as religious intolerance – popery was not confined to Rome. Dissenters could be branded as closet papists, since they upheld their own variety of 'the deposing doctrine', reserving the same power to their synods and assemblies which catholics notoriously ascribed to the papacy.[15] By the 1760s anglican consciences had become troubled by the realisation that the political, social and economic disabilities imposed upon their catholic country-men might also qualify as persecution, and it had become fashionable to boast of the slack enforcement of the penal laws as evidence of the moderate and enlightened disposition of protestant Ireland.[16]

The spread of pure Christianity, of course, was inextricably linked to the progress of civility, and for Irish protestants civility signified the language, learning, customs and common law of their mother country.[17] Although the Rev. John Richardson of Belturbet and a handful of anglican clergymen were zealous advocates of evangelisation in the native tongue, the predominant view associated the strength of super-stition in Ireland with the persistence of a barbarous and backward culture.[18] In 1698 Bishop Foy of Waterford and Lismore had linked the survival of superstition and idolatry amongst the Irish to 'their wild

---

[13] *The ax laid to the root: or, reasons humbly offered, for putting the popish clergy in Ireland under some better regulations* (Dublin, 1749), p. 22.

[14] Arthur Dobbs, *An essay on the trade and improvement of Ireland* (2 vols., Dublin, 1729), II, pp. 91–2.

[15] Nathaniel Foy, *A sermon preached in Christ's-Church, Dublin; on the 23d of October, 1698* (Dublin, 1698), p. 8; Theophilus Bolton, *A sermon preach'd in St Andrew's, Dublin . . . October 23, 1721* (Dublin, 1721), p. 29. For later echoes, see *A second letter to the people of Ireland on the subject of tythes. . . . By a friend to the constitution* (Dublin, 1758), p. 16; *Fragment of a letter to a friend relative to the repeal of the test* (Dublin, 1780), p. 8.

[16] Edward Young, *A sermon preached in Christ-Church, Dublin; on Sunday, October 23, 1763* (Dublin, 1763), p. 7; Richard Woodward, *A sermon preached at Christ-Church, Dublin, on the 13th of May, 1764, before the Incorporated Society for Promoting English Protestant Schools in Ireland* (Dublin, 1764), p. 10.

[17] For an emphatic statement of the superiority of English culture see [Richard Cox], *An essay for the conversion of the Irish* (Dublin, 1698), esp. pp. 10–12.

[18] T. C. Barnard, 'Protestants and the Irish language, c. 1675–1725', *JEH*, 44 (1993), 243–72.

savage way of Living in single Cottages, and dismal Unhabitable places', and proposed that 'the Irish Nation' should be corralled into towns and villages and compelled to attend English-speaking schools.[19] Similar schemes followed, as clerical and lay leaders argued the necessity of de-gaelicising Ireland. Proselytism and anglicisation went hand in hand, most notably in the foundation of the Charter School movement in 1733. Although Bishop Hutchinson and Bishop Nicolson (both Englishmen) displayed a scholarly interest in the Gaelic tongue, the majority of their colleagues rejoiced in the eradication of a primitive, squalid and depraved culture. By the 1730s patriots such as Samuel Madden were able to rejoice that the natives were being assimilated to English customs, manners and habits; even the Irish language was being laid aside, breaking down the 'great Partition Wall, that kept us estranged and divided'.[20]

These perceptions of catholicism, crystallised while memories of the Williamite wars were still fresh, persisted throughout the next century, their currency rising and falling with the vicissitudes of Anglo-French rivalry. On ceremonial occasions anglican preachers dutifully mounted the pulpit to deliver their annual warnings that the church of Rome, even if 'too Politick to let fly her Fire-brands, Anathemas, Depositions of Princes, Crusadoes, Armys of Holy Cut-Throats . . . has this Artillery of Hell still in her Stores'.[21] One useful barometer of sectarian anxieties is supplied by the annual totals of catholic gentlemen persuaded to conform. Conversion rates peaked in 1740–1, 1745–9, after 1756, and 1761, as each invasion scare produced a fresh crop of recruits to the established church. Numbers reached a new height during 1766–8, this time against the background of agrarian agitation in Munster, before falling away in 1770s.[22] A similar pattern is evident from the popularity of Sir John Temple's *The Irish rebellion*, reprinted in 1713, 1714, 1724, 1746, 1766, each new edition a testimony to the resilience of atavistic animosities.[23]

In their shared fidelity to the reformation, and in other ways too, Irish protestants had all the makings of fully-fledged Britons. They laid claim to an inheritance of civil and religious liberty which was thought to distinguish the British empire from the despotic, catholic regimes of

[19] Foy, *Sermon preached in Christ's-Church, Dublin*, pp. 27–8.
[20] Samuel Madden, *Reflections and resolutions proper for the gentlemen of Ireland* (Dublin, 1738), p. 103.
[21] William Henry, *A philippic oration against the pretender's son and his adherents* (Dublin, 1745), pp. 9–10.
[22] L. M. Cullen, *The emergence of modern Ireland 1600–1900* (1981), pp. 195–6.
[23] For Temple, see Toby Barnard, '1641: a bibliographical essay', in Brian MacCuarta, ed., *Ulster 1641: aspects of the rising* (Belfast, 1993), pp. 173–86.

continental Europe. Along with the other inhabitants of the various kingdoms and colonies yoked together under the British crown, they shared a common historical identity rooted in the constitutional and ecclesiastical struggles which had taken place under the Stuarts in the previous century and they prided themselves on the rights guaranteed by the British constitution and enshrined in Magna Carta and in the revolution settlement. Although the early patriots generally referred to their community as 'the English interest',[24] the term 'British' was frequently used in the two or three decades after the Boyne, and still occasionally found in the middle of the century. As late as 1745 one County Tyrone curate was still able to write of 'the Spirit of Liberty which Exalts us *Britons* above all other People on Earth'.[25] Ulster presbyterians, whose anomalous position as Scottish settlers in an English colony gave rise to a troubled relationship with both church and state, also found good reasons to subscribe to 'true *British* patriotism'.[26] Yet by the 1770s both groups had jettisoned their earlier aspirations to the name of Briton and were moving towards a more insular definition of an Irish nation which played down denominational divisions.

The sources of this divergence lie in the inferior position – political, economic, and psychological – occupied by the Irish within the British state-system, and symbolised by the constitutional subordination of the Dublin legislature. At this point it is necessary to bear in mind the paradox of the Glorious Revolution when considered in a three-kingdoms context. While the political upheavals of 1688–91, combined with the fiscal and military reorganisation necessitated by continental warfare, had produced a revival of parliamentary institutions in all three kingdoms, the very same factors had accelerated existing centralising tendencies within the British multiple monarchy, producing a dramatic

---

24 [Francis Brewster], *A discourse concerning Ireland and the different interests thereof, in answer to the Barnstaple petitions* (1698), *passim.*

25 William Henry, *Philippic oration*, p. 13. For earlier examples see Walkinton, *Sermon preached Octob. 23. 1692*, p. 12; Ezekial Burridge, *A short view of the present state of Ireland* (n.p., 1708), pp. 20, 31; Synge, *Thankfulness to almighty God*, p. 13; Maule, *Sermon preached . . . the twenty-third day of October, 1733*, p. 3; Dobbs, *Essay on the trade and improvement of Ireland*, I, p. 74; [James Arbuckle et al.], *A collection of letters and essays on several subjects, lately published in the Dublin Journal* (2 vols., 1729), I, p. 187; [Patrick Delany], *The tribune* (1729), p. 38. Molyneux had described the 'Protestants of Ireland' as British in the MS of his *Case of Ireland* but deleted the adjective from the printer's copy: see P. H. Kelly, 'The printer's copy of the MS of William Molyneux, "The case of Ireland's being bound by acts of parliament in England, stated" 1698', *Long Room*, 18–19 (Spring/Autumn 1979), 13.

26 John Abernethy, *The nature and consequences of the sacramental test considered* (Dublin, 1731), p. 4. See also John MacKenzie, *A narrative of the siege of Londonderry* (1690), p. [iii]; [John McBride], *A vindication of marriage, as solemnized by presbyterians in the north of Ireland* ([Belfast?], 1702), p. iii; [John Smith?], *A short account of the late treatment of the students of the University of G[lasgo]w* (Dublin, 1722), p. 35.

shift in the balance of power between centre and periphery. One logical consequence was the abolition of the Edinburgh parliament in 1707; another was the assertion of Westminster sovereignty over Ireland in the 1720 declaratory act. Unlike the Scots, however, the Irish were left with the formal structures of an independent kingdom; and just as the Westminster parliament provided a focal point for British consciousness, so the very existence of a parliament in Dublin inevitably stimulated the development of a separate corporate identity within the Irish elite.

II

Anglo-Irish patriotism has its roots in the parliamentary struggles of the 1690s.[27] The economic causes of Anglo-Irish grievance – notably the suppression of the Irish woollen industry – are well known, but equally important was the unduly lenient attitude adopted by the London government towards the defeated catholics after the battle of the Boyne. The conflict between the Dublin parliament and the court over the terms of the treaty of Limerick demonstrated the tensions which could arise when the interests of the local protestant elite clashed with the strategic needs of the 'fiscal-military state', and exposed the dangers of an excessive dependence on English goodwill. In the 1690s, as MPs met in regular sessions for the first time, they were able to use their control of supply as a lever to secure the effective disabling of catholic Ireland which they had sought repeatedly but unsuccessfully under the restoration monarchy. Just as the Dublin legislature emerged as an integral part of the machinery of government, it thus came to acquire special significance as the guarantor of protestant security.

The demand for equal status within the empire rested on the doctrine of the ancient Irish constitution, given its classic statement in William Molyneux's *The case of Ireland's being bound by acts of parliament in England, stated* (1698). The substance of Molyneux's *Case* was taken up with a discussion of historical and legal precedents designed to prove that Ireland was not a dependent colony like the English territories in America, but a self-contained political entity, united to England only by a shared allegiance to the crown.[28] The historical roots of this independence were located in Henry II's annexation of Ireland: its civil and ecclesiastical estates had not been conquered in battle, it was argued, but had made a voluntary declaration of loyalty to the Anglo-Norman

[27] Patrick Kelly, 'Ireland and the Glorious Revolution: from kingdom to colony', in Robert Beddard, ed., *The revolutions of 1688* (Oxford, 1991), pp. 163–90.
[28] William Molyneux, *The case of Ireland's being bound by acts of parliament in England, stated* (Dublin, 1698), p. 148.

monarch. Here was an original contract, which Molyneux compared to the orthodox whig theory of the Glorious Revolution, by which Henry II had extended the common law and granted Ireland its own parliament 'as a separate and distinct Kingdom from *England*'.[29]

Molyneux drew liberally upon the antiquarian researches of earlier constitutional writers such as Bishop Anthony Dopping of Meath (*Modus tenendi parliamenta in Hibernia*, 1692), his own father-in-law Sir William Domville (*Disquisition*, 1660) and the catholic lawyer Patrick Darcy (*Argument*, 1643). The doctrine of an ancient constitution, derived ultimately from the dispossessed 'Old English' – those settlers of medieval origin who had mostly remained faithful to Rome – constituted a bridge between protestant patriotism and older catholic notions of an Irish nation.[30] Molyneux also attempted an appeal to natural rights, acknowledging the influence of his 'Excellent Friend' John Locke, again offering the possibility of a more inclusive patriotism.[31] But this tactic, while it has attracted much attention, was peripheral to his thesis. The essentially colonial basis of the *Case of Ireland* was starkly revealed when Molyneux produced his second line of defence against England's claim to govern Ireland by right of conquest. Supposing Henry II had acquired Ireland by conquest, he considered, it was only 'the *Antient Race* of the *Irish*' that had thereby lost their rights; 'the *English* and *Britains*' who had fought on the winning side 'retain'd all the Freedoms and Immunities of *Free-born* Subjects'.[32] This strain of thought, often overlooked by historians, survived even in heyday of the volunteers.[33]

The Case of Ireland maintained a tyrannical hold over Irish protestant constitutional thought in the eighteenth century. Although the initial reaction was unfavourable – contemporaries regarded the book as counterproductive – 'the famous Mr Molyneux' had become recognised as the standard authority on the Irish constitution by the time of the Wood's halfpence controversy.[34] The book was reprinted four times in the first quarter of the eighteenth century (1706, 1719, 1720, 1725); a single isolated issue appeared in 1749; and four more paved the way for legislative independence (1770, 1773, 1776, 1782). It was this '*manual*

---

[29] Ibid., pp. 29, 37–8.
[30] Aidan Clarke, 'Colonial constitutional attitudes in Ireland, 1640–1660', *Proceedings of the Royal Irish Academy*, 90C: 2 (1990), 357–75.
[31] Molyneux, *Case of Ireland*, pp. 3, 26–7, 113.   [32] Ibid., p. 19.
[33] [Charles Francis Sheridan], *Observations on the doctrine laid down by Sir William Blackstone, respecting the extent of the power of the British parliament, particularly with relation to Ireland* (1779), pp. 46–7; *The alarm; or, the Irish spy* (Dublin, 1779), p. 51.
[34] Patrick Kelly, 'William Molyneux and the spirit of liberty in eighteenth-century Ireland', *Eighteenth-Century Ireland*, 3 (1988), 137; see also Isolde Victory, 'The making of the 1720 declaratory act', in Gerard O'Brien, ed., *Parliament, politics and people: essays on eighteenth-century Irish history* (Dublin, 1989), pp. 9–29.

of Irish liberty' rather than revolutionary theories imported from America, which supplied the ideology of the volunteers in 1782.[35] While a few pamphleteers sought to place the discussion of imperial organisation in a wider theoretical framework, the majority remained mired in the labyrinthine precedents which purported to show that acts of the English parliament had not been binding in Ireland.[36]

It is true that, while the ideological artillery of Irish patriots remained relatively stable, their national self-image was dramatically transformed. Terms such as 'the English interest in Ireland', which had dominated the literature of the 1690s, had been largely displaced by a clear preference for Irish identifications by the middle of the next century.[37] In addition to the passage of generations, this new self-reliance reflected continuing resentment at the economic and legislative restrictions imposed by London and the controversial appointment of Englishmen to lucrative posts in the Irish civil and ecclesiastical administration.[38] During this long transitional period, identity was defined situationally, with protestant writers imagining themselves as Irish, English or even British according to the context – constitutional relations, domestic politics, or the slights and humiliations suffered by those politicians and intellectuals who spent time in England. While it is undeniable that these layered identities were gradually being reordered, however, this process should not be allowed to obscure the basic continuities in the religious and cultural sentiments of protestant Ireland.

As we have already seen, the first generation of patriotic writers invoked the common name of *Englishman*. For several decades they hesitated between Molyneux's ancient constitution and the option of a parliamentary union, which they believed would provide the surest foundations for their civil rights and economic interests.[39] Although they appealed to universal ideals – that government, for example, should

---

[35] *The alarm; or, the Irish spy*, p. 53; Kelly, 'Molyneux and the spirit of liberty', pp. 141–7. See also Jacqueline Hill, 'Ireland without union: Molyneux and his legacy', in Robertson, ed., *Union for empire*, pp. 271–96.

[36] See, for example [R. French], *The constitution of Ireland, and Poyning's [sic] laws explained* (Dublin, 1770); [John Dunn], *Plain reasons for the new-modelling of Poynings' law* (Dublin, 1780).

[37] See David Hayton, 'Anglo-Irish attitudes: changing perceptions of national identity among the protestant ascendancy in Ireland, *ca.* 1690–1750', *Studies in Eighteenth-century Culture*, 17 (1987), 145–57; Gerard McCoy, 'Local political culture in the Hanoverian empire: the case of the Anglo-Irish' (D.Phil. thesis, University of Oxford, 1994).

[38] For the latter see Patrick McNally, '"Irish and English interests": national conflict within the church of Ireland episcopate in the reign of George I', *IHS* 29 (1995), 295–314.

[39] James Kelly, 'The origins of the act of union: an examination of unionist opinion in Britain and Ireland, 1650–1800', *IHS*, 25 (1987), 240–4.

rest upon the consent of the governed – they viewed these totemic liberties as the historical birthrights of Englishmen, translated into an Irish context in the act of colonisation. Samuel Madden, a nephew of William Molyneux who described himself as 'a native of Ireland', insisted that ties of blood, political principles, religious beliefs and dynastic allegiance bound his community to Britain: 'Are we not therefore, in the truest Sense of the Word, *Englishmen*, as well as *English subjects* . . . and have we not spent our Blood as freely, like true *Britons*, when, and wherever those noble Calls invited us, and the Glory and Service of *Great Britain* wanted our assistance?'[40] Unfortunately, however, the English had already acquired an irritating habit of confounding the loyal protestants of Ireland with their popish enemies. David Hayton has shown how traditional stereotypes of the Irish as bellicose and bibulous were expanded to include the protestant gentry in the first half of the eighteenth century.[41] Despite all that they had suffered in the service of England, Irish protestants found themselves treated as foreigners by the mother country; henceforth they would have to 'rest satisfied with the odious Character of an *Irish-man*'.[42] In constitutional terms, Ireland's inferiority was underlined by the rejection of a series of petitions in 1703, 1707 and 1709 for a legislative union, a rebuff which prompted Swift's first Irish pamphlet, *The story of an injured lady*, written in 1707.[43]

Many historians of eighteenth-century Ireland, engaged in the search for the cultural origins of Grattan's parliament, have taken as their theme the growing consciousness among Irish patriots of a distinct group solidarity defined in opposition to England. It has been suggested by several historians that the growth of interest in Irish history stimulated the development of a new national consciousness which underpinned the constitutional revolution of 1782.[44] A number of recent studies have shown how the interests of protestant and catholic historians began to converge on the neutral territory of pre-Norman Ireland.[45] Most prominent on the catholic side were Charles O'Conor and

[40] Madden, *Reflections and resolutions*, pp. 25, 107–8.
[41] David Hayton, 'From barbarian to burlesque: English images of the Irish c. 1660–1750', *Irish Economic and Social History*, 15 (1988), 5–31.
[42] [Brewster], *Discourse concerning Ireland*, p. 44.
[43] For Swift see Oliver W. Ferguson, *Jonathan Swift and Ireland* (Urbana, IL, 1962); Joseph McMinn, *Jonathan Swift: a literary life* (1991).
[44] See, for example, F. G. James, 'Historiography and the Irish constitutional revolution of 1782', *Éire-Ireland*, 18 (1983), 14–16.
[45] Colin Kidd, 'Gaelic antiquity and national identity in enlightenment Ireland and Scotland', *EHR*, 109 (1994), 1197–214; J. R. Hill, 'Popery and protestantism, civil and religious liberty: the disputed lessons of Irish history 1690–1812', *P&P*, 118 (1988), 96–129.

Sylvester O'Halloran, whose writings were clearly related to the catholic campaign against the penal laws, while protestant enthusiasm for Celtic civilisation was stimulated by Walter Harris, Charles Vallancey, Henry Brooke, Charlotte Brooke and Joseph Walker. It is important to recognise, however, that while Irish protestants came to reject the *name* of Englishman they did not reject the wider ethnic framework explored by Linda Colley and others. The ambiguities, complexities and evasions characteristic of Anglo-Irish culture can be seen if we turn briefly to examine the antiquarianism which flourished in Georgian Ireland.

It is undeniable that the defence of Gaelic antiquity carried political overtones: its origins, after all, lay in the response of Gaelic scholars to the charges of racial inferiority propagated by colonial apologists such as Spenser and Davies. But the Gaelic enthusiasms demonstrated by the Anglo-Irish elite can be viewed better as another expression of the protestant mission than as a more ecumenical brand of cultural nationalism. Early Irish Christianity – portrayed as scripturally based and independent of Roman authority – had held attractions for protestants since Archbishop James Ussher's pioneering *Discourse of the religion anciently professed by the Irish and British* (1622), which sought to establish a line of descent from St Patrick to establishment anglicanism. In Anglo-Irish historiography, dominated by clergymen of the established church, the recovery of pre-Norman culture offered a means of appropriating Celtic Christianity and learning, and of divesting Irish culture of its popish associations.[46] Similarly, scholarly interest in the native tongue was not revivalist but philological, and continued to be linked with conversionist fantasies. Irish language enthusiasts, such as the prominent antiquarian Charles Vallancey distanced the ancient language from 'the jargon yet spoke by the unlettered vulgar'; like the Rev. John Richardson he appealed to the examples of Bishop Bedell and Robert Boyle, asking whether his unfortunate countrymen would forever be deprived of the privilege of 'reading the scriptures, and judging for themselves'.[47]

Equally interesting, although less noticed by historians, was the reconstruction of the ancient system of government in the image of the revolution settlement. The starting point here was Geoffrey Keating's *Foras feasa ar Éirinn* (c. 1634), an account of the Milesian high civilisation influenced both by renaissance ideas of centralised monarchy and

[46] Clare O'Halloran, '"The island of saints and scholars": views of the early church and sectarian politics in late-eighteenth century Ireland', *Eighteenth-Century Ireland*, 5 (1990), 7–20.
[47] Quoted in Clare O'Halloran, 'Golden ages and barbarous nations: antiquarian debate on the Celtic past in Ireland and Scotland in the eighteenth century' (Ph.D. thesis, University of Cambridge, 1991), pp. 102–3.

by the counter-reformation ideology imported from the continental universities.[48] Translated into English as *The general history of Ireland* (1723), with 'catholic' obligingly rendered as 'Christian' throughout the text, Keating's analysis of the Irish high kingship was ransacked by patriotic writers for evidence of parliamentary government and civic virtue. Thirty years later another landmark was reached with the publication of Charles O'Conor's *Dissertations on the antient history of Ireland*, which presented a whiggish characterisation of the Gaelic polity as 'a mixed Monarchy . . . in the general, too much under the Controul of aristocratical Principles'.[49] Amateur historians like Henry Brooke subsequently employed the vocabulary of whig constitutionalism to analyse the Gaelic world in the image of post-1688 Britain.[50] Anti-quarian inquiries were thus shaped by contemporary political allegiances, not the other way round; the exotic shores of Gaelic civilisation, vacated by their aboriginal inhabitants, were now safe for protestants to colonise. In looking to pre-plantation Ireland protestant scholars were not attempting to establish a common bond with their catholic countrymen; on the contrary, they were able to appropriate the name of Irishman only because catholic Ireland had been so completely eliminated from political calculations.

III

In 1719 Archbishop William King posed the underlying question in eighteenth-century Irish political thought when he asked, 'How [will] the Protestants . . . secure themselves, or England secure Ireland when all the commonalty are Papist?'[51] As King's language suggests, this was first and foremost a military problem, and such pragmatic considerations had outweighed purely religious motives in the framing of penal legislation during the previous twenty-five years. But this is not to say that Irish protestants had abandoned their duty to instruct the natives in the true faith. Deliverance from the Jacobite army had placed them under a clear obligation: in return for God's mercies they must not only promote piety among their own people but bring their enemies into the light and liberty of the gospel through a combination of coercion and

---

[48] Brendan Bradshaw, 'Geoffrey Keating: apologist of Irish Ireland', in Brendan Bradshaw, Andrew Hadfield and Willy Maley, eds., *Representing Ireland: literature and the origins of conflict, 1534–1660* (Cambridge, 1993), pp. 166–90.

[49] Charles O'Conor, *Dissertations on the antient history of Ireland* (Dublin, 1766), p. 48.

[50] Hill, 'Popery and protestantism', p. 106.

[51] Thomas Bartlett, *The fall and rise of the Irish nation: the catholic question 1690–1830* (Dublin, 1992), p. 29.

conciliation.[52] A wide and confused range of 'solutions' to the catholic problem was discussed, from the reinforcement of penal legislation to state supervision of the clergy. Most shared one common assumption, however: that the key to the popish system lay in the absolute dominion of the priesthood over the consciences of their people. If that one link could be removed from the 'fatal chain' which led to Rome, the whole edifice of idolatry and superstition would surely collapse.[53]

The enactment of penal legislation as late as 1756, and the savage anti-catholic sermons of the succeeding decade, testify to the longevity of coercive thinking; each modification of the popery laws from 1778 onwards only revitalised the determination of conservatives to defend their remaining privileges. Increasingly, however, the trend was towards regulation rather than restriction. As early as 1723, Lord Molesworth recommended that the government should attach the catholic clergy to the state by granting them state salaries, a proposal echoed by Samuel Madden in the next decade.[54] The patriotic school of political economists, of which Madden was a prominent member, attributed Irish backwardness to sociological and environmental factors as well as religion: consequently it was possible to believe that the mere fact of cohabitation and communication with protestants had introduced 'a sort of Reformation'.[55] The conviction of the economic patriots that the native inhabitants were 'improvable' was consonant with the more latitudinarian tone of anglican preaching, evident even in a few of the 23 October sermons, preached in commemoration of the 1641 massacres. In many ways, however, the impact of enlightenment thought was to reinforce rather than mitigate hostility to Irish catholicism. The liberal strand in protestant thought rested on the optimistic assumption that a relaxation of the penal policy would expose Roman catholics to the irrefragible logic of rational Christianity.

The best-known exponent of this approach was Edward Synge, whose controversial *The case of toleration consider'd with respect both to religion and civil government* (1725) discussed church–state relations on a theoretical level rarely attained by his colleagues. His criticism of coercion, though it may have owed something to the Bangorian controversy in England, clearly reflected his hopes for the emergence of a

---

[52] Foy, *Sermon preached in Christ's-Church, Dublin*, p. 25; Maule, *Sermon preached . . . the twenty-third day of October, 1733*, pp. 23–4; John Richardson, *A proposal for the conversion of the popish natives of Ireland, to the establish'd religion* (Dublin, 1711), pp. 2–3.

[53] *The ax laid to the root*, p. 4.

[54] [Molesworth], *Some considerations for the promoting of agriculture, and employing the poor* (Dublin, 1723), p. 30; Madden, *Reflections and resolutions*, p. 92.

[55] Ibid., p. 100.

gallican wing in Irish catholicism.[56] Less familiar is another 23 October sermon published ten years later by the respected Dublin dissenter John Abernethy, entitled *Persecution contrary to Christianity*. Like Synge, Abernethy was indebted to Hoadly and Locke, and condemned the attempts of the civil magistrate to enforce religious uniformity. 'Such a notion', he warned, 'has too much of the leaven of Popery itself.'[57] Indeed Abernethy's muted critique of the penal code, like his earlier assaults on the sacramental test, rested on a redefinition of popery to include any state intervention in matters of conscience. Roman catholicism was dangerous not because of its errors, but because it denied the right of private judgement which was seen as pivotal to Christianity. The final, much later, example to be considered here was the first to directly question the protestant interpretation of 1641. In 1770 the anglican clergyman Thomas Leland laid the ultimate blame for the rebellion at the door of 'papal superstition', but broke with the anti-catholic diatribes customary on that occasion by acknowledging the hardships suffered by the catholics before 1641 and examining the part played by 'the errours and iniquities of our forefathers' in igniting the rebellion. By implication, Leland's sermon could be taken as criticism of the penal code. As Ireland's foremost 'philosophical historian', Leland self-consciously belonged to an enlightened age which had banished sectarian passions, but his desire to be impartial did not mean that he looked any more favourably on catholic doctrine. He urged his audience to hope that popery 'hath been softened by a kind of tacit reformation'.[58]

In the first half of the eighteenth century pleas for the legal toleration of Roman catholicism went unheeded. Synge's sermon met with hostility from his fellow clergy, and in later works he himself returned to a hardline stance. But his central proposition – the extension of a measure of state protection in return for a repudiation of the temporal dominion allegedly claimed by Rome – would resurface in later decades. The outbreak of the Seven Years War prompted further attempts to draw up a statement disavowing the doctrines that the papacy had the authority to depose protestant princes and that it was lawful for catholics to break faith with heretics, but these foundered upon the opposition of the holy see and the more conservative bishops in Ireland. Loyal addresses,

---

[56] Edward Synge, *The case of toleration consider'd with respect both to religion and civil government, in a sermon preach'd in St Andrew's, Dublin, before the honourable House of Commons; on Saturday, October 23. 1725* (1726).

[57] John Abernethy, *Persecution contrary to Christianity: a sermon preached in Wood-Street, Dublin, on the 23d of October 1735* (Dublin, 1735), p. 26.

[58] Joseph Leichty, 'Testing the depth of catholic/protestant conflict: the case of Thomas Leland's "History of Ireland", 1773', *Archivium Hibernicum*, 42 (1987), 17.

published in 1727, 1759 and 1760 cut little ice as long as Rome recognised 'James III' as king of Great Britain and Ireland. Following papal recognition of the house of Hanover in 1766, however, renewed efforts were made to devise a compromise formula acceptable to both the state and the church authorities. Frederick Augustus Hervey, bishop of Derry (1768–1803), whose study of church–state relations on the continent confirmed his opinion that catholicism was 'a silly but harmless religion', drafted a test of loyalty designed to disable the Irish church by driving a wedge between the 'gallican' and ultramontane tendencies.[59]

By 1774, when Hervey's test oath received parliamentary approval, the case for toleration had been given a vital boost by the appearance of a pro-Hanoverian revisionism among a section of the catholic intelligentsia. Before the 'shipwreck' of 1690–1, catholic ideology had combined loyalty to the divine hereditary monarchy of the Stuarts with a counter-reformation defence of papal authority in political as well as ecclesiastical matters and a profound hatred of reformed religion, especially its Calvinist manifestations.[60] After the treaty of Limerick, however, the publication of such sentiments was not tolerated. In the half century which elapsed between Hugh Reily's *Case of Ireland briefly stated* (1695) and the foundation of the Catholic Committee in 1756, Irish catholics had good reason to avoid public discussion of their principles: what little evidence we have suggests that their political thought continued to operate within the old parameters set by Jacobite allegiance and catholic confessionalism.[61] From the 1750s, however, a public relations exercise was launched as a new generation tried to break the equation of popery and disloyalty which provided the intellectual justification for the penal code.

The mastermind behind this campaign, which set the tone for catholic propaganda right up to the 1790s, was Charles O'Conor, whose linguistic and antiquarian expertise had secured him a foothold in fashionable ascendancy circles. O'Conor challenged the popular stereotypes of

[59] Eamon O'Flaherty, 'Ecclesiastical politics and the dismantling of the penal laws in Ireland, 1774–82', *IHS*, 26 (1988), 35.

[60] Breandán O Buachalla, 'James our true king: the ideology of Irish royalism in the seventeenth century', in Boyce *et al.*, *Political thought in Ireland*, pp. 7–35; Patrick Kelly, '"A light to the blind": the voice of the dispossessed elite in the generation after the defeat at Limerick', *IHS*, 24 (1985), 431–62.

[61] S. J. Connolly, *Religion, law and power: the making of protestant Ireland 1660–1760* (Oxford, 1992), pp. 157–9, 233–49; C. D. A. Leighton, *Catholicism in protestant kingdom: a study of the Irish ancien régime* (Basingstoke, 1994), pp. 56–7; Vincent Geoghegan, 'A Jacobite history: the Abbé MacGeoghegan's *History of Ireland*', *Eighteenth-Century Ireland*, 6 (1981), 36–55; Breandán O Buachalla, 'Irish Jacobitism and Irish nationalism: the literary evidence', in Michael O'Dea and Kevin Whelan, eds., *Nations and nationalisms: France, Britain, Ireland and the eighteenth-century context* (Oxford, 1995), pp. 103–16.

Irish catholicism on all fronts – dynastic allegiance, economic capacity and political ideology. Appealing to the protestant improvers, he argued that the penal laws drained the country of specie and acted as a disincentive to three-quarters of its inhabitants. The removal of restrictions on catholic landownership would not only produce economic benefits, he maintained, but would give catholics a common interest in their country which no spiritual or temporal power could override.[62] To this end he advocated a test of political orthodoxy which would allow catholics to separate temporal and spiritual allegiance, arguing that 'Disaffection to the *Religion* of the State, is one Thing; and Disaffection to the *Constitution* of our Country, quite another.'[63] At a deeper level he sought to show that catholicism was not incompatible with a spirit of liberty, pointing to the pre-reformation foundations of the British constitution.[64] Missionaries from Rome had not interfered with free government in Ireland; on the contrary, 'during the whole Time of the *Hy-Niall* Oeconomy', the island had become 'the Temple of Liberty, and the Emporium of Learning to all *Europe*'.[65] Assuming the role of an opposition patriot, O'Conor talked of popular sovereignty and the right of resistance, and condemned 'our domestic Enemies, *Faction, Luxury,* and *clerical Prejudices*'.[66] Most interesting of all, he portrayed the extension of religious toleration to Roman catholics as the logical completion of the work of reformation. No sooner had the reformed churches been established, he explained, than popery had resurfaced as state persecution.[67] The imposition of pains and penalties on the grounds of religious faith was '*Popish Ecclesiastical Policy, in Disguise*'.[68]

Caught between the hostility of the establishment and the desire of the church hierarchy to maintain its monopoly over catholic public utterances, O'Conor found pamphleteering a risky and complicated business, as the many references in his letters to the need for 'the greatest caution and secrecy' attest. The statements of the Catholic Committee were often penned by sympathetic protestants like Edmund Burke, hired hacks like Henry Brooke, or by O'Conor himself writing 'in the character of a moderate Protestant'.[69] His tracts were thus necessarily tailored towards a protestant audience, and there are doubts

---

[62] [Charles O'Conor], *Seasonable thoughts relating to our civil and ecclesiastical constitution* (Dublin, 1753), esp. pp. 32–3 .

[63] Ibid., p. 25.

[64] [Charles O'Conor], *The case of the Roman-catholicks of Ireland. Wherein the principles and conduct of that party are fully explained and vindicated* (Dublin, 1755), p. 19.

[65] [O'Conor], *Seasonable thoughts*, p. 27.

[66] Ibid., pp. 11, 39.   [67] Ibid., pp. 14–16.   [68] Ibid., p. 42.

[69] Walter D. Love, 'Charles O'Conor of Belanagare and Thomas Leland's "philosophical" history of Ireland', *IHS*, 13 (1962), 7, 10.

as to how far the arguments represented his own private opinions, let alone those of his community. Nevertheless, it was through this propaganda exercise that a new generation of catholic leaders was schooled in the language of whig constitutionalism. While this process remains largely unexplored, there can be no doubt that it was the necessary precondition to their participation in the United Irish coalition of the 1790s.

IV

The challenge of transcending the confessional basis of Irish patriotism was taken up by Henry Grattan in 1781 when he dared to ask 'whether we shall be a Protestant settlement or an Irish nation?'[70] In the brief moment of euphoria which followed the attainment of legislative independence, much was heard of the need to 'incorporate' the catholics and thus blend Ireland's three great denominations into one people.[71] On the radical fringe of the patriot group, the first hesitant attempts were made to construct a more inclusive definition of Irishness which would bridge the gaps between protestant, catholic and dissenter. Before the French revolution, however, it was taken for granted that, whatever concessions were on offer, the machinery of government itself would remain a protestant monopoly. Paternalistic overtures towards the catholics were made on the assumption that the majority of the population would remain in a state of subordination. For most protestants toleration signified freedom of worship, but stopped short of access to political power; the very term, as Bishop Woodward later pointed out, implied 'superiority and a *right* of control'.[72]

Initially, the movement for legislative independence resembled the traditional, defensive variety of colonial self-assertion. In the 1770s British policy in Ireland was recast once more in an imperial context, as the outbreak of war with the American colonists, and then their French and Spanish allies, forced the state to mobilise its resources on an unprecedented scale. The first significant breach in the penal code, the 1778 catholic relief act, was a direct product of the transatlantic crisis, intended to stimulate catholic recruitment into the British armed forces. As in the 1690s, it seemed that local protestant interests were being sacrificed on the altar of imperial security, emphasising once more the

---

[70] Quoted in Maureen Wall, *Catholic Ireland in the eighteenth century*, ed. Gerard O'Brien (Dublin, 1989), p. 139. The context was the reading of Gardiner's Relief Bill of 1781.

[71] See, for example, Barry Yelverton, quoted in R. B. McDowell, *Irish public opinion 1750–1800* (1944), p. 70.

[72] Richard Woodward, *The present state of the church of Ireland: containing a description of its precarious situation* (Dublin, 1787), p. 18.

dangers of constitutional dependence. The limited concessions proposed in May 1778 were compared to the Quebec act of four years earlier; fresh murmurs of Romish conspiracies were heard from the patriot opposition, and were particularly well received among the Ulster presbyterians, whose demand for the abolition of the sacramental test had been (temporarily) rejected at the same time.[73] Such alarms, of course, were but a faint echo of the anti-catholic rage which engulfed Glasgow and Edinburgh in 1779 and London the following year; rumours that presbyterian leaders were planning a protestant association on the Gordon model came to nothing.[74]

If the imperial crisis re-energised the assailants of Rome, it also prompted a reconsideration of the catholic question in the longer term. Confronted with the possibility of a new rapprochement between the catholic leadership and the government, patriot leaders were reluctantly forced to enter the 'race for the Catholic'.[75] In his celebrated *Letters of Owen Roe O'Nial*, the presbyterian Joseph Pollock had appealed to the patriots to 'lay aside all rancour of prejudice on account of distinctions either political or religious'. Pointing to the examples of Switzerland and the United Provinces, where protestants and catholics shared a common citizenship, he looked forward to a gradual enlargement of religious toleration at home.[76] Vague professions of 'liberality' became a routine feature of patriot propaganda, demonstrated most spectacularly by the manifesto issued at Dungannon in 1782, which included a crucial resolution supporting the relaxation of the penal code. At the same time, on a local level, the recruitment of catholics into volunteer regiments was openly encouraged. The image of a population united behind the protestant elite was carefully fostered; it was in this context, indeed, that the 'common name of Irishman' made its first appearance.[77]

This new latitude must also be set in the context of the changing confessional landscape on mainland Europe. After 1750 several developments, including the refusal of the pope to recognise Charles Edward Stuart in 1766, encouraged those who felt that the penal code was

---

[73] Robert E. Burns, 'The catholic relief act in Ireland, 1778', *Church History*, 32 (1963), 181–206.

[74] O'Flaherty, 'Ecclesiastical politics', 42.

[75] The term is John Foster's: Bartlett, *Fall and rise of the Irish nation*, p. 121.

[76] Owen Roe O'Nial, 'Letters to the men of Ireland', reprinted in J. Lawless, ed., *The Belfast politics enlarged* (Belfast, 1818), pp. 131, 134.

[77] *Moderation unmasked; or, the conduct of the majority impartially considered. By the author of a scheme for a constitutional association* (Dublin, 1780), p. 68. The anonymous author asked, 'Why should we recollect that we have different Appellations – *Protestants, Roman Catholics, Dissenters?* – Let them be forgotten, and they are forgotten – We remember only that we have the common one of *Irishmen*.'

unjust, anachronistic and counter-productive. The decline of papal authority in Europe, signalled by the expulsion of the Jesuits from Portugal (1759), France (1764) and Spain (1767), leading to their dissolution in 1773, was apparently confirmed in Ireland by the political writings of the Capuchin monk, Arthur O'Leary, who played a vital public role as the acceptable face of Irish catholicism. O'Leary had attracted notice for his pamphlets in favour of the oath of allegiance of 1774 and his conspicuous loyalty during the French invasion scare of 1779. Having consistently disowned both the House of Stuart and the deposing doctrine, he went on to compose *An essay on toleration* (1781) which paid homage to Locke and Voltaire. His novel teachings on church–state relations won the admiration of dissenting radicals, while his popularity in Dublin protestant circles was demonstrated by his election to the Monks of St Patrick and his appointment as chaplain to the Irish Brigade of volunteers.[78] O'Leary's public pronouncements, like the earlier revisionism of O'Conor, enabled protestants to enjoy the feeling that ancestral animosities were fading, without actually having to consider the price to be paid in concrete concessions.

Unity, however, did not mean equality, as the radical fringe of the reform movement soon discovered to its cost. In the run-up to the Grand National Convention of Volunteers of November 1783, Peter Burrowes, a delegate from the Irish Brigade, had urged the admission of catholics to the franchise, arguing that persecution had done more harm than 'all the doctrine of the Jesuits'.[79] Observing that the Roman catholic religion was in retreat throughout Europe, Burrowes reasoned that popery in Ireland would diminish as catholics acquired more property, 'unless we prop up their superstition with their resentment, and keep their prejudices alive by maintaining our own'.[80] In the north, catholic grievances were articulated by William Todd Jones, the radical MP for Lisburn, who pointed to seventeenth-century examples of catholic 'patriotism' including even the Jacobite parliament of 1689 to refute the assumption that 'their faith is not favourable to a free state'.[81] But perhaps the most utopian reformer was Francis Dobbs, who drew up a comprehensive plan of constitutional, legal, military and ecclesiastical reform for the Dungannon reform convention of 1783. His draft

---

[78] M. S. Buckley, *The life and writings of the Rev. Arthur O'Leary* (Dublin, 1868), p. 197.

[79] *History of the proceedings and debates of the volunteer delegates of Ireland on the subject of a parliamentary reform* (Dublin, 1784), pp. 19–21.

[80] [Peter Burrowes], *Plain arguments in defence of the people's absolute dominion over the constitution* (Dublin, 1784), p. 53.

[81] William Todd Jones, *A letter to the electors of the borough of Lisburn* (Dublin, 1784), pp. 41–7; quotation from p. 29.

constitution included a simplified liturgy based on the ten commandments, the lord's prayer and the sermon on the mount, and public provision for congregations of every denomination; if implemented, he predicted that 'there would soon be but one religion in this country'.[82] Such optimism, as he made clear elsewhere, was sustained by the experience of volunteering, which had promoted social and cultural exchange between the different denominations. Once again, however, the rhetoric of convergence and union barely concealed the desire for assimilation: 'the Papist, with an orange cockade, fires in honour of King William's birth day. He goes to a Protestant church, and hears a charity sermon. He dines with his Protestant associates, and perhaps a Popish chaplain says grace.'[83] The protestant, it was assumed, would be the element that absorbed.

As the campaign for reform lurched onward, the debate on catholic enfranchisement entered a more focused, theoretical phase. When the Ulster Committee of Correspondence began to consider a reform programme in 1783, Henry Joy, editor of the reformist *Belfast News-Letter*, consulted a number of politicians and political writers on the question of whether their Roman catholic countrymen were capable of exercising the rights of citizenship. While the Irish volunteer leaders, Charlemont and Flood, warned against any transfer of political power, the English authorities consulted were more favourable. Richard Price, the 'rational dissenter', replied that it was unjust to deprive any man of his rights on account of his religion, although he subsequently admitted that peculiarities of the Irish situation justified the restriction of catholic rights.[84] John Jebb, the unitarian convert who had resigned his Cambridge fellowship following the failure of the Feather's Tavern petition, was confident that the extension of the suffrage to catholics would stimulate industry and commerce as well as setting an example to catholic countries with protestant minorities.[85] Predicting that a reformed parliament would only be obtained with the co-operation of all persuasions, he proposed that the vote should be given to propertied catholics for a probationary period. He was in no doubt as to the outcome: 'the Roman Catholic religion, or at least the worst part of it,

---

[82] Francis Dobbs, *The true principles of government, applied to the Irish constitution* (Dublin, 1783), pp. 50, 58, 63.

[83] Francis Dobbs, *Thoughts on the conduct and continuation of the volunteers of Ireland* (Dublin, 1783), p. 20.

[84] Price to William Sharman, 7 Aug. 1783, in D. O. Thomas, ed., *The correspondence of Richard Price* (2 vols. to date, Cardiff, 1983–), II, pp. 188–91; Price to Henry Joy, 23 Sept. 1783, Linenhall Library Belfast, Joy MSS, 11/5.

[85] Jebb to Joy, n.d. [1783], Linenhall Library Belfast, Joy MSS, 11/8.

would gradually decay. Persecution being removed, light, and learning, and industry would effect the rest.'[86]

Wolfe Tone's famous 'great discovery' – that the foundation of English power was the 'disunion of Irishmen' – was obviously not new.[87] Why then did the abolition of the penal laws, widely canvassed in the 1780s and rejected by the vast majority of Volunteers, suddenly become a political option in the next decade? Part of the answer no doubt lies in the appearance of a more aggressive spirit of political, economic and perhaps even cultural competition with the English. A gulf of fifty years, seldom explored by historians, separates Swift's concern with Ireland's 'Imperial Crown' from the vindication of Ireland's *independent national rights* by the generation of 1782.[88] The language of nationhood was becoming charged with modern connotations of popular sovereignty, citizenship and statehood. By the 1780s we also find the first explicit intrusions of Gaelicism into political discourse. Todd Jones dismissed the shades of Hampden, Harrington and Falkland in favour of the Gaelic and Old English rebels Tyrone and Desmond; William Drennan informed the volunteers that they were 'all *native Irish*, under the controul of an *English pale*', and encouraged them to forget all about Alfred, Hampden and Sydney and the heritage of the freeborn English-man.[89] Although the nation was still viewed primarily as a community of laws and political institutions, patriots also made hazy references to the cultural and linguistic roots of Ireland's separateness. It was during this same period, after all, that the expansion of new modes of communication – the press, the novel, the satirical print – combined with the rise of primitivism and the cult of sincerity to shape a greater awareness of a distinctive cultural personality in England.[90]

These vague intimations of Gaelocentric nationalism, which historians find so arresting, seem to have caused little stir among contemporaries.[91] The transition from commonwealthsman to United Irishman owed less to any national awakening than to external political factors,

[86] Jebb to Hamilton Rowan, 5 Mar. 1785, 29 Sept. 1785, William Hamilton Drummond, ed., *The autobiography of Archibald Hamilton Rowan, esq.* (Dublin, 1840), pp. 127–32.

[87] The quotation is from Marianne Elliott, *Wolfe Tone: prophet of Irish independence* (New Haven, 1989), p. 105.

[88] [Frederick Jebb], *The letters of Guatamozin on the affairs of Ireland* (Dublin, 1779), p. 5.

[89] Jones, *Letter to the electors*, p. 53; [William Drennan], *Letters of Orellana, an Irish helot* (Dublin, 1785), pp. 7–8.

[90] Gerald Newman, *The rise of English nationalism: a cultural history 1740–1830* (1987).

[91] Mary Helen Thuente, *The harp re-strung: the United Irishmen and the rise of Irish literary nationalism* (New York, 1994), rightly draws attention to the literary and cultural dimensions of late eighteenth-century radicalism. It was only after the union, however, that a full-blown cultural nationalism emerged: see Joep Leerssen, *Remembrance and imagination: patterns in the historical and literary representation of Ireland in the nineteenth century* (Cork, 1996).

beginning with the dislocation of the imperial system. The American secession, interpreted as a civil war between members of a single transatlantic community of British protestants, had ended in the establishment of a republican form of government, derived from but apparently superior to the British constitution. Despite occasional literary gestures towards Gaelic Ireland, patriot discourse remained resolutely Anglo-Saxon in content; during the American war, however, the volume and hostile tone of opposition propaganda was unprecedented. England, wrote one presbyterian clergyman, was 'a country where . . . men speak of liberty without understanding it . . . whose power had been baneful to every people who had the misfortune to be connected with them'.[92] The same war had also called forth volunteer units on massive scale. While this citizens' militia never saw action, the military spectacle and civic ritual of these years, and the rhetorical and symbolic expressions of volunteering found in poems, slogans, banners and belt-buckles, all presented new and exciting ways of imagining an Irish national community.[93]

Another factor was the instability caused by the settlement of 1782, which had disrupted the traditional methods of British control in Ireland; legislative independence raised too many difficult questions, especially in the field of foreign policy. As the demand for a more representative House of Commons threatened to undermine parliamentary management, British ministers came to recognise that the only sure means of preserving the Anglo-Irish connection was by the creation of a single, unified kingdom.[94] At exactly the same moment a number of radicals, who quickly grasped that the 'constitution' of 1782 was largely symbolic, declared their support, in private at least, for complete separation. The hardening of a new conception of the national interest was already evident before the French revolution and the Burke–Paine debate polarised Irish politics. During the Nootka Sound war scare the administration had suppressed Wolfe Tone's *Spanish war!* (1790), which dared to ask why Ireland should continue to fight Great Britain's battles. Although Tone repeated the classic view of the Anglo-Irish connection as a dual monarchy, his demand for an independent foreign policy, a navy and national flag, pointed to outright separatism.[95]

---

[92] William Campbell, 'Sketches of the history of presbyterians in Ireland', unpublished MS dated 1803, Presbyterian Historical Society of Ireland, p. 235.

[93] I. R. McBride, *Scripture politics: Ulster presbyterians and Irish radicalism in the late eighteenth century* (Oxford, 1998), ch. 5.

[94] Kelly, 'Origins of the act of union', pp. 253–8.

[95] [T. W. Tone], *Spanish war! An enquiry how far Ireland is bound, of right, to embark in the impending contest on the side of Great Britain* (Dublin, 1790), pp. 8, 22, 30–3, 42. For Tone see Elliott, *Wolfe Tone*; Thomas Bartlett, 'The burden of the present: Theobald

The crucial precondition for the United Irish project, however, was the dissolution of anti-catholicism as a unifying force following the collapse of the Bourbon monarchy. France, as one presbyterian minister remarked, was that 'mighty nation in which above any other was shed the Blood of Saints and Martyrs, that nation defiled by the . . . massacre of St Bartholomew worse than even that of Ireland and by the Dragooning at the revocation of the Edict of Nantes'.[96] Reformed theologians everywhere had long viewed the catholic kingdom as an instrument of antichrist; in the protestant prophetic tradition the collapse of the Bourbon monarchy was frequently linked with the fall of the papacy. The French revolution, which saw the nationalisation of the French church and the appropriation of its lands by the National Assembly, could be read as an assault on Roman catholicism and on all religious establishments. So it was interpreted by Richard Price, whose famous sermon to the Revolution Society on 4 November 1789 envisaged 'the dominion of priests giving way to the dominion of reason and conscience', and so it appeared to Edmund Burke, who could find no other analogy for Jacobinism than the *theoretick dogma* of the reformation.[97]

Like their brethren in Britain and America, Irish protestants welcomed the French revolution as the harbinger of the millennium, and drew their own, peculiarly Irish, conclusions. 'A catholic country' as Thomas Emmet later noted, had 'contradicted the frequently repeated dogma, that Catholics are unfit for liberty; and the waning glory of the British constitution seemed to fade before the regenerated government of France'.[98] On St Patrick's Day 1792 the Catholic Committee issued the clearest repudiation to date of the temporal jurisdiction and the deposing power of the pope, the principle that no faith be kept with heretics and the doctrine of papal infallibility.[99] The Dublin Society of United Irishmen responded triumphantly with an address explaining that Irish catholics had become 'Political Protestants' since they

Wolfe Tone, republican and separatist', in David Dickson, Dáire Keogh and Kevin Whelan, eds., *The United Irishmen: republicanism, radicalism and rebellion* (Dublin, 1993), pp. 1–15.

[96] Samuel Barber, MS sermon on Revelations 18:20 [June 1791], Presbyterian Historical Society of Ireland, p. 19.

[97] Richard Price, *A discourse on the love of our country* (1789), p. 50; Conor Cruise O'Brien, *The great melody: a thematic biography and commented anthology of Edmund Burke* (1992), p. 452.

[98] T. A. Emmet, 'Part of an essay towards the history of Ireland', in W. J. MacNeven, *Pieces of Irish History* (New York, 1807), p. 12.

[99] *Declaration of the General Committee of the Catholics* (Dublin, 1792).

protested against the errors of the state and endeavoured to establish the reformation of the constitution.[100]

IV

Anglo-Irish attitudes in the eighteenth century were often recognisably colonial in character, inviting transatlantic parallels with other settler communities.[101] But protestant Ireland also belonged, culturally as well as constitutionally, to the Hanoverian multiple monarchy. For students of the 'new British history', the case of Ireland illustrates the limitations of protestantism as an integrative force within the three kingdoms during the great age of Anglo-French hostilities. Protestantism, it is clear, could act as a vehicle for separatist impulses as well as a unifying agent. In their attempts to explain the coalescence and dissolution of national communities within these islands, historians are ultimately driven back to the political and social contexts which determined relations between local elites and the metropolitan power. Allegiance, as John Brewer has written, 'depended not just on the ideological construction of a cultural identity but upon the political gravy-train and upon the distribution of economic spoils'.[102]

For Irish historians, on the other hand, the recent emphasis on the protestant basis of British identities confirms 'the transient and conditional nature of Anglo-Irish nationalism' detected by Thomas Bartlett and others.[103] Irish protestant patriotism was defined in religious and constitutional, rather than ethnic, terms: its spokesmen were not rejecting their British heritage, but asserting their own equal claim to it. After 1789, however, the spectacular implosion of French despotism left radicals free to direct their fire against what William Drennan called 'the *papistical* spirit of the Protestant Ascendancy'.[104] The conversion from commonwealthsmen to United Irishmen was made possible by the belief that Roman catholics were throwing off the chains of priestcraft and superstition to adopt political protestantism, a belief which could not survive the reassertion of sectarian identities that culminated in

---

[100] 'Address to the nation', 14 Sept. 1792, in *Society of the United Irishmen of Dublin [Proceedings]* (Dublin, 1794), p. 22.

[101] See, for example, Nicholas Canny, 'Identity formation in Ireland: the emergence of the Anglo-Irish', in N. P. Canny and A. R. Pagden, eds., *Colonial identity in the Atlantic World* (Princeton, 1987), pp. 159–212.

[102] John Brewer, 'The eighteenth-century British state: contexts and issues', in Lawrence Stone, ed., *An imperial state at war: Britain from 1689 to 1815* (1994), p. 68.

[103] Thomas Bartlett, '"A people made rather for copies than originals": the Anglo-Irish, 1760–1800', *International History Review*, 12 (1990), 18.

[104] William Drennan, *A letter to the right honourable Charles James Fox* (Dublin, 1806), p. 27.

1798. The common name of Irishman, then, did not replace traditional protestant identities, but was awkwardly superimposed on top of them. Once this relationship is properly understood, it becomes easier to explain the limitations of the United Irish project, and to understand the willingness of many protestant radicals, following the disastrous rebellion of 1798, to see Irishmen 'melted' into Britons.[105]

[105] [William Drennan], 'Monthly retrospect', *Belfast Monthly Magazine*, 1 (1808), 385.

Britain, Ireland and the world

11 The island race: Captain Cook, protestant evangelicalism and the construction of English national identity, 1760–1800

Kathleen Wilson

> My object [is] nature in its greatest extent; the Earth, the Sea, the Air, the Organic and Animated Creation, and more particularly that class of Beings to which we ourselves belong.
> J. R. Forster, *Observations made during a voyage round the world* (1778)

> The philosophical traveller, sailing to the ends of the earth, is in fact travelling in time; he is exploring the past; every step he makes is the passage of an age. Those unknown islands that he reaches are for him the passage of human society.
> J.-M. Degerando, *The observation of savage peoples* (1800)

> A new world hath lately opened to our view . . . the innumerable islands, which spot the bosom of the Pacific Ocean . . . which seem to realise the fabled Gardens of the Hesperides . . . But amidst these enchanting scenes, savage nature still feasts on the flesh of its prisoners – appeases its Gods with human sacrifices – whole societies of men and women live promiscuously, and murder every infant born among them.   Thomas Haweis, sermon to the London Missionary Society, 1795.[1]

'The island race': the phrase is used as the title to part I of Winston Churchill's *History of the English speaking peoples*, a section covering the history of the island of Britain from Celtic society to the Norman conquest. In Churchill's view this period shaped and bequeathed to modernity that mixture of customs, characteristics and racial stock that constituted 'Englishness', a composite that would leave its mark, in his words, on 'every faith, fashion, practice and doctrine' that came its way. Reviewing the polyphonic mixtures of tribes and cultures that made up

For comments on an earlier version of this essay, I would like to thank Nicholas Mirzoeff, and my colleagues and graduate students in the history department, State University of New York at Stony Brook. Funding for the research came in part from the National Endowment for the Humanities, University Fellowship, and an NEH–Newberry Library Fellowship; both institutions have my continuing gratitude.

[1] 'The apostolic commission', *Sermons preached in London* (1795), p. 12.

early British society and acknowledging the role of Roman imperialism
in laying the foundations of modern civilisation among the 'wild barbarians' of the island, Churchill none the less upheld the primacy of Anglo-
Saxon blood and custom in producing the distinctive 'island race' that
would one day stamp its imprint on the globe.[2] Churchill's understanding of the various tributaries of English racial stock may have owed
much to nineteenth-century race science,[3] but his notion of the 'island
race' also articulated a conception of the national identity that eighteenth-century Britons would have recognised. This saw Englishness as
defined by a conjuncture of territorial boundaries, topographical features and historical continuities that included language, character and
physical attributes – a conceptualisation in which 'race' played a central,
if complex, role. It was in this capacity (that is, as a social and cultural
rather than biological category) that 'race' had become an important
form of self and group identification in the second half of the eighteenth
century, its significance and relationship to the national character
vigorously debated in political, scientific and religious circles.

This chapter will explore how some contemporary debates about
'race' were articulated and reflected in English representations of
Captain Cook and the South Seas. Specifically, I want to argue that
through the figure of Cook and the widely circulated stories of his and
early protestant missionary voyages to the south Pacific islands, an
important component of English ethnicity – that of England as a unique
'island race' – was authorised and renewed as central to Britain's
national identity and imperial mission. Such an undertaking requires
some preliminary cautions, for the discussion of both 'race' and 'nation'
in the early modern period is fraught with controversy and confusion.
Nineteenth-century conceptions of 'race' as a largely biological inheritance identifiable through physical characteristics are too frequently
read back onto earlier periods in the quite reasonable effort to illuminate
the genealogy of modern discourses of racism and difference.[4] Yet as a
number of influential studies have recently demonstrated, 'race', like
gender and ethnicity, is a historically contingent construction that does
not describe empirical, static or absolute conditions in societies, but

---

[2] Winston Churchill, *A history of the English-speaking peoples* (4 vols., 1956–8); a shortened
version was also published as *The island race* (1964).
[3] See George Stocking, Jr, *Victorian anthropology* (New York, 1992); Robert Young,
Colonial desire: hybridity in theory, culture and race (1995) and Nancy Stepan, *The idea of
race in science: Great Britain, 1800–1960* (1982).
[4] See the otherwise excellent study by Londa Schiebinger, *Nature's body: gender in the
making of modern science* (Boston, 1993). For a reading of 'race' closer to that presented
here see H. L. Malchow, 'Frankenstein's monster and images of race in nineteenth-
century Britain', *P&P*, 139 (1993), 90–129; Catherine Hall, *White, male and middle class*
(1992), esp. pp. 25–6; and the works in footnote 6.

positional relationships made and unmade in historical circumstances and manipulated in the pursuit of power. In the early modern period, 'race' was identified and signified through religion, cultural practice, custom, language, climate, aesthetics and historical time, as much as physiognomy and biology (although certainly the latter two played important, if contested, roles).[5] Similarly, recent work on nations and nationalisms, by foregrounding the nation-state as a 'road to modernity', have tended to obscure the complex and multiform ways in which nations and national identities were imagined, represented and consumed in earlier periods.[6] Histories of national identities, in particular, cannot be reduced to histories of 'nationalism(s)' *per se*, but must be recovered instead in the fragmentary and often paradoxical modes and meanings of cultural expression that constructed identities themselves. 'Englishness' from this perspective appears to be less a stable entity (revolving, for example, around the supposed perennial fixities of protestantism, king, parliament, liberty and Englishmen's birthrights)

[5] Henry Louis Gates, Jr, *'Race', writing and difference* (Chicago, 1985), pp. 1–15; Dominick LaCapra, ed., *The bounds of race: perspectives on hegemony and resistance* (Ithaca, 1991); Margo Hendricks and Patricia Parker, *Women, 'race' and writing in the early modern period* (1994); Etienne Balibar, 'The nation form: history and ideology', in Balibar and I. Wallerstein, *Race, nation, class: ambiguous identities* (1991); Elizabeth Bohls, 'Standards of taste, discourses of "race" and the aesthetic education of a monster: critique of empire in *Frankenstein*', *Eighteenth Century Life*, 18 n.s. (1994), 23–36. In the Georgian period as in other periods, 'race' and 'nation' bore several competing systems of meaning. Used in their widest senses to denote groups distinguished or connected by common descent or origin, each sought to identify political, religious, social and territorial particularity, and as such were frequently used interchangeably in much of the cultural, political, scientific and travel literature of the day. Although there was a trend by the later decades of the century in scientific and ethnographic writing to use 'race' to define the broad differences among mankind, and 'nation' to denote particular ones, the older meanings of 'race' and 'nation' as inheritance, lineage and group particularity were still at play, confusingly often in the same scientific or travel document. Similarly, cultural notions of 'race' continued to compete with biological ones throughout the century. See the works of John R. Forster, George Forster and James Cook, footnote 14, and Nicholas Hudson, 'From "nation" to "race": the origin of racial classification in eighteenth century thought', *Eighteenth Century Studies*, 29 (1996), 247–64. 'Ethnic' (which was used in the eighteenth century to refer to cultures and humans that were heathen, pagan or otherwise beyond the realm of Judaeo-Christendom) and 'ethnicity' are used in this chapter in their late twentieth-century sense as systems of cultural difference based on ethnocentric roots and perspectives, existing within or across national boundaries – a terrain covered by 'race' in the eighteenth century.

[6] See, for example, Benedict Anderson, *Imagined communities* (1983); Eric Hobsbawm, *Nations and nationalism since 1780* (Cambridge, 1990); Liah Greenfeld, *Nationalism: five roads to modernity* (Cambridge, MA, 1992); Linda Colley, *Britons: forging the nation, 1707–1837* (New Haven, 1992). For criticism of these positions, see Partha Chatterjee, *The nation and its fragments* (Princeton, 1993); *Representations*, special issue, ed. Carla Hesse and Thomas Laqueur, 47 (1994); and Kathleen Wilson, *Britannia's children: configurations of the nation in the eighteenth century* (forthcoming, Routledge, 1999).

than a continually contested terrain, a 'sign of difference', the specific meanings of which depended upon the contexts of its articulations.[7]

This chapter will highlight the ambiguous meanings and interconnections of eighteenth-century notions of race and nation in constituting and naturalising English difference and distinctiveness. As the rhetoric of travellers' and explorers' tales shifted from the fantastic, exotic and economic of earlier periods, to the scientific reportage of the eighteenth century, the systems of classification initiated in natural science were extended to, or imitated in, comparative social description. This enabled the varieties of both humans and nations to be ranked in order of 'nature', history, culture and civilisation; and this ranking became integral to eighteenth-century European imperialism and its larger taxonomic projects of ethnology, natural history and global knowledge. In the process, a type of 'scientific' reportage, based on observation, classification and comparison of data, would be a rhetorical technique adopted across a range of discursive media and cultural forums to represent colonial encounters. These representations were themselves cultural events that allowed the exotic, unknown and 'discovered' to be appropriated, domesticated and rendered plausible.[8] Their impact on articulations of English national identity is strikingly illuminated in the apotheosis of Captain Cook. Here theatrical extravaganzas, scientific classificatory systems and religious imperatives converged to set the English (and, secondarily, the British) apart as an 'island race'. This notion idealised past national and imperial experiences, and shaped expectations about the national destiny in ways that would indeed – as Churchill testified – leave its indelible imprint on the globe.

Contexts

In the years surrounding Cook's exploits, a convergence of political, cultural and imperial crises had worked to give ideas about race and its relationship to the national identity a particular salience. After several decades of enthusiastic expansionist sentiment among British publics, the peace of Paris (1763) had brought to the fore a growing unease at

---

[7] See, for example, Hall, *White, male and middle class*, p. 26; Young, *Colonial hybridity*, p. 2; Kathleen Wilson, 'Citizenship, empire and modernity in the English provinces, 1720–1790', *Eighteenth Century Studies*, 29 (1995), 80–1; the quotation is from Homi Bhabha, 'Signs taken for wonders', in *The location of culture* (1994), p. 108.

[8] For discussions of this point, see James Hevia, *Cherishing men from afar: Qing guest ritual and the Macartney embassy* (Durham, 1995), pp. 84–5; Thomas Richards, *The imperial archive* (1993); Jonathan Lamb, 'Introduction', *The South Pacific in the eighteenth century*, *Eighteenth Century Life*, 18 (1994), pp. 5–6.

the enormity of British possessions, their racial and religious diversity and the authoritarian techniques used to govern them. The East India Company and its conquests on the sub-continent became a source of scandal when the full extent of the fortune amassed by Robert Clive, and the means he used to acquire it, became known in 1773. West Indian and North American debacles also underscored the unsavory aspects of an empire of conquest. British attempts in the late 1760s to expatriate or exterminate the Caribbs on the island of St Vincent in order to appropriate their lands produced a particularly gruesome and bloody war on the island that forced English observers to confront the realities of conquest and question the long-vaunted moral superiority of British imperialism over its European competitors. American colonial revolt and the massive war effort to suppress it did little to quell these questions about the supposed virtue and superiority of the imperial project and the character of Englishness. Britannia's rule of the waves had begun to look like a trial by fire that incinerated justice and liberty in the name of the national interest.[9] If white, protestant English people living abroad were not able to claim the same liberties as Englishmen at home, what hope was there for the other, proliferating ranks of peoples under British rule?

Above all, abolitionist sentiment and the plight of black Britons living within England raised troubling questions about the nature and accessibility of English rights and liberties for those whose Britishness could not be taken as self-evident. Beginning in the mid-1760s (and after two centuries of comparative indifference), hostility to the slave trade and to the plantocratic justification for slavery's continuation in the New World steadily grew, invigorated by British protestant evangelical outrage and periodically amplified by bloody incidents that made even the most phlegmatic portions of the English public queasy.[10] Chief among them was the *Zong* affair of 1781, when 133 captive Africans aboard a slave ship bound for Jamaica were thrown overboard and drowned for the insurance money. The Sierra Leone resettlement project of 1786–7, hatched in the aftermath of an influx of black immigrants from America at the end of the war, also forced a confrontation between differing claims to national belonging, and ultimately made clear the contingent nature of black British claims to citizenship and the cultural and physical

[9] See Kathleen Wilson, *The sense of the people: politics, culture and imperialism, 1715–1785* (Cambridge, 1995), pp. 274–5.

[10] See, for example, James Walvin, ed., *Slavery and British society, 1776–1846* (Baton Rouge, 1982); Moira Ferguson, *Subject to others: British women writers and anti-slavery* (1992); Claire Midgely, *Women against slavery: the British campaign, 1780–1870* (1992); and, for the critical role of black Britons, Peter Fryer, *Staying power: the history of black people in Britain* (1984).

requirements of 'Englishness'.[11] Such events underscored the role of race in legitimating forms of domination to which Britons themselves would not submit. They also demonstrated that the terms of national belonging within an imperial polity could not be rendered capacious or elastic enough to accommodate all of the 'others' within.

Finally, the voyages inaugurating what is Eurocentrically called the second age of discovery – Bryon, Wallis and Carteret to the Pacific, Cartwright to Labrador, Phipps and Pickergill to the Arctic – provided new information about the diversity of humanity and its lifestyles which renewed old questions about the relative positions of European and indigenous peoples. If all peoples enjoyed a 'natural' equality, as some enlightenment thinkers had suggested, then why were some so much more advanced than others? If all were alike morally and anatomically, then how could the rights and privileges enjoyed by Europeans in general and English people in particular be justified? The result was an appeal to nature and history that gave philosophers, scientists, clergymen and cultural entrepreneurs alike the task of sorting out the 'facts' of human similarity and difference and bestowing them with moral and political significance.

A new kind of national hero

In these contexts, the Pacific explorations of Captain James Cook and their widely publicised results gave a much-needed lift to the collective national psyche and imperial self-confidence alike. Indeed, despite the European internationalism, in personnel and goals, of the exploration projects launched in this period, they could still be used for patriotic and narrowly nationalistic purposes. 'Maps, names, lists and taxonomies were the plunder of the later eighteenth century', Jonathan Lamb has remarked, and the writing up and translation of accounts of voyages were very real weapons in the wars for empire.[12] Cook's three voyages (1768–71, 1772–5, 1776–9) accordingly generated an industry of highly ethnocentric commentary, praise and critique that commenced with publication of Hawkesworth's *Voyages* in 1773 and continues to the present day. Marking new departures in scientific discovery, observation and collection of data, the voyages captured the national imagination with their tales of vast oceans, giant coral reefs, wild cannibals, erotic maidens and Arcadian tropical islands populated by uncorrupted island

---

[11] Wilson, 'Empire, citizenship and modernity', pp. 82–4; Stephen Braidwood, *Black poor and white philanthropists* (Liverpool, 1994).

[12] Lamb, 'Introduction', *South Pacific*, p. 5; see also Philip Edwards, *The story of the voyage* (Cambridge, 1994), ch. 1.

races. Cook himself was lionised by the English public in ways that few figures of the era could match, coming to symbolise and embody the combination of intrepidity and humanism that was quickly vaunted as a central feature of the national identity.

The instant interest in and acclaim generated by Cook's Pacific feats can be quickly demonstrated. Official and unofficial accounts of the voyages proliferated in the 1770s and 1780s, quickly becoming the most popular books at circulating libraries in the metropolis and provincial towns, and these were endlessly condensed, excerpted, reprinted and otherwise recirculated in print culture.[13] To cite just one example, Hawkesworth's three-volume *Voyages* was based on the journals of Cook, naturalist Joseph Banks and draftsman Sydney Parkinson, and was lavishly illustrated with detailed and highly romanticised engravings of South Sea scenes. Despite its high price and the controversy sparked by its incipient cultural relativism, the *Voyages* went into multiple editions in Britain and America, followed by French, German, Italian and Spanish translations from 1774 to 1794, and was excerpted in virtually every London and provincial magazine. The vast troves of information on distant lands and peoples garnered on the voyages swelled the seven lines devoted to the South Pacific in the first edition of the *Encyclopaedia Britannica* to forty double-columned pages in the third edition of 1788–97.[14]

In addition, Cook himself was immortalised in biographies, plays, painting and poetry. All served as fulsome encomiums to the low-born man who became a great commander by virtue of his own talents; the supreme English explorer whose amazing forays into undiscovered countries spread friendship and arts among native peoples while furthering the national reputation and standing throughout the world. Fanny Burney called him 'the most moderate, humane and gentle circumnavigator that ever went out upon discoveries', and this verdict

---

[13] Alan Frost, 'Captain James Cook and the early romantic imagination', in his *Captain James Cook: image and impact* (Melbourne, 1972), pp. 90–106; for the popularity of voyage literature in general in the eighteenth century and of Cook's voyages in particular, see Edwards, *Story of the voyage*, chs. 1, 5 and 6.

[14] John Hawkesworth, *An account of the voyages . . . successively performed by Commodore Byron, Capt. Wallis, Capt. Carteret and Captain Cook* (3 vols., 1773); for excerpts see *Gentlemen's Magazine, London Magazine, Lady's Magazine, Town and Country Magazine, Annual Register,* and *Universal Magazine* for summer/autumn 1773. Other accounts include: Sydney Parkinson's *Journal of a voyage to the South Seas on the Endeavor* (1773); Cook's *Voyage to the South Pole* (1777); John Forster's *Observations made during a voyage round the world* (1778), and his son George Forster's *Voyage round the world in the years 1772–5* (1777); and Cook and Lieut. James King, *A voyage to the Pacific Ocean* (Admiralty version, 1785) and *A compendious account of Capt. Cook's last voyage* (1784). See also W. E. Pearson, 'Hawkesworth's alterations', *Journal of Pacific History,* 7 (1972), 45–72.

was confirmed by Hannah More, Anna Seward and William Cowper among others. The scientific and humane orientation of Cook's voyages appealed to members of the literary *beau monde*, like Dr Johnson and Mrs Thrale, who had been repelled by the crass commercialism and aggressive militarism of earlier endeavours. Similarly, Cook's reputed respect for the diversity and commonalty of humankind made him the exemplar for abolitionists of what could be accomplished once the progress of all was privileged over the profits of a few. As Hannah More declared in her poem, *The slave trade*:

> . . . [His] social hands,
> Had link'd disserv'd worlds in brothers' bands,
> Careless, if colour, or if clime divide
> But lov'd, and loving

was how Cook lived and died. Even his resistance to the sexual charms of Tahitian women (in marked contrast to most of the rest of his officers and crew) was celebrated for confirming his credentials as a man of sensibility and an upholder of non-aristocratic morality.[15] After decades of war and the celebration of leaders whose fame rested on more militaristic and sanguinary acts performed in the service of their country, Cook represented not only an alternative masculinity, but also a new kind of national hero, one who demonstrated both English pluck and humanity, sense and sensibility, to best advantage. He was the explorer's 'man of feeling' who died on the altar of national service with more blood brothers than bloodshed to his credit. That such idealisations ignored what his journals hinted at and what those of his fellow officers and crew spelled out (a quick temper that could quickly become violent) is important for what it reveals about Cook's instantly mythical stature.[16] He was a figure capable of reconstituting British imperial authority and English superiority through what was now seen as the essentially humanitarian and philanthropic enterprise of empire-building.

Island of history

The role of Cook's apotheosis in this reconfiguration is amply displayed in a theatrical extravaganza in his honour that is worthy of detailed

---

[15] Fanny Burney, *Early diary* (1908), p. 267; T. M. Curley, *Samuel Johnson and the age of travel* (Athens, GA, 1976), pp. 66, 69; Hannah More, *The slave trade* (1784); *The Lady's Magazine*, 4 (1773), 345–6. Cowper wrote of Cook in *The task* (1785). The most celebrated Cook biography of the day was Andrew Kippis, *Life of Captain James Cook* (1788).

[16] For which see Gananath Obeyesekere, *The apotheosis of Captain Cook: European mythmaking in the Pacific* (Princeton, 1992); Marshal Sahlins, *How 'natives' think, about Captain Cook, for example* (Chicago, 1995).

attention. In the age of the 'first empire', English theatre did much to consolidate and popularise ideas about English distinctiveness, and to socialise audiences into the *mores* of gender, class and national differentiation. Lauded as a key element in the emergence of a polished and polite urban culture, the eighteenth-century stage represented and disseminated topical 'knowledge' about the world as a central part of its respectability and 'civilising' function. Indeed, through its representations of conquest (both sexual and territorial), of 'otherness' (both racialised and gendered) and of desire, Georgian theatre supplemented the encyclopaedic gaze of print culture in staking out the grounds of identification in the formation of alterity and sameness. It thus incarnated what Michael Taussig has called that 'compulsion to become the other' that was crucial in socialising English people into recognising difference, and especially the historicity and distinctiveness of the English compared to other nations.[17] The Cook play amplified and reconfigured some of the visual and figurative tropes at work in other dramas of the day, and enabled English audiences to come to terms with their histories and destinies in particular ways.

Omai, or a trip around the world, a pantomime written by the Irish playwright John O'Keeffe and the composer William Shields, was produced at Covent Garden in December 1785, one and a half years after the official accounts of Cook's final voyage had been released by the admiralty. It was central to the process of Cook's heroization.[18] Omai was the name given by the English to the first Polynesian visitor to England (brought in 1774 by Captain Furneaux of the *Adventure*, the consort vessel of the second voyage), who became the darling of London society for the two years of his stay and was even presented to George III. Although a commoner from the island of Ulaietea, he quickly

---

[17] Michael Taussig, *Mimesis and alterity: a particular history of the senses* (New York, 1993), p. xvii. Following Taussig, I am using 'mimesis' here in its anthropological rather than literary sense; unlike Taussig, however, I consider mimesis to be less a universal faculty than a *political* move, an instrument of mastery at the heart of the imperial enterprise that attempts to neutralise alterity's radical potential by re-presenting it in order to claim it as its own.

[18] This pantomime has been extensively studied, but its richness as a representation of colonial encounter warrants its further examination here. This account is indebted to, but differs significantly from, those by Rudger Jöppien, 'Philipe Jacques de Loutherbourg's pantomime *Omai, or a Trip Round the World* and the artists of Captain Cook's Voyages', in *Captain Cook and the South Seas* (1979), pp. 81–133; Bernard Smith, *European vision and the South Pacific* (New Haven 1985), pp. 115–22; and Greg Dening, *Mr. Bligh's bad language: passion, power and theatre on the Bounty* (Cambridge, 1992), pp. 270–6, 293–8; and is based upon John O'Keeffe, *Harlequin Omai* (1785); Newberry Library, Microprint of O'Keeffe, Airs, etc. for *Harlequin Omai*; BL, Add. MS 38622, Plays, Coker Collection, fs. 164–187v; and *Recollections of the life of John O'Keeffe* (2 vols., 1826), II, pp. 113–14.

became the noble savage for the patrician set, and was lauded for his 'natural' grace, politeness and manners, and was painted in suitably neo-classical style by Reynolds. Significantly, the stage production that borrowed his name bore little resemblance to his or to Cook's 'real' circumstances.

Instead, the pantomime had a whimsical and romantic plot, which involved Omai (here made heir to the throne of Tahiti) and his betrothed, the beautiful Londina, daughter of Britannia, setting chase across the world to escape the evil spells of his rival who wants to prevent their union and hence that of the two kingdoms. The lovers' flight provided the theme of the show, whisking them across all the islands Cook had visited or discovered, including Kamchatka, the Ice Islands or Antarctica, New Zealand, the Tongan or Friendly Islands and the Sandwich Islands. In doing so, the pantomime set new standards in scenery and costume for topographic and ethnographic accuracy. Indeed, the sets were technologically breathtaking, designed by Phillipe Jacques de Loutherbourg, who closely consulted the paintings, sketches and engravings from all three voyages, and painted under the direction of John Webber, the artist aboard the *Resolution*, the flagship of the second voyage. They brought to stage design the same arts of perspective, light and motion that had helped make navigation such a spectacular science. The key performances of popular actors – especially the stately Elizabeth Inchbald as Britannia and Ralph Wewitzer as a native prophet who paid homage to Cook in extempore gibberish that was supposed to be Tahitian and was 'translated' in the programme – added a different kind of appeal to a show that sparkled with its jumble of exoticism, science, spectacle and 'fact'. 'What can be more delightful than an enchanting fascination that monopolizes the mind to the scene before the eye, and leads the imagination from country to country, from the frigid to the torrid zone, shewing as in a mirror, prospects of different climates, with all the productions of nature in the animal and vegetable worlds, and all the efforts of man to attain nourishment, convenience and luxury, by the world of arts', gushed the critic for *The Times*; while the critic in *Rambler's Magazine* called it 'a school for the history of Man'.[19]

As an entertainment about encounters in the 'contact zone' when English islanders confronted the 'otherness' of Pacific islanders, the pantomime enabled what Walter Benjamin has called the 'flash of recognition' between divergent historical subjects and periods that staked out the grounds of similarity in the construction of historical

[19] *Times*, 22 Dec. 1785; *Rambler Magazine*, Jan. 1786, 53.

difference.[20] Capturing Pacific peoples in the encyclopaedic gaze of the period's nascent social science, the representation allowed 'travel' – geographic and temporal – by aid of the latest in visual sciences and technologies, while the Pacific islanders so arrayed provided examples to English audiences of their earlier selves, 'mirrors' of a past once deemed lost, but now paraded before them in proof of present-day English ingenuity, civility and cosmopolitanism. At the same time, through the dissemination of apparently neutral topical and 'scientific' knowledge, the pantomime demonstrated the role of theatre in formulating a notion of an (idealised) history 'as it really was' that was also at the heart of burgeoning vogues in painting and fiction.[21] The music, too, was praised for its realism. Shield's songs were described as 'beautifully wild' and 'capturing the vernacular airs of Otaheite' by including Tahitian words as well as imitations of the sounds of conches and exotic animals. The pantomime thus permitted 'science . . . [to] approach barbarity' as the critic for the *London Chronicle* so evocatively remarked.[22]

Not coincidentally, these genres are brought together in the final scene of the pantomime, which takes place in Tahiti. Omai, successfully wed to Londina, is installed as king and a grand procession of all the peoples of the Pacific islands takes place: Tahitians, New Zealanders, Marquesans, Tongans, Hawaiians, Kamchatkars, Easter Islanders, Eskimos and Indians of Nootka and Prince William Sound. This scene of happy miscegenation, instrumentalised by both the generic form and the princely status of Omai, inverts that practised by (lower-class) English sailors and Tahitian women. Its implications are in the event displaced and contained by the entry of the real hero of the piece, for as soon as the marriage procession ends, an English captain steps forward, gives a sword to Omai, and begins to sing a grand lament for Captain Cook. A giant painting of the *Apotheosis of Captain Cook* (the first of what would be a long line of similarly titled paintings) simultaneously descends on the stage, portraying Cook, resting in clouds over the Hawaiian bay where he had been 'sacrificed', being crowned by Britannia and Fame (p. 276). As a member of the last in the series of 'original' island races, Cook represents their final and most advanced form. Like the pantomime of which it was a part, the painting thus

---

[20] Walter Benjamin, 'Theses on the philosophy of history', in Hannah Arendt, ed., *Illuminations* (New York, 1969).

[21] For the 'contact zone', see Mary Louis Pratt, *Imperial eyes: transculturation and travel writing* (1992); for this idealised notion of history, see Dening, *Bligh*, p. 292 and Smith, *European vision*, pp. 117–18; and for naturalism in history painting see Smith, *European vision*, p. 121.

[22] O'Keeffe, *Recollections*, II, p. 114; *London Chronicle*, 22 (1785).

The apotheosis of Captain Cook
Source: From a design of P. J. De Loutherbourg RA copyright British Museum.
Reproduced courtesy of British Museum.

transforms through mimesis the 'real' into the ideal, a higher form of knowledge. The tripartite structure of the painting attests to this progression. The picture is divided into the space of exploration and discovery (where the exact representation of landscape and British ships evoke an objective mapping of the 'discovered' and exotic terrain where Pacific islanders lived); an intermediate space separating the human and celestial; and the space of the divine – rococo in style – where Cook, in a pose clearly influenced by Benjamin West's *Death of Wolfe* (1773), is deified while looking nobly and sympathetically at the human scene below. The voices of all the various peoples proclaim:

> The hero of Macedon ran o'er the world,
> Yet nothing but death could he give
> 'Twas George's command and the sail was unfurl'd
> And Cook taught mankind how to live.
> He came and he saw, not to conquer but to save.
> The Caesar of Britain was he:
> Who scorn'd the conditions of making a slave
> While Britons themselves are so free
> Now the Genius of Britain forbids us to grieve
> Since Cook ever honour'd immortal shall live.[23]

Cook, Omai and the Pacific islanders thus became figures in the panorama of English progress and achievement, lessons in the 'school for the history of man', the 'mirror' of past and present. It was, as the playwright himself noted, an immensely gratifying moment for English audiences, who thereby participated in the progress and ultimate canonisation of English imperialism itself as the agent of enlightened civilisation. George III was moved to tears during the numerous performances of the pantomime he attended during its long initial run, and the finale became one of the most popular songs of the late 1780s and 1790s, demanded by audiences at theatres, concerts and assemblies and sung at tavern societies.[24]

Omai's lengthy run and revivals were limited to the London theatres, but audiences in the localities were similarly dazzled by *The death of Captain Cook*, a French ballet enthusiastically received in the capital in 1789 before going on a three-year tour of provincial England and Ireland. Its gorgeous, naturalistic scenery also served to heighten the romantic plot about love and betrayal among Hawaiian islanders, rendering Cook's death all the more tragic and heroic. Indeed, the play's emotive force was attested to by the hysterical sobbing that broke out among theatre audiences at the moment of Cook's deadly stabbing. According to Greg Dening, in one performance an actor playing a

---

[23] O'Keeffe, *Harlequin Omai*, IV, chorus.   [24] O'Keeffe, *Recollections*, II, p. 114.

marine was pierced by a real sword left out by accident, and his death throes received animated applause by the incognisant spectators – the ultimate melding of mimesis and authenticity.[25]

The tropes, images and techniques of the Cook plays must be seen as part of an emergent new style that was taking hold in London and provincial theatre in the last quarter of the century, one that similarly melded topical events, scientific knowledge and mythic histories into fable and visual spectacle.[26] For example, the reification of English heroics occurred in the various versions of the siege of Quebec and the death of General Wolfe, which were first staged in provincial theatres in 1763 (and perhaps influenced West's famous painting) and which remained a favorite afterpiece into the 1800s. These contained idealised 'historical' tableaux similar to those in the Cook plays, which aimed at exalting another recent exemplar of a glorious national past. Similarly, exotic settings appeared in a series of 'island' plays appearing in the 1780s and 1790s that explored the topos of the island itself as it related to Great Britain – such as *Robinson Crusoe* and *Hannah Hewit, or the female Crusoe*. And other 'historical' dramas, such as *Alfred, a masque*, drew upon contemporary English interest in Saxon history to meditate upon the origins of the distinctiveness of the English national character (a theme concurrently emphasised by the Scot, David Hume, in his *History of England*, as well as English radical journalists).[27] This patriotic spectacle, also designed by Loutherbourg, used transparencies and eidophusikons to transmute past into present, namely the 'naturalistic' scenery of ancient Britain into a representation of the late naval review at Portsmouth, replete with an ocean in prospect, merchant ships, men of war and English sailors. Alfred is enjoined by a hermit to

> backward cast your eyes
> on this unfolding scene; where pictur'd true
> As in a mirror, rises fair to sight
> Our England's genius, strength and future fame!

as the tars jump ashore to sing a specially revised version of Arne's *Rule Britannia*:

> The nations, not so blest as thee,
> Must in their turns to tyrants fall,
> While thou shalt flourish great and free

[25] Dening, *Bligh*, p. 295.

[26] See my *Britannia's children* for full citations to the plays mentioned in this paragraph.

[27] For which see David Hume, *History of England from the invasion of Julius Caesar to the revolution in 1688* (2nd edn, 8 vols., 1763), I; *Encyclopaedia Britannica* (2nd edn, 1778–83), II; O. Hulme, *An historical essay on the English constitution* (1771); and Asa Briggs, *Saxons, Normans and Victorians* (Bexhill-on-Sea, 1966).

The dread and envy of them all . . .
The Muses still, with freedom found
Shall to thy happy coasts repair,
Blest isle, with matchless beauty crown'd
And manly hearts to guard the fair![28]

Liberty, the arts and (feminine) beauty are destined to flourish on the 'blest isle', secured under the dual protections of topography and a paternalistic, yet ultimately coercive, masculinity. Such panoramas thrilled audiences for the next two decades, providing, like *Omai*, a 'mirror' of English history and futurity that reflected current English manliness, ingenuity and achievement. The Cook plays, then, with their blend of fantasy and ethnography, were part of this turning point in the finesse with which theatre transformed historical idealisations into historical realities that helped structure and confirm beliefs about the historicity, distinctiveness and promise of the English compared to other nations. The island race, it seems, even in its infancy, would never ever be slaves.

The progress of nations

Cook's voyages had a huge impact on the British imagination, initially fostering a craze for descriptions of the customs and manners of South Sea islanders, feeding the appetite for the exotic, eroticising the primitive, and initially bolstering neoclassical views about the natural equality, universal reason and similarity of human life in the state of nature.[29] However, this revival of primitivism proved to be short-lived, for the publication of the details of the voyages stimulated contending interpretations of the nature of Pacific peoples that revealed the inadequacy of classical traditions in interpreting 'primitive' cultures. Indeed, Cook's second and third voyages had the effect of validating a longer-held and more ferociously enacted anti-primitivism that had shaped English colonial relations for some time, not least with the Irish, Welsh and Scots.[30]

First, natural and social scientists, including some of those who had

---

[28] *Alfred: a masque* (1773); Sir Augustus Harris, 'A collection of newspaper cuttings relating to London theaters, 1704–79'.

[29] For the interest in Tahiti, see Dening, *Bligh*, pp. 265–8; Lars E. Troide, ed., *The early journals and letters of Fanny Burney* (Montreal, 1988), I, pp. 322–7; Anne Raine Ellis, ed., *Early diary of Frances Burney* (1907), pp. 320–33; and nos. of the *Gentlemen's Magazine, London Magazine, Lady's Magazine, Town and Country Magazine* for 1773, 1775, 1777, 1780. For the cult of soft primitivism, see Hoxie Sissy Fairchild, *The noble savage: a study in romantic naturalism* (1933); and Lois Whitney, *Primitivism and the idea of progress* (Baltimore, 1934).

[30] See, for example, Nicholas Canny, 'The ideology of English colonization: from Ireland

accompanied Cook on his second and third voyages, described the island races encountered in a good deal less romanticised way.[31] The Maori 'massacre', and dismemberment of an entire boat crew from the *Adventurer*, was revealed in the separate accounts of Cook, Lieutenant James Burney and naturalist J. R. Forster (a German *émigré* who for a time believed fervently in the superiority of the British imperial project over its European competitors[32]); and it perhaps horrified the reading public in Britain more than those who had witnessed it. 'Such a shocking scene of Carnage and Barbarity as can never be mentioned or thought of, but with horror', Burney asserted, recalling the blood and body parts that lay strewn along the beach near the wrecked boat. Reports of cannibalism and human sacrifices among the Maoris and Tahitians respectively confirmed traditional beliefs about 'savages' abroad that had titillated and horrified English and European publics for two centuries; while detailed accounts of the 'shivering wretchedness', 'treachery' or 'stupidity' of other islanders, such as the aborigines of New Holland, also did much to qualify visions of uncorrupted noble savages. Hence despite the efforts of Cook and his officers to assess indigenous peoples against their own backgrounds and not against European standards, the second and third voyages suggested to many observers that the force of 'climactic' variations on human, animal and vegetable kingdoms alike had produced some unthinking and nasty brutes whose absolute difference from Europeans of any rank could not be more marked.

Accordingly, the tropics began to be used to promote the idea that

to America', *William and Mary Quarterly*, 3rd ser., 30 (1973), 575–98; Nicholas Canny, 'Identity formation in Ireland: the emergence of the Anglo-Irish', in Nicholas Canny and Anthony Pagden, eds., *Colonial identity in the Atlantic world 1500–1800* (Princeton, 1987), pp. 159–212; David Cairns and Shaun Ricard, *Writing Ireland: colonialism, nationalism and culture* (Manchester, 1988); and John Gillingham, 'Foundations of a disunited kingdom', in Alexander Grant and Keith J. Stringer, eds., *Uniting the kingdom? the making of British history* (1995). Thanks to Karl Bottigheimer for this reference. For eighteenth-century Scottish intellectuals' use of primitivism as a means of fostering appreciation for ancient Ossian, and hence contemporary Scottish manliness and virtue, see Richard B. Sher, *Church and university in the Scottish enlightenment* (Princeton, 1985), pp. 151–74. Thanks to Ned Landsman for this reference.

[31] The following is based on: Cook, *Voyage to the South Pole* and *Voyage to the Pacific Ocean*; Forster, *Observations*; George Forster, *Voyage round the world*; Cook, *The journals of Captain James Cook on the voyages of discovery*, ed. J. C. Beaglehole, I, *The voyage of the Endeavor, 1768–1771* (Cambridge, 1955); II, *The voyage of the Resolution and Adventure, 1772–75* (Cambridge, 1961); and *The Resolution journal of John Reinhold Forster* (4 vols., 1982).

[32] In his journal he refers to the 'free and spirited Sons of Liberty, who inhabit this Queen of Islands' [i.e., Britain], and lauds the 'great Impartiality and Justice of the English nation': he later changed his mind. See Edwards, *Story of the voyage*, pp. 102–24; quotations from Forster's *Resolution* journal cited on pp. 108–9.

man had risen stage by stage from a lower to higher form of existence, a progression in which primitive peoples lagged far behind. This early version of socio-economic evolution, although overtaken by the unlikely convergence of comparative anatomy, physical anthropology and evangelicalism in the early nineteenth century (until its revival, in altered form, by Darwin in the 1850s),[33] none the less marked a distinctive initiative in the later eighteeth century's efforts to understand human diversity that impacted on theories of natural and human history and political economy. Forster, imbued with classical and Linnaean learning and influenced by the contemporary Scottish social scientists, became a leading proponent of this view. He devoted over half of his *Observations* to classifying the various 'nations' of the South Pacific into two 'races', distinguished according to 'Custom, Colour, Size, Form, Habit and natural Turn of Mind', and ranked according to manners, morals, cultivation and religion (or the 'progress towards Civilization', a rubric under which the treatment of women was accorded great significance).[34] While physical differences loomed larged in Forster's descriptions about what was distinctive about each island race in the Pacific, it was the historical stage of their existence, identified through population size and mode of subsistence, that 'explained' the variations in culture and physiognomy: 'such are the beginnings of arts and cultivation, such is the rise of civil societies; sooner or later they cause distinctions of rank, and the various degrees of power, influence and wealth . . . Nay, they often produce a material difference in the colour, habits and forms of the human species.' His extensive descriptions were used to argue that tropical peoples showed both the importance of environment and the role of chronological degeneration in the formation of different races.[35]

Philosophers and social scientists seemed willing to go further. In his *Origin and progress of language* (1773–9), which drew on accounts of Cook's first voyage, Lord Monboddo claimed that man's departure from his earliest state was a progression, not a decline or degeneration, and that the capacity for rational thought and moral improvement was not inbred but developed by hard work and struggle. 'There cannot be virtue, properly so called, until man is become a rational and political animal; then he shows true courage, very different from the ferocity of the brute or savage . . . the infant of our species.' Clearly, the climate of the tropics was unable to foster the improvement of the moral sense and rationality through which civilisation progressed; the capacity for improvement was the touchstone by which such societies must be measured. Despite Monboddo's notorious idiosyncracies, the arguments for

[33] For which, see Stocking, *Victorian anthropology*, pp. 18–25.
[34] *Observations*, p. 418; see also pp. 231–40, 431–5.   [35] Ibid., 322–6.

the 'stages' through which human civilisation progressed in time were bolstered or amplified by other stars of the Scottish enlightenment (such as John Millar) as well as some continental scientists; and they were popularised in periodicals, fiction and travel accounts which outlined a version of socio-economic evolution in which rationality itself, as well as custom, skin color and physical characteristics, became intractable parts of a progression from lower to higher humanity, however 'climactic' they were in origin.[36] Nature becomes culture, and culture nature, in this mental universe, and mimesis fails the less advanced races as a form of knowledge production. As Cook remarked, when reflecting on Omai's lack of application on returning to his native land in 1776, 'this kind of indifference is the true character of his nation. Europeans have visited them at times for these ten years past, yet we find neither new arts nor improvements in the old, nor have they copied after us in any one thing.'[37] From the perspective of explorers, social scientists and their interlocutors, Pacific islanders occupied a different historical temporality than Europeans, whose civilisations were older and hence more advanced, if also in certain respects more degenerate. The understanding of history itself had changed as a result of the perception that economic and cultural growth entailed both progress and corruption.[38]

Cook's own death at the hands of one of these races aided immeasurably in the transformation from noble to ignoble savages. In the aftermath of his death, the Hawaiians and other primitive peoples of the Pacific began to be compared to the Hottentots and Eskimos – races notorious for their cannibalism, harshness towards their women, hostility to Europeans and disgusting personal habits. Certainly not all indigenous peoples were degenerate and inferior, but they all seemed to fit into the evolutionary progression of the races that scientists as well as philosophers were advancing. Whether immature or degraded, the South Sea peoples were irretrievably behind the Europeans in customs, progress and intelligence. They were located in an anterior historical

[36] James Burnet, Lord Monboddo, *Of the origin and progress of language* (Edinburgh, 1773), I, pp. 133, 440, quoted in Peter Marshall and Glyndwr Williams, *The great map of mankind: British perceptions of the world in the age of enlightenment* (1982), p. 274; see also John Millar, *The origin of ranks* (Edinburgh, 1800), pp. 45–6. For a discussion of Monboddo and other Scottish thinkers on race, see Marshall and Williams, *Great map of mankind, passim*; Ronald Meeks, *Social science and the ignoble savage* (Cambridge, 1976), esp. ch. 6; and for continental scientists, see Schiebinger, *Nature's body*, p. 200.

[37] *Cook's* Resolution *Journal*, p. 241. It is only fair to point out that Cook was not consistent on this point: when he visited Tahiti 1774, he had been astonished at the improved houses and canoes which he attributed to the iron tools acquired by the islanders from English ships: *Voyage to the South Pole*, II, p. 346.

[38] Johannes Fabian, *Time and the other* (Columbia, 1983); J. G. A. Pocock, 'Modes of political and historical time in early eighteenth-century England', in his *Virtue, commerce and history* (Cambridge, 1992), p. 95.

time that, if it allowed Europeans and especially English islanders 'to behold, as in a mirror, the features of our own progenitors', as enthusiasts such as Adam Ferguson and J.-M. Degerando proclaimed,[39] also ensured their permanent place on the lower rungs of the ladder of civilisation. In this guise the historical differences among the races could serve as guides to understanding the cultural differences among the classes in Europe. In both cases human progress was contingent upon a willingness as well as capacity for self-improvement through the exertion of rationality and the reigning in of baser instincts. Such was the argument, at least, of the anglican clergyman Thomas Malthus, who placed the South Sea peoples only just above the Tierra del Fuegans and American Indians in the 'stages' of human civilization by which men learned to exercise the 'moral restraint' necessary to control the sexual instinct and avert demographic disaster. Naturally, the European, and especially English, middle classes were seen to have excelled at liberating reason from the forces of instinct, and as such were taken to be the guarantors of future progress.[40]

Protestant island

Such theories were supported and expanded by the various strands of evangelical protestantism that had been gaining ground in religious and political circles in the last three decades of the century. Protestantism itself, of course, was in Britain a great deal more than anti-catholicism or the last resort of national bonding, as Linda Colley and Liah Greenfeld have recently reminded us. It demonstrated and embodied the old testament image of a chosen, godly people who were 'an elite and a light to the world because every one of its members was a party to the covenant with God'.[41] As such, it secured to Britons the assuredness of their own excellence and entitlement. Protestantism was considered to be the most 'rational' of religions, the one that 'philosophers would chuse . . . which has given evident Sign . . . how nearly its interest is united with the Prosperity of our Country', as Thomas Sprat wrote in 1667. 'The equity of her laws, the freedom of her political constitution, and the moderation of her religious system' were cited over a century later by William Guthrie as the elements that made Britain the happiest

---

[39] Ferguson, *Essay on the history of civil society* (1767), quoted by Meeks, *Ignoble savage*, p. 150. For Degerando, see quotation above, p. 265.

[40] See Thomas Malthus, *An essay on the principles of population*, ed. Patricia James (2 vols., Cambridge, 1989), I, bks. 1–3, 21, 47 and *passim*. Thanks to Ruth Cowan for referring me to this source. See also Stocking, *Victorian anthropology*, pp. 34–5.

[41] Colley, *Britons*; Greenfeld, *Nationalism*; quote from latter, p. 52.

country in the world.[42] In this context, protestantism, a rational, improving religion – in stark contrast to the superstitious idolatry that dominated across the Channel – could serve as both a marker of English preciosity and an avenue of contestation and survival for marginalized or persecuted groups within Britain.[43]

However, the sense of superiority, entitlement and 'chosen-ness' that protestantism bestowed on the British could also be used to advance national political, cultural and spiritual power abroad. Here the growing influence of evangelicalism among the upper and middle reaches of British society had a powerful impact.[44] In the decades surrounding Cook's voyages, evangelicalism – dissenting, methodist and anglican – worked to discover, and endow with great urgency, the national mission to save the debased savages from themselves, a project which cultural and imperial rivalries with France accelerated. Evangelicals were among the first to denounce the romanticisation of Pacific islanders that followed the publication in English of Bougainville's *Voyage* and then Hawkesworth's *Voyages*. John Wesley, avid and critical purveyor of indigenous peoples in their 'natural' states, sat down to read the latter with 'huge expectations' but was quickly stunned and appalled. 'Men and women coupling together in the face of the sun, and in the sight of scores of people!' he exclaimed, 'Men whose skin, cheeks, and lips are as white as milk. Hume or Voltaire might believe this, but I cannot!' Other anonymous and self-styled 'protestants' attacked Hawkesworth's *Voyages* in the newspapers for attempting to 'debauch the Morals of our Youth at home', exclaiming that his book gave English women 'stronger excitements to vicious Indulgences than the most intriguing French Novel'.[45] From this perspective, South Pacific peoples in general and Tahitians in particular exemplified the sloth and sensuality not of the state of nature but of original sin. Over the next two decades – in a spirited riposte to enlightenment niceties – sermons, letters, essays and missionary reports denounced the iniquities of human sacrifice, infanticide, nudity, lasciviousness, uncontrolled sexuality and total absence of revealed religion that the accounts of the voyages had shown. The conversion of the South Sea islanders accordingly became a *cause célèbre* in evangelical circles that sparked the formation of a new spate of

[42] Sprat, *Observations on Mons. de Sorbiere's voyage into England, 1665* (1709), p. 179, quoted in Greenfeld, *Nationalism*, p. 85; William Guthrie, *A new geographical, historical and commercial grammar* (1785), p. iv.

[43] See my 'Citizenship, empire and modernity'.

[44] See Ernest Marshall Howse, *Saints in politics: the 'Clapham Sect' and the growth of freedom* (Toronto, 1952); John Henry Overton, *The evangelical revival in the eighteenth century* (1886); C. F. Pascoe, *Two hundred years of the SPG* (1901).

[45] *Journal of Rev. John Wesley* (1836), pp. 286, 686–7; *Public Advertiser*, 3 July 1773.

missionary societies geared towards saving the debased savages from heathenism and French enlightenment alike. The Baptist Society, founded in 1792 by William Carey, who led the mission that set out for Bengal the next year; the ecumenical London Missionary Society (1795), founded by a handful of Bristol and London clergymen; the Anglican Church Missionary Society (1795); and the Africa Society (1795) all claimed to have been galvanised into action by the accounts of the Pacific peoples provided by the Cook voyages.[46]

Of course, the ultimate goal of evangelicalism was to create universal Christian subjects equal in the eyes of God. But the evangelical belief in good works, benevolence, and also the essential sinfulness of man, legitimated ideas of both savage backwardness and the central role that protestant England (God's chosen nation) must play as the 'Teacher of Nations', showing the way forward to progress and salvation.[47] There was, after all, no apparent contradiction between a potential spiritual equality and a national, social and racial hierarchy, as evangelical efforts to Christianise African slaves in America had long made clear, and as current campaigns for reformation of manners and abolition of the slave trade reinforced. The crop of missionary societies were well connected to the abolitionist cause and to each other in personnel as well as goals, and were equally clear in their insistence that the salvation of heathen souls was the key to the advancement of Britain's imperial and commercial, as well as moral, ascendancy in the world.[48]

The London Missionary Society or LMS demonstrated the materiality of these imperatives to convert, subdue and possess through the cultural power and superiority of English protestantism. Conceived in a spirit of competitive zeal with baptist and anglican missionary societies

[46] William Carey, *An enquiry into the obligations of Christians, to use means for the conversion of the heathen* (Leicester, 1792), quoted in Richard Lovett, *The history of the London Missionary Society, 1795–1895* (2 vols., 1899), I, p. 4; see also ibid., I, pp. 18–21, 117–18; Rev. Dr Bogue, 'To the evangelical dissenters who practise infant baptism', *Evangelical Magazine*, 1 (1794), quoted in Lovett, *History of the LMS*, I, pp. 6–10; John Williams, *A narrative of missionary enterprises in the South Sea islands* (1835), pp. 2–37; C. Duncan Rice, 'The missionary context of the British anti-slavery movement', in Walvin, *Slavery and British society*, pp. 150–63; Ernest S. Dodge, *Island and empires: western impact on the Pacific and east Asia* (Minneapolis, 1976), pp. 87–117.

[47] Rev. George Burder, *An address to the serious and zealous professors of the gospel, of every denomination respecting an attempt to evangelize the heathen* (1795), quoted in Lovett, *History of the LMS*, I, pp. 22–3. See also Rev. Melville Horne, *Letters on missions; addressed to the protestant ministers of the British churches* (1794), reviewed by Haweis in *Evangelical Magazine*, 3 (1794).

[48] See Dodge, *Island and empires*, pp. 87–91; Rice, 'Missionary context', pp. 156–7; Stuart Piggin, 'The American and British contributions to evangelicalism in Australia', in Mark A. Noll, David W. Bebbington and George A. Rawlyk, eds., *Evangelicalism: comparative studies of popular protestantism in North America, the British Isles and beyond, 1700–1990* (New York and Oxford, 1994), pp. 292–3.

on the one hand and catholic missions on the other, its leaders quickly fixed on the 'well-tempered' but culturally degraded South Sea 'heathens' as most urgently in need of their ministrations. Thomas Haweis expounded on this theme in an early sermon to the organisation, noting the sharp contrast between the lush natural beauty of Tahiti and the spiritual and moral turpitude of its inhabitants. 'Amidst these enchanting scenes', he warned, 'savage nature still feasts on the flesh of its prisoners, appeases its Gods with human sacrifices – whole societies of men and women live promiscuously, and murder every infant born amongst them'. From this perspective, it was up to the worthy individuals of the society and their missionary representatives to correct and complete the tasks the Cook voyages had initiated. The society dispatched the *Duff* to Tahiti in 1796, carrying thirty men, six women and three children, to do God's and Britain's work, and their subsequent reports soon began to circulate among the British public in newsletters, travel collections, prints and paintings, joining the accounts of Cook's and Bligh's voyages as authorities on Polynesian culture in the British imperial archive.[49]

In the missionary accounts, however, cultural relativism was eschewed in favour of a more uncompromising view of antipodean savagery that sought to establish simultaneously the redemption, superiority and proprietary rights of the English settlers. For example, the Tahitian chieftain's agreement to cede the district of Matavai to the missionaries was deemed sufficiently important to Britain's official claim to the island for the directors of the LMS to have it immortalised on canvas. Exhibited at the Royal Academy in 1799, the scene was disseminated to a wider public thorough Bartollozzi's engraving. It depicted sober, respectable and thoroughly dressed English confronting half-naked islanders – 'the untutored offspring of fallen nature anxiously awaiting the Christian revelation', as Bernard Smith has noted.[50] Letters, diaries and reports, published separately and excerpted in periodicals, also circulated details about native polygamy, promiscuity, infanticide and human sacrifice that made clear that the mistakes and indulgences of Cook and his crews would not be tolerated. Here it was spiritual, not sexual, commerce that was to be the coin of the realm, and the success of the colonial encounter was to be measured by the degree to which the

---

[49] Captain James Wilson, *Missionary voyage to the southern Pacific Ocean* (1799); Lovett, *History of the LMS*, I, pp. 117–237, *passim*; see also a condensed account of the voyage in R. M. Forster, *A collection of celebrated voyages and travels from the discovery of America to the present time* (2nd edn, 4 vols., Newcastle upon Tyne, 1817), II, pp. 431–52. Wilson's account became so well known that Malthus only had to refer to it as 'the late Missionary Voyage' in his second, extended edition of the *Essay on population* of 1803.

[50] Smith, *European vision*, pp. 146–7.

settlers mastered themselves through fortitude, suffering and faith, and their native charges through example, enlightenment and ultimately conversion. On landing in Tahiti, the missionaries found their 'passion . . . more powerfully excited to find their population greatly diminished, and, through the prevalence of vice, tending to utter extinction' – an assessment which neatly reversed the responsibility for the plague of venereal disease which Cook had lamented as a direct consequence of European contact onto the indigenous islanders themselves. Not that Cook and his crews were held to be blameless: the missionaries attributed the surprise with which the Tongatoboo islanders greeted their refusal to sleep with native women to 'the practices of our abandoned countrymen making them believe this was a favour we could not well do without'.[51] In the event, such a drastic transformation in the cultural frame of reference as that represented by the missionaries led the locals to 'suspect we are not Englishmen, or like any others they have seen who have ever visited their island'. The dangers (in the missionary view) of such mis-recognition and identity confusion led them to adopt, by unanimous vote, strict rules governing their interactions with the Polynesians, and to eschew those of their own number who transgressed them or otherwise threatened to go native. Hence in the second year of the mission on Tahiti (1798), Thomas Lewis's decision to marry a native woman caused great distress among the rest of the fellowship, who had no choice but to excommunicate him from their church, although he continued to attend the public religious services, and 'to bring this native with him'. John Jefferson, secretary to the society, justified this resounding rejection of English–Tahitian miscegenation as absolutely central to the maintenance of the cultural boundaries upon which the success of the mission depended:

It must be borne in mind in this and in all similar circumstances that the woman remained heathen, not only ignorant of Christianity, but addicted to all the abominable practices of a savage life. It was not a case of a missionary marrying a native convert but of a Christian man uniting himself to a heathen woman, and that on an island where the testimony of the missionaries, after a residence of eighteen months, was that in all probability not one single female on the island over ten or twelve years of age had escaped pollution.[52]

Lewis's wife, in other words, was not only willfully incognizant of the spiritual authority of English protestantism as the representative of Christendom, but also tainted by the possibility that she had contracted

---

[51] Wilson, *Missionary voyage*, pp. 275–6; 166. See also Lovett, *History of the LMS*, I, pp. 134–45; *Evangelical Magazine* (1798); and 'Journals and letters of the missionaries, 1798–1807', in *Transactions of the Missionary Society* (3 vols., 1803–13).

[52] Lovett, *History of the LMS*, I, pp. 156–7.

venereal disease through earlier sexual encounters. Acceptable intermarriage depended upon cultural, spiritual and bodily submission to 'English' values on the part of the colonised, without which carnal knowledge could not be sanctified.

Through such representations, the LMS, like other missionary efforts of the day, provided the moral counterpart and corrective to the changing ethnographic representations of so-called primitive races. 'The missionaries have done a great deal for us in clearing up our notions of savage nations', Coleridge reportedly asserted, for they have shown that '[t]here scarcely ever existed such a set of blood-thirsty barbarians'.[53] Only through the interventions of the holy spirit and British civility in protestant/Christian conversion could such peoples be transformed into obedient Christian subjects, thus confirming the pedagogical relationship set up between them.[54] As 'God's elect among the islanders' (as the missionaries were wont to remind themselves in times of hardship), their duty was to endure intense provocation, temptation and tribulation in order to effect the salvation of the corrupted and debased whose conversion would constitute the ultimate homage to English superiority and resolve. Interestingly, in the evangelical publications of the next two decades, the original 'scientific' repertoire of images – plants, animals, landscapes, native peoples – that dominated the earlier accounts of the voyages were supplanted by appropriately evocative scenes of native brutality, superstition and backwardness. Hence Webber's *Human sacrifice at Tahiti* was retrieved from Cook and King's *Voyage to the Pacific Ocean* of 1784 to become one of the best-known illustrations of the nineteenth century; while the new editions of Cook's voyages were both purged of their 'indecent' contents and extended with new illustrations of brutish-looking savages whose skin and intentions grew ever darker.[55]

Certainly not all primitive peoples were seen to be sunk in the same degrees of sloth and superstition. Africans, for example, who possessed an 'idolatrous' religion were held to be lower in rank than, for example, Tongans and Society Islanders, who seemed to have religions that were neither idolatrous nor animistic, and who possessed distinguishable political structures with regulations and laws. Nevertheless, as with anti-

---

[53] Quoted in Smith, *European vision*, p. 147.

[54] Smith, *European vision*, pp. 317–18; John Barrow, *Voyages to the Pacific* (1836).

[55] Ibid. These representations fitted neatly with the new science of comparative anatomy being developed in the early nineteenth century by Georges Cuvier, Lamarck and the British anatomist Sir William Lawrence, which treated differences in cranial and nose shapes as signs of deeper differences in biological organisation and hence civilisation: see Stepan, *Idea of race*, ch. 1–2; and Schiebinger, *Nature's body*, where she notes that Reynold's portrait of Omai stands as 'type' for one of the five major races of humankind in Blumenbach's *Natural varieties of mankind* (1810).

slavery, missionary work combined genuine humanitarianism with hierarchical notions of British superiority and English difference in ways
that bolstered conceptions of the gulfs between and distinctiveness of
'the races'. Significantly, the great victory of conversion the missionaries
proclaimed to have achieved among the Tahitians by 1820 did little to
dislodge this perception of the hierarchical and pedagogical relationship
that existed between them. The English success in 'transforming . . .
[the] barbarous, indolent and idolatrous inhabitants' of the Tahitian and
Society islands 'into a *comparatively* civilized, industrious and Christian
people', the celebrated LMS missionary John Williams argued, had
inaugurated for the Polynesians a 'new era . . . not only in their moral
history, but also in their intellectual'. This bringing of savage peoples
into history, and gratitude and filial piety it inspired, was acknowledged
by the former heathens themselves, according to Williams, who recalled
a Raiatean chief telling him 'although we have ten thousand instructors
in Christ, we have not many fathers, for, in Christ Jesus, you have
begotten us through the Gospel'.[56]

An island race supreme

Captain Cook, 'famous civilizer and secret terroriser', in Marshall
Sahlins' words,[57] reached a heroic stature in the English national
consciousness that few figures before or since have matched. His
continued importance in academic and popular historical mythology is
demonstrated in the quantities of biographies, monographs and journals
that continue to be devoted to assessing his impact and legacy. In the
later eighteenth century, in the aftermath of war and imperial dismemberment, the representations of Cook's achievements helped recuperate
British political and imperial authority, rescue the national reputation
for liberty and restore faith in the superiority of the English national
character. Cook's explorations also inaugurated a period of intensive
British imperialism and settlement in the South Seas, undertaken with
all the fire and zeal of the missionaries themselves, that their present-day
aboriginal descendants still lament. In these and in other ways, Cook,
Tahiti and the South Seas gave the English both a history and a future.

Cook's voyages also had the effect in his own day of embroiling an
array of religious, cultural and scientific spokespersons in controversies
over the meaning and results of human diversity. Tahitian islanders,
once seen as uncorrupted 'noble savages', became transformed into
'backward' primitives incapable of progress and providing irrefutable

---

[56] Williams, *Missionary enterprises in the South Seas*, pp. 3, 465, 467; emphasis mine.
[57] Sahlins, *How natives think*, p. 1.

evidence of the lower evolutionary stage of savage races. In this context, the historical, cultural and physical difference of South Sea islanders became proof positive of a natural inequality that even a change in climate or environment could not brook. In the cultural progression that was the story of European and especially English civilisation, indigenous peoples across the globe clearly lagged behind. As such, they provided, much more dramatically than the French, a mirror image of Englishness that bolstered Britons' sense of superiority and resolve. Significantly, Job Nott, Birmingham buckle-maker, could think of no greater insult to hurl against French Jacobins them to compare them unfavorably to Hawaiian 'savages': 'bloody minded barbarians . . . worse than the Antipoads that kill'd and chop'd our brave sailor Captain Cook to pieces . . . they [Jacobins] cut out Gentlemen's hearts, and squeezed the blood into wine and drank it'.[58]

Evangelical protestantism had a key part to play in this transformation. It was not only that religion played a larger role in scientific debates in Britain than on the continent;[59] it was also that protestantism secured to the English and, secondarily the British, the asssuredness of their own entitlement, superiority, pulchritude and difference. The English sense of cultural distinctiveness as well as British conceptions of the national destiny relied heavily on this inheritance, facilitating the English nation's ascendancy in the British isles and beyond. Through this convergence of religious, scientific and nationalistic myths and imperatives, Cook – the low-born English islander who charted brave new worlds – would become the emblem of an 'island race' which was forged through ingenuity, protestantism and liberty; whose character marked it out to become the 'teacher of nations'; and whose destiny was to impose a *Pax Britannica* on the world.

[58] Cited in John Brewer, ' "This monstrous tragi-comic scene": British reactions to the French revolution', in David Bindman, ed., *The shadow of the guillotine* (1992), p. 21.

[59] Stepan, *Idea of race*, ch. 1.

12 A transatlantic perspective: protestantism and national identities in mid-nineteenth-century Britain and the United States

John Wolffe

In the history of protestantism and national identities, the period between the beginnings of legislative toleration of Roman catholicism in the late 1770s, and its substantial achievement in 1829, has an evident unity. Despite their many differences of interpretation, both Linda Colley and J. C. D. Clark push their analysis of the influence of protestantism in eighteenth-century Britain on into the first third of the nineteenth century, and then conclude it in the 1830s. Both see the enactment of emancipation as a profoundly significant event, even if Clark interprets it primarily as a cause of change, and Colley primarily as a consequence of changes that had already been taking place over the preceding decades. Colley in particular recognises that strong protestantism was conspicuous in Britain for many decades after 1829, but 'none the less', she concludes, '1829 was the end of an era'.[1]

This chapter, however, is concerned with the period after 1829 and explores the mechanisms and the contexts in which the cultural and ideological frameworks analysed in earlier chapters survived beyond 1829. There is also consideration of the ways in which they were replicated across the Atlantic, in the north-eastern United States. The intention is not to dispute the essential judgement that 1829 was a watershed. Catholic emancipation was profoundly significant in that it left the composite British state no longer defined by its exclusion of Roman catholicism; and because it meant that protestantism, at least in the negative sense of the word, had ceased to be a matter of national consensus. Moreover, in the ensuing decades the impact of the 'Oxford movement' rendered the protestant character of the church of England more ambivalent; and, eventually, theological liberalism became a potent solvent of traditional protestant dogmatic positions. Nevertheless it would be quite wrong to see the period after 1829 as merely some

[1] Linda Colley, *Britons: forging the nation, 1707–1837* (1992), p. 334 and *passim*. Cf. J. C. D. Clark, *English society 1688–1832* (Cambridge, 1985).

kind of long epilogue of protestant decline, following the eighteenth-century golden age. Expressions of protestant feeling continued to be strong, notably in the campaign in support of the church of Ireland in the mid-1830s; in the opposition to the permanent state endowment of Maynooth College in 1845; in the resentment stirred by the so-called 'papal aggression' of 1850; and in a variety of popular disturbances, particularly the Stockport riots of 1852 and the unrest associated with the activities of William Murphy in the 1860s. Even in the late nineteenth century and early twentieth century, protestantism was still sustained by anti-ritualist agitation; enjoyed considerable political and cultural importance in the polarised communities of Lancashire and central Scotland; and – albeit in a diffuse sense – gave important ideological legitimacy to the empire. Even if the pressure eventually began to fall, there was too much head of steam for it all to have been produced by a furnace which had ceased to be stoked in 1829. Even if militant protestants became a minority, they still retained for many decades the potential to stir broad public sympathy, especially at times of perceived crisis.[2]

Quite apart from the evidence of the continuing strength of protestant sentiments, there are two further reasons why it is worthwhile to pursue the themes of this volume into the early Victorian period. First, it was in these decades that nationalism in the generally received sense of the word – bringing together 'the vital aspirations of the modern world: for autonomy and self-government, for unity and autarchy, and for authentic identity'[3] – established itself as a major ideological force on the European and world stage. It is therefore a curious historiographical paradox that recent historians of nationalism and national identity in Britain have concentrated their attention primarily on the seventeenth and eighteenth centuries while the nineteenth century has been relatively neglected.[4] No pretensions can be made to rectify that deficiency in a single essay, but in concluding the present volume it is important to assess the extent to which nineteenth-century forms of nationalism in Britain grew out of earlier assertions of the linkages between protestantism and national identity.[5] Second, during the middle years of the

[2] John Wolffe, 'Change and continuity in British anti-catholicism, 1829–1982', in Frank Tallett and Nicholas Atkin, eds., *Catholicism in Britain and France since 1789* (1996), pp. 67–83.

[3] John Hutchinson and Anthony D. Smith, eds., *Nationalism* (Oxford, 1994), p. 4.

[4] Gerald Newman, *The rise of English nationalism: a cultural history, 1740–1830* (1987) also illustrates this chronological focus, even though only limited attention is given to religion.

[5] For more wide-ranging assessment of linkages between religion, national identity and nationalism in the nineteenth- and early twentieth centuries, see John Wolffe, *God and greater Britain: religion and national life in Britain and Ireland, 1843–1945* (1994) and

nineteenth century, British protestantism was in effect exported to other parts of the English-speaking world. In 1849, Hugh McNeile, one of the most influential protestant clergymen of his day, asserted that the mission of England was 'to extend over the world a pure and reformed church'.[6] The case of the United States provides a particularly instructive illustration of this process.[7] The exploration of such geographical transmissions and transmutations of protestantism serves to provide valuable additional perspectives on the nature of the tradition in Britain itself.

From the standpoint of eighteenth-century scholarship it is understandable that the period up to 1829 has been interpreted as one of substantial continuity with the past; from the nineteenth-century perspective, however, it was also one of significant new developments which helped to ensure the survival of a changed but vigorous sense of protestant identity well into the Victorian era and beyond. Obviously there were continuities in tradition and prejudice: Foxe's 'book of martyrs' was still being extensively republished in the nineteenth century; Guy Fawkes' day was still boisterously celebrated. But new developments gave a changed character and a considerable intensity to early Victorian anti-catholicism. The union with Ireland in 1800 had given British protestants a new sense of political and religious responsibility for a predominantly catholic nation, while it also cemented their awareness of a common identity with the protestant minority. Emancipation, moreover, not only brought Daniel O'Connell and his co-religionists into parliament, but it gave a new confidence to priests and people at the grass-roots. Even before the major surge of Irish immigration in the 1840s, Roman catholicism had become a forceful and visible presence in Britain itself, whereas in the past it had been either foreign or obscure. The other side of the coin was the remoulding of protestant ideology by the evangelical movement, which in the 1820s began to acquire a more dogmatic and more explicitly anti-catholic temper than it had possessed in the eighteenth and early nineteenth centuries. Evangelical protestant conviction was fuelled by eschatological expectation,

David Hempton, *Religion and political culture in Britain and Ireland from the Glorious Revolution to the decline of empire* (Cambridge, 1996).

[6] H. McNeile, *National sin – what is it? A letter to the Rt. Hon. Sir George Grey, Bart., MP* (1849), p. 30.

[7] There is obviously also potential for investigation of the diffusion of protestant ideas within the British empire. On contemporary developments in Canada, see Scott W. See, *Riots in New Brunswick: Orange nativism and social violence in the 1840s* (Toronto, 1993) and J. R. Miller, 'Anti-catholic thought in Victorian Canada', *Canadian Historical Review*, 66 (1985), 474–94. On Australia see C. M. H. Clark, *A history of Australia* (3 vols., Melbourne, 1962–87), II, pp. 170–4, 200–1, 240–2; III, pp. 345–6; and Michael Hogan, *The sectarian strand: religion in Australian history* (Ringwood, Victoria, 1987).

stimulated particularly by the very public and popular ministry of Edward Irving. If, as Irving maintained, the Roman church was to be identified with the Babylon of the *Apocalypse*, and the second advent of Christ was to be imminently expected, uncompromising protestant witness was a vital responsibility for individual and nation alike. In the years after 1829 such theological rationalisation of protestantism had a significant attraction for erstwhile ultra-tory opponents of emancipation, whose pre-existing constitutional theory had been exploded by the irreversible reality of concession. The consequent resurgence of protestantism was focused by the formation of numerous protestant societies, notably the Protestant Association in 1835 and the National Club a decade later. It contributed both to the revival of conservatism in the 1830s and to its internal tensions in the 1840s and 1850s.[8]

In the year of Queen Victoria's accession, the fourth duke of Newcastle, who had been one of the most die-hard opponents of emancipation, published his *Thoughts in times past, tested by subsequent events*. England, he believed, had stood forth first among the nations at the reformation, when it had been selected by providence as the asylum and sanctuary of true religion, occupying 'a very similar position to the Jews of old'. 'National character' had been 'ameliorated, ennobled and confirmed' by the reformed religion. Such national virtue had been a protection from the moral pestilence of the French revolution and had enabled England to emerge victorious in 1815 as the beacon and paragon of the world. Thereafter, however, things had begun to go wrong. Destructive opinions multiplied and in 1829 'we . . . crucified the great propitiatory cause of the peculiar blessings which had been heaped upon us by a bounteous hand'. Divine favour had now been withdrawn and as a direct result of this heinous religious and political sin the nation had become prey to disastrous instability and decline.[9] It would be tempting, but wrong, to dismiss such pronouncements as the ramblings of an isolated and disillusioned old man. Newcastle was only fifty-two in 1837 and was to live for another thirteen years, politically active almost to the last. His close associate, the earl of Winchilsea, survived until 1858. In the pamphlet quoted, Newcastle was not resigning himself to the course of events, but seeking to reverse it. He did see some glimmerings of hope, believing that the public mind was now 'fast returning to its ancient good sense and proverbial patrio-

---

[8] For detailed discussion and substantiation of the points made in this paragraph refer to my book, John Wolffe, *The protestant crusade in Great Britain, 1829–1860* (Oxford, 1991), *passim*.

[9] 4th Duke of Newcastle, *Thoughts in times past, tested by subsequent events* (1837), pp. xix-xx, xxx-xli.

tism'.[10] Although his own dream of repealing emancipation was never to become practical politics, he detected an upsurge of protestant patriotic feeling, which gave a curious populism to the language of this most conservative of aristocrats.

It had been widely noted that in voting for catholic emancipation the House of Commons had been in advance of the opinion of the electorate, which was predominantly opposed to concession.[11] Subsequently Daniel O'Connell was to observe that the parliament elected under the provisions of the 1832 reform act – and therefore presumably more in tune with public opinion – was more protestant than its predecessor and would never have voted for emancipation.[12] From late 1834 the campaign in defence of the Irish church sought to give a sharper direction and political focus to such popular sentiment. Evangelicals took a prominent part in this movement which culminated in the formation of the Protestant Association in 1835, and religiously derived protestant convictions proved a potent means of harnessing the loyalty of former whigs and even radicals. One such was John Campbell Colquhoun, who speaking in Glasgow in October 1835, stressed the socially comprehensive nature of the appeal of protestantism, and founded it on an emotive appeal to Scottish history:

> To the peer we say enrol yourself in our ranks . . . There will your name be enrolled with the good and great of past times – with the men who in dark and declining days stood firm for their faith, with Knox and Melville, the patriots of Scotland, and our martyred fathers . . . But if you will not come, then to you, my countrymen, I turn to you of every class, and of every occupation. I commit this cause into your hands. They were the poor of former days, who fought for it and who won it. It is your cause still.[13]

Protestantism was thus explicitly linked with the rhetoric of resistance to oppression and authoritarian dictation, and in this form it could enjoy a significant popular appeal, expressed in the formation during the late 1830s and early 1840s of protestant operative associations and protestant classes. The protestant nation defined in opposition to Rome might be labelled as 'England', 'Britain' or, north of the border, as Scotland, but such distinctions were probably largely unselfconscious: common protestantism was what counted.[14]

[10] Ibid., p. x.
[11] Newcastle himself made this point in *An address to all classes and conditions of Englishmen* (1832), pp. 14–15.
[12] *Hansard*, 3rd ser., xv. 483, 11 Feb. 1833.
[13] Mortimer O'Sullivan and Robert J. M'Ghee, *Romanism as it rules in Ireland: being a full and authentic report of the meetings held in various parts of England and Scotland* (2 vols., 1840), I, pp. 426–7.
[14] *In God and greater Britain* (1994) I have suggested (p. 199) that by the early twentieth century a divergence could be discerned between an liberal anglican 'English' identity

An important specific illustration of the mind of mid-nineteenth-century British protestantism is provided by the career and views of Hugh McNeile, who was a central figure in the process of redefinition and resurgence after 1829.[15] McNeile was born in County Antrim in 1795 and educated at Trinity College, Dublin. He was ordained in the church of Ireland in 1820, but, after his first curacy, spent his whole ministry in England. He was thus representative of the important Irish strand which became more closely woven into British protestantism in the decades after the union. In 1822 he was presented to the living of Albury in Surrey by Henry Drummond, an MP and country gentleman, and a prominent lay supporter of Edward Irving. McNeile himself was strongly influenced by Irving, and at the end of the 1820s was the moderator at the series of Albury conferences on the interpretation of biblical prophecy, which fostered firm belief in the imminence of the premillenial advent of Christ, when Roman catholicism would be judged and pure protestantism vindicated. As Drummond and Irving moved into perceived heresy in the early 1830s, McNeile broke with them and in 1834 moved to St Jude's, Liverpool. He remained on Merseyside for more than thirty years, with his strong theologically based protestantism blending with and reinforcing local sectarian antagonism. He was a figure of national renown, one of the most powerful orators of his generation, and a man who in his person bridged social and cultural milieux which historians perhaps too readily assume were wholly distinct from each other.

McNeile's protestant convictions found an early expression in 1826 in a sermon preached on behalf of the Continental Society, a body concerned with proselytism among Roman catholics in Europe. For him the identification between 'popery' and the biblical Babylon was axiomatic, and he described the abominations which he considered to arise from the Roman root: power ecclesiastical, power temporal, infidelity and radicalism.[16] Three years later, vigorously opposing emancipation, he gave his views an explicitly national character. He maintained that the histories of Israel and Judah were a rehearsal of the pre-ordained histories of the nations of Christendom, and that 'our modern Judah' had been preserved from the fearful judgements experienced by papal nations. England's blessings were the fruit of its historic protest against popery, and all the Jeremiahs in the land should speak out now to

and a protestant 'British' one, but I would not apply this distinction to the period under discussion in the current paper.

[15] For biographical detail see J. A. Wardle, 'The life and times of the Rev. Dr Hugh M'Neile, DD 1795–1875' (unpublished MA thesis, Manchester University, 1981).

[16] H. McNeile, *The abominations of Babylon* (1826).

prevent them being compromised.[17] With the measure passed, however, McNeile had no intention of conceding that the battle for national protestantism had been lost. In a speech to the Protestant Association in 1839 he advocated what he termed 'nationalism in religion', the tenacious maintenance of the established church as the linch-pin of national character. It was wrong for spirituality and charity entirely to supersede patriotism, and the papal system remained a 'national usurpation to be resisted by national exclusion'.[18]

Like many other staunch protestants, McNeile was sadly disappointed in the second Peel ministry of 1841–6. Whereas in 1839 he had pinned his hopes on toryism, in 1846 he addressed a long open letter to the new whig prime minister, Lord John Russell. He urged Russell to recall 'the high, the noble, the patriotic, the Christian and Protestant Whig of 1688' and to stake his political existence 'on the recovery of our national Protestantism'. The slumbering protestantism of Britain, was, McNeile claimed, only waiting for a leader.[19] In 1849 in an open letter to Sir George Grey, the home secretary, McNeile explored the nature of what he termed 'national sin'. He suggested that the current cholera epidemic was a divine visitation on the nation as a punishment for its sinful official acts, above all the Maynooth act of 1845 which McNeile portrayed as a breach of the second commandment:

Against remonstrances, against the light of revealed truth, in defiance of the plainest language of God's law, England has persevered, 'in a friendly and liberal spirit', to encourage idolatry; and now in 1849, England stands aghast at a second visitation of the cholera. God is not mocked, whatsoever a nation soweth, that shall it reap.[20]

Such exhortations and denunciations seemed to fall on deaf ears at the time, but in 1850 Russell, at least, provoked by the restoration of the Roman catholic hierarchy, was dramatically to display the protestant strand in his make-up in the famous 'Durham letter'. He stirred an extensive popular response. Meanwhile McNeile's patriotism continued to be fundamentally derived from his protestantism: in 1860 he spoke

[17] H. McNeile, *England's protest is England's shield, for the battle is the Lord's* (1829).
[18] H. McNeile, *Nationalism in religion* (1839). It is worthy of note that a computer search of the British Library *Catalogue of printed books* suggests that this pamphlet was the only British publication before the 1860s to contain the word 'nationalism' in its title. The word occurs in the text of G. S. Faber's *The primitive doctrine of election* (1836), presumably McNeile's source for its use, where it denotes a theological doctrine defined as 'the election of certain whole nations into the pale of the visible Church Catholic, which Election, however, relates purely to their privileged condition in this world, extending not to their collective eternal state in another world' (ibid., p. 20).
[19] H. McNeile, *The state in danger. A letter to the Rt. Hon. Lord John Russell, M.P.* (1846), pp. 55–8.
[20] McNeile, *National sin*, p. 35.

out about the Italian question and the current invasion scare. National security depended on national character, which was itself dependent above all on the institutions of the reformed religion and the national church, which were safeguards of balanced liberty.[21]

It will not have escaped notice that the most forceful advocates of national protestantism after 1829 were anglicans, or adherents of the church of Scotland. Now that Roman catholics were no longer excluded from parliament, those who sought institutional buttresses for protestantism were forced back on the established churches. Protestant motives are thus important in explaining the tenacity with which the church of Ireland was defended, and the establishment of the church of England indefinitely maintained. At the same time, patriotism as well as theology stirred vigorous resistance to the 'Oxford movement' and to ritualism: if the protestant character of the church of England were to be undermined not only would individuals be deprived of the priceless spiritual blessings of pure reformed Christianity, but the nation would lose an essential pillar of its distinctive identity. In Scotland, meanwhile, a sense of the necessity for presbyterianism to reclaim its reformation heritage contributed to the tensions which exploded in the 'Disruption' of 1843 and subsequently sustained the rival churches for the remainder of the century. Protestantism thus derived much strength from becoming interwoven with other important strands of political and ecclesiastical ideology.

Nevertheless, the perception that national protestantism meant the maintenance of an established church inevitably limited the appeal of the idea among nonconformists, who were now becoming increasingly numerous and articulate. It was true that some, notably Wesleyan methodists, were sufficiently hostile to Rome and sympathetic to the church of England for them to support the establishment in principle even while they competed with it in practice.[22] An Independent minister, in a fast day sermon in 1832, condemned emancipation as an 'aggravated and appalling national sin' and denounced as infidels those protestant dissenters who had been implicated in it.[23] In Scotland, the Free Church rejection of the existing establishment was consistent with continuing advocacy of a purified national church. It was also true that early Victorian nonconformists were vigorously protestant in a theolo-

---

[21] H. McNeile, *Speech of the Rev. Dr M'Neile on the Italian and national defence questions* (1860).

[22] On Wesleyan anti-catholicism see David Hempton, *Methodism and politics in British society, 1750–1850* (1984).

[23] Joseph Irons, *Jehovah's controversy with England: the substance of a sermon preached at Grove Chapel, Camberwell March 21 1832, the day appointed for a general fast* (1832), pp. 13–14.

gical sense. But among the radicals who pressed for general disestablishment true protestantism implied the severing of all links between religion and the state. Thus *The Nonconformist* newspaper, which took as its motto the 'dissidence of dissent and the protestantism of the protestant religion', observed in January 1845:

The fact is at length obtruding itself stark naked upon public notice, that the state, in connecting itself with the religious institutions of a people, contemplates one object, and one only – the security and increase of its own power. Hitherto the majority, perhaps, of our own countrymen have seen in the alliance nothing but a national deference to the truth, and have acquiesced and even gloried in their own servitude, under the impression that they were thereby maintaining a bulwark for Protestantism.

In reality, however, in the opinion of *The Nonconformist*, state support of religion was playing into the hands of the Roman catholic church.[24] The tension between the radical nonconformist and the anglican strands of protestantism was to come very much into the open later in 1845 when a minority seceded from the Anti-Maynooth Conference, insisting that opposition to the grant must be primarily on voluntarist grounds, rather than on the basis of national protestantism.[25] It is also noteworthy that bodies of dissenters, apart from Wesleyans, were under-represented in the agitation against the Roman catholic hierarchy in 1850 and 1851.[26]

British nonconformists might reject the idea of a state church as a bulwark of protestantism, but in the mid-nineteenth century they lacked an alternative model of the relationship between protestantism and national identity: the logic of the voluntarist argument was that the nation as such would have no distinctive religious character. Moreover, there was a practical tension between voluntarist opposition to the church and protestant cooperation with it against Rome. This was notably apparent in a pastoral address on the 'papal aggression' by the leading independent, John Angell James. On the one hand, he called for united action with anglicans and characterised the contest as not just one between rival hierarchies, but between Rome and protestant England. On the other, he denounced the union of church and state and called for standing forth 'against the popery of Protestantism, as well as of Rome'.[27]

The dilemmas facing English nonconformists serve as a bridge to discussion of the case of the United States, where the absence of state

[24] *The Nonconformist*, 15 Jan. 1845, p. 38.
[25] A. S. Thelwall, ed., *Proceedings of the Anti-Maynooth Conference* (1845), pp. xcviii- cii.
[26] D. G. Paz, *Popular anti-catholicism in mid-Victorian England* (Stanford, 1993), p. 45.
[27] J. A. James, *The papal aggression and popery contemplated religiously: a pastoral address* (1851).

churches meant that no such twofacedness was necessary. In other respects, however, it will be argued that the American experience showed striking parallels with the situation in Britain, and suggests that British protestant states of mind were in the early Victorian years not only sustained at home, but also exported overseas.

It is true that the received historical interpretation of protestantism in the United States in the mid-nineteenth century has portrayed the intensity of the anti-catholicism there apparent as one aspect of American exceptionalism, a product of the particular political, religious and social conditions prevailing in a young nation and a new continent. Such a view is derived in particular from Ray Allen Billington's seminal work, first published in 1938, *The protestant crusade 1800–1860*. Billington started with the seventeenth-century puritans, arguing that the early colonial generations, themselves refugees from religious persecution, inherited in particularly full measure the intense European anti-catholicism of the period. He continued:

> The isolation of the people, the introspection to which they resorted in their wilderness homes, the distance which separated the colonies from the mother country and from Europe, all fostered the bigotry which they had brought from the old world. The liberal currents that gradually diminished the intolerance of the people of those lands did not flow towards America.[28]

This is, however, to draw a false contrast. As earlier chapters of this book have demonstrated, the sentiments that Billington termed 'bigotry' remained very much apparent in Great Britain throughout much of the eighteenth century. On the other hand, the liberalising waves of the enlightenment lapped on the shores of the Connecticut and the Potomac as well as on those of the Forth and the Thames. On both sides of the Atlantic a less polemical but still essentially orthodox protestantism was being mediated to the intelligenstia by university institutions such as William Robertson's Edinburgh and John Witherspoon's Princeton.[29] In America, as in Britain, puritan anti-catholicism became overlaid by more recent theological and historical deposits. In the early nineteenth century even leading New England exponents of the traditions of the 'Pilgrim Fathers' did not dwell particularly on the anti-catholic strand in their outlook.[30] In both the

---

[28] R. A. Billington, *The protestant crusade, 1800–1860* (New York, 1938), p. 4.

[29] R. B. Sher, *Church and university in the Scottish enlightenment* (Edinburgh, 1985); Mark A. Noll, *The scandal of the evangelical mind* (Grand Rapids and Leicester, 1994), pp. 83–90.

[30] Lyman Beecher, *The memory of our fathers: a sermon delivered at Plymouth on the twenty-second of December 1827* (Boston, 1828); G. B. Cheever, *Some of the principles according to which this world is managed . . . delivered as an address at the religious celebration of the fourth of July in Salem* (Boston, 1833).

United States and Britain, therefore, nineteenth-century protestantism was stirred and reshaped by contemporary influences as well as drawing on inherited tradition.

There is, moreover, a striking similarity in the broad pattern of mid-nineteenth-century protestant activity in the United States and in Britain. There were comparable upsurges in the early to mid-1830s and in the mid to late 1840s, reaching a climax in the early 1850s. In the United States organised protestantism enjoyed a short period of real political power, following the electoral triumphs of the 'Know-Nothings' in 1854. In both countries the theologically motivated anti-catholicism of evangelical clergy blended with the more secular concerns of politicians and the raw prejudices of the crowd. In America, however, protestantism was linked to greater excesses of violence than occurred in nineteenth-century Britain, notably in the burning of the Ursuline convent at Charlestown, Massachusetts in 1835 and the Philadelphia riots of 1844, events which might perhaps more constructively be compared with the Gordon riots of 1780 than with any strictly contemporary events in Britain.

An obvious common factor immediately apparent from this chronology is that a sense of protestant identity in both countries was reinforced by the heightened atmosphere of religious competition engendered as a result of the Irish diaspora. In both Britain and the United States Irish migration between the 1820s and the 1850s provided the person-power to transform the Roman catholic church from being a small and relatively inconspicuous group to become a major force in the religious life of the nation. The success of the church in retaining the loyalties of the Irish poor was the fruit of hard pastoral labour at the parochial level and vigorous leadership at the national one, and it was inevitable that such endeavours would attract protestant notice and concern. The grandiloquent pronouncements of prelates such as Cardinal Wiseman, archbishop of Westminster, and John Hughes, archbishop of New York, even if intended primarily for internal catholic consumption, could not escape protestant notice. The earl of Arundel, a leading English lay catholic, acknowledged in the House of Commons in 1847 that the church of Rome was antagonistic to protestantism 'and will be while the world lasts, until Protestantism is extinguished'.[31] In November 1850, just as England was being convulsed by protest against the restoration of the catholic hierarchy, across the Atlantic John Hughes spoke on what he called the decline of protestantism and affirmed that the ambition of his church to convert

---

[31] *Hansard*, 3rd ser., xcl, c. 764, 14 Apr. 1847.

the world in general and the United States in particular was no secret.[32] Even if the fevered imaginations of militant protestants meant that they were, as J. H. Newman put it, 'prompt to believe any story, however extravagant, that is told to our [Roman catholic] disadvantage',[33] the perception that they were engaged in a struggle for ultimate religious and cultural ascendancy was no illusion.

Within this framework of parallel stimulus and development five particular ways can be identified in which American protestantism resembled that in Britain and Ireland, and indeed was directly shaped by influence from across the Atlantic. First, at a popular as well as an elite level, Ireland exported her protestantism as well as her catholicism. Sectarian rivalries continued to be played out on American soil, most notably in Philadelphia. In 1819 Matthew Carey, a Roman catholic pamphleteer and publisher who had fled from Ireland in the 1780s, published his *Vindiciae Hibernicae* intended to refute protestant versions of the history of his native country, notably the charge that protestants had been massacred in 1641.[34] Carey initially believed that the 'prejudices on the subject which it was intended to combat, had scarcely any existence here' (in the United States), and intended his book for circulation primarily on the other side of the Atlantic.[35] However, by 1826 Carey had come to the conclusion that attacks on catholicism were all too current in the United States, and he was particularly outraged by a 'scurrious and abusive' address which had originated with a Gideonite Society, whom he believed to be really a body of Orangemen.[36] Subsequently, in June 1831, a meeting was convened in Philadelphia to make arrangements for celebrating 12 July as 'the one hundred and forty-first year of freedom from Popery and arbitrary power'.[37] The allusion was evidently to the protestant victories in Ireland in 1690, not to any event on American soil. The outcome was a public demonstration which ended in violent confrontation with Roman catholics. Allegations were made that the protestants had carried an orange flag and had played 'God Save the King' and 'Boyne Water'. A defence of the protestants as 'sound Republicans' served to illuminate the ambiguities in their consciousness. They

---

[32] *Complete works of the most Rev. John Hughes, DD* (2 vols., New York, 1865), II, pp. 87–102.

[33] J. H. Newman, *Lectures on the present position of catholics in England* (1892 edn), p. 1.

[34] Matthew Carey, *Vindiciae Hibernicae: or Ireland vindicated* (Philadelphia, 1819); James N. Green, *Matthew Carey: publisher and patriot* (Philadelphia, 1985), pp. 4–5, 30.

[35] Broadside dated Philadelphia 5 Dec. 1825 (American Antiquarian Society, Worcester Mass).

[36] Matthew Carey, *Letters on religious persecution* (Philadelphia, 1826).

[37] *The Protestant*, 2 July 1831, pp. 210–11.

happened to play a tune called by Europeans '*Boyne Water*', but by the Americans '*Siege of Plattsburgh*' – in commemoration of the triumph of our armies over the British Empire at the village of Plattsburgh during the late war, from which circumstance the tune has become a national air. These insults were given not to the Protestants of Ireland in their country but to the American people and to our institutions.[38]

This incident gives a fascinating insight into how the culture of Irish protestantism could merge almost imperceptibly into that of American patriotism, with a fairly direct transfer of Irish sectarian rivalries on to American soil, just as they were translated to mainland Britain in similar unrest associated with 12 July at the same period.[39] Indeed, the very proximity of 12 July to 4 July probably allowed American nationalism to capitalise on sentiment initially stirred by Orangeism without significant prior ideological transformation.[40]

Second, there was the adoption of similar conspiracy theories and the assumption of a polarity between protestantism and catholicism which had profound political and social implications as well as religious ones. James Welch, a travelling agent of the American Sunday School Union, spending the Christmas of 1835 on the Mississippi, found time to write down his reflections on the state of the nation:

> The United States have been more highly blessed of God than any people, I believe, that ever lived on earth. Like Carpurnium [sic] they have been '*exalted to Heaven*', but such has been the pride, infidelity, injustice, oppression and worldlymindedness that the God of nations has abundant cause to be offended with us . . . I have for years had my fears that He was about to let loose upon us, by emigration and other means, the whole power and intrigue of Popery; and . . . unless the government and the parents of the country awake from their indifference and inattention to the subject of enlightening the public mind, there are not a few boys *now living*, who *will* live, to hear the funeral knell of this last hope of liberty on earth . . . I believe the Catholics have a secret and deep laid scheme to subvert the liberties of my country.[41]

Welch had probably been reading a book published earlier in 1835 by Samuel Morse, better known as the inventor of the electric telegraph, in which it was alleged that the absolutist powers of Europe were deliberately encouraging catholic emigration to the United States in order to subvert republican liberties.[42] Morse's work had been written after extensive travel in Europe and in his mind the antagonism of 'Popery and Protestantism' was directly convertible into that between

[38] Ibid., 6 Aug. 1831, pp. 249–50; 27 Aug. 1831, pp. 276–7.
[39] Wolffe, *Protestant crusade*, pp. 92, 192–3.
[40] For discussion of the parallel adaptation of the Orange tradition in Canada see See, *Riots in New Brunswick*.
[41] Presbyterian Historical Society, Philadelphia, James E. Welch Diary, 26 Dec. 1835.
[42] Samuel F. B. Morse, *Foreign conspiracy against the liberties of the United States* (1835).

'Absolutism and Republicanism'.[43] Welch's diary is significant evidence of how such views were being mediated through a man whose travelling ministry over several decades brought him into contact with large numbers of children across much of the country.

Thus, in America, as in Britain, Roman catholicism was identified with the 'other', inherently foreign and hostile to essential features of the constitution and national character. Whereas in the eyes of a British aristocrat like the duke of Newcastle the Roman catholic priest was in league with the forces of democratic revolution, to an ardent American republican like Morse he was the agent of monarchical absolutism. In positive terms, Newcastle's conviction that 'Protestantism gives life and being to our Constitution' was mirrored by the belief of the American Thomas R. Whitney that it was on 'the good old Protestant Bible' that 'our fathers built up this glorious fabric of independence'.[44] Whereas in Britain religious establishments were defended as a primary bulwark of protestantism, in America their absence was celebrated as an equally vital safeguard against Rome. In the eyes of W. C. Brownlee, 'the Romish hierarchy invariably puts forth its influence over all lands, in proportion as it gains strength, to unite church and state'.[45] Conversely, for Robert Breckinridge, the thorough independence of religion from the state was a central foundation of the American mind, but this ideal was now threatened by 'herds of foreign ecclesiastics' seeking to proselytise the nation 'to a system hostile to liberty'.[46] Nathaniel Beman went so far as to define the papal world as characterised by the union of church and state, two aspects of the same spiritually and politically repressive order which were 'as vitally united as the Siamese twins'. He went on to define American freedom in opposition to Rome:

What! this country to become papal, and receive all the dogmas of the Roman Church! Will the American mind, accustomed to think for itself, and irradiated by human learning and the Bible, ever subscribe to her articles of faith and submit to *her* dictation in matters of religion? No, never, while the sun shines, and the sweet stars are in heaven. *Never*, while the earth is green, and Mercy is on the throne![47]

[43] Morse to A. J. Willington, 20 May 1835, Library of Congress, Washington DC, Morse Papers, Container 11.

[44] 4th Duke of Newcastle, *Thoughts*, p. liv; *The Republic*, II (Aug. 1851), 93; cf. T. R. Whitney, *A defence of the American polity* (New York, 1856).

[45] W. C. Brownlee, *Popery an enemy to civil and religious liberty and dangerous to our republic* (New York, 1836), p. 122.

[46] R. J. Breckinridge, *A discourse on the formation and development of the American mind* (Baltimore, 1837), pp. 27, 32.

[47] Nathaniel S. S. Beman, *Characteristics of the age: a discourse delivered in the first presbyterian church, Troy, NY, on thanksgiving day, December 12 1850* (Troy, 1851), pp. 25, 28.

Despite the radical contrast in the political and constitutional frameworks existing in Britain and the United States the mental processes stirred by the identification of protestantism and national identity were very similar.

Third, British modes of agitation and organisation were imitated in the United States. Public debates between protestants and Roman catholics were a central part of the British Reformation Society's operations in Ireland from 1827. When a spectacle of this kind was first held in London in 1828 it attracted the critical interest of a visiting American minister, W. B. Sprague. As Sprague feared, these confrontations were counterproductive in relation to their initial objective of convincing Roman catholics of the errors of their church, but they were very effective in mobilising protestant enthusiasm.[48] However, during 1830, a recently established weekly magazine in New York, *The Protestant*, took a less critical view, reprinted extensive reports of further public debates held in Britain, and advocated the organisation of similar events in American cities, believing that they would lead to triumphant results 'for the cause of civil liberty, genuine Protestantism, and "Bible religion"'.[49] From 1832 the idea was indeed picked up in the United States with the holding of a number of well-publicised debates during the next few years, some in writing in the columns of newspapers, others in face-to-face meetings.[50] Meanwhile, Americans were also noting the other activities of British anti-catholic organisations, such as the Continental Society and the British Reformation Society, and during the course of the 1830s, formed comparable organisations to promote similar agitation in the United States.[51]

Fourth, British protestant literature circulated in the United States, and some of it was reprinted there. In a volume now in the Presbyterian Historical Society in Philadelphia, American protestant controversial tracts were bound together with several of the publications of the Protestant Association in London.[52] There was a considerable vogue in nineteenth-century Britain for the republication of that staple of protestant polemic, Foxe's 'Book of martyrs',[53] a trend which stirred more

---

[48] Wolffe, *Protestant crusade*, pp. 38–42; W. B. Sprague, *Letters from Europe in 1828* (New York, 1828), pp. 34–5.
[49] *The Protestant*, 19 June, 16 Oct., 20 Nov. 1830.
[50] Billington, *Protestant crusade*, pp. 61–5.
[51] *New York Observer*, 18 July 1829, 20 Nov. 1830, 2 July 1831; Billington, *Protestant crusade*, pp. 58, 95–6. Billington was incorrect (p. 95) in stating that the British Reformation Society was formed to combat catholic emancipation: in fact it eschewed political involvement (Wolffe, *Protestant crusade*, pp. 43–5) and was thus an even more relevant model for American organisation than Billington supposed.
[52] It is impossible to date the binding precisely, but it would appear to be contemporary.
[53] Wolffe, *Protestant crusade*, p. 112.

than an echo across the Atlantic. A Philadelphia edition of 1830 was a straight reprint of an English one of 1813; and a London edition of 1824 appeared in abridged form, with additional material relating to alleged recent Roman catholic persecution in Europe, in Hartford in 1820, Cincinnati in 1832 and Middletown in 1833. It was reprinted in Hartford in 1845 and 1854.[54] Meanwhile, the works of the intensely protestant contemporary British novelist Charlotte Elizabeth Tonna were enjoying a substantial American market. They were reprinted in New York by John S. Taylor in the early 1840s, but in 1844 a rival publishing house, M. W. Dodd, launched a competing collected edition. Taylor countered with the claim that he had published several works, amounting to 3,257 pages of text, which were not in Dodd's edition, and offering his edition in uniform sets at 50 cents a volume with 'liberal discounts' to the trade and to Sunday schools. Meanwhile, a review of Dodd's collected edition observed that 'the works themselves are so well known as not to need commendation'.[55] By 1850 it had already gone through eight printings. Dodd's edition was also noteworthy for an introduction by Harriet Beecher Stowe, in which the leading American woman writer evidently felt some embarrassment over the virulence of Charlotte Elizabeth's anti-catholicism. Nevertheless, 'It is to be considered also; in allowance for the severity with which she always portrays popery, that she has seen the system carried to its full and appropriate results in Ireland, in a manner in which an American can scarcely form a conception.'[56] In reading these volumes, as in the other respects already noted, American protestants were being encouraged to impose a slanted reading of European conditions on to their own catholic neighbours.

Finally, there was a consciousness of protestantism as a common cause and a bond of brotherhood that spanned the Atlantic. In April 1836 the scurrilous New York periodical *The Downfall of Babylon* published an appeal to the inhabitants of Great Britain urging mutual support and exchange of information in the joint struggle against popery.[57] At a more elevated level, at the time of the formation of the Evangelical Alliance in 1846, the essential free spiritual unity of evangelical protestantism was extolled and contrasted with the allegedly despotic uniformity of Rome.[58] In 1846 *The New York Evangelist* greeted

[54] John Malham and T. Pratt, eds., *Fox's* Book of martyrs *or the* Acts and monuments of the Christian church (Philadelphia, 1830); Charles A. Goodrich, ed., *Book of martyrs* (Hartford, 1830).
[55] *New York Observer*, 25 Jan. 1845, 1 May 1847 (advertisements).
[56] *The works of Charlotte Elizabeth with an introduction by Mrs. H. B. Stowe* (8th edn, 2 vols., New York, 1850), introduction.
[57] *Downfall of Babylon*, 30 Apr. 1836, pp. 96–7.
[58] John Wolffe, 'Unity in diversity: North Atlantic evangelical thought in the mid-

with great relief the settling of the Oregon dispute. It considered that war with England would have been a disaster for the gospel, and that by united effort the two nations could bless the world enormously by united mission in the cause of 'true Christianity'.[59] In January 1851, while Britain was being stirred by anger at 'papal aggression', a preacher in New York portrayed the parallel advance of British and American civilisation in triumphalist protestant terms:

What mean the vast enterprise, skill and industry of Britain – her extended commerce – her empire, upon which the sun never sets – her laws, extended over millions of India – her protection of the right wherever her flag floats? . . . They show the advance of Protestantism.

What mean the rising cities of these free states . . . those rapidly multiplying churches for the worship of God in every direction . . . the building of cities and churches by the waves of the Pacific, and where, until recently, nothing in the way of religion dare be lisped save popish mummeries. They mark the advance of Protestantism.[60]

A specific biographical case study will serve further to illustrate the parallels, interconnections and differences between protestantism in Britain and the United States. In May 1839, the month in which Hugh McNeile addressed the Protestant Association on 'nationalism in religion', George Barrell Cheever became minister of Allen St Presbyterian Church in New York. Cheever was born in Maine in 1807 and throughout his life relished the puritan heritage of his native New England. Initial religious doubts gave way during his twenties to revivalistic spiritual intensity. After some years as a congregational minister in Massachusetts he went on an extended journey to Europe between 1836 and 1839.[61] He was in Britain for much of 1837 at a time of considerable protestant excitement. The experience, together with his subsequent direct encounters with continental catholicism, substantially reinforced his latent protestantism. At the same time, his prejudices against the union of church and state were confirmed by contact with English nonconformists and Scottish voluntaryists, and he asserted that 'the entire annihilation of her Church Establishment would be a second reformation, as important for the literature and religion of Great Britain, as the reformation of Luther was for that of Europe and the world'.[62]

---

nineteenth century', in R. N. Swanson, ed., *Unity and diversity in the church*, SCH, 32 (1995), 363–75.

[59] *The New York Evangelist*, 25 June 1846.

[60] N. Murray, *The decline of popery and its causes: an address delivered in the Broadway Tabernacle on Wednesday evening, January 15, 1851* (New York, 1851), pp. 29–30.

[61] For biographical information see Robert M. York, *George B. Cheever: religious and social reformer 1807–1890* (Orono, Maine, 1855).

[62] *The New York Observer*, 23 Dec. 1837, 6 Jan. 1838.

Such were the formative influences on a man who immediately on his return to the United States began more than three decades of ministry in New York, a city which, like McNeile's Liverpool, was currently experiencing the rising tide of Irish catholic immigration and accordingly provided fertile soil for militant protestantism. Cheever quickly became a popular preacher and lecturer, not only in New York itself, but also back in New England.[63] In *God's hand in America*, published in 1841, he asserted that America had a special place in divine purposes which were now moving towards their consummation. In December 1842, Cheever asserted that the American race had grown out of 'the noblest principles of the Reformation' and that it had been a beneficent providence that had kept Columbus' ships, and the consequent contagion of catholic Spain, away from the northern shores of the continent. Private judgement of the scriptures and justification by faith were not only spiritual imperatives but essential foundations for the development of freedom and national distinctiveness. The potential tyranny of the union of church and state and the creeping 'imperium in imperio' of the Roman catholic church must be strenuously resisted.[64] Cheever's polemic against Rome as a civil as well as a spiritual despotism was further developed in crowded lectures at the Broadway Tabernacle in January 1844. Against this challenge Americans should cherish the memory of their puritan ancestors and demonstrate to the whole world the success of what 'we believe to be ultimately connected with the possession and preservation of liberty for all mankind, A CHURCH WITHOUT A BISHOP, AND A STATE WITHOUT A KING'.[65]

There is a sense in which the place of protestantism in earlier nineteenth-century American national identity merits comparison with eighteenth- as well as nineteenth-century Britain, in respect of the manner in which, to apply Linda Colley's phrase, it was central to the forging of a new nation. The primary contention of this chapter, however, is that the American dimension is a centrally important aspect of the development of protestantism in the North Atlantic world in the aftermath of those two ambiguous revolutions of 1775–80 and of 1829–32. Political and constitutional discontinuities fragmented the ideologies and alignments of the earlier eighteenth century, but did not deprive protestantism of its formative power. Indeed the very uncertainties and conflicts of the nineteenth-century world fuelled statements of

---

[63] York, *Cheever*, pp. 104–6.

[64] G. B. Cheever, *The elements of national greatness* (New York, 1843), pp. 8, 11, 14–15, 38–40.

[65] G. B. Cheever, *The hierarchical despotism* (New York, 1844), p. 63; York, *Cheever*, p. 106.

national protestantism which in some respects outrightly contradicted each other. Although in the long term such tensions may well have contributed to a loss of credibility, in the medium term they gave added intensity to protestant convictions. Moreover there was a suggestion that protestantism itself ultimately united Britain and America far more than it divided them. Such assertions, debatable though they were, well illustrate the vital importance of the continuing contribution of protestantism to national identities in the decades after 1829.

Index